THE JEWEL IN THE CROWN

STIG KVAAL AND PER ØSTBY

THE JEWEL IN THE CROWN

KONGSBERG DYNAMIC POSITIONING SYSTEMS

1975–2015

PAX FORLAG A/S, OSLO 2015

© PAX FORLAG 2015
COVER: AKADEMISK PUBLISERING
PRINT: PRINT BEST OÜ, ESTONIA
PRINTED IN ESTONIA
ISBN 978-82-530-3788-2

CONTENTS

FOREWORD

ON SEPTEMBER 10TH 1988 we sat in the office of Professor Jens Glad Balchen at the Norwegian Institute of Technology (NTH) in Trondheim. Preparing to write our thesis about the development of the cybernetics community in Norway during the 1950s and 1960s, we were to interview one of Norway's foremost pioneers in this field. During the meeting, Balchen talked about dynamic positioning and highlighted Albatross as a «general success».

At that time, we could not imagine the events that would transpire, or that Kongsberg Maritime – almost 25 years later – would ask us to write a technological biography about dynamic positioning. Saying yes to such a request was easy. Now that we are finished, we can say that writing this book has been both fun and educational. And of course, it is rather exciting to continue something that marked the beginning of our academic life. At that time, one of the biggest challenges for researchers and engineers was how to apply cybernetics in industry. This DP book project has given us first-hand insight into what happens when research and industry intersect, and how visionary automation dreams have created a Norwegian industrial adventure.

The project has enjoyed good support and stewardship from all those involved, and there are many to be thanked. First and foremost, thanks to Kongsberg Maritime for this assignment. The book committee has followed us closely throughout the project and invested considerable effort, and they also deserve our sincere thanks. The committee consisted of two historians, professor Håkon With Andersen of NTNU and associate professor Stein Bjørnstad of BI, as well as Øystein Andreassen, Morten Breivik, Nils Albert Jenssen, Rolf Arne Klepaker and Roy Larsen of Kongsberg Maritime. In addition, Nils Albert contributed several technological background notes, and he and Øystein have done a formidable job as photo editors. Morten, who took the initiative for the project, was the first chairman of the book committee. Halfway through the project he left Kongsberg Maritime to head up the Department of Engineering

Cybernetics at NTNU, turning the chair over to Roy Larsen, but he continued to provide considerable support to the book committee. Sadly, Rolf Arne passed away in the middle of the project. With his passing we lost a skilled, congenial and insightful partner. Special thanks to Stein for sharing the source material from his thesis on the Kongsberg industrial phenomenon and innovations in deep-water technology. Thanks also to publishing editor Marianne Bjørndal of Pax, for her invaluable help in turning an unfinished manuscript into a finished book. She has been an insightful and pleasant sparring partner and advisor during the final phase of the work. Thanks also to our translators Blue-C.

Current and former employees of Kongsberg Maritime, Albatross and Simrad contributed in various ways. Whether through interviews or conversations, their experiences and knowledge have been imperative to the quality of the book. Several attended a technology seminar arranged by the book committee and specifically addressed the key issues and aspects of DP technology. Several more were present during an evening of reminiscing at Kapteinshaugen. Many provided their own technology memos and gave crash courses in a range of areas from Kalman filtering to hydroacoustics, redundancy and GPS. It was also exciting to experience simulator technology live, but we admit that earning our DP certificate may not be realistic. Roald Holstad and Geir Hasnes read the beta version manuscript and provided valuable input and feedback. Thanks to all who have contributed!

We would also like to thank NTNU for allowing us to take on this project, and our colleagues at KULT for contributing to a strong and exciting academic community and an enjoyable workplace. Last but not least, we, as fathers and partners, would like to thank our families for their patience during times when we were both physically and mentally absent.

Trondheim, March 2015
Stig Kvaal and Per Østby

1

THE ART OF PERFECT POSITIONING

WHEN THE FIRST seafarers began to venture beyond familiar waters and mastered the art of sailing and navigation, they also changed conditions for the development of human society. With a knowledge of sailing, the sea became more than just a source of food. It became a thoroughfare, linking people and cultures through commerce and the exchange of information and ideas. As the degree of human interaction and the demand for foreign goods increased, shipping became ever more important. As stated in a well-known ancient Roman quote – «Navigare necesse est» – to sail is necessary. Though not as well known, the quote ends, «Vivere non est necess» – to live is not necessary.

These words, spoken by the political and military leader Gnaeus Pompeius Magnus in 56 BC, witnessed a Rome at war, and their desperate need for grain to feed a starving population. The grain had to be transported by ship, but due to threatening weather, the crew refused to leave port. The order was, however, clear. They had to sail. Their lives were subordinate to the Roman Empire. There was little the crew could do when faced with the needs of society and the whims of nature.

This quote gives us insight into two things: modern civilizations are dependent on shipping and shipping is associated with major hazards. It also reflects a time in history where the value of a seafarer's life was much less than that of today.

The Bible tells a different story about the sea, seafaring danger and a crew exposed to the forces of nature. The Old Testament book of Jonah reads:

> Then the Lord sent a great wind on the sea, and such a violent storm
> arose that the ship threatened to break up. All the sailors were afraid
> and each cried out to his god. And they threw the cargo into the sea to

«Shipwreck on the Norwegian coast» by Johan Christian Dahl (1832).

lighten the ship. But Jonah had gone below deck, where he lay down and fell into a deep sleep. The captain went to him and said, «How can you sleep? Get up and call upon your god! Perhaps he will pay heed to us that we may not perish.»[1]

The crew's solution to appeasing God's wrath and calming the frothing ocean was to throw Jonah overboard. In all cultures, belief has affected humanity's relationship to nature and the forces of weather. Rituals and sacrifices have been used to calm the storms and appease the gods that controlled the weather.

But seafarers haven't just relied on the good will of the gods. Throughout history, they have developed and implemented a number of technologies in the battle against the elements. Larger and safer vessels, better methods of navigation and the construction of lighthouses have improved the chances of reaching distant shores and getting safely home. Despite these improvements, seafarers have for centuries relied on their seamanship, sails or motors when encountering raging storms. In some cases and in the midst of rough waters, dropping anchors to keep the ship steady and free from treacherous rocks and cliffs has been the only option. History is full of tragic stories about sinking ships and crews taken after battling the powerful forces of wind, currents and waves. Even the «invincible» Spanish Armada was no match for severe weather when it set sail for England in 1588. There was little the sailors could do in the face of a terrible storm.

In the late 1800s, however, someone did find a solution to taming the sea, at least in theory. Jules Verne, in his short story «L'ile à hélice» (Propeller Island), writes about a French string quartet being diverted to Standard Island when on route from the port of San Francisco to San Diego. This artificial island navigated the Pacific Ocean and was able to lie calmly throughout rough weather though not being 'moored in the strictest sense'.

Verne writes:

> In other words, anchors were not used, as this would have been impossible at depths of one hundred meters or more. Thus, by means of the machines, which manoeuvre ahead and astern throughout its stay, it is kept in place, as immobile as the eight main islands of the Hawaiian Archipelago.[2]

Published as science fiction in 1895, the basic premise of Verne's adventure fantasy novel later materialized with revolutionary technology just a few generations after his death.

In March 1993, nearly one hundred years after Verne had described «Propeller Island», the drillship *Discoverer 534* was assigned to the Gulf of Mexico. Though not equal to the dimensions of Verne's fantasy island, the 160 meter-long ship, with a displacement of over 20,000 tons, was huge in its own right. The vessel's seven diesel generators powered two six megawatt (MW) main propulsion units and six 1.6MW tunnel thrusters.[3]

Drilling for oil 106 nautical miles south of Mobile, Alabama, the ship encountered strong easterly winds that eventually reached speeds up to 86 knots (160 km/h). The Beaufort scale classifies a wind force of 64 knots as a hurricane. This storm was later referred to as «The storm of the century» and «The killer storm». The sea convulsed and waves cascaded over the bow, crashing into the ship's bridge. Visibility was almost zero. During the peak of the storm and subject to massive waves, the vessel rose and fell twelve metres at a time. And as nature unleashed a force of fury, the crew, similar to the Roman seafarers and Jonah's fellow passengers, feared an unkind fate: «... huge forces of nature were thrown hard against us, making demands on people and equipment beyond their utter maximum. We, during the battle, lost engines, prop motors, SCRs, and thrusters, but we DID NOT lose our composure, position, nor heading, and therefore kept all our crew dry and safe.»[4] This time, however, the crew didn't need to throw the captain overboard to conquer nature. Instead, they relied on a dynamic positioning system from a little town in the interior of Norway.[5]

A DP FROM KONGSBERG

The *Discoverer 534* was equipped with an AD703, known as Kongsberg's Albatross Dynamic Positioning System. This advanced technology and system, speculated by Verne in the late 1800s, stationed the vessel without the use of anchors and ropes. This book tells the story of the Dynamic Positioning Systems, or so-called DPs, that have been developed, produced and sold by the DP team in Kongsberg.

The story of these systems is about more than just machines and technical solutions. It's about the events and the people who since the mid-1970s have driven and shaped the technology, thus expanding its application both commercially and geographically.

The little group that made up Dynpos, Kongsberg Våpenfabrikk's first DP project, has evolved over the past four decades to become a significant business area for Kongsberg Maritime and its staff of 4,650 employees.[6] Founded and integrated in Kongsberg Våpenfabrikk (KV), the project was organised under various groups in KV, then became a company called Albatross prior to joining the Simrad Group. A lot of water has passed under the bridge since the early days when major financial issues threatened closure, and system pioneers prayed for a speedy DP sale to keep the project, and their heads, above water. Kongsberg Maritime's DP is a billion kroner business. In 2014 Kongsberg Maritime had a turnover of nearly NOK 9.7 billion.[7]

The DP system underwent several name changes, including ADP, SPT and K-Pos, all of which reflect new generations of technology and owners. From the soaring Albatross on the first system deliveries to Simrad's blue wave, the logo has changed and today is visually recognizable by Kongsberg's logo and stamp of quality, a gold and royal-crowned K monogram on a red background. While the name and logo speak of ownership and lend the system an identity, they say little about the DP system itself.

DYNAMIC POSITIONING

Seagoing vessels are continually exposed to the harsh forces of wind, currents and waves and are driven off course if not controlled by the crew. Traditionally ships were anchored and stationed through a combination of rudders, sails and motor driven propellers. Just more than 50 years ago, ships began to use automatic control systems to stay in position. Called Dynamic Positioning, this computer-controlled system automatically positions the vessel to a fixed point on the sea bottom or a determined distance from another ship or rig.[8]

A vessel moves in six degrees of freedom. The DP controls motion in the horizontal plane, i.e. the movement longitudinally and laterally, as well as rotation around the vertical axis. However, DP cannot control heave, roll and pitch, and thus is not a preventive solution for seasickness.

The International Maritime Organization (IMO) defines a DP system as having three main components: a DP control system, a power supply system and a thruster system. However, it is the control system that people mostly think about when discussing a DP system. Without this, the other two components compose a traditional propulsion system.

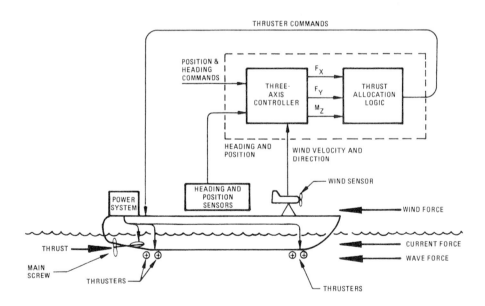

A simplified schematic diagram of a dynamic positioning system from the early days of DP. The solutions have become more sophisticated, but the principles are the same today. The illustration is taken from the 'DP bible' of the time, Max J. Morgan's book *Dynamic Positioning of Offshore Vessels* from 1978.

Dynamic positioning is based on feedback control. To maintain a specific position, information as to vessel whereabouts and targeted position must be accessible. Calculating a vessel's position demands various measurements from one or more reference systems to determine the vessel's exact location. When servicing an oil platform, a supply ship must know the exact distance from the structure, whereas a pipe-laying vessel must know its correct position to follow a defined pipe-laying track.

One of these reference systems is generally a satellite-based positioning system. The most common of these is GPS, which accurately calculates position anywhere in the world within an error radius of one metre. Additionally, positioning sensors showing actual position in relation to one or several fixed points are often used. Hydroacoustic position sensors, for example, calculate position based on signals between a transducer on a vessel's hull and transponders on the seabed. Another possibility for determining vessel position is the so-called taut wire application, a wire maintained in constant tension with a depressor weight on the seabed. Position is calculated through knowing the exact length and angle of the wire in relation to the weight.

Radio signals, radar or laser, are examples of other systems used to determine position. These systems have different advantages and disadvantages and are often bundled together to increase precision and safety. Further, position data from reference systems are supplemented with directional information from several gyrocompasses. In alliance, these systems provide several measurements for determining ship position, relative or absolute.

Once the actual position is determined, the next challenge is to precisely position the vessel in the exact spot. Fixed or azimuth rotatable propellers or thrusters guide the vessel to where the distance deviation between the actual and target position is least. This process not only requires exact calculations for power supply and the distribution of power between the different propulsion systems, but demands advanced mathematical models and calculations. These are part of the cybernetic DP control structure, the very brain of the system. A guidance component calculates programmed desired movements to bring the vessel to its desired position. Another main component is the model-based estimator, which gathers information about wind, position, the use of thrusters and other forces to calculate real-time vessel movement. Often referred to as the Kalman filter, the estimator continues its calculations despite any short or lengthy disappearance of key measurement data. By comparing the programmed movements of the guidance unit with the actual movement of

Azimuth thrusters installed on the icebreaker *Fennica*. The propellers are over five metres in diameter. Each of them has a motor that can deliver 7.5 MW and a thrust of more than 130 tons. Photo: KM.

the estimator, a regulator then determines the overall thruster forces needed to accurately position the vessel. The regulator sends signals to the thruster allocation unit, which then calculates optimal command distribution to the propellers and thrusters. Together, the guidance unit, the estimator, regulator and thruster allocation unit are the most important components in the brain of a DP system brain.

Main propellers located aft and one or more thrusters are used to manoeuvre a vessel. Thrusters can have both fixed direction, such as tunnel thrusters, mounted in a tube running through the hull, or controllable direction, such as azimuth thrusters, which are mounted under the vessel and can be rotated 360 degrees. These devices are driven by the vessel's power supply system. Today, modern DP vessels are based mainly on diesel-electric propulsion. The vessel's diesel engines drive power generators supplying energy to the electric motors for the thrusters.

How the forces of nature affect a DP vessel is dependent on vessel size and design, resulting in a large variety of thruster equipment and power supply systems. Vessels towing heavy anchor chains while moving an oil rig or securing precision tension control during the installation of subsea pipelines have much higher demands for power and heavier equipment.

A modern supply ship is generally equipped with four to five thrusters, representing an aggregate power demand of some fifty cars, that is about 5 MW. Annually, these thrusters consume several million litres of diesel, corresponding to energy consumption in some one thousand Norwegian homes. A drilling rig, on the other hand, is equipped with five to eight giant thrusters representing a capacity of 30 MW. Its annual power consumption is five to ten times higher than a supply ship, the same amount used by a medium-sized Norwegian hydropower plant. In comparison, almost double the total capacity of the Gamlebrofoss power station in the river Numedalslågen, a river just a stone's throw from Kongsberg Maritime's main office, Carpus.[9] The annual energy consumption of a drilling rig could power 6000 homes, that is, half the residences in the city of Kongsberg.

Major forces are set in motion when conducting ocean operations. These represent significant operational costs and heavy investments, especially in the vessels themselves. The price tag of a modern supply ship is some one-half billion NOK. A drilling rig can be ten times that amount. The day rate for a supply ship is a couple hundred thousand NOK, while a drilling rig may cost over one million per day. Significant fuel costs come in addition, though they are usually paid by the contractor. If one utilises time well, huge profits can be made. Dynamic positioning is more than just precise positioning; it's about the efficient use of time.

The fifty-plus years of DP systems history began with an American drill ship operating in the Pacific during 1961. Sixteen years later, Kongsberg delivered its first Norwegian-produced DP system to a North Sea diving vessel. Since then, DP has been developed for a series of new applications and installed on board a number of vessel types including drilling, supply, pipe and cable laying, rock installation, shuttle tankers, crane and lifting, mine sweeping, cruise, floating accommodation and yachts. DP is no longer just about being positioned, but about following a predefined track or staying within a defined area.

MORE THAN TECHNOLOGY ALONE

Dynamic positioning is seldom mentioned without it being referred to as a system, that is, a dynamic positioning system most often called a DP system. This term implies that it is composed of several parts, which not only belong together, but are necessary for the system to function as a total unit. Though a DP system usually refers to several technical entities including an operator station, a control unit, position sensors, power supply and thrusters, it is more than just technical components. Its operation is based on a broad range of non-technical elements. System use is regulated by numerous safety regulations, specific legislation covering equipment and operational requirements, and global international standards stipulated by classification companies. Additionally, the DP system is dependent on software applications that enable communication between the control system and all other on board units and systems.

Once created, technology evolves and must be maintained to meet regulatory requirements and new demands. The system is dependent on developers, technical service professionals and others to upgrade components and keep it functioning as a whole. It is also dependent on a large sales and market organisation to relay user feedback to system developers who undertake necessary upgrades and then pass them on to the benefit of all system users. Ultimately,

The DP console on the aft bridge of the diving vessel *Stena Constructor*. Stena was a very important customer for Albatross during its early years. Between 1979 and 1981 the shipowner ordered Albatross DP systems for six of its diving vessels. This picture is from 1979 and shows, from left, Oddvar Rusten, Leif Gulliksen and Sjur Bøyum. Photo: Mediafoto.

the many operators using the system determine how successful it is in performing its intended tasks. However, a DP system cannot function without documentation and relevant education and training. Operational understanding is a prerequisite to people using the technology.

A DP system is dependent on the efforts of a significant number of people, who ensure that each part of the system collaborates together. In fact, many technologies found in a DP system were not developed for this purpose. Without a computer it would be impossible to operate a DP system. More powerful, quicker and cheaper machines have played an important role in system development. Other factors such as new data storage technology and communications protocols, and improved operating systems and programming languages, have played an integral role in DP structure. Take GPS for example. This technology, though not developed with a DP in mind, has become a major component. When understanding DP, as a system, it's not easy to define where one technology stops and the other begins.

THE ART OF PERFECT POSITIONING

The discovery of oil in the North Sea the day before Christmas Eve in 1969 presented industry with a package of previously unimaginable DP opportunities. The original Albatross Dynamic Positioning System evolved through the dynamic synergy between research ideas, modern high-tech industry vision and maritime tradition. Who would have thought that a state-owned business in a small village deep in Norway's interior would not only establish itself in this market, but become a global leader?

Today virtually all offshore operations are entirely dependent on dynamic positioning. It is hard to picture modern offshore oil or gas production without DP. Conversely, it is difficult to imagine the development of DP systems without the growth of the petroleum industry. Though many factors played diverse roles in the development of DP technology, the petroleum industry had the greatest impact. The scope of this industry, combined with developments in downstream, upstream and transport operations, has deeply affected DP design and development.

Though external market demands and developments stand as major drivers, they alone have not created the DP unit. Technology is not created by external conditions, but by the initiatives and dedication of entrepreneurs. The DP system has risen through the collaborative involvement of individuals, that is, their unique contribution of expertise, experience and determination to exploit

Wind and waves create significant risks and demands for vessels that have to work close to platforms, as they can constantly be pushed away from, or in the worst-case scenario into, rigs. This picture is from the brochure 'Dynamic Positioning Systems ADP100' from 1984.

new opportunities. What others could not see, they created. Without these personalities, the first Albatross system, and its many successors, would have never seen the light of day.

It is a truly remarkable accomplishment for these DP pioneers to have created such an advanced dynamic positioning system. Even more impressive is that they succeeded in establishing a business that grew to be the market leader in just a few years, and that they retain their DP pole position year after year. This not only reflects solid technology and the determination and ability to improve the product over time, but that the company has managed to incorporate feedback from clients and position itself in the market by setting the standard for what a DP system should be, and what clients can expect from it. How did they manage this?

It all started when someone decided to master the art of perfect positioning. This book is about how this seemingly simple aspiration has evolved into the Kongsberg DP.

2

EUREKA

IN 1971 NTH Professor Jens Glad Balchen contacted the management of Kongsberg Våpenfabrikk (KV) with a business idea. Balchen explained that international companies were now selling systems for dynamic positioning (DP) to drilling vessels in the offshore market.[1] He believed, due to recent theories of cybernetics, that it would be possible to create better DP systems than those that the foreign firms delivered. Wouldn't it, therefore, be an idea for KV to develop its own DP system, based on these theories, which it could offer to the offshore industry?

Balchen pointed to Norway's long history as a seafaring nation. Soon, the huge Ekofisk field in the North Sea would start production of oil and gas. He was convinced that operations in such inhospitable waters would require new and more advanced technological solutions. As Balchen saw it, KV had established a good reputation for its high level of industrial expertise and ability to deliver. Furthermore, he noted, it was his opinion that the company had a responsibility to contribute to the development of Norwegian industry within the potential offshore market.

Balchen spoke at length, and with passion, about his idea, but it didn't help. The KV management saw no immediate market for the product, and the professor had to leave the meeting without the success he'd hoped for. Despite this setback he didn't give up, contacting KV on several occasions afterwards, but always with the same result.[2] What was it that gave Balchen the drive to take the initiative and push ahead?

A HOLE IN THE BOTTOM OF THE SEA[3]

In 1962, the oil company Shell launched a semi-submersible drilling rig called *Blue Water 1*, which, utilising anchors and positioning, could maintain a set

Jens Glad Balchen, the leading authority in the field of Cybernetics in Norway, graduated from Norges Tekniske Høgskole (NTH – Norwegian Institute of Technology) in 1949. He was a central figure in building up the most important educational and research community for cybernetics in Norway, at NTH and the research organisation SINTEF. Numerous engineers were trained in automation, servo engineering or control engineering, as cybernetics was often referred to in Norway. The knowledge they transferred to Norwegian companies helped to modernise industry in the country. Balchen was also behind a number of technological innovations, some of which became successful products. Photo: Image archive at the Institute for technical cybernetics, NTNU.

position. This was enabled with a so-called tiltmeter – a wire attached to a weight on the seafloor – and, by measuring the angle of the wire, it was possible to determine if the rig maintained the same position. The rig was capable of operating at depths of more than 200 metres. With this advance, the dream of being able to drill from an installation that was not resting on the seafloor became a reality. In the years after 1950, the oil companies moved from the wetlands along the coast of the Gulf of Mexico and out into the shallowest waters beyond the coastline. At that point, a depth of 20 metres was the long-established limit for fixed rig operations. Since the oil companies considered it very likely that there were significant petroleum reserves in deeper water, there were experiments with floating devices, of which *Blue Water 1* was one. The rig was not the only innovation that Shell pulled out of its sleeve, as another team was working almost simultaneously with its own deep-water project not far from Los Angeles.[4]

In 1961, the drillship *CUSS 1* was launched in California. The ship was owned by a consortium of oil companies, including Continental, Union, Shell and Superior Oil – namely CUSS, giving the ship its name. Originally built as a marine barge for World War II, it was transformed into a kind of technological research station for drilling in the ocean in 1956. In 1958 the ship had drilled holes in the seabed between 14 and 100 metres deep, moored to just four buoys to hold it in place. However, compared to the waters it would later operate in, this was just a cautious test for *CUSS 1*.

The drillship *CUSS 1* at anchor off the Californian coast. Launched in 1961, the ship was a marine barge that was repurposed to perform core drilling in bedrock at great depths. It had four azimuthing thrusters and was manually controlled by operators who determined positioning visually, or with sonar. The operators could hold *CUSS 1* in position within a radius of 180 metres while drilling was ongoing. Core samples of rock on the seabed were taken at depths of down to 3500 metres. Photo: Howard Shatto private archives.

In 1960, the vessel was upgraded, giving it the capacity to drill in much deeper water. To cope with such operations, the ship had to be virtually stationary. It was therefore equipped with four azimuth thrusters (rotatable propellers) of 147 kilowatts (kW) each, one in every 'corner' of the vehicle. The thrusters were manually controlled by two operators following the ship's position visually, and on a sonar screen.

Four buoys on the water's surface defined an area with a radius of 180 metres. This gave the operators a picture of the zone that the ship had to stay within. Sonar, a hydro acoustic instrument developed during World War II to detect submarines, showed objects in the water on a screen and, in the case of *CUSS 1*, was used to indicate where the vessel lay in relation to four deep-lying underwater buoys.[5] In March 1961 an operation to drill down to 945 metres off La Jolla in California was successful. Several core samples were later taken near Guadalupe Island off Mexico.[6] While the first drilling operations were performed by the ship's owners to test its capabilities, its final task was conducted by a group of scientists who hired the vessel for something called Project Mohole.[7]

The initiative for Project Mohole stemmed from Walter Munk, a famous American oceanographer and geophysicist from Scripps Oceanographic Institute in the US. In 1956 he had approached the National Science Foundation (NSF) and applied for research assistance for test drilling to investigate the bedrock in the ocean off the coast of California and Mexico, and later near Hawaii, where the ocean was up to 6,000 metres deep.[8] The idea was followed up by a research group with the exotic name of American Miscellaneous Society (AMSOC), an informal collaboration between different types of scientists from the US Navy. The researchers had backgrounds from disciplines such as biology, oceanography and geology, but shared a strong common interest in the unsolved mysteries of the ocean's depths. The leader of the group was oceanographer Willard Bascom.[9] Both Munk and Bascom were inspired by the Croatian geologist Andrija Mohorovicic, who had given his name to *The Mohorovicic Discontinuity*, the transition between the Earth's warm core and its crust. According to contemporary theories the surfaces (plates) of the crust were in motion. Today these theories have been scientifically verified, and surveys show that the release of tension in the transition between these various plates is the most common cause of earthquakes. In the 1960s the theories were still controversial, and the researchers wanted to find out more about this phenomena.[10]

The exploration drilling at Guadalupe Island must have been deemed satisfactory, as the project took core samples of rock 200 metres below the seabed, at a depth of 4,000 metres. This was more than 30 times the previous record for deep water drilling. Even through vessels could move a significant amount under deep water drilling without damage to the drill string, it was nevertheless quite an achievement to hold a four kilometre long drill string in virtually the same surface position under operation.

A SHIP CALLED *EUREKA*

Another drillship, *Eureka*, was launched in 1961. It was significantly smaller than *CUSS 1*, but was a newbuild specifically designed for drilling at great depths. This time it was Shell alone, and not a consortium, which owned the

Eureka was launched in the same year as *CUSS 1* and shared the same purpose – to drill at great depths while being held in position. While the position of *CUSS 1* was determined by a combination of visual observation and sonar, Eureka utilised a so-called taut wire. The vessel's movements were calculated from the cable's angle. With these calculations the analogue steering device that controlled the two thrusters could move it back, forth and sideways by adjusting the thrusters' azimuth and speed. Tests proved that it worked as constructor Howard Shatto had envisaged. With this development, the world's first automatic positioning system was born. Photo: Howard Shatto private archives.

Howard Shatto, often referred to as the 'father of Dynamic Positioning', was born in Minnesota. After graduating from Yale as an electrical engineer in 1946, he gained employment with the oil company, Shell. He quickly rose through the ranks, taking on various positions before moving to Shell's development division for underwater technology at Long Beach, outside Los Angeles, in 1960. In 1961 he headed the development of a control unit for the drillship *Eureka*, solving the challenge with a groundbreaking innovation. Photo: Howard Shatto private archives.

ship. In addition, *Eureka* was equipped with a system that could keep the ship stationary during drilling operations. At the outset, the plan was to use the same type of instrumentation and manual control as *CUSS 1*. However, in large part due to the influence of Howard Shatto, a young American electrical engineer connected to the construction project, these plans were changed.[11]

Shatto was born in Minnesota and educated at Georgia Tech and Yale. He graduated in electrical engineering in 1946 and was hired by Shell that same year. Thereafter he worked his way up through the ranks, acquiring a broad range of experience that proved to be valuable when it came to *Eureka*'s construction. The first task he was charged with after his training period at Shell was coordinating the construction of three small diesel-electric drilling rigs outside New Orleans. One of them later exploded after having drilled into a gas pocket. The result was a gigantic crater in the swamp where the rig had once stood. The rig itself was never found.[12]

During the Korean War Shatto was drafted by the US Navy, where he was tasked with educating military engineers. Once back in Shell, he led maintenance operations on the automation systems at a gas plant in New York. It was there that he gained insight into how modern industrial control systems worked, but it was what would happen after 1960 that would set his career on a new trajectory. It was then that he began working with Shell's underwater technology development division at Long Beach, outside of Los Angeles, in what was called the 'deepwater group'. This group worked towards the objective of building Shell's knowledge and technological expertise so that it would be well-positioned if oil production had to move out into deep water. The group performed tasks relating to the development of wellheads, unmanned underwater vehicles (called Mobots) and experiments with control systems for ships.

Shatto's boss, Bill Bates, wanted to build a similar vessel to *CUSS 1*, but with smaller dimensions. The assignment was given to the Orange shipyard in Texas and Shatto was asked to work on equipping the ship. When Shatto arrived at the yard the plan was to construct and install a control system that could keep the ship stationary over a given time. Two azimuth thrusters, with engines boasting power outputs of, respectively, 147 and 294 KV, would ensure adequate power for this task. Basically, Bates wanted to control the ship manually, in the same way that *CUSS 1* was operated.

Shatto himself said that he was terrified of the thought that *Eureka* would be manually controlled. The ship would be drilling in shallower water than *CUSS 1*, and the shallower the water, the less deviation the drill string would withstand. In his opinion it was madness to believe that a manual steering system had the capacity to react quickly enough if the ship began to drift off.[13] One day as he sat in the blazing heat of his car on the way home from Ventura to Los Angeles, he got the idea for an automatic control system: «It was out of this angst that the first concept was born.»[14] Just before Christmas 1960, Shatto wrote to Bates and expressed both his concern for the control system and an outline of what he believed to be a better approach. Bates replied that such a system was unnecessary, but if Shatto wanted to, he would let him try out a new solution. Bates also promised to treat Shatto and his wife to a slap-up dinner if it worked.[15]

Shatto's control system was based on concepts and equipment from the processing industry, so his experience with the automation of industrial processes came in handy. The main part of the steering mechanism consisted of three standard electronic PID controllers (Proportional-Integral-Derivative), one controller for each horizontal degree of freedom. A PID controller is a basic technical control principle implemented in countless control units and used to control electrical and mechanical devices such as engines, pumps, heaters, fans, valves and other elements to achieve stable levels, temperatures, thicknesses, weights, volumes, or amounts of other types.[16] The PID controllers, which were supplied by Honeywell, were quite modern for their time. At this time, controllers were typically pneumatic, but in this case they were electronic and connected to an electromechanical device that relayed command signals to the ship's two azimuth thrusters.

The new control unit, christened 'APE', was designed and patented by Shell, but built by Hughes Aircraft, which took USD 50,000 for the assignment. This firm, founded by the legendary industrialist, filmmaker and eccentric Howard Hughes, would also be important in the next stage of dynamic positioning's development. In this instance, Hughes Aircraft made Shell's new system in

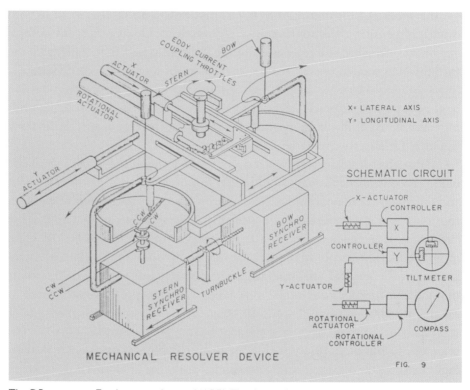

The DP system on Eureka was nicknamed 'APE'. This figure shows a sketch of the electromechanical mechanism that converted the commands from three PID controllers (one for each degree of freedom) to azimuth and RPM commands for the two thrusters. The solution was patented. Illustration: Howard Shatto private archives.

accordance with Shatto's specifications. The steering unit could move the boat back and forth and sideways by adjusting the thrusters' azimuth angle (orientation) and speed, and hence bring the world's first marine thrust allocation functionality to life. Compared with today's advanced systems, it was relatively primitive, but at that time it was groundbreaking, marking a major step towards precise positioning without anchoring.

Although the goal of the control systems on both the *CUSS 1* and *Eureka* was to allow the vessels to maintain the same position relative to a point on the seabed, there were major differences in the control systems and positioning sensors. While the position of the *CUSS 1* was determined by a combination of visual observation and sonar, *Eureka* utilised a taut wire. To keep an eye on how the ship's position changed, the tiltmeter connected to an oscilloscope, an instrument used to measure the temporal variations in electrical signals.

The *Eureka*'s positioning system was first tested manually, but it proved impossible to keep the ship in position. However, when the automatic control system was switched on a little 'miracle' occurred. The people on the bridge saw the luminous spot on their screen move slightly back and forth at first, before it moved into the centre of the oscilloscope, where it then stayed. Thereafter the boat remained in the same position for an entire hour and a core sample was obtained from a drilled depth of some 350 metres. Shatto was not on board for the test, but Bates was. Bystanders claim that Bates just about hovered three feet above the ground when he came ashore. Shatto got the promised dinner with his wife. *Eureka* thus became the world's first fully-automated positioned ship. Dynamic positioning had been born.[17] Shatto would later be involved in the construction of other and more advanced DP systems.

Development occurred within just a few years in the early 1960s, gaining momentum from a variety of different fields within research and industry. During the Second World War Britain and the United States developed many new technologies, such as the radar, echo sounder and sonar, as well as equipment and control algorithms that could measure and control various systems and industrial processes. The US Manhattan Project, which led to the development of the atomic bomb, was also the origin of new knowledge and technological concepts.

TRANSFERRING TECHNOLOGY TO NORWAY

Although the most important technologies were of foreign origin, they did reach Norway after some time. A large-scale transfer of technology was made possible first through the Marshall Plan, and later by the Organisation for European Economic Cooperation (OEEC) and the military alliance NATO (North Atlantic Treaty Organisation). Both the economic assistance programme for the reconstruction of Europe after World War II and the military cooperation between the US and the European countries were important in stimulating technology transfer and industrial development. It was not just about moving products and production processes across borders, but equally about the transfer of professional people and knowledge. In the years between 1950 and 1970 many Norwegian engineers, and other professionals, were either educated or trained in the United States. Several major scholarship programmes catered for that demand.[18]

At the same time as people, knowledge and technology circulated between the US and Europe, post-war institutions for technical research were under development in Norway. In 1946 The Royal Norwegian Council for Scientific and Industrial Research (NTNF) and the Defence Research Establishment (FFI) were founded. Thanks to funding from NTNF more technical research institutions could be financed in the years that followed, namely the Central Institute for Science and Industrial Research (SI) in Oslo, the Institute for Atomic Energy (IFA) at Kjeller and in Halden, and the Foundation for Scientific and Industrial Research (SINTEF) at the Norwegian Institute of Technology (NTH) in Trondheim. Another well-known research organisation, the Chr. Michelsen Institute (CMI) in Bergen, had already been established in 1930.[19] These institutions were crucial hubs for the knowledge that was transferred from the UK and USA. It was here that foreign technology could be understood and built upon. An example of arguably one of the most important types of research and knowledge transfer in this period was cybernetics.

Cybernetics takes its name from the Greek word kybernetes, meaning helmsman. A central figure in the development of this interdisciplinary field was the American mathematician Norbert Wiener. His book *Cybernetics: or Control and Communication in the Animal and the Machine* from 1948, became a theoretical framework for the control of complex dynamic systems.[20] The principles were perhaps complicated, but the goals were simple. It focused on how different factors in complex systems influence one another and how such processes can be controlled to achieve goals without unwanted side effects. The central point is measuring the result (output) of a process and controlling the factors that affect (input) the process.[21] The systems can be anything from living organisms to systems within society, and machines. Cybernetics became the foundation and the theoretical basis for applied fields with dynamic names such as: power engineering, control engineering and automation engineering.

The cybernetic principle of feedback can be easily explained by looking at a typical manufacturing process in a factory. A liquid is heated to a certain level and then needs to be kept at that temperature. The operator feels the temperature during the process and opens or closes a valve depending on what he determines the temperature to be. For a more accurate measurement the operator's hand can be replaced by a thermometer. The operator's role can be further reduced by a computer that determines the temperature and decides when the operator should open or close the valve. This part of the process can also be replaced by a servomechanism that opens and closes the valve itself. At this stage, measurement, assessment and regulation have been replaced by a servo technical system that can manage processes automatically, and there is no need for human intervention.[22] With such cybernetic principles as a starting

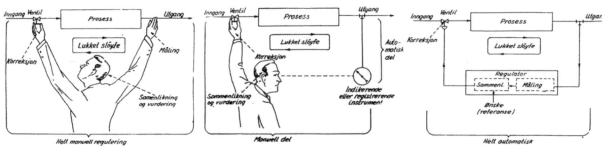

The illustration shows the cybernetic principle as explained in the text. It is taken from the *Teknikken og framtiden*, 1956.

point, a number of prototypes of technologies intended to streamline and auto-mate Norwegian industry were developed. Norwegian engineers were trained by US experts to this end, as the latter travelled around Europe on something akin to missionary expeditions. Donald P. Campbell from the Massachusetts Institute of Technology (MIT) travelled around Europe from 1949, lecturing on various ways to make industry more efficient. In that same year he gave a lecture in Oslo and many of the rising stars of Norwegian research and industry attended, including Haakon Sandvold, Erik Klippenberg, Karl Holberg and Fredrik Møller.

JENS GLAD BALCHEN AND CYBERNETICS

There was one important person missing when Campbell held his lecture in Oslo, namely Jens Glad Balchen. In the decades that followed he was to become the undisputed leader of Norwegian cybernetic research and develop-ment. However, at the time of the lecture he was about to complete his elec-trical engineering education and fully focused on exam preparations. After graduation from NTH in 1949, Balchen applied for a grant from the Foreign Ministry to study servo technology in the United States. His application was successful and he spent the year at Dunham Laboratory, Yale University, where he received a Master of Science in Engineering in 1951. Yale University is only two hours by car from MIT, paving the way for Balchen to make contact with one of the recognised servo groups there. By spring 1951 he was involved in the prestigious Whirlwind project. The US military planned, amongst other things, to use automated machining to make components for its fighter planes. The computer that the researchers used to control the milling machines was seen as particularly advanced, as it had its own display and could operate in a real-time mode. At this stage it was tested together with a lathe to investigate ways in which the lathe could be governed.[23] Control of milling machines was therefore one of the tasks Balchen took on when he returned to NTH in 1952. Automated machining was also one of the areas where KV, with assistance from SINTEF and SI, would come to invest heavily in from the end of the 1960s onwards.[24]

The term cybernetics was first adopted when Norbert Wiener launched his landmark book in 1948, but the principles and tasks that this branch of mathematics was to solve were not new. Many of the fundamental practical aspects of cybernetics were developed from the 1920s on. There were three areas in particular where the principles were applied: different mechanisms were used to control industrial production processes; in addition, Bell Labs and AT&T, the two big US telephone companies, used simple control mechanisms to amplify telephony signals over long distances; and the third example was when MIT built their first analogue computers in 1930.[25] These different cybernetic applications had different terminologies and cultures to understand and conceptualise the same principles. It was only later, when the automatic control tasks were described theoretically, that a common but interdisciplinary discipline emerged. The first time a PID controller was described in theoretical terms was in 1922, by Russian-American researcher Nicolas Minorsky. He experimented with, amongst other things, different principles for automated ship control.[26] The need for speed and precision in various weapon systems during World War II, such as radar-controlled anti-aircraft guns, led to the development of electronic calculating machines and servo technical controls. In the wake of inter-war progress, the development work connected to the Manhattan Project and research activities in the MIT Radiation Lab were of great significance to the development in understanding of the theoretical and practical aspects of cybernetics.[27]

Around 1949, when servo technology was introduced in Norway, «computations» and control were performed by various mechanical or semi-automatic relays. With the introduction of computers, calculations could be performed much more accurately and eventually with greater flexibility. During the 1950s, Docent (Associate Professor) Balchen and his colleagues at the NTH institute of automatic control technology (one of the first institutes of its kind in the world) and SINTEF's department for automatic control built up extensive expertise in the various aspects of cybernetics. The same happened at SI in Oslo and FFI at Kjeller. Efforts to find effective methods for the automation of industrial processes coincided with a growing interest in computers. At this

In 1954 Jens G. Balchen and the people at the Department of Control Engineering at NTH constructed an analogue computer called DIANA (DIfferential ANAlyser). This occurred at the same time as the digital computer NUSSE (Norsk Universell Siffermaskin Selvstyrt Elektronisk, or Norwegian Universal Autonomous Electronic Counting Machine) was assembled at the Norwegian Computing Centre in Oslo. While NUSSE was in principle a number cruncher, DIANA was designed to solve differential equations in real time, which was important for control technology tasks. Photo: Image archive at NTNU.

time the technological research groups in Norway bought or built their own computers. For example, NUSSE (Norsk Universell Siffermaskin Selvstyrt Elektronisk, or Norwegian Universal Autonomous Electronic Counting Machine), a digital computer, was built by the Norwegian Computing Centre. With the Norwegian machines DIANA, NUSSE, FREDERIC and LYDIA, all built in the 1950s, as the starting point, computer technology was used to develop different concepts for the automation of industrial production.[28]

THE CHALLENGE OF COMMERCIALISATION

Balchen led the construction of analogue computer DIANA (DIfferential ANAlyzer) in 1953 and, by 1962, NTH had acquired its first digital computer, the Danish GIER (Geotechnical Institute's Electronic Regnemaskin – meaning calculator). It was used to develop a variety of concepts for numeric control of machine tools and the automation of industrial processes.[29] In the years from 1955 to 1970, several types of automatic control systems for machine tools, flame cutters and drafting machines were developed by Balchen's institute. The systems Konrad, Polykon and Monokon came in quick succession. However, it was only Monokon that reached production stage, a CNC machine (Computerised Numerical Control) being produced by KV.

From 1954, the digital computer NUSSE was used to perform various mathematical and statistical arithmetic. This machine proved to be the cornerstone for the development of an automated cutting machine for steel plates, called the ESSI unit, and later for the drafting machine Kingmatic, which was acquired by several of the world's leading manufacturers of cars, ships and planes. The Monokon and Kingmatic became important products for KV.

Not everything that was developed by Balchen and his team was equally commercially successful. In 1965 a prototype for the automation of cement kilns was unveiled at Dalen Portland Cement Factory in Brevik. Over 100 executives from a variety of Norwegian manufacturing businesses attended the demonstration. According to Balchen himself the system worked perfectly, but none of those in attendance were interested in acquiring such equipment for their own companies.[30] Although no one wanted to buy this kind of automation system, Balchen still found backing. He persuaded Kåre Torp, the owner and director of NOBØ Factories in Trondheim, to finance the creation of the Comtec business in 1967. Comtec's objective was to develop and manufacture automation systems for smelters, cement factories and glassworks. When the company began, six employees from SINTEF's department for automatic control were key members of the workforce.[31] In the five years from 1967 to 1972, a number of successful units were delivered, but because of the large development and customisation costs only a few of the contracts achieved a profit. The focus and investment in industrial automation was therefore discontinued. Comtec then achieved real success as a supplier of typesetting equipment for European publishers and newspaper groups, achieving a market share in excess of 70 percent, but this wasn't to last. When major international companies entered the market the company lost customers and was eventually sold to Norsk Data in 1981.[32] Comtec's example is in many respects indicative of the situation facing those involved in the commercialisation and industrialisation of cybernetics in Norway between 1965 and 1980.

In other words, the commercialisation of industrial activity tied to concepts developed in research institutes proved to be difficult in a small country like Norway. Technological concepts and prototypes were not necessarily transferrable from research to industrial environments. Nor could it have been easy to transfer technologies from large and standardised manufacturing companies in the US to small and relatively non-standardised enterprises in Norway. In both cases, both the sender and receiver had to adapt for the process to succeed. The many challenges related to technology transfer and development are worth bearing in mind when considering the manner in which the KV management evaluated Balchen's suggestions.

THE ESTABLISHMENT OF NORCONTROL

Balchen's first stay in the US in the early 1950s was certainly productive. In the years that followed, he was there several times for research purposes. These stays often took place where his friend from his first years at MIT, the engineer Albert Conrad, was dean, namely the Engineering Faculty at the University of California, Santa Barbara (UCSB). Conrad's expertise lay in the control of electric motors. It was also there, in 1959, that Balchen became aware of the new research and development field of ship automation.[33]

At the end of the 1950s the US Maritime Administration (MARAD) had started development work on various forms of automating tasks on board vessels. In the same way that some envisioned automated factories, many others dreamed of automated ships controlled from the bridge.[34] Four enthusiastic Norwegian civil engineers were drawn to this optimistic, but as yet technologically unproven, 'future world' in 1959. They already knew each other, but travelled separately and had different assignments in the United States, primarily at universities in California. Alongside Balchen, there was Jan Getz, a director of Skipsteknisk Forskningsinstitutt (SFI, or Institute of Marine Technological Research) in Trondheim, who researched vessel corrosion problems. Arild Økland was Balchen's fellow at the institute of automatic control and was at Berkeley to learn about ship automation. The fourth was Ibb Høivold, who at this time was employed by CMI in Bergen. All four were excited about what they saw and could hardly wait to introduce these new possibilities to Norway.

In 1963, Noratom, Norsk Hydro and KV, under the leadership of Ibb Høivold, began a collaboration to develop automation systems for the main engine on the ammonia tanker *Haugvik*. SINTEF and Balchen were also involved periodically in this assignment. The automation solutions chosen for the system were pneumatic and relay-controlled, as opposed to computerised. At this time there were no computers that were small, robust and cheap enough to be used for this type of system. This push for machine room automation would later lead to the launch of the automation system Autochief, which remains a leading brand within engine automation. The project was successfully completed in 1964, to the great satisfaction of all participants. Classification society Det Norske Veritas (DNV) thereafter developed a new certification, namely E0 (Engine Zero). This certification meant that the engine room on ships could be largely unmanned while the engine was running. It also meant that shipowners could pay lower insurance premiums.[35] The experience from *Haugvik* paved the way for the creation of ship automation company Norcontrol in 1965, with Hoivold as its director.[36]

By the time the vessel *Taimyr*, owned by Wilh. Wilhelmsen, launched in 1969, Høivold and his people had developed a new automation system. This time it was supported by the brand new mini computer Nord-1, which was designed and built by the firm NORDATA – Norsk Data Elektronikk (later Norsk Data). The company was established and operated by Lars Monrad-Krohn, Per Bjørge and Rolf Skår, all with backgrounds from the Defence Research Institute.[37] With the system's installation on *Taimyr*, the vessel became the first Norwegian ship boasting automation of the bridge, power supply and cargo monitoring control, and one of the world's first radar-based anti-collision systems.[38] Throughout the 1970s, Norcontrol developed a variety of advanced control systems that were sold in Norway and Asia.[39]

A NEW ALGORITHM

When Balchen was in the US at the beginning of the 1960s, he met a researcher who was on his way to becoming a new star within cybernetics and the space age world of automation. It was the Hungarian-born Rudolf Emil Kalman. The meeting between the two marked not only the beginning of important research work, but also the start of a lifelong acquaintance. Just like Norbert Wiener, Kalman was to visit Balchen and the cybernetics community at NTH in Trondheim on several occasions.

Kalman's cybernetic theories implied a completely new way of handling measurements for control systems, regardless of whether they related to ships, submarines or spacecraft. The Kalman filter, which is an advanced mathematical algorithm, was a crucial part of the spacecraft navigation system utilised in the US Apollo programme, which led to man setting foot on the moon for the very first time on July 20 1969.[40] Kalman's theories and the Kalman filter were also crucial when KV began developing its DP system. It's therefore worth delving into Kalman's dramatic background and the factors that led to the development of his groundbreaking work in cybernetics.

Rudolf Kalman was born in Budapest, Hungary on 19 May 1930. As a result of the German occupation during World War II, his father decided that the

In 1969, the prototype of Norcontrol's DataChief engine control system was installed on board the *Taimyr*. The development of this computer system made it possible to leave the engine room unmanned for parts of the day. The system could also control a number of other functions on board. Norsk Data's Nord-1 computer operated as the system's 'brain'. Photo: KM.

The control console DataBridge on board *Taimyr*. The radar-based collision avoidance system (ARPA) attracted considerable attention. DataBridge contained a number of system modules to handle various aspects of ship operation, position determination and navigation. Photo: KM.

family had to flee, leading them on a journey through Turkey and the Middle East to North Africa. There they were taken care of by Allied forces and eventually sent to the United States. When the war was over, they were repatriated to postwar Germany, where they lived under difficult conditions until they were allowed to return to the US in 1949.[41] Kalman began to study electrical engineering at MIT, where he became interested in various aspects of mathematics, such as the Laplace transform. At MIT, he was told that such transforms were most commonly used in conjunction with servomechanisms, which were developed during the war and used to control, amongst other things, gun turrets and anti-aircraft weaponry. Thus he was guided into the field of applied mathematics for control-theoretical problems from an early stage. During his studies, Kalman, by chance, was introduced to a new mathematical world while waiting for an exam in electromagnetic theory. The examiner was delayed and Kalman had a whole hour in which to study a book he found on the examiner's office desk. The book was about nonlinear oscillations and was written by Nicolas Minorsky.[42] This book became hugely significant for Kalman's view of mathematics and subsequently also for the development of his career. He received a Bachelor degree from MIT in 1953 and a Masters degree the following year.

In 1955 Kalman began a doctorate at Columbia University in New York City. He defended his thesis just two weeks before the Soviet Union surprised the whole world by sending the satellite Sputnik into orbit on October 4 1957. Little did he know at that point that his own research in the years to follow would be important for the success of the American space programme.

In autumn 1958, Kalman got a job as a research mathematician at the Research Institute for Advanced Studies (RIAS) in Baltimore, Maryland. It was here that he developed the algorithm that bears his name, and broke through as a researcher of the very highest order. His 'eureka moment' arrived in November 1958 on the train ride home after a conference at Princeton University. At 1am the train encountered problems and stopped just outside Baltimore. Kalman was worn out and sleepy, but in the course of the next hour it suddenly hit him that he might be able to use the state space approach used in control theory to address the problem with Wiener filtering. The Wiener filter was an algorithm that was used to control processes in real-time, named after Norbert Wiener. Following the journey, Kalman continued working on his idea and, by the end of January 1959, he had developed the foundation of what would later become known as the Kalman filter. The result was first published in 1960 as «a new approach to linear filtering and prediction problems».[43] The paper was published in a journal outside his academic field since its result was so groundbreaking

The Hungarian-born mathematician and engineer Rudolf Emil Kalman is the originator of the Kalman filter. The algorithm, which removes 'noise' from data streams, was first presented by Kalman in an article published in 1960. It played a crucial role in landing the first astronauts safely on the moon and was later used for dynamic positioning and other technical systems. In 2008 Kalman received both the Charles Stark Draper Prize and the National Medal of Science, the highest honours awarded to researchers in the US. The latter was presented by President Obama during a ceremony at the White House in October 2009. Photo of Kalman: IEEE Global History Network. Photo of Obama and Kalman: Ryan K. Morris / National Science & Technology Medals Foundation.

that Kalman's contemporaries did not immediately understand its implications. In 1961 a further article was published with his colleague Richard Bucy.[44]

In short, the Kalman filter provides an intelligent filtering of measurements by combining a mathematical model of a system with the actual measurements from that system. Based on the statistical characteristics of the measurements, the model and the measurements are weighted optimally relative to each other in order to achieve far more accurate and stable signals than using only measurements alone. It is this model-based filtering that makes it possible to separate measurement noise in an unrivalled way.

In 1960, the International Federation of Automatic Control (IFAC) arranged its first World Congress in Moscow. One of the keynote speakers was the barely 30-year old Kalman, another was Norbert Wiener. In the following years Kalman was to be invited to hold speeches at all the major international conferences and universities. In 1964 he became a professor at Stanford University in California, moving to the University of Florida, Gainesville, as a professor from 1971. In 1973 he also received a position at ETH Zurich in Switzerland. With his mathematically advanced and also practically applicable results, Kalman contributed to the founding of modern control theory. System-theoretic concepts, such as state space, controllability and observability were central in his work.

Unlike the Wiener filter, the Kalman filter is a recursive algorithm that is particularly suitable for implementation on a computer. The algorithm therefore made a huge industrial breakthrough in a short period of time, starting with NASA and Stanley Schmidt, who learnt of the filter in autumn 1960 and subsequently developed it further for use in the Apollo vessels' navigation systems.[45] Using inertial navigation and star observations, the paths of spacecraft could be estimated with near perfection. Countless applications in everything from nuclear-powered submarines to GPS systems, and eventually dynamic positioning of ships at sea, would follow. Although Kalman's original findings still apply, the solutions have been continuously developed for the best possible practical use, especially to tackle challenges related to numerical effects in computers. When Balchen and his colleagues began working with solutions for DP systems, Kalman's algorithm became an essential element of their developments.

A NORWEGIAN COMPUTER INDUSTRY

Computers became a key technology for cybernetics and its practical applications. It is therefore difficult to picture what happened without mentioning the activities that took place at the FFI in the years after 1962. In the 1950s FFI bought a huge Mercury computer from England, called FREDERIC (Ferranti Electronic Defence Research Institute Computer). Mercury was actually the first computer that was produced in quantity and sold in component parts. The Norwegian astronomer and mathematician Jan W. Garwick arranged its purchase from Ferranti, a company with ties to Manchester University's computer research milieu, which has long led the world in terms of computer development.[46] The components cost a total of NOK 700,000 and were driven by 2000 radio valves. The story goes that once the computer was purchased, the FFI didn't have any money left for the customs duties. Machine parts were therefore smuggled into the country as diplomatic mail. SI, SINTEF and CMI also assembled similar computers. These helped to give Norwegian technology researchers the tools and fundamental skills they needed.

The first computers were, however, too expensive, large and unreliable for use in anything other than development exercises at research institutes. The major electronics companies of the time, such as DEC, Hewlett-Packard and IBM therefore began the development of something called mini-computers in the 1960s. These mini computers would be more flexible and robust, cheaper and smaller than the major stationary computers that were their precursors. FFI was keen to be involved in this movement and, in 1962, started the development of something called the Simulator for Automatic Machinery (SAM).[47] This development coincided with another important project FFI was involved in.

KV had given FFI an assignment to design a surface-to-surface missile, called Penguin, «the bird that could not fly».[48] The management at FFI claimed that they needed better equipment to analyse missile flight paths during test firing. NOK 700 000 of Penguin's development budget was therefore set aside to construct the mini-computer SAM. FFI's desire to build a mini-computer, instead of buying one from abroad, was probably the main driving force behind this creative use of the military's money. In this intense computing environment, there were several people, such as Karl Holberg – who was, amongst other things, central in the development of KV's anti-submarine missile, Terne – who saw the possibilities for establishing computer firms, and perhaps even a Norwegian computer industry.[49] SAM was completed in a few years, with the project spearheaded by Yngvar Lundh and Lars Monrad Krohn. The team also simultaneously developed the software SAMBA (Sam's Binary Assembler).[50]

When the work on SAM was completed in 1964, FFI began work on its follow-up. ODIN was a trajectory computation system for Field Artillery mortars. It was based on the SM3 computer, which was a further development of the SAM. When this system was completed in 1969, KV received a substantial order for its production, putting it into direct and fierce competition with Norsk Data (ND). This was seen by some at ND, and their supporters within the Norwegian academic computing arena, to be unfair, with the state-owned KV profiting from a position of favouritism. The historian Knut Øyangen writes that KV, with this delivery to the Armed Forces, broke an unwritten rule that state-owned companies should not compete with privately owned ones.[51]

In addition, there was another military project that helped increase the competence levels of KV's computer specialists. The Armed Forces ordered a new series of submarines from Germany, the Kobben-class submarines, which were delivered to the Navy between 1961 and 1967. However, the fire control systems the submarines were delivered with were unsatisfactory and needed replacing. In response, KV developed the fire guidance system MSI 70U, which utilised the same computer as the Field Artillery, namely the SM3. A less complicated and more affordable version of the SM3, the SM4, was created for the civilian market. The successor to both of these, KV's proprietary KS500, was, for the time, a high quality computer, but primarily suited to different types of process control.[52]

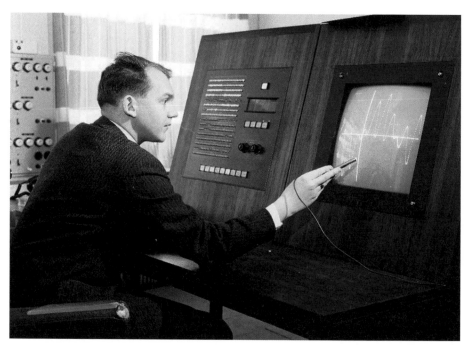

Rolf Skår in front of the mini-computer SAM, which was built by the Norwegian Defence Research Establishment (FFI) in 1964. Work on SAM spawned the idea of creating a Norwegian company to manufacture computers. In 1967, Skår, Lars Monrad-Krohn and Per Bjørge, together with investors Terje Mikalsen and Tarald Glastad, founded the company that eventually became Norsk Data. They are often referred to as Norway's first computer entrepreneurs. Nord-computers were sold in large numbers until well into the 1980s. Photo: FFI.

THE STRATEGISTS OF INDUSTRIAL POLICY

Norcontrol eventually achieved real success as a provider of ship automation in Norway and abroad, but initially experienced great difficulties in returning an operating profit. This situation was not unique to Norcontrol. From 1960 until well into the 1970s, the electronics industry had to be nurtured with great care.

Between 1956 and 1970, technological research and development work was mainly funded by the Norwegian government through NTNF and channelled through research institutes. In the wake of the institutes' concept development projects, private firms such as Comtec and Norsk Data were established, or the concepts were fed into state enterprises such as KV. KV's strategic role as a midwife for computers, electronic control systems and industrial automation is important in understanding the continuing narrative. The legitimacy of this 'system', often called the linear model, provided the authorities with justification for the high share of state funding the Norwegian technological research institutes received.[53] A far-reaching discussion about the politics of research was ongoing from 1964. The starting point was a critique of the substantial allocations of funding given to nuclear research. A conflict over the optimum use of large-scale state subsidies relating to technological research and development projects soon emerged. As a result, the handling of policies relating to the potentially important electronics industry and research fields became an industrial political theme well into the 1970s.[54]

The industrialisation of technological research proved difficult after 1960. The few private companies that emerged often went bankrupt or survived on the thinnest of margins. However, the state-owned enterprises could plough on with potential loss projects thanks to transfers of new capital or loans from the government. A final instrument for both private and state enterprises to take advantage of were the public sector 'District Development Funds', from 1960, and the Development Fund, from 1965. This became another way to use public funding to reach very specific political goals.[55] The build up and organisation of the research system, as well as the availability of public funding, represented an important structural framework for what happened to the part of the industry that sold high-tech products in this period. Key industrial political strategists, such as Jens Chr. Hauge and Finn Lied, watched over developments with interest.[56]

Hauge had been head of the resistance movement 'Milorg' during the war, Defence Minister from 1945 to 1952 and was vice chairman of KV from 1953 to 1982. Finn Lied led FFI in the periods 1957–1971 and 1972–1983, and was Secretary of State for Industry from 1971 to 1972. Lied was also Chairman of Statoil, the Norwegian state oil company established in 1972, in the years between 1974 and 1984. Together with Bjarne Hurlen, KV CEO from 1956 to 1975, and Arve Johnsen, Statoil CEO from 1972, this influential coterie acted as a driving force in the development of Norwegian industry. Separately and together they tried to control the electronics industry, as well as the operations of KV and Statoil. The comradeship that formed when they participated in the resistance movement during the war lived on in their common struggle for Norwegian industry and business development in the post-war years.

As Norwegian ship automation technology was developing, and onwards through the 1970s, Hauge and Lied endeavoured to make the businesses within the maritime electronics sector stronger and more viable by joining them together. Those that struggled were swallowed up by, or merged with, those that proved to be more successful. Historian Francis Sejersted writes with reference to his colleague Knut Sogner: «The idea was to commit to three cornerstone companies – the privately owned Tandberg, representing consumer electronics,

Finn Lied and Jens Chr. Hauge in 1974. These two Arbeiderparti (Labour party) men were, together with leading industry executives such as Kongsberg Våpenfabrikk's Bjarne Hurlen and Statoil's Arve Johnsen, important strategists in the creation of Norwegian industrial policy in the 1960s and 1970s. Photo: NTB scanpix.

the state-owned KV, catering for the professional electronics segment, and the foreign-owned Elektrisk Bureau, representing the telecommunications sector, which was bought back as part of the strategy. Operations were then streamlined and coordinated with a basis in publicly supported research and development work. This ambitious plan failed completely.»[57]

The result of these management experiments was often competition or conflict between the individual businesses, particularly between those that were privately and state-owned. As previously mentioned, Norsk Data ended up in a competitive situation with KV when the defence department wanted to invest in new computer systems for Field Artillery, and KV was selected. Hauge and Lied stood behind the scenes here, eager to have KV as the sole Norwegian computer manufacturer.[58]

A BUSINESS WITH A MISSION

Knowledge of KV's position in Norway and its corporate development in the post-war period is essential in understanding the creation of a Norwegian system for dynamic positioning. The KV factory was established in 1814 and has a long history as an important weapon supplier for the national armed forces. One of its key developments, amongst other things, was the Krag-Jørgensen rifle, an early Norwegian manufacturing and export success.[59] After World War II was over, KV, along with Raufoss Ammunition Factory (RA) and the main Naval yard, became holding companies under the umbrella of the Armed Forces. These were businesses with close connections to the state and were not operated according to usual market considerations. However, it was quickly determined that this was an organisational model unsuited to further success, and in 1948 KV was reorganised under a more conventional business model, with a supervisory board, a board of directors and a CEO. In 1968, KV was converted into a limited company. The firm would now operate in the same way as similar concerns – something that could lead to problems.[60] KV also had a strategic role as a supplier of military equipment, in addition to the fact that it had a degree of responsibility for employment in the region.

In 1948 there were 900 employees at the weapons factory in Kongsberg, but by 1968 this figure had grown to 2000, a formidable increase. There was an expectation that the business would be financially self-sufficient, but no dividends were paid out between 1948 and 1968. The turnover rose every year, but profit did not increase proportionally. Descriptions of the business display a general pattern of low equity, small returns and a large and steadily growing debt. However, this didn't necessarily imply a crisis situation for the firm – at least until well into the 1980s – as the owner, the Norwegian state, consolidated the deficits. During this time, the business also transformed itself academically, as the proportion of highly qualified engineers increased.[61] During the 1960s and 70s the business changed both in terms of ownership, organisation, expertise and products. Sales of weapons and weapons systems stagnated, and the management reacted by increasing the portfolio of civilian products.

Hauge and Lied fronted the company politically, recruited customers and ensured financial support when it was needed. They worked in close collaboration with Hurlen, who led KV in the key years between 1956 and 1980, first as CEO until 1975 and then as chairman. This trio – Hauge, Lied and Hurlen – were important when it came to planning and strategic choices, and they directed the company's ongoing assignments until well into the 1980s. When KV was reorganised in 1968, the plan was for the company to play a strategic role as a producer of modern technology developed by the country's technological research institutes. Using concepts that were previously developed at SINTEF, FFI and SI, KV was able to offer a variety of electronic equipment and machinery. From the late 1960s the business developed both machining tools and drafting machines, with control systems incorporating numerical control (NC) or computerised numerical control (CNC).[62]

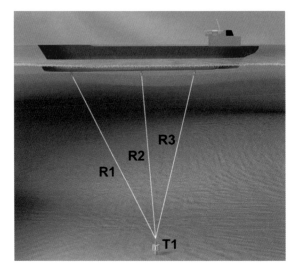

Short Baseline (SBL) was the first hydroacoustic measuring principle used to compute position in DP systems. The distance between the transponders (the units 'answering' the transmitted audio signal) on the bottom (T1) and hydrophones mounted under the hull (R1, R2 and R3) were calculated from the elapsed time from the ship's acoustic source to the responses from the transponder being received by the hydrophones on board. When the speed of sound in water is known, ca. 1500 m/s, distances can be calculated and the ship's position relative to the transponder is determined by geometric calculations. Illustration: KM.

FROM PROJECT MOHOLE TO THE *GLOMAR CHALLENGER*

In 1950, Balchen had been in the US, learning about the computer control of machining tools through MIT's Whirlwind project. In 1959 he gained insight into ship automation. During another sabbatical in 1968, he came across yet another technology that captured his interest. In a break between two lectures at UCSB, he began chatting with some doctoral students who were associated with AC Electronics, which was owned by General Electric (GE). The students told him that they had been involved in a project where they developed the DP system for the vessel *Glomar Challenger*.[63]

Balchen saw the potential of this for Norwegian conditions and kept in touch with these students while he was in California. This was 'Balchen's method'. He came in contact with people who worked with new technological concepts and took notice of what they did. He then took the ideas home and developed his own solutions, adapted for the Norwegian market.

The students' descriptions of *Glomar Challenger* gave him an insight into the issues surrounding DP.[64] The ship would perform the same tasks as *CUSS 1* and *Eureka*, taking samples of the earth's crust at great depths. The first two did not succeed penetrating deep enough into the earth's crust. Now it was time for a new ship, with completely different dimensions. *Glomar Challenger* was launched in 1968 and went into operation for Scripps Institution of Oceanography at the University of California, San Diego (UCSD). The American Miscellaneous Society (AMSOC) had now been disbanded, and the National Science Foundation had taken over the task of 'investigating the depths'. The

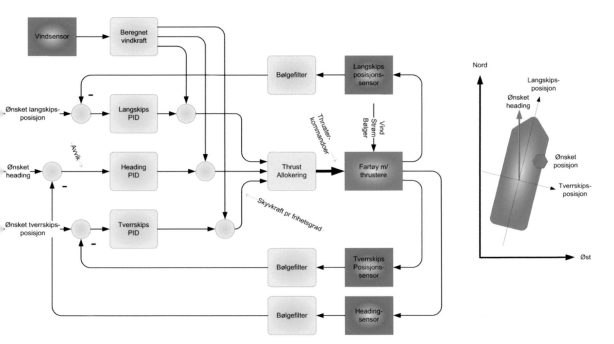

As with the DP system on the *Eureka*, the *Glomar Challenger's* system utilised three PID regulators – one for each degree of freedom – although these were now in the form of computer algorithms. The same applied for the thrust allocation mechanism. The principle innovation that was introduced was 'wind feed forward coupling', whereby measured wind speed and direction were used to calculate the wind's influence on the ship and immediately compensate for this, meaning that wind would not push the ship out of position. In addition, there was better filtering of measurement signals to reduce the influence of waves motions. Illustration: KM.

Mohole Project had now evolved into a new and more professional operation, 'The Deep Sea Drilling Project'.[65] *Glomar Challenger* was on a different scale to *CUSS 1* and *Eureka*. The ship was equipped with a derrick standing some 43 metres high, capable of drilling more than 1,700 metres below the seabed, at depths of down to 7,000 metres. The ship was eventually used to take core samples from more than 600 locations in the Atlantic, Pacific and Indian oceans, which were then analysed by geologists.[66]

In the aftermath of *Eureka*, US companies Honeywell and Delco worked in parallel to develop a digital computerised DP system.[67] It was Delco, however, which won the commission to develop and build *Glomar Challenger's* DP system, utilising a new technology for determining vessel positioning, namely ultrasound hydroacoustics. This was already a known methodology that was used by the US Navy, amongst others, for oceanographic purposes.[68] The ship was therefore equipped with an acoustic transmitter and three hydrophones (underwater microphones), which listened to pulses sent from a source on the seabed (transponder). The transponder was used to send out a return signal when it received a signal from the transmitter on board the *Glomar Challenger*. When knowing where the different hydrophones were located and measuring the time between the transmitted pulse from the transmitter on board and the 'answer' from the transponder as detected by the different hydrophones on the hull, the vessel's position in relation to the transponder could be calculated. The concept is today known by the name Short Base Line (SBL).

Glomar Explorer, *Glomar Challenger*'s sister ship, was built by the Howard Hughes owned company Global Marine Development Inc. The DP systems in both vessels were based on the classical control theory, with PID controllers, and were in principle very similar to the analogue system in *Eureka*. After launching in 1972, the US Central Intelligence Agency (CIA) and Special Activities Division (SAD) operated the *Glomar Explorer*, performing the secret mission 'Project Azorian'. The motivation for this task had been the CIA's discovery of a sunken Soviet submarine, K-129, in deep water outside Hawaii. It now wanted to raise the vessel and obtain whatever classified information and equipment was on board. The mission was carried out under the false premise of investigating the possibility of harvesting magnesium nodules on the seabed. However, the project was only partially successful as the submarine broke in two, and the most valuable part, containing the codebooks and nuclear missiles, sank back into the depths.[69]

The *Glomar Challenger*'s DP system boasted the introduction of so-called wave filters that removed the wave-induced component of the ship's movement. The measurements of the movements caused by high frequency wavelets represented 'noise' in the measurements and therefore had to be kept away from the controllers, so the thrusters could be operated as smoothly as possible. Large and rapid variations in commands to thrusters leads to wear and unnecessary energy consumption. At the same time, it is pointless to try to compensate for such rapid wave motion. As a result, the filter separated the measured movement into two components: a slowly varying part caused by the vessel's exposure to wind, current and wave drift, and a rapidly varying part caused by the waves' rapid pulsations. The slowly varying component was used in the control loop. Designing a good wave filter was complicated because the wave frequency varies over time. Such a filter also degrades the DP system stability and can, in worst-case scenarios, lead to a breakdown in position control. Eventually DP systems also featured so-called 'wind-feed forward control', which was based

The first drilling vessel with dynamic positioning, which also had a riser and blowout preventer (BOP), was *SEDCO445*, which was delivered to Shell in 1971. It was 145 metres long, weighed 17,500 tonnes and was equipped with two propellers for propulsion and eleven transverse thrusters. Several mini computers were employed to operate the DP system from Honeywell. After 1971, the ship has had many owners and names such as *Foresight Driller II, Flex LD, Deepsea Worker, Peregrine VII* and *Deepwater Navigator*. Photo from 'History of DP' by Howard Shatto.

on the idea that it is possible to measure the wind speed and direction and from these measurements calculate the effect of the wind force on the ship. The thrusters can then compensate for these forces before they affect the ship position. In a graphic description of this, wind-feed forward control represents an addition to the thrust command calculated by the PID-controller.

SEDCO 445

1971 was an important year for the development of DP technology. It was then that the drillship *SEDCO 445* was launched with a Honeywell DP system on board. In addition, Howard Shatto was a key figure in the project.

After Shatto had finished work on *Eureka*, he busied himself with a variety of tasks for Shell. Then, in 1967, he received a request to travel to the Netherlands and lead the installation of dynamic positioning on a vessel under construction, the *SEDCO 445*.[70] This was a large vessel, with impressive thruster power. It was 145 metres long, weighed 17,500 tonnes and had two propellers for propulsion and a total of eleven transverse thrusters under the keel. It was said that the new DP system gave a more accurate positioning than any other competing systems of the time, and was certainly more reliable. It had not just one, but several mini computers set up to drive the system. It also introduced the idea of computer redundancy by installing two machines, where one watched over the other – basically, if one computer stopped, the second would assume control. In addition, the system also offered redundancy in terms of position measurement, as it was equipped with taut wire, and hydroacoustics and riser angle measurement on the blowout preventer (BOP). The riser enclosed the drill string between the ship and the BOP, which is a valve positioned above the bore hole that closes in the event of dramatic pressure changes in the drill pipe, or as a result of an uncontrolled blowout.[71]

These mini computers provided the platform for Honeywell's new Automatic Station Keeping (ASK) system. According to the firm, the ship offered redundancy in all system functions, as well as a guarantee of 150 days of continuous operation, which at this time, when computers were quite unstable, was considered impressive. After the ship was launched in 1971, it sailed to Borneo where the system was tested. Thus the world's first modern drillship for oil and gas drilling, with a computerised digital DP system and risers for positioning, was ready for operation. *SEDCO 445* came before *Glomar Explorer*, but after *Glomar Challenger* and was perhaps the first serious signal that the use of DP technology had moved from science and geology to the oil and gas industry. Professor Balchen, who recognised the commercial opportunities offered by DP technology, noticed this important change. The perceived success of both the ship and its dynamic positioning only stoked the enthusiasm of the nascent DP supplier base.[72]

NORWAY IN THE OIL AGE

In 1962 the Norwegian government received a letter from the oil company Phillips. The discovery of a sizable gas field in the seabed off Groningen in the Netherlands in 1959 had piqued the interest of oil companies, motivating them to explore resource potential further north. Phillips wanted to explore for oil in the North Sea and was willing to pay USD 160,000 a month for rights to test drill on the Norwegian continental shelf. To ensure Norwegian rights over potential resources, on 31 May 1963 the country proclaimed that the seabed and subsoil of the areas outside the Norwegian coastline were Norwegian.

Agreements were then made with Denmark and the UK on the division of the continental shelf by the so-called median line principle. From 1965 a framework for regulations for licences was in place, and the first concessions were announced. In summer 1966 the first exploration well was drilled, but was found to be dry. Several years went by before a commercial discovery was made, but when it happened, it was worth the wait.

The Ekofisk field was discovered by Phillips in the autumn of 1969 and was, at that time, the largest oil field ever found at sea. The Norwegian company Hydro had a small portion and thus became a part of this early oil 'fairy tale'. Ekofisk was located in the southern part of the Norwegian sector and was the first petroleum field that came into operation on the Norwegian shelf. Trial production started from the mobile rig *Gulftide* in June 1971, before the field was eventually developed with several fixed platforms and pipelines transporting oil and gas to the UK and Germany. In the early days, until around 1973, foreign companies dominated exploration activities and were responsible for the development of the first oil and gas fields. When Statoil was created in 1972, the rule governing a 50 percent 'state participation' in each production licence was introduced. This was later altered, allowing Parliament to consider adjusting the proportion in individual cases.[73] Francis Sejersted describes this early phase with the term 'enclave model', meaning North Sea developments took place almost untouched by what happened on the mainland and almost without Norwegian industrial participation. This situation would come to change significantly in the years to come.[74]

The discovery of oil in the North Sea in 1969, and the fact that its recovery had already started by 1971, was of great importance to Norwegian society, business, and industrial policy. The authorities were taken by surprise and several years went by before the enclave was broken. The foreign dominance in offshore was mirrored in the education sector, with Norwegian institutions lagging behind their international counterparts. The management at NTH was, like many others, surprised by the rapid pace of oil activity and, after the news of the Ekofisk field went public, a hectic restructuring was instigated.[75] Even though it was the marine, chemical and geological science disciplines that were affected first, the intense discussions about oil education also reached the Institute of Control Engineering, which, in 1973, was renamed the Institute of Technical Cybernetics. When Balchen sought out KV in Oslo in 1971, it was therefore not only DP developments abroad that occupied him, but equally what was happening 'at home' in the North Sea.

JUST AN EXCITING IDEA?

When the American pioneers developed automated solutions for precise positioning at sea, Jens Glad Balchen seized on them with immediate interest. The DP systems had their origins in Balchen's pet subject and relied on what he saw as the main component of a cybernetic system, namely the computer. The suggestion that KV should develop a separate DP system has to be considered against the backdrop of what happened in the US: modern cybernetic principles such as the Kalman filter and their implementation into the DP systems' software. By combining the two he believed it was possible to make a better product than anything that had been developed so far. Such a concept simultaneously represented a new opportunity for both the cybernetics technicians at NTH and those at SINTEF. An environment of young, ambitious technology researchers had emerged and without their knowledge it is difficult to imagine the creation of a Norwegian-developed dynamic positioning system. But in the Norway of 1971 DP was, at most, nothing more than an interesting idea.

To make a Norwegian DP system a reality, there was a need for an industrial company with the necessary expertise and financial resources to take the idea 'from the desktop and into production'. KV was such an enterprise. Alongside the fact that the company had a management willing to invest in risky development projects, KV also had a solid knowledge base, with a large group of engineers and technicians who had experience with the advanced control of machine tools and weapons systems. Balchen himself had previously been involved in several of the company's projects. Despite this, KV's management was still not interested in what Balchen described as a superior principle for dynamic positioning, instead focusing on the fact that there was no market for such equipment in Norway in 1971.

To develop a product makes little sense without a market. Norway has a long maritime history with shipowners who have a reputation for being willing investors. However, in 1971, Norwegian shipowners were in a minority in the North Sea and, among those who were active, DP was not yet seen as a strong alternative to anchoring. KV, therefore, felt they had little reason to follow Balchen's advice.

3

THE DYNPOS PROJECT

WHILE KONGSBERG VÅPENFABRIKK (KV) had given the thumbs-down to Professor Jens Glad Balchen's idea of developing an in-house dynamic positioning system, several reputable international companies were already delivering DP systems in the USA and Europe.[1] Among these were Honeywell (USA), Delco (USA), General Electric Company (UK), CIT Alcatel (France) and Thomson-CSF (France). In the years between 1971 and 1975, these companies delivered DP systems to vessels like the SEDCO 445, Global Explorer, Saipem Due, France's Triton and Pélican, and the British Wimpey Sealab. The market was limited, though, and in 1975 there weren't more than ten or so drilling vessels with DP, and under 20 installations globally.[2] However, the vessels were increasing in size and positioning precision, and able to handle strong winds and high seas. In 1973 it was calculated that SEDCO 445 could hold her position to within a radius of 15 metres while drilling at 300 metres depth. This could be maintained in winds up to 49 knots, in four-metre waves, and with currents of 1.5 metres per second. Reportedly, in some instances, ships had maintained position in winds over 65 knots.[3]

Balchen followed developments abroad closely, and in 1973 he once again contacted KV. He informed them that in the short time since presenting his business case, there had been significant changes in technology, and in the market. Shortly after this inquiry Kongsberg proposed a pilot project to study the possibility of a Norwegian-developed DP system, even though it still wasn't clear that Balchen and the SINTEF team would succeed this time either. So what made them change their mind?

The Norwegian Institute of Technology (NTH) was established in Trondheim in 1910 and became the premier technological research and educational institution in Norway. In 1950, SINTEF (The Foundation for Scientific and Industrial Research) was established as a parallel research institution in close cooperation with NTH. Through overlapping human resources and project collaboration the Institute of Automatic Control, NTH, and the department of Automatic Control, SINTEF, created a powerful cybernetic research community that contributed to industrial development within a variety of disciplines, from medical technology to industrial development. In 1996, NTH merged with the University of Trondheim to form the Norwegian University of Science and Technology (NTNU). Photo: Image archive at Universitetsbiblioteket, NTNU.

THE NORWEGIAN R&D COMMUNITY GATHERS MOMENTUM

At the same time as international companies were increasing the capacity and precision of their DP systems, activities in Norway were centred around building up competence and experience with DP. In 1973 Christian Michelsen's Instute (CMI) in Bergen applied to The Royal Norwegian Council for Scientific and Industrial Research (NTNF) for funding to finance a research project that would simulate the effect of wind, current and waves on a Norwegian-built H3 rig. Aker Yards would build the rig on order from the American company Deep Sea Drilling. Two other companies would be involved as well, Frank Mohn and Odfjell Drilling. Frank Mohn would deliver the thrusters and CMI would do testing of models for thruster control. The application stated that the project focused on «positioning», rather than dynamic positioning, which demanded competency that CMI did not possess. According to the project initiators, climatic conditions in the North Sea were so challenging that only semi-submersible rigs could be used for year-round exploration drilling. The area of the North Sea that had been opened for exploration up to that time had moderate water depth, and positioning could be secured by anchoring. If exploration was to be carried out north of 62°N, it would be in deeper water with more challenging conditions. Demands on both rig construction and positioning would force the development of better solutions.[4] According to the newbuilding specs, a Honeywell DP system was to be installed on the rig.[5] However, CMI's participation was terminated with the conclusion that DP was not «practical».[6]

The first years of the 1970s saw various research projects with relevance for dynamic positioning initiated at NTH. In 1973, Balchen asked one of his interns, Steinar Sælid, to intensify development of the theoretical and practical principles of dynamic positioning. Like his colleagues at the department, Sælid was a cybernetics specialist, and had in 1972 submitted his thesis on *Sensitivity analysis in optimal systems.* When he defended his doctoral thesis four years later it would be on automatic steering of cement kilns, one of the automation concepts that Balchen had sold to Comtec toward the end of the 1960s.[7] From 1973 and until the defence of his thesis in 1976, Sælid would divide his time between work on the thesis and development of the principle elements of dynamic positioning.

Balchen's main strength was not merely his technical prowess, which no one disputed, but perhaps more so his ability to gather the best minds around him, and Sælid would prove to be no exception. Giving Sælid the task of determining how Kalman filtering could be used in dynamic positioning, for example, typified Balchen's ability to challenge his best people. Sælid was one of the select few who played key roles in developing concepts for model testing, vessel simulation and the development of algorithms for DP systems. Others seeking to work with the same subject matter would soon follow him.

At that time, the Norwegian cybernetics community was familiar with Rudolf Kalman's theories, but no one had yet attempted to exploit the theories in relation to DP. That would soon change. From 1974 on, several theses on dynamic positioning would emerge from the NTH/SINTEF environment. The first of these was Kjell Åge Auen's thesis from 1974 in which he described a *System for dynamic positioning of a ship.* In subsequent years Bjørn Fossum addressed *Calibration of inertial navigation systems using a simplified Kalman filter,* and Karstein Vestgård, *Navigation system for dynamic positioning during*

Steinar Sælid graduated from the NTH department of cybernetics in 1971, and later received a doctorate in the management of cement kilns. He was then employed at SINTEF, where he contributed to the development of the Albatross DP system. After this intense development work, Sælid left SINTEF to become a Docent at NTH. One of his research tasks was the mathematical oceanographic modelling of the Barents Sea. This photo from 1978 shows Sælid while he considers results from the Barents Sea simulation carried out on a Nord-50 computer. Sælid joined KV in 1983, where his work had great significance in the development of dynamic positioning and AIM. Photo: Steinar Sælid private archives.

pipelaying.[8] The first academic presentation that linked the algorithm to DP was given at the International Federation of Automatic Control (IFAC) annual conference in 1976. Not unexpectedly, it was co-authored by Balchen, Sælid and the third key figure in DP development in Norway, Nils Albert Jenssen.[9] By this time Jenssen had joined the same NTH/SINTEF group as Sælid. In 1974 he defended his thesis at the NTH Institute of Technical Cybernetics.[10] He was later approached by Balchen, in a similar way to Sælid, to work on dynamic positioning. In the years to follow Jenssen worked on dynamic positioning projects and completed his doctorial thesis on the same subject. Jenssen and Sælid became the key contributors to the development of cybernetic steering algorithms and software for Norwegian DP systems.

However, the NTH/SINTEF groups that shared offices in D-block at Gløshaugen were not the only ones looking into new and technologically advanced solutions for DP systems. While SINTEF was perfecting its contribution to a possible DP concept, Simrad experts in Horten and Oslo were investigating other aspects of positioning. Simrad, founded as Simonsen Radio in 1948, had over the years developed and produced a series of different hydroacoustic underwater instruments, including echo sounders and sonar. Now the company was developing hydroacoustic positioning equipment.

Dynamic positioning demands reliable position reference systems. While *CUSS 1* employed sonar, *Eureka* utilised taut wire. The two vessels *Glomar Challenger* and *Glomar Explorer* used hydroacoustics, which had existed longer than DP. While servo technology and DP systems were developed in the USA, it was technical research from Great Britain during World War II that resulted in the various acoustic measurement systems such as echo sounders and sonar (asdic). Attempts to track German submarines between Scotland and Murmansk spurred these initiatives. Final development work was carried out at the Allied testing station in Scotland.[11] Norwegian engineers also participated in this work, thereby gaining first-hand knowledge of these critical hydroacoustic systems. Fredrik Møller, who would later serve as managing director at the Norwegian Defence Research Institute (FFI), was at the time heading up the Armed Forces Supreme Command's technical committee (FOTU), which served as the common body for the Norwegian contribution to Allied defence research. Møller brought this invaluable knowledge home and employed it at FFI after 1945, contributing greatly to FFI's leading echo sounding and sonar initiatives. From 1957 on, Simonsen Radio took over the rights from FFI for production and sales of echo sounders on the private market. The business was not without its problems as foreign currency restrictions limited the purchase of foreign supplies and components. With help from Erik Brofoss, Minister of Finance in Einar Gerhardsen's administration, Møller was given enough leeway on import restrictions to allow production to continue. Simonsen Radio was shortened to Simrad in 1957, and the company eventually emerged as a brand name and achieved commercial success with its most important products: echo sounders, radio telephones and sonar.[12]

Towards the end of the 1960s the company would undergo major changes. The North Sea herring disappeared for an extended period, and other fish stocks were also substantially reduced. As a result Simrad was forced to carry out major rationalisation measures. Decreased sales in traditional products spurred investment into the development of more advanced products. And as a rule, specialty competence in hydroacoustics was the starting point for any new product development.[13] In the years that followed, Simrad developed a series of

Nils Albert Jenssen graduated as an engineer in engineering cybernetics at NTH in 1974. From 1975 he was employed in SINTEF's department for automatic control. Along with Steinar Sælid and Eldar Mathisen, Jenssen wrote the extensive software code for the first DP systems Albatross sold. Although the code was changed and comprehensively expanded, it represented the very foundation of what happened at Kongsberg in the years that followed. In 1981 Jenssen received Norway's first doctorate in dynamic positioning. He was hired by KV in 1982 and continued the development of the DP expertise that contributed to Albatross' breakthrough from the 1980s on. The picture shows Jenssen at work developing a Position Mooring System. Leif Palmstrøm is in the background. Photo: Mediafoto.

new echo sounders and sonars for smaller boats and the fishing fleet. During this time, on assignment for the Institute of Marine Research in Bergen, they also began experimenting with a more advanced type of sonar, one that would feature screen display instead of the old paper formats. Additionally, Simrad developed an all-new multi-beam transceiver, i.e. an instrument that could send and receive multiple signals simultaneously and thereby provide higher quality position measurement.[14] This transceiver became the basis for development of the important Hydroacoustic Position Reference (HPR) product line.

A separate project was established in Horten to work with what was called HPR100. The purpose was to create a multi-beam system that could be used in navigation. Kåre Hansen, who would later take over as Director of Simrad, headed the project, while Rolf Arne Klepaker and Karstein Vestgård were two of the other major contributors. The project received financial support from the National Development Fund and research-related assistance from CMI, SINTEF and the Central Institute for Industrial Research (SI). However, development proved difficult and was nearly terminated on several occasions. Fortunately, Simrad was able to sell the first system for determining the position of risers on a rig to the Norwegian shipowner Fearnley. Eventually the HPR100, in a later version, became an important reference system for dynamic positioning.[15]

AN INTERESTING AND PROFITABLE NICHE

The North Sea oilfields resembled more construction sites in the 1970s. From the modest exploration activities in the early 1960s to production and pipelaying through the 1970s, deep sea divers were the construction workers of the North Sea. This was before remotely operated vehicles (ROV) that today have virtually taken over tasks previously performed by divers. Up until the mid-1970s, divers often operated from fixed installations equipped with diving facilities, or from supply boats with diving equipment on deck. The first dedicated diving vessels were usually anchored, operating in the southern reaches of the North Sea where water depths were generally shallow, making anchoring feasible.

But as oil and gas were discovered in ever-deeper waters, divers also had to explore new limits. While water depth at Ekofisk was 70 metres, at Statfjord divers had to go down to 150 metres. The Norwegian trench, with a depth of more than 300 metres, lies in between the North Sea basin and mainland Norway. There, new diving technologies had to be employed, including saturation diving, where divers inhale primarily helium instead of air. Diving to great depths is in any case a risky business. As more divers began to work further down in the cold and inhospitable North Sea, accidents became more frequent, often with tragic outcomes. From 1968 and through the 1970s nearly 100 divers perished in the Norwegian and British sectors. Even more North Sea divers were damaged for life from extensive saturation diving over many years.[16] A number of measures were initiated to secure the divers' safety. One of these was equipping ships with a so-called moon pool, a well built into the hull of a ship where the diving bell is lowered and hoisted without being slammed by waves against the hull. Use of diving bells was common, and divers often lived in the bells for weeks on end. The bells could be raised and lowered without altering the internal pressure. But these operations using mooring as the tool for station keeping were time consuming and difficult and early on shipowners

The divers are supplied breathing gas from the surface (a mixture of oxygen and helium – normal air would be 'thick as soup' under such pressure, while nitrogen would cause poisoning). In addition, the divers wear hot water suits, supplied with temperate water. All the supply services and the dive management activity take place in a separate dive control centre on the surface. After a period that can last days or weeks, the divers are gradually brought back to the normal air pressure. The picture shows dive control on-board *Seaway Eagle*. Photo: Mediafoto.

When divers perform underwater assignments they move from the vessel's accommodation chamber to the diving bell, as both are pressurised to the corresponding depth where the tasks are to be carried out. When the bell is lowered to the working depth and the water pressure is the same as the pressure inside the diving bell, the bottom doors open and divers enter the water and proceed to the workplace. One diver is always left in the bell as a reserve. This picture shows the diving bell aboard the *Seaway Eagle* as it is hoisted into the depths. Photo: KM.

began to show interest for specially equipped DP vessels able to save time and increase safety.[17]

Against this backdrop, diving services became an attractive business idea for a risk-taking shipowner from Haugesund named Jacob Stolt-Nielsen, and soon after his equally bold employee Bjørn Bendigtsen. The Stolt-Nielsen company had profited in the parcel tanker market, that is, mid-sized chemical tankers. During the oil crisis in 1973, Stolt-Nielsen sold eight tankers and had expendable capital to invest in other activities.[18] While other shipowners like Fred Olsen, Odfjell, Smedvig and Ugland put their money into drilling rigs, Stolt-Nielsen invested in a helicopter base and a fleet of ships designed for various oil-related service assignments.[19] The fleet was highly recognised in the North Sea, not only for taking on critical assignments in the hectic build-up phase of North Sea oil, but also for the characteristic canary yellow of its hulls.

Jacob Stolt-Nielsen jr. was born in Haugesund in 1931. Both his grandfather and father were shipowners. After completing business school Stolt-Nielsen jr. went to London to gain experience as a shipbroker. In 1959 he bought his first ships and began to build up a significant business transporting chemicals. In the 1970s, he sold out and focused on activities in the North Sea. This involved the creation of one of the world's largest companies for subsea operations. Photo: *Dagens Næringsliv.*

In 1973 Stolt-Nielsen placed the following job announcement in the Norwegian daily Aftenposten: «It's the man that counts.» The company needed people to operate its ships, seafarers and divers for installations in the North Sea. Bjørn Bendigtsen was one of those who saw the ad, applied and was given a job. Born in Lofoten, he held degrees in both economics and engineering. This dual expertise was important in his new position as head of fleet development, responsible for equipping vessels as they were acquired or built. The shipowner viewed his new employee as a man of great determination and courage. He gave him considerable responsibility and soon after joining the company, Bendigtsen negotiated outfitting contracts for new diving and fire fighting vessels with Germany's Jahnsen Werft.[20] Prior to these negotiations, Bendigtsen had attended an offshore exhibition in Houston, where the big buzz was about pipelines on the seabed, and how the North Sea floor would soon be covered with this «spaghetti». This development would make anchoring even more demanding and time-consuming. According to Bendigtsen, these discussions were fresh on his mind when ordering equipment for the new ship.

Bjørn Bendigtsen grew up in Lofoten and went on to study engineering at Narvik University College. He was employed at KV for several years before being recruited to a leadership position at Aukra Bruk. While employed by KV he took an economics education at BI Norwegian Business School. This dual expertise came in handy when Jacob Stolt-Nielsen hired him to lead his North Sea business in 1973. Bendigtsen ordered Norway's first DP system for *Seaway Falcon* and played an important 'mediating role' when KV began developing the first DP systems. Photo: Bjørn Bendigtsen's private collection.

Seaway Falcon became the first of several new ships that Stolt-Nielsen would order for North Sea engagements, all fitted with the latest technology. *Seaway Falcon* was equipped to support saturation diving, but perhaps even more significantly, the vessel featured a DP system from Honeywell, making *Seaway Falcon* the first ship in Norway with dynamic positioning. The ship was to be used not only for diving, but fire fighting as well.

Safety issues were discussed widely in the media at the time. The contract with Jansen Werft included a gigantic fire fighting installation mounted on the aft deck. The fire fighting monitors were to be steered in the same way as guns on a war ship, and could be kept on a target even during wavy conditions. Bendigtsen was employed at KV for a short period before joining

Bjarne Hurlen's name is closely associated with KV's rise to become Norway's leading high-tech company. Hurlen transformed the business from a work place characterised by its handcraft to an engineering company with modern scientific methods as the foundation for its production and management. KV became an industrial-political instrument for the industrialisation of Norwegian research results. Hurlen is seen here with among others Prime Minister Einar Gerhardsen and director at FFI, Finn Lied. The photo is taken in 1964. Photo: Ivar Aaserud / Aktuell / NTB scanpix.

Stolt-Nielsen. While there he had worked in the department that developed steering systems for the L/70 anti-aircraft gun, produced on licence from Swedish Bofors. During WWII, anti-aircraft guns were guided by two operators, which proved reasonably successful against propeller-driven aircraft. But with the advent of jet aircraft the guns had to move much quicker, and with greater precision. So from 1956, gun carriages were equipped with small electric motors steered by servo-technical principles. Experience that Kongsberg gained from these steering systems was later employed in development of fire guidance and industrial equipment for ships.[21] Bendigtsen requested the assistance of Kongsberg's competence in the development of a steering system for water cannons on the *Seaway Falcon*. Records show that shipowner Odd

Berg in Tromsø built a similar ship, the *Arctic Surveyor*, which also featured DP from Honeywell.[22]

The *Seaway Falcon* order was the start of an extensive collaboration between Stolt-Nielsen and Kongsberg Våpenfabrikk. Bendigtsen recalls seeing the value of this cooperation early on. Kongsberg was under standing orders to assist Norwegian industry in exploiting the opportunities in the North Sea. Cooperation with Kongsberg could therefore prove to be useful when new North Sea contracts were being negotiated.

But the establishment of this new relationship was not a given. The ship-owner himself, Jacob Stolt-Nielsen, had little sympathy for KV director Bjarne Hurlen, or his «Labour Party bastion», as he referred to the company. Following repeated encouragement from Bendigtsen, he conceded to meet with the Kongs-berg management to discuss «possible common interests», as it was referred to. The meeting between Bjarne Hurlen and Jacob Stolt-Nielsen took place in the autumn of 1974 and was described by Bendigtsen as chilly, formal and without concrete results. Had it not been for Bendigtsen's perseverance, contact would have been terminated.[23] At the same time, the meeting must have had some effect, as the DP initiative was continued. That same autumn, Kongsberg's Rolf Qvenild, Bjørn Jahnsen and Olav Berdal met with representatives from Simrad, CMI and SINTEF in Kongsberg's Oslo office.

THE PARTIES UNITE

Between 1973 and the autumn of 1974, KV took several different initiatives. They had collaborated with CMI, Simrad and Aker Group from 1972 on the outfitting of an H3 rig. They also had a project under the administration of what was called NTNF's Deep Water Committee. The project goal was to investigate problems related to petroleum installations, in particular where to locate oil and gas pipelines on the North Sea floor. The resulting report cited dynamic positioning as a potentially useful tool in pipelaying. According to KV, both operators and shipowners had become aware of the technology.[24] And, as it looked, this applied to KV management as well. In any case, the company performed a simple market survey that indicated annual sales potential of one to two DP systems per year to drill ships and rigs, and the equivalent to working boats and supply ships.[25]

Meanwhile, NTH/SINTEF people turned up suddenly at KV's Oslo office. Balchen had heard that KV had revived the DP idea and was ready to promote his case. This time it was not director Bjarne Hurlen, but Development Manager

In 1978, three years after Hurlen's departure, Rolf Qvenild was appointed KV's new CEO. By this time he had held a prominent position within the business for several years. Like Hurlen, Qvenild was an engineering graduate from NTH. Hurlen was chosen to lead KV through an important phase of modernisation and Qvenild continued this drive, and also took KV into the oil age. In the period from 1970 to 1980 the 'weapons factory' was in many ways a development laboratory for new technology. Not all projects were commercially realised in Qvenild's time, but several of them are today key businesses within the Norwegian maritime industry. The picture shows Qvenild introducing the ADP503 to interested visitors in 1977. Photo: Mediafoto.

Olav Berdal and Head of Planning Rolf Qvenild who met with Balchen. Steinar Sælid accompanied Balchen, and he later recalled Balchen saying that Qvenild received him in an entirely different manner than Hurlen in 1971. He wrote further that Berdal seemed genuinely interested in the project, and shared his opinion on dynamic positioning with Qvenild.[26]

This shaky interaction, with cautious initiatives, investigations and conversations, led nonetheless to KV, CMI and NTH/SINTEF initiating a modest collaboration in January 1974. It was termed a preliminary project, with a budget of NOK 600,000. NTNF was to invest NOK 200,000, with the partners footing the rest of the bill themselves. The numbers seemed to indicate that the project was not given the highest priority, and Balchen's idea floundered along without strong stewardship until autumn of the same year, when the situation changed dramatically.

On 23 September 1974, Kongsberg Våpenfabrikk was invited to yet another meeting in their Oslo office. Representing KV this time were Olav Berdal and Bjørn Jahnsen. Simrad brought Arnulv Borud, Per Pettersen and Alf Solbakken, and Frode Galtung attended from CMI. Jens G. Balchen, Steinar Sælid and Knut Grimnes represented NTH/SINTEF. The parties agreed to commence development of a Norwegian DP system.[27] Prior to the meeting Berdal had sent an outline describing the initiation of the project and the conditions for future collaboration. The outline also contained specifications for a potential DP system, in addition to defining roles and responsibilities for the various partners. Aside from certain technical details, the parties agreed on most of the terms.[28] Simrad would develop and produce the hydroacoustic position reference system. Two alternative reference systems were also to be procured from third parties, namely taut wire and Artemis. KV would contribute computers and systems competence. According to Berdal, the computers had a memory of between 16 and 32 kB, extremely modest by modern standards. Berdal felt that KD's SM-4 machine would be a good choice.[29] Since CMI already possessed experience in simulating the effect of wind, current and waves on the H3 rig, they were assigned responsibility for necessary simulations. Balchen noted that NTH/SINTEF were already well underway in generating cybernetic algorithms and software for a potential DP system.[30]

The market situation, and whether there were customers for this product, was not addressed at the meeting, even though it was no secret that KV had been in contact with Jacob Stolt-Nielsen and Bjørn Bendigtsen. At that point no agreements had been entered into, much less anything that resembled a contract with the owner. Nonetheless, KV's management strongly believed that Stolt-Nielsen would sign a contract in time. This belief was perhaps the strongest incentive for holding the meeting.[31]

Neither Norsk Data nor Norcontrol were invited to the meeting, leading some to call the conclusion into question. Because Norcontrol, Simrad and KV all sold maritime electronics, they were in principle competitors. Until 1970 there was an unspoken agreement that state-controlled enterprises should not compete with private ones. This «truce» was based on the companies dividing markets between themselves. While Norcontrol was the key supplier of shipboard electronics to the merchant fleet, Simrad served primarily the fishing fleet. That KV should sell electronics to the military was also a given. Several culminating factors were threatening the harmony of this arrangement. The previous chapter referred to the build-up of a modest computer industry with KV and Norsk Data as the key players. The other factor cutting through the unwritten rules and handshakes was development in the North Sea, where no single party could claim ownership. When the initiative for a Norwegian-produced DP became more than Balchen's bright idea, there arose several possible constellations and collaborative models in the offshore market. But Norsk Data and Norcontrol were not invited to the party. For some, this was not a good solution. That it was controversial is evidenced in a memo penned by KV's Olav Berdal, where he outlines the possible areas of conflict. He writes that selection of partners would have to be «cleared at a high level», referring to the old conflict between KV and Norcontrol, who cooperated with Norsk Data. KV's choice of partners revealed not only a conflict between public and private, but a conflict between two companies producing computers, KV and Norsk Data.[32]

Just days after the key meeting in Oslo, a representative from Honeywell met with Norcontrol's general manager Ibb Høivold to discuss possible cooperation on a competing solution for dynamic positioning. The meeting did not, however, bear fruit.[33] Subsequent meetings between Norcontrol and KV on possible collaboration never got beyond informal agreements on mutual support of each other's products. The differences between the two companies were too great, as both aspired to be systems suppliers. State-owned KV had out-manoeuvred privately controlled Norcontrol, an unthinkable outcome before 1970. But victory often has its price: When KV applied for economic support from the government development fund, they were refused on the grounds of the «solo run» that KV had just completed.[34] This relatively small controversy between Norcontrol and KV shows that development of a new and exciting concept requires not only new technical solutions, but also the ability to form new alliances.

KV AND THE NORTH SEA

From January 1 1975, several things started to happen. One was the establishment of a petroleum division in Kongsberg Våpenfabrikk. Another was the start of a project that would lead to the launch of a complete DP system. By the time the petroleum division was up and running, KV had already undergone extensive structural changes. Modernisation of the organisation, new products and methods of production were key factors for KV between 1968 and 1972. Delivery of highly advanced equipment to the military was an important part of the business. High-tech solutions to the civilian market were becoming increasingly important. Up until the crisis following the Arab oil embargo in 1973, automated flame cutters for steel plates and drafting equipment (for making technical construction drawings), as well as control systems for machine tools (machines for shaping metal or other rigid materials, e.g. a

From the 1950s onwards NTH, SINTEF and the Central Institute for Industrial Research (SI) in Oslo developed numerical control systems for cutting torches, milling machines and drafting machines. Both the control
unit ESSI, which was used for the automatic cutting of steel plates (see photo), and the drafting machine
KINGMATIC blossomed from SI's experiments with the computer NUSSE. In Trondheim the Department
of Mechanical Engineering, with SP Andersen and Eiliv Sødahl, and the Department of Automatic Control,
with Torbjørn Brataas and Jens G. Balchen, spearheaded the development of several numerical control
systems for milling machines. Of Konrad, Nukon, Polykon and Monokon, only Monokon was commercially
successful. KV was involved in these projects at an early stage and sold many systems to carmakers, aircraft
manufacturers and shipyards. Early in the 1970s KV had 50 percent of the market for control systems for
drafting machines in Europe. Photo: Bjørn Quistgaard.

milling machine) were sold successfully to European automobile and airplane
factories and shipyards.

When the crisis hit the shipbuilding industry, the production of control
systems for flame cutters was gradually reduced. For a while, KV compensated this loss by selling drafting machines and the CNC2000 and NC2000
machine tolls. The former was directly programmable and minted for the
European market. Since the Coordinating Committee for Multilateral Export
Controls (COCOM) rules prohibited sales of the more advanced CNC2000,
the NC2000 was sold to companies in Eastern Europe. Computer guided
systems were products that fit with managing director Hurlen's desire to build
KV's profile as a modern, high-tech company. For that reason KV steering
systems for flame cutters, drafting and machine tools were exhibited at trade

fairs. They were to serve as proof of the company's success. In fact, they were all loss projects for Kongsberg Våpenfabrikk, along with computer systems.[35] The discovery of oil in the North Sea in 1969 was an event that would benefit Kongsberg greatly. By 1973, there was a great deal of activity taking place on the Norwegian Continental Shelf. The major Norwegian field Ekofisk was in production, and the Frigg field was being prepared for production start. At the same time, several foreign oil companies were busy exploring for new petroleum sources to develop. The oil embargo that year also resulted in consequences other than empty order books for the shipyards. The price of oil shot up, making oil and gas discoveries in the North Sea even more valuable. Though KV's sales of flame cutters to the shipbuilding industry were down, the company compensated losses by entering the offshore market. With this in mind, KV's board gave Rolf Qvenild the assignment to find petroleum-related activities that would link the company to the offshore industry.

As a crisis swept over Europe a change of character in Norway's petroleum politics was taking place. The historian Francis Sejersted writes: «'Norwegiani-fication' politics not only led to discriminatory policies favouring national interests, but to discrimination between private Norwegian interests, and the introduction of competition between public and private companies.»[36] From 1972 the political message was to support Norwegian business differently than before. This political change of direction would benefit Norwegian companies looking to enter this attractive market.

The Norwegian Petroleum Directorate (NPD) and Statoil were established that same year. While the NPD was to regulate and oversee the fast-growing offshore segment, Statoil was to manage the state's interests and be instrument through which greater Norwegian share of offshore activities could be achieved.[37] Companies operating in the oil sector quickly understood that this state-owned company would be a centre of power and exercise great influence on the future of the Norwegian offshore industry. KV had previously served a strategic role in Norway's industrial development. It came as no surprise, then, that Statoil and KV formed a partnership with a common goal to develop Norwegian business in the offshore market. The new oil policies, combined with the Statoil alliance, must have had a positive effect on the re-evaluation of Balchen's DP idea. Could dynamic positioning be an oil-related activity that KV could concentrate on? KV's management had no idea as to how important DP could become, other that what it had gained through the simple market survey from 1973. For this reason, no dramatic changes were made. But as with many other potentially big oil-related business concepts, the idea matured into a possible project. When KV established its petroleum division under Rolf Qvenild in 1975, dynamic positioning was not the only thing on his mind.

Initially, Qvenild had a name for the division, but nothing more. This situation was short-lived, though, and various oil-related projects were soon transferred to Qvenild's portfolio. The first of these was the subsidiary STATEX in Stavanger, specialists in computer-aided analysis of seismic data. At the time, 50 people were involved in the production of seismic maps for North Sea exploration. Another project was the Coast Center Base (CCB) at Ågotnes outside Bergen, which delivered service and repair work for the oil industry. Thirty-five employees performed welding on rig jackets and repair of wellheads. In Kongsberg, cooperation with the American company Cameron Iron Works led to a series of orders for wellheads that were adapted to the large automatic lathes in the factory. Some of the staff at the time were also testing various underwater oil and gas production systems. Eventually this business concept would become a successful business owned and run today by the American corporation FMC Technologies (Food Machinery Corporation), with a branch in Kongsberg.[38] The petroleum division's fourth area of focus during the spring of 1975 was Supervisory Control And Data Acquisition (SCADA); a control and information system for production platforms in the North Sea that KV wanted to develop and market. The idea was a good one, but SCADA would remain on paper during the mid-1970s.[39]

THE DYNPOS PROJECT IS ESTABLISHED

Following the founding meeting in September of 1974, representatives from KV, Simrad, CMI and SINTEF met several times to plan future work. In January of 1975, KV's management determined to start a project that would secure the various initiatives to that point. During the course of the pre-project, KV had dealt with NTNF's Deep Water committee (NTNF's dypvannskomité), but now the Continental Shelf committee (NTNF's kontinentalsokkelkomité) at NTNF would assume payments for part of the development work. The Continental Shelf committee held a significant share of the responsibility for financing research related to the North Sea petroleum industry in the 1970s. The «Dynamic Positioning» project was awarded NOK 340,000 for 1975, with allocations of roughly the same size to follow in subsequent years. The NTNF board would later reduce the amount for 1975, approving NOK 150,000 to CMI, and NOK 60,000 to Simrad. Applications to the Development Fund (Utviklingsfondet) were largely unsuccessful. KV was offered loan financing from the fund in 1977. At that time the project could cover its own expenses.[40]

A steering group consisting of KV's Bjørn Jahnsen, Simrad's Per Pettersen, and Frode Galtung from CMI was given the task of leading the work.[41] Soon after, Bjørn Bendigtsen became Stolt-Nielsen's representative in the group. The minutes of one meeting noted: «Stolt-Nielsen is potentially the largest customer for DP equipment and will take delivery of a support vessel within 3-4 months, and offers this project highly valuable user experience.»[42] As one of only a few in the country soon to have a Honeywell DP system installed on one of their vessels, Stolt-Nielsen's involvement was strategic to the project, and, perhaps of equal importance, to becoming potentially KV's first customer. However, the significance of the group faded quickly as KV took sole ownership of the project. Due to limited funding from NTNF and the rejection from the Development Fund, the bulk of the work was financed with the partners' own money, in large part KV's. Kongsberg Våpenfabrikk's initiative was now gaining momentum.[43]

Olav Berdal, serving under Rolf Qvenild, headed development projects in KV's new petroleum division. As chief of development, he was responsible to find the right people and ensure the necessary working conditions for the various sub-projects. Starting in April of 1975, Thor Skoland was assigned responsibility for hardware in the Dynpos project. Skoland had gotten his degree from MIT in 1966. Following that, he worked in the US for some years prior to joining KV in 1972. He was known for his quiet and orderly nature, with formidable technical knowledge and a proven ability to complete tasks. Highly qualified, management had no problem in assigning him responsibility for the daily running of the project.

During the first phase, only a handful of people were located in what was called building 11. Skoland was here, together with certain KV employees working with control algorithms for flame cutters, drafting machines and weapon guidance systems. Skoland had also worked on MSI-80S, the control system for Penguin missiles on torpedo boats. MSI-80S was the «brother» of the fire control system, MSI-70U, fitted on the German-built, Kobben class submarines delivered to Norway from the 1960s.[44] The experience gained from both of these systems would prove invaluable, especially regarding hardware and software applications, when the first DP machines were later built.[45]

Dynamic positioning soon found its way into the Petroleum division without much fanfare. No large personnel movements or financial transactions took place at the start of the project. By January 1975, DP was not yet a winning

Thor Skoland is one of the fathers of Albatross' DP success. He was educated at MIT in the US and, together with Bjørn Barth Jacobsen, given the task of leading the development of dynamic positioning from the outset. He fronted the technical development work, oversaw the daily operations of the business and acted as a stabilising force in Albatross – an organisation that was, in its early years, small but made up of many individual characters. The picture shows Skoland (rear left) demonstrating a DP system at an oil exhibition in Stavanger in 1976. Photo: Mediafoto.

ticket for divisional director Rolf Qvenild. This low-budget project requiring a minimum of staff, had a minimal risk when compared to the more than NOK 100 million invested in gas turbine development the same year. The KV approach when it came to initiating new development projects resembled the shotgun effect. Each pellet costs very little, but the chances of hitting a target increase significantly as more pellets that are fired. In fact, KV seemed at that time to possess many of the elements needed to realise the project. This applied not least to the most expensive and most central element in a DP system, the computer. The previous year saw the launch of KV's new flagship, the KS500 computer, which management intended to market both in Norway and abroad. The machine was also being pushed for all of KV's larger projects. Production of computers would eventually grow in importance for the state-owned company. At its peak the Computer division employed more than 400 people. Qvenild's growing interest for dynamic positioning can also be understood in

Stolt-Nielsen's newbuild diving ship *Seaway Falcon*, was the first to be equipped with dynamic positioning and automatic control for its aft deck water cannons – of which the latter were also delivered by KV. The same year that the ship came to Norway, 1975, there was a fire on Ekofisk's Alpha platform. The fire was extinguished after the *Seaway Falcon*'s water cannons were trained on it for several hours. The incident received substantial media coverage and was good publicity for Stolt-Nielsen's new ships, demonstrating the importance of having DP systems on-board. The picture shows *Seaway Falcon* tackling another fire, this time on the Ekofisk Bravo platform in 1977. Photo: Scanpix.

the context of developments in the Computer division. Sales were reasonably good in 1974, but dipped in the years that followed. From 1975 to 1985 this KV division lost more than NOK 300 million.[46] A public audit performed in the wake of KV's crash landing in 1987 reported: «KV's civilian computer business was one of the enterprises that transformed KV into a high-tech company, and was a key to the company's vision of becoming a locomotive for Norwegian industry.»[47] All projects requiring computing power after 1974 must have been highly welcome. It may not have been perfect, but the KS500 became the only alternative for a KV-developed DP system.

A MODERN DIVING SHIP

In February 1975 the Norwegian daily Verdens Gang (VG) ran a full-page story presenting the *Seaway Falcon*. The story focused on safety on board North Sea petroleum installations and questioned the type of emergency preparedness the authorities could provide in the event of fire on board. The report was illustrated by a photo of a ship showering a burning oil rig with water. The *Seaway Falcon's* fire fighting capacity was of obvious significance for the journalist, who reported that KV had delivered the system. But the article also gave a lot of attention to Honeywell's DP system. According to the paper, the ship could remain stationary just metres from the burning rig while it extinguished the fire.[48] The article was invaluable for Stolt-Nielsen, and surely for Honeywell, but also sent an important message to the authorities that dynamic positioning could become important for many vessel types in the North Sea.

Around the same time that VG featured DP, Stolt-Nielsen representatives were invited to Kongsberg again. This time with divisional head Qvenild as host, the shipowner received a royal welcome, including being transported in KV's impressive limousine. Following a short tour of the factory, new possibilities for collaboration were discussed. The atmosphere at this meeting was quite different from the last. Qvenild and Stolt-Nielsen seemed to hit it off, enjoying each other's company. Though no contract was signed this time either, the visit later proved to be greatly significant for the Dynpos project. The KV team sincerely hoped that the seeds of future sales had been sown, and that Stolt-Nielsen would order more than just the one control system for his water cannons.

When *Seaway Falcon* arrived in Haugesund early summer in 1975, it didn't waste much time at quayside. The crew and divers boarded the ship and set course for the North Sea on assignment for Phillips. The oil company originally intended to hire the ship without divers, but Stolt-Nielsen refused. He had invested large sums, not just in the ship, but also in preparing the crew and the divers. In the period between ordering and launching, he had trained divers that were to follow the ship. Now he insisted that they be used for what they were trained to do. Phillips had their own divers, but Stolt-Nielsen ended up getting his way. While the *Seaway Falcon* was carrying out diving work at sea, Stolt-Nielsen and KV started to discuss yet another contract. Engineers kept development work simmering on the back burner. During the spring and summer of 1975 information and specifications were gathered on previous DP installations. For example, while *Seaway Falcon* was moored one weekend in Stavanger, Skoland came on board to examine Honeywell's DP system. He observed that it was located in a separate computer chamber behind the bridge. On the bridge itself was a monitor connected to the system. The screen provided continuous information on the ship's position, but gave no feedback to the DP. Skoland was sceptical of what he saw. He felt the installation resembled more a data room in a bank than a marine dynamic positioning system. The hydroacoustic position reference system was derived from a military application, and operators had reported weaknesses. In rough seas the propellers could spin in the air, sending air bubbles under the ship and disabling positioning capabilities.[49]

According to Skoland the problem was about different ways of looking at ship instrumentation. While Honeywell was good at industrial process equipment, Kongsberg had experience with military systems for vessels operating with limited space and in harsh conditions. These were submarines and torpedo boats, not factories. Honeywell's installations were obviously inspired by dry land industry, and less suited to diving and supply ships in the extreme climate of the North Sea. This experience would shape the framework of KV's version of DP systems.

Over the summer, the team drew up detailed sketches of their system. Skoland then visited CMI, NTH/SINTEF and Simrad to settle on a time frame for work on the various elements of the system.[50]

A BOUNDLESS LEADERSHIP

During work on sketches and system functionality, the Dynpos team was visited by someone who would leave his restless fingerprint on the future development of the Dynpos project. Bjørn Barth Jacobsen would eventually lead the project together with Thor Skoland, from 1975 to 1980. Barth Jacobsen had earned his degree in electronics from NTH in 1969. After a stint with the Norwegian

Bjørn Barth Jacobsen was born and raised in Bodø, and a graduate in engineering from NTH. In the summer of 1975 he, along with Thor Skoland, was assigned to lead the DP project. This job was tailor-made for the purposeful Barth Jacobsen. While Skoland took care of ongoing tasks, technical issues and deliveries, Barth Jacobsen was an indefatigable powerhouse. To the staff in the small organisation he proclaimed a vision of world domination, while he used his forceful determination to convince doubting customers. Against all odds, Albatross broke through and achieved the market dominance Barth Jacobsen had envisioned, despite no one really believing it to be possible. Photo: Mediafoto.

state television station NRK, and some years with Shell, including assignments in the North Sea, he was hired at KV's Oslo office in Bygdøy Allé.[51] He made a notable impression there, not least because of his blunt and at times devil-may-care style. He was soon given responsibility for Kongsberg Engineering, one of KV's early petroleum-related projects, located in Lier. The next stop would be the factory in Kongsberg.[52]

Barth Jacobsen and Skoland were fairly similar when it came to backgrounds and professional interests, but strikingly dissimilar as people. When Barth Jacobsen celebrated and sang, standing on the nearest table, Skoland would be the one to coax him down. The two became good friends, moved to the same street, attended the Free Church together, and shared enthusiasm for the DP project. Like many unconventional leaders, there were many stories about Barth Jacobsen; some true, and some not. And when he shared his desire to lead the DP initiative forward into a world-leading dynamic positioning company, many simply shook their heads. How could KV compete with huge multi-nationals like Honeywell, with their economic muscle and tens of thousands of employees?

By the summer of 1975, the project was still mostly an idea. There were outlines, specifications and dreams, but no customers and no specific plan for turning the dream into reality. There was the one possible customer, but that was it.[53] According to the Dynpos team, Bendigtsen had on several occasions commented that the Honeywell systems were not up to skippers' expectations. They were too expensive, not user-friendly and robust enough. Spare parts were also expensive, and service unsatisfactory. If this was the case, there were many reasons to change suppliers.

Signals by the Norwegian authorities to prioritise domestic suppliers of products and services were vital to the business appraisals of a shipowner. KV already had strategic agreements with Statoil. Statoil was still a small company, not yet well established compared to other major oil players. But the authorities' intention to use the company to strengthen the Norwegian offshore industry in competition with foreign interests made the alliance attractive for those interested in serving the offshore market. This would prove to be the trump card.

By cultivating a good relationship with KV, Stolt-Nielsen could become attractive for Statoil. And there is no reason to believe that Qvenild and Stolt-Nielsen omitted this key topic from their conversation while on way to lunch in the back seat of the Kongsberg limousine. Many factors were in KV's favour, but many issues had to be ironed out before a contract could be signed.[54] Several involved at this time talk about shuttle traffic between KV and Stolt-Nielsen's office. In particular, Barth Jacobsen and Bendigtsen made the trip between the offices frequently.

Eventually a proposed contract was drafted. And for some reason the proposal was made for *Seaway Heron*, a fictitious H-3 rig. Since *Seaway Heron* was launched some time later, and was a ship and not a rig, the proposal was probably meant for the rig *Seaway Swan*. A report and a brochure from that time both indicate that this was a redundant DP system with three KV computers. Three conditions were highlighted in the proposed contract: First of all, CMI's experience with simulation on comparable rigs was weighted heavily. Next was use of standard KV instrumentation from the weapon control systems MSI-70U and MSI-80S. In addition, service was guaranteed on three-hour notice. The price for a «Complete dual DP-system» was NOK 5.3 million and approx. one million for optional auxiliary equipment such as taut wire.[55]

In the autumn of 1975, toward the end of negotiations, Rolf Qvenild questioned Jacob Stolt-Nielsen about how KV was doing in comparison to their competitors. To everyone's surprise Stolt-Nielsen replied: «We are being completely overrun by Bjørn Barth Jacobsen, and have for that reason not had time to speak with any of your competitors.» It remains difficult to verify this statement completely, but history indicates that Barth Jacobsen ran an intense

In September 1970 Phillips delivered an application to the Norwegian Ministry of Industry for permission to initiate test production at Ekofisk. The company initially wanted to get an overview of both the reservoir and the weather conditions in the area before they began an extensive and costly development programme with permanent platforms. Exploration activities in the area developed rapidly, and the preconditions for the development changed constantly, with the result that the technical solutions also altered. Both builders and shipowners learned important lessons through the development of Ekofisk, which became the first major offshore 'construction site'. Many Norwegian offshore solutions were tested here. Photo: NPD.

and focused sales strategy. As far as Stolt-Nielsen was concerned, he operated in an industry where taking chances was part of the job, where high risk was an everyday occurrence, and where trust was a prerequisite. He had fought tooth and nail to prove that his divers on *Seaway Falcon* could get the job done. Perhaps he recognised some of his own drive in KV's people? Regardless, a dramatic event was soon to put negotiations on hold.

In November of 1975 fire broke out in the North Sea. The Alpha platform on Ekofisk was burning, and Stolt-Nielsen got his chance to prove what his ship and crew could do. *Seaway Falcon* laid for hours only a few metres from the burning platform. The powerful water cannons on the aft deck sprayed huge volumes of water up on the towering platform. The battle against the blaze seemed hopeless for a time, but after hours of tireless fire fighting the flames subsided. By cooling down the steel areas beneath the fire, *Seaway Falcon* had hindered major structural damage. The platform had been saved and the owners saved millions by not having to replace the jacket.[56] The event received massive media coverage and served to remind those in the petroleum sector about how important DP systems were to offshore safety.

On November 22 1975, not long after the Ekofisk fire, Kongsberg Våpen-fabrikk signed its first contract with Stolt-Nielsen for a DP system on the service rig *Seaway Swan* – and not a day too soon. When the development project first started in January 1975, Qvenild informed the Dynpos team that they were safe for half a year. But after a contract was needed to keep the project afloat. Qvenild extended his deadline over the summer, and when the DP lights started flashing in November and the contract was safe in hand, he, undoubtedly, wasn't the only one breathing a bit more easily. The Dynpos project might have been stranded in 1975 had KV not landed the contract. The signing was in any case just one step on the way to an operative system. Now the product had to be delivered.

THE PIECES FALL INTO PLACE

In 1971, KV saw no point in competing with international industrial giants for only a few DP systems each year. When they eventually took the initiative for a development project in

1974, several factors had come to bear: CMI, SINTEF and Simrad had each gained competence in their respective specialties. KV was heading full steam ahead into the era of oil and needed new projects and ideas. And together with Statoil, KV would play a strategic role in strengthening Norwegian companies' contribution in the North Sea.

In September of 1971, DP was just a daring initiative. In 1974 the enthusiasm had spread to a dedicated group, but still rested on shaky ground. DP still existed only as an idea, a principle and a concept. The concept was gradually cemented, not just with national interests, but in national politics. Political signals made it clear that Norwegian suppliers were to be favoured. Good relationships were established between KV's DP team and shipowner Jacob Stolt-Nielsen in 1975. And by 1975 the bonds were even stronger. To be «on the same team» with KV, and then Statoil, gave the shipowner major advantages when competing for new contracts. Perhaps most importantly, Stolt-Nielsen was now interested in ordering a system he had not yet seen, that his company knew little about and that would end up costing «a fortune». Would an enthusiastic group with only new ideas, plenty of knowledge, and a formidable drive, be able to succeed?

4

ALBATROSS

WHEN THE CONTRACT between Kongsberg Våpenfabrikk and shipowner Stolt-Nielsen Seaway was signed in the autumn of 1975, a milestone was gladly passed. Finally, KV could begin its work on a DP system for *Seaway Swan*, a drilling rig of the H-3 type, one of the most sold rigs during the 1970s.

After the 1973 Arab oil embargo led to overcapacity in the rig market, Stolt-Nielsen chose to convert *Seaway Swan* into a working, construction and diving platform. The conversion, which was ordered at Rauma-Repola yard in Mantyluoto, Finland, also included new equipment. The rig was to be fitted with automatically controlled water cannons, with KV assigned to deliver the automation as well as a DP system. KV was now challenging market leader, Honeywell.[1]

This meant that the DP concept had to be developed into a prototype, and then a finished product. Then it had to function to Stolt-Nielsen's satisfaction. In addition, it was critical that the product was such a success that other customers would be interested. But there were many challenges that had to be solved before reaching that stage. Simrad had not yet completed its HPR100 position reference system. There were weak points that the engineers wanted to resolve before it was released to the market. Balchen had been successful in pitching the Kalman filter, but Rudolf Kalman's cybernetic principles had not yet been applied to a DP-system. KV's KS500 machines were completed but what is now called the Data and Systems Division, reported production challenges.

Once the order was in the bag, Olav Berdal established a separate DP team for the *Seaway Swan* contract. The team had several offshoots: the main team concentrated on hardware, system software, operator communication and measurement systems and was stationed at Kongsberg. This group included

Seaway Swan was contracted as a drilling rig, but was converted to a construction and diving vessel prior to delivery from the shipyard in Finland in 1978. Its first job was for the British National Oil Company working on the Thistle Field in the UK part of North Sea. Seaway Swan had limited DP capabilities by modern standards, with two azimuth thrusters in each pontoon, one 30-tonne unit in the bow and one in the aft with a thrust of 14 tonnes, together with two main propellers of 20 tonnes. The vessel was later sold and converted back to an anchored drilling rig. Photo: Mediafoto.

Thor Skoland, Sverre Corneliussen, Egil Ørbeck and Nils Tore Østerbø. Their remit covered everything except the cybernetic control algorithms. The task of developing this crucial part of the DP system was assigned to SINTEF employees in Trondheim who cooperated closely with the Kongsberg team. The Christian Michelsen Institute (CMI) in Bergen was awarded various simulation tasks related to the effect of wind, currents and waves on a rig.[2] Meanwhile, in Horten, Simrad engineers were busy developing a DP-customised HPR solution. This was a comprehensive project, which led to Simrad creating a new HPR concept.

Although the contract for the first DP system was signed, not everything went as planned. The development team quickly got the message from the shipowner that the rig would be delayed from the yard. Fortunately, KV soon landed a contract for the supply of a DP system, once again from Stolt-Nielsen shipping. The deal was for the diving vessel *Seaway Eagle*, which was a sister ship to *Seaway Falcon*. *Seaway Eagle* was scheduled for delivery in May 1977.[3] As it turned out, Kongsberg Våpenfabrikk would build and supply two DP systems instead of one, a large and complex system with full redundancy for the *Seaway Swan* rig and a smaller and simpler system for *Seaway Eagle*.

THE EMERGENCE OF DP

The most important hardware component in a DP system is the computer. The path of development from Norwegian Defence Research (FFI), SAM, Odin and Kongsberg's SM3 and SM4 is described previously, now it was the KS500 that mattered. To many people at the time, this new computer seemed to perform pure magic. It was launched in 1974 and was already being used in a number of KV products. This machine was built with process control in mind. KS500 was used in weapon control systems for the military, but better suited for flame cutters and machine tools. As a general computer, it was vaguely useful. At KV it was Thor Stensrud who was responsible for KS500 in the DP system.[4]

KS500 was built on a 16-bit address/data bus with control signals and was a word-based machine (Word = 2 bytes) with a maximum of 64 kW address range. The physical module size was a separate KV standard resembling a «prolonged double Europe». The engineers did however modify most KS500 modules with braces to reduce vibration when used in a maritime environment.[5] The components were laid out on double-layer circuit board, which was common at the time. So-called 'Schottky logic' was used, which

An inside view of the KS500 as it was delivered in ADP503 systems. The computer is in the left cabinet. In the upper section the red panel used to adjust the computer program on board (called patching) can be seen, together with the Tandberg cassette player used to load the computer program into the machine. The section below is the computer rack with the KS500's printed circuit boards; first the Stansaab screen electronics in the low shelf, followed by two higher shelves with the computer itself. On the bottom there is a fan cage to ensure that the temperature in the cabinet is kept under control. The right cabinet contains mainly power supply components and fuses. Photo: Mediafoto.

created significant noise sensitivity on double-layer circuit boards, since the cards did not have the noise-protecting layers that are now deemed necessary. It was only after a major review of the components in 1978 that the sensitivity problem was solved.

Several years working with both military and civilian systems meant that KV could offer a well-functioning operating system, Kongsberg Operating System (KOS), which was specialised in controlling real-time tasks. That the Dynpos team didn't have to develop such an operating system was an important time saver. The application programs managed the entire DP system and recorded wind speed, and position. Using the computer, they also calculated in which direction the thrusters should be used, and at what power level. The software code for all these functions was developed and programmed by SINTEF's Trondheim team, which consisted of Nils Albert Jenssen and Steinar Sælid. From 1975 to 1980, Jenssen and Sælid developed the software for *Seaway Eagle*, *Seaway Swan* and the other deliveries from KV during this period.[6]

While Jenssen worked with optimum control and thrust allocation, Sælid was responsible for the Kalman filter and measurement systems. They often engaged in passionate discussions in their office in D-block in Elektrobygget Gløshaugen at NTH/SINTEF. Hans Roar Sørheim, who later received his doctorate in DP-assisted offshore loading, also participated in the discussions, which often continued over lunch, with drawings and mathematics scribbled on serviettes. Jenssen and Sælid were eventually joined by the third central software developer in this period, Eldar Mathisen, who was employed by KV in 1976. His role was to integrate computer applications in KS500 machines. For those who knew Mathisen, this came as no surprise. He, like many of the others who worked with the development of the DP system, was a cybernetics specialist and a student of Jens G. Balchen. The highly skilled Mathisen became the point of contact between the communities in Trondheim and Kongsberg.[7]

Together, Jenssen, Sælid and Mathisen wrote the extensive software code for KV's first DP systems. Although the code was updated and vastly expanded in later years, the original version provided the foundation. Thousands of lines of code were written in the programming language Fortran IV. With the hardware and software being developed at different sites – the former in Kongsberg and the latter in Trondheim – the two tasks had to be integrated. Eldar Mathisen therefore commuted between Trondheim and Kongsberg with the programs – recorded in hole-punched ribbon that was safely stashed at the bottom of his bag. In Kongsberg, the computer programs were loaded into the computer and tested with the hardware and the other programs. The development teams

Eldar Mathisen was a freshly qualified engineer from NTH when he was assigned the challenging task of stitching together all the software that was developed at Kongsberg and Trondheim, so that computer interfaces, sensors and software could function as one system. Everything was new and there was no one with a complete overview or experience to provide support. Mathisen was the linchpin of the first deliveries until he took on another job in 1980. The picture is taken aboard the *Seaway Sandpiper* where Mathisen is explaining the ADP system to a customer representative. Photo: Mediafoto.

discovered quite early that KS500 lacked the capacity to run the demanding algorithms.[8] At that time, KS500's limited internal memory was the DP system's Achilles' heel. The programs had to be adjusted, which meant that the much-vaunted Kalman filter could not be properly implemented. To solve this, clever mathematical transformations and simplifications needed to be devised.

ALBATROSS IS BORN

In the spring of 1976, with the development of the two Stolt-Nielsen vessels well underway, Dynpos attended the Offshore Northern Seas (ONS) exhibition in Stavanger, the Norwegian offshore industry's flagship event. Bjørn Barth Jacobsen decided that the project needed a suitable name and a logo that could represent the group and the products it was developing. He delegated

Albatross employees were proud of their group. The exotic albatross with its enormous wingspan was an important symbol of identity.

the task to Kari Paulsen (later Kari Larsen) who was employed as a secretary for the Dynpos project. Paulsen, like the other employees in the project, was up to the task.

There was a tradition of using bird and animal names for successful KV products during this period, with Terne and Penguin the most notable. Terne was a ballistic boat-to-submarine missile KV had developed for the Norwegian Navy, and Penguin was a surface-to-surface anti-ship missile first developed by KV in the early 1970s, and updated several times since. Penguin MK1 was also known as the world's first «fire and forget missile» for sea targets.[9]

Paulsen flicked through bird names in an encyclopaedia. She did not have to look long before she found her bird, the magical, majestic and magnificent albatross that lived its life on the vast, deserted ocean expanses. Along with the condor, the albatross has the biggest wingspan of all birds and can grow up to 3.6 metres from wing tip to wing tip. Albatross wings are also long and narrow to harness the wind optimally, enabling them to soar for hours without beating their wings once. An albatross therefore tends to spend little time on land, other than to breed. Paradoxically, in the past, sailors have associated the albatross with bad luck, which is reflected in the famous poem «The Ancient Mariner» by Samuel Coleridge.[10] Those who were involved in the Dynpos project at the time, however, felt that luck was on their side. They liked both the name and the logo, and the logo was used exactly as Paulsen had drawn it from the picture in the encyclopaedia. This was a name and logo that everyone

From the wheelhouse on the diving vessel Seabex One, where Albatross staff are engaged in hectic activity prior to the handover in June 1981. Alf Bævre, Sverre Corneliussen, Hans Jørgen Dyrnes, Helge M. Landsverk, Steinar Gregersen, Knut Lagim and Find Søberg were some of Albatross people involved in this project. Photo: Mediafoto.

involved could be proud of, and this was long before the business community embraced the concept of brand.[11] In time, the logo could be seen on everything from DP consoles to service engineers' coveralls, or carry bags that were used for the advertising material on stands at exhibitions and fairs that the Albatross team attended around the world.

At the time, when Dynpos personnel became 'albatrosses', the group was still a project in KV's Petroleum division. The creation of a name and logo signalled a new phase in the group's development. Over time, they acquired the reputation of being unconventional and strong-headed, but above all as outstanding professionals. Management clearly saw no reason to change this culture and continued to attract graduates from Balchen's cybernetics programme at NTH in Trondheim.

SEAWAY SWAN

Although work on *Seaway Swan* was abandoned in favour of *Seaway Eagle*, a separate development team continued to prepare the delivery of the former. A brochure published in autumn 1975 was the first product description of the DP

The ADP503 system was heavy and took up a lot of space. This picture, from 1977, shows the DP unit set up in KV's premises to be presented to potential customers. On the right side the cabinets with A-, B- and C-computers and peripheral equipment, can be seen. Operator consoles are situated in the middle, with a battery-backed power supply unit (UPS) to the left. Ingvar Løvdal, on the right, is explaining the technology. Photo: Mediafoto.

system that KV wanted to deliver to customers. The brochure gave a thorough description of «The Kongsberg Dyn. Pos System», the computer, Kongsberg System 500, and the position reference system HPR100. The computer was afforded plenty of space in the brochure. It was described as having a high degree of modularisation, and the brochure declared that more specialised component modules could be applied as necessary. The DP was equipped with three full KS500 computers, two of which ran parallel and one that stood on standby.[12] This made the system highly reliable, which the brochure highlighted as a key selling point.

Reliability was an important parameter. Today it is very rare that computers break down, but in the 1970s it was a common phenomenon. The systems were particularly sensitive to external electromagnetic interference. Sverre Corneli-ussen says that one of the first tasks the team worked on was to explore how vibrations and electromagnetic noise would affect DP systems. He describes how he crawled around on the deck of *Seaway Eagle* with a measuring device. Meanwhile, the skipper threw one propeller forward and one into reverse, which gave strong vibrations in the hull.

Even this challenge was overcome quickly. On *Seaway Swan*, the «synchros» received much attention. The so-called synchros were used in measuring angles of rotation and interfacing, that is, the connection between the thrusters and the computer. Such devices were widely used in military systems and were known to be reliable, accurate and virtually immune to electromagnetic interference. This was something KV had plenty of experience with, and therefore such a solution was chosen for the first DP systems. Noise was still a problem, however, and although this was initially blamed on the synchros, many hours of testing showed that the interference was not necessarily coming from the vessel itself, but probably from a nearby coastal radio.[13]

That a computer could break down brought renewed attention to the issue of redundancy, as was highlighted in the sales brochure. The design was later delivered under the name Albatross Dynamic Positioning (ADP) 503 and was equipped as described in the brochure. The system had two computers, A machine and B machine, which ran DP simultaneously, as well as a third computer, C machine, which checked if A and B were in sync. Both A and B were online but only one of them at a time controlled the thrusters. Unofficially, the latter was often referred to as the «online machine». The online machine could be either A or B. If the online machine stopped, the other machine would automatically take over. The C machine had a common memory area with the A and B machines via a so-called node module, and, if A and B started running out of sync, the C machine would show the message «AB difference». If the «AB difference» message came up, the operator had to restart the machine that was not running the thrusters, after having first checked that the «online computer» was operating properly.[14]

Because ADP503 was a dual system with two machines running in parallel, both machines had to receive information about key commands. For this reason, the buttons were equipped with two sets of switches, one for each computer. The controls were sensitive though. If they were pressed with either too little pressure or not held down for the right amount of time, there was a risk that only one computer would detect the command. This would result in the 'AB difference' message appearing, much to the confusion of the DP operator. Correctly pushing the buttons was therefore an important element of operator training. Their construction was robust, for operators with a heavy hand. Users were instructed to press the button fully, with a fair amount of force, and hold it for at least one second.[15]

Alarms not only gave important information to operators, but also documented both the DP operation and any errors. An alarm panel showed errors

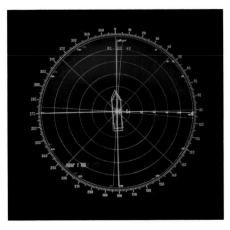

Here the so-called 'pos plot' can be seen, showing the position and orientation of the vessel as it appeared on the Stansaab display on the first ADP502 and ADP503 systems. The 'pos plot' could be presented with the north axis up and a vessel symbol that moved in relation to the desired position (in the centre of picture), or as a relative plot with a fixed vessel symbol in the centre of the screen. The axis then rotated with the vessel's heading, while the symbol for the desired position moved around. The image also indicated wind and current speed and direction. The DP operator could also follow the position of the HPR transponders and taut wire weight on the seabed. The 'pos plot' was inspired by the radar screens of the time. It was also introduced as a requirement for DP systems in DNV's first regulations. Photo: Mediafoto.

in computers, thrusters, generators, sensors and other devices connected to the system. All alarms were also printed on a long, continuous data printout typical of the 1970s. If the printer ran out of paper, for example, an alarm would go off. But because this alarm was considered of low priority, it was only printed, and since the printer was out of paper, the message was not conveyed. The system was designed so that «everything» was duplicated. Both output and input was run through both computers. The machines consisted of around 20 components in a computer rack. Many of the modules came in various editions, and altogether there were close to 40 different modules.[16]

Of course, there was more to the user interface than buttons and printers. The most important information could be read on the various screens. For ADP503, a graphics system was used that had been adopted from KV's installations in torpedo boats. This technology was called «random scan display». It consisted of a 30 centimetre round Stansaab monochrome display, with orange or green text, and symbols on a black background. It resembled contemporary radar displays, with an extensive graphics system that filled an entire 5 x 19 inch rack. The graphics were not very user-friendly compared to today's standards though, and there were only a handful of people who knew how to program this system. The operator could only see lines and text. This is when «posplotet» was born. Posplotet was the new graphic symbol that showed the vessel's position and heading in relation to where it should be located, and included both wind and ocean currents.[17]

However, the need for a better graphical interface became apparent, and in 1979 DP systems came with colour display, controlled by a modern graphics system Ramtek. This consisted of three huge printed circuit boards and was priced accordingly. The resolution was 640x480 pixels, which was very advanced for its time. Interestingly, the first DP systems used equipment with military specifications, which meant that absolute precision was required. It was said that once the top of the DP console was taken off, even if you were lucky enough to get it back on, you would never get the screws back in place. If you removed the side panels, the same thing happened – it was completely impossible to get them back in place. It was no wonder then that one of the service engineers, Roald Holstad, jokingly defined the KV standard as follows: «The holes are in the right place, it's just that the screws don't fit.»[18]

CALCULATING THE POSITION

The DP system needed to be able to recognise a vessel's position in order to function, and it was therefore important to have good position references. This was in a time before the global satellite-based navigation systems such as GPS had been put into operation (and long before they became available for civilian use).[19] This meant that the DP systems had to be based on other methods to get a continuous measurement of the position. Both *Seaway Swan* and *Seaway Eagle* were equipped with a hydroacoustic position reference system from Simrad.

When Simrad started developing HPR for DP, there were two established concepts in ordinary use. These were 'short base' (Short Baseline – SBL) and 'long base' (Long Baseline – LBL) solutions. Short base had been introduced back in the 1960s with *Glomar Challenger*, which has been described earlier. The drawbacks of this solution were that several holes had to be made in the hull where pipes were inserted so that a hydrophone could be lowered beneath the keel. All hull penetrations represent a safety risk to a ship, so it was critical to develop solutions that guaranteed against water intrusion, should the underwater equipment be damaged in any way. This was very expensive – often at least as expensive as the measuring equipment itself. The alternative was the so-called long base system (LBL), which used a combined transmitter and receiver on the ship and three or more transponders on the seafloor. The principle was the same as for SBL. If the location of each transponder was known, the vessel's position could be determined using geometry. The LBL principle enabled more accurate measurements than SBL because it allowed for calculations with longer baselines. A baseline is the distance between the transponders in the LBL system or between the hydrophones on the ship in SBL. The disadvantage of LBL was that several transponders had to be placed, with each one needing to be localised accurately. This was both time consuming and resource intensive.[20]

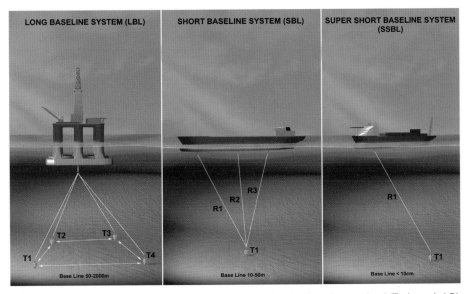

The figure illustrates the various acoustic positioning principles that have been utilised. Today only LBL and SSBL are in use. LBL has advantages in very deep water, as its accuracy is independent of water depth. Simrad broke new ground when the company developed HPR100. By using a more advanced receiver the direction in which the sound signals were received could be measured. In this way it was possible to get away with only one hull implementation. Creating holes in the hull always carries a certain risk. Illustration: KM.

Simrad chose a completely different solution, the so-called super short base principle (Super Short Baseline – SSBL). With the SSBL principle, the distance between a combined transmitter/receiver under the hull and a transponder on the seabed was measured. The direction of the sound response from the transponder was also taken into account. The former unit consisted of a connector and three sets of receivers located in an L-shape. Each set consisted of multiple listening elements mounted side by side. By selecting the number of elements in each group, receiver directivity could be controlled, that is, the ability to listen in a certain direction. By using all of these elements, it was possible to listen in the direction of the transponder, resulting in immunity to interference sources coming from other directions. This improved accuracy significantly. Using fewer elements would widen up the listening sector, but at the expense of noise immunity. On the other hand, this enabled any missing transponders to be located. Such beamforming was essentially sonar technology. Angle measurement could be performed by comparing the signals from the three groups of receivers.[21]

When the acoustic position sensors on the rig *Seaway Swan* were tested, the quality of signals was mixed. If the vessel moved too far from transponders on

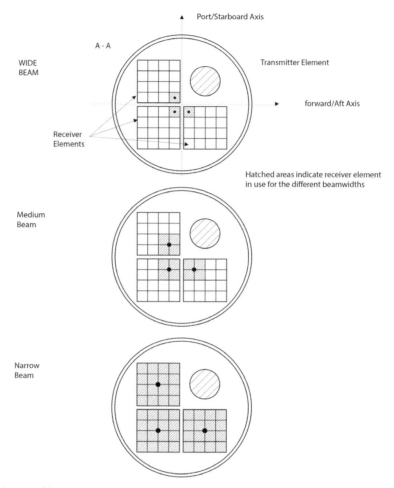

Principle drawing of the acoustic elements of the HPR100 transducer (1976). By using different combinations of elements, it was possible to control the transducer's listening capabilities. Using all elements allowed listening in a narrow vertical cone with an opening of 30 degrees (narrow beam), while activating four elements in each group provided a listening range of 60 degrees (medium beam). Using only one element in each group gave a listening range of 160 degrees (wide beam). Range and accuracy of detection was determined by the width of the cone; the narrower the cone, the longer the range and the better the accuracy. Using wide beam provided only half the range of narrow beam. To achieve good accuracy, a transducer with extremely narrow opening angle was required. Illustration: KM.

the seabed, the signals were poor and the transponders had to be moved. The acoustic reference system was therefore supplemented with taut wire.[22]

A third example of the position reference systems was Artemis, which consisted of a transmitter that sent microwaves between the ship and one responder located at a fixed point nearby. This point could be a fixed beacon, a fixed platform or something else that was stationary. The system was based on radar signals and antennas that resembled those used for small radars. Like the first two systems, this system also had its drawbacks. Although the specifications stated that the system could utilise a fixed point within a range of six kilometres, in practice the point had to be within about one to two kilometres. The three reference systems had quite different properties and complemented each other. They were all used simultaneously by the control system and their inputs mixed together according to their accuracy. The DP system would hence work as long as at least one of the reference systems provided adequate data.[23]

GROWING PAINS

As KV's development team worked busily on the first delivery to Stolt-Nielsen, Bjørn Barth Jacobsen travelled north to Tromsø. He had heard that the shipowner Odd Berg was expanding his fleet of vessels that would service oil companies in the North Sea. According to Barth Jacobsen, the master on Berg's *Arctic Surveyor* complained that the DP system they were running often had to be operated manually with a joystick because it was unstable in automatic mode. In addition, the shipowner felt that the spare parts were too expensive and that the American supplier was too far away when service was needed. They also had several challenges with the hydroacoustic system and wanted to change to Simrad HPR. Due to these issues, Odd Berg wanted a DP system from Kongsberg Våpenfabrikk. The Tromsø shipowner required, however, that the system had to be installed during the summer of 1977.[24] The order would mean that KV had to develop and install additional deliveries in parallel to its existing obligations, and Barth Jacobsen realised that this would create concern among KV's management. With this in mind, on 12 January 1976, Barth Jacobsen wrote to Rolf Qvenild: «... Bergship would like to place an order for KV's DP system including one to two backup systems (radar and radio (NB) with a potential contract value of NOK 7.7 to 8 million, for delivery by 05.01.77 ... we have been requested to provide an official offer for DP outfitting by 01.17.76.»[25] Qvenild responded firmly that no new contracts could be entered into with such short deadlines. He wrote that a prototype was already under construction, referring to the DP system for *Seaway Eagle*. Whether it would work, was not yet known. Qvenild added that there were too few people with the necessary expertise. He concluded his letter by stating that this was also about KV's reputation because customers would assume that KV was pulling out of the first deliveries.[26]

Barth Jacobsen responded quickly and made the point that by building more units at the same time, KV could achieve «economy of scale». This was the way large international companies became competitive. In addition, he wrote: «... we risk having to run another 'hobby workshop' to support the few units we have delivered.» He concluded by asserting that in this industry there was only room for winners.[27] But Qvenild could not be persuaded and he stopped the order.

The correspondence is interesting for several reasons. Firstly, it was striking that Qvenild and Barth Jacobsen sat in separate locations and wrote letters to each other. Why didn't they communicate by phone? The correspondence also contrasts Barth Jacobsen's aggressive ambitions with the KV leadership's apparently 'responsible approach'. Further, that Barth Jacobsen didn't comply without first questioning reflects the assertiveness of the albatrosses. This attitude was reassuring to customers, despite the fact that not one single DP system had been delivered. Barth Jacobsen also gained a reputation for being fearless in any given situation.

Forgetting his coat at a customer's office on purpose so he could return to continue a sale, is just one of the more innocent rumours that went around. Such an enthusiastic and persistent salesman and manager could be positive in the initial phase, but became a challenge as the Dynpos project became a division and later a separate subsidiary. It is not surprising that most of these stories stem from the turbulent 1970s. Barth Jacobsen's ability to create interest among customers and impart a sense of courage in his co-workers was one of the ingredients in the shaping of an entrepreneurial culture. In the early days, Building 11 was buzzing around the clock. Staff in the other KV departments were in awe – and sometimes envy – at these intense and skilled 'albatrosses', who spent long days developing new and exciting technology.

A SUPERIOR SYSTEM

Although NTH Professor Jens Glad Balchen initiated the Dynpos project, he had lost interest by the time it finally started, and was already occupied with new projects. In particular, his new research passions concerned modelling and control of fish. But true to his character, Balchen explained to his colleagues how a DP system should look before he withdrew. Since installing dynamic positioning aboard a ship or rig was different from equipping a control room for an industrial plant, it was important that the DP system be adapted to the oil industry's working conditions. As Balchen saw it, DP systems would

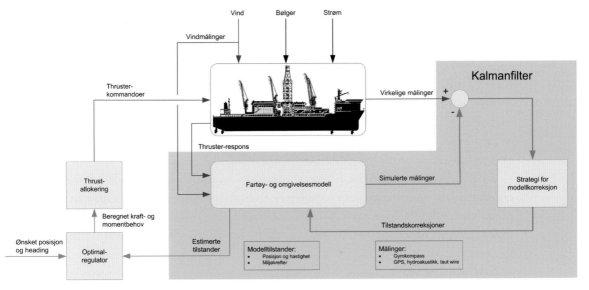

One of the Kalman filter's earliest applications was in navigation, but using this technique on ship motions was new. Sketches explaining the Kalman filter were used actively in marketing to show the new and revolutionary difference in the product compared to the competition. Illustration: KM.

mainly be used on small vessels that operated in harsh conditions. This meant the systems had to be simple, user-friendly and robust. Balchen was especially interested in computer programs and control algorithms. In order to achieve his vision, the DP systems were equipped with both feed-forward control and Kalman filters. In this respect, the Norwegian DP systems could prove themselves significantly better than those delivered by Honeywell.[28]

A Kalman filter is an algorithm that combines a mathematical model of a dynamic system with noisy measurements of the actual behaviour, or the state, of the system. This combination makes it possible to estimate a less noisy version of the system's state, and the algorithm is therefore referred to as a filter. Such a filter can also estimate elements of the system's state that cannot be measured directly, but only indirectly.

Essentially, the mathematical model is used to predict, or forecast, what the system's state will be in the next time step. The next incoming measurement is then used to correct the model-based estimate of the state. If the measurement contains a lot of noise, the system will compensate less than if the measurement contains little noise. With high measurement noise, the filter will therefore rely more on the model than on the measurement, and vice versa. This weighting is done automatically through so-called covariance matrices, which are a measure of the statistical properties of the filter's components, as well as the coupling between these.

The Kalman filter is a recursive algorithm because it retains the entire measurement history in its current state estimate and therefore only needs to use the next measurement to update this estimate for the next time step. This avoids having to store all previous measurements for use in demanding calculations each time a new measurement comes in. The filter will then work recursively on an incoming stream of noisy measurements in order to produce a statistically optimal estimate of the system's state.

In the context of DP, the Kalman filter uses a mathematical model of the DP vessel and its surroundings together with noisy measurements of the vessel position, heading, thruster use, wind effects, and so on. Balchen's research group reported their first experiences with the filter for use in dynamic positioning in an article from 1976.[29]

The filter made it possible, for example, to use several different types of position reference systems simultaneously, so that these could be combined to achieve an optimal position estimate. This is a very important feature, as the use of different measurement principles leads to far greater reliability than the use of a single principle. By comparison, Honeywell's DP system primarily relied on hydroacoustics.[30] The Kalman filter's mathematical model could also provide an estimate of the vessel position even if measurements were lost, otherwise known as dead reckoning. Furthermore, the Kalman filter could distinguish between the high- and low-frequency components of motion measurements, so that only the low-frequency components were used for position control, which both reduced fuel consumption and wear and tear on the thrusters. The so-called 'DP Current', a measure of the unknown forces affecting the vessel, was also calculated by the filter and used by the controller.

The new Kalman filter based DP system was described in detail in a research paper from 1980, with results from full-scale operations, which indicated «excellent system performance».[31] In the aftermath of this pioneering work, Balchen is rumoured to have said: «There are only three people in the world who really understand control technology, and the other two are former students of mine», referring to colleagues Sælid and Jenssen.[32]

When it came to sales, the Kalman filter attained an almost magical quality. There are many anecdotes about the filter, mostly revolving around the enthusiasm of customers and the imagination of salesmen. One such story regards a contract that the salesman secured by including an extra Kalman filter free of charge. Of course, as the filter was an algorithm implemented in software and

Photo showing the diving ship *Seaway Eagle*, launched in 1975. When the ship docked in Haugesund on the 17th of May 1977, the first Norwegian DP system had been installed, tested and approved. The vessel would serve on various diving assignments in the North Sea. Photo: Gary Markham.

not something tangible, this part of the contract was most likely not fulfilled. According to another urban legend, Rolf Qvenild approved an invoice for the purchase of alcohol for cleaning the filter – something he would never have seriously done, as he himself was qualified in cybernetics from NTH.[33] What is beyond doubt, however, is that the use of this algorithm proved a superior solution, and created a better and more robust dynamic positioning system. Use of the Kalman filter was also testimony to KV's ability to deliver state-of-the-art systems.

THE DELIVERY OF *SEAWAY EAGLE*

The technical challenges were numerous in the early days. The development teams worked with both projects simultaneously, but priority was given to the DP system for *Seaway Eagle*, which was the least challenging project. *Seaway Eagle* was 63 metres long and 13 metres wide, with a draught of less than five metres. The vessel was equipped with two engines of 2720 kW propulsion and two 680 kW side thrusters, while it was also outfitted for saturation diving and had a moon pool.

Sverre Corneliussen brought critical systems competence to Albatross, and would prove to play an important part of the team during the development of the overall system. He was also the mind behind the redundancy concept that would emerge a decade later. The photo is taken aboard the sand barge *Cobla 1* (GC 306) and shows from right, Sverre Corneliussen, Jan Erik Faugstadmo (Simrad) and Olav Robstad. Photo: Mediafoto.

In addition to Thor Skoland, Olav Berdal had selected Sverre Corneliussen to work on the hardware.[34] Corneliussen's background was from NTH and FFI, and in 1974 he travelled around to various shipyards that were to adopt the new KS500 machine. His responsibility was mainly related to the computers and their configuration, and he assisted with installation or service on these computers. His experience was useful when installing the DP system aboard *Seaway Eagle*.

Since the DP didn't require redundancy, there was only a need for one KS500 computer. The system included taut wire, HPR and Artemis position reference systems.[35] *Seaway Eagle's* hardware was assembled in Kongsberg during 1976. In the new year of 1977, all the components were in place, and the completed system could be tested.

Then it was time for installation onboard. The ship was already in dock at the Haugesund Mekaniske Verksted (HMV), where an opening in the hull was made for the HPR100 pipe to be welded. Simrad employees were responsible for installing the HPR unit. Those participating from KV were Sverre Corneliussen and Vidar Djønne, who lived aboard the ship during the entire delivery process. Later, Olav Robstad and Eldar Mathisen also joined the team. Although they worked according to KV's drawings, they sought the advice of the shipyard workers, acquired their own parts, and improvised with customised solutions.[36]

Behind the wheelhouse there was a large fixed metal box with a door. The plan was that this space would house both the computer and an additional power source (Uninterruptible Power Supply, UPS). When the KS500 machine was winched aboard, however, they couldn't get it through the door. A cutting torch was used to cut an opening on top of the box so that the computer and power supply could be winched down into the space. Afterwards, the hole in the roof was welded together. The two control consoles, one each for the DP system and HPR, were mounted on the port side of the wheelhouse. The DP installation used the same display as the HPR console.[37] Some features were also taken from the motor torpedo boats where KV had installed Penguin missiles. The workers lived aboard and worked without interruption from March to May 1977. The installation became an uncompromising race to deliver DP systems according to time, specifications and budget. Those involved were under immense pressure, as were their families. On more than one occasion, when the sessions dragged out, staff had to pack up and go home to 'save the marriage,' as it was called.

On May 17 1977, Norway's national day, the installation was declared ready for initial testing. Early in the morning the captain headed towards 'Sletta', an area of open sea not far from Haugesund. Aboard the ship were representatives from both Simrad and Kongsberg Våpenfabrikk. Sverre Corneliussen, who had lived on board for months and been awake for the previous 36 hours, was desperately trying to keep his eyes open. Finally the skipper brought the ship to a standstill. A transducer for the Simrad HPR was lowered into the sea with just one orange floating buoy on the surface marking where it lay. Then, the first Albatross-installed DP system was switched on.

Everyone on the bridge was quiet. The ship lay perfectly still, remaining in the same position minute after minute. After an hour everyone was satisfied and went down to the mess hall where the chef served coffee and cake to celebrate the event. When they emerged half an hour later, the ship was still in the same position. The system was then seen as approved and *Seaway Eagle* returned to shore. When the ship with the first Norwegian developed DP system slid into the docks in Haugesund, national day celebrations were in full swing throughout the city. Now the exhausted Albatrosses could also celebrate.

A QUICK TRIP TO MILAN

The third DP contract won by KV was to provide a system for the Italian ship *Capalonga*.[38] In December 1976, Thor Skoland heard rumours that Shell and the Milan-based Italian company, SSOS/Talassa, had plans to equip a ship for diving and fire fighting services in the North Sea.[39] Bjørn Barth Jacobsen got the message and travelled to Italy together with Eldar Mathisen. They arrived in Milan on Monday morning, but when they met at the company's office, no one from either company would meet with them. The ladies at reception conveyed the message that a DP system was of no interest. In a similar situation, most people would have returned home. But in keeping with his 'doctrine' of 'world domination', Barth Jacobsen had another strategy. He and Mathisen sat in the lobby until the office closed for the evening. They returned on Tuesday and again on Wednesday. Surely, they thought, the strategy would work eventually. On Thursday, they were finally invited in to meet the technical staff at SSOS/Talassa. The Italians were nice enough but again said that they had no need for a DP system. Of course, they invited their guests to stay a while if they wished.[40] According to the Italian engineers, the ship had a small engine capacity, in terms of both propulsion and water cannons. They were therefore attempting to calculate how much extra turbine power the ship needed. Barth Jacobsen and Mathisen were engineers at heart, so they rolled up their sleeves and threw themselves into the problem. After several rounds of calculations, they eventually concluded that six additional turbines should suffice. Barth Jacobsen suggested that Kongsberg Våpenfabrikk could deliver the turbines, and suggested that they should also consider a DP system. At this point, the hosts agreed and expressed that they would like to buy turbines from KV so long as the terms were good, and also conceded that a DP system might be required after all.

Significant power was required for *Capalonga*, which was 100 metres long, 15 metres wide and weighed 5,000 tonnes. Four 750 kW azimuth thrusters provided the propulsion. For this particular project, one of the few ADP502 systems that Albatross designed was proposed as the most suitable. According to rumours, the DP system was sketched by Barth Jacobsen on the back of a napkin, and the tender price was set after he had accidentally come across competitor pricing among papers that lay scattered around the Italian company's office.[41] In the meantime, ADP502 was developed and installed as an expanded version of the ADP501 system that was aboard the *Seaway Eagle*. The main difference between the two was that ADP502 had a separate graphical display. During discussions on the selection of the DP system, however, a minor issue arose. It was Mathisen who discovered that there was not enough thruster power at the stern of the ship. The problem was quickly solved by the engineers incorporating azimuth thrusters mounted outside the hull in the design, 'bulbs' on each side – almost like outboard motors, which was a totally new way of thinking for offshore vessels. Nothing was impossible for the Norwegian-Italian partnership. Friday and Saturday went by with more work, restaurant visits, work and restaurant visits, and so they proceeded until Sunday morning when the contract was finally signed. Now the Dynpos crew could finally return home.[42]

It turned out, however, that not everything had been done by the book. The payment for the delivery was approved, but the contract contained terms that Qvenild did not particularly like. Given his opposition to the delivery of equipment to Odd Berg, he didn't really appreciate another new order for DP systems to be delivered just six months later. Moreover, the contract contained clauses stipulating that KV had to cover any variations in exchange rates. Upon his return, Barth Jacobsen was therefore immediately summoned by a raging Qvenild. Barth Jacobsen quickly calmed Qvenild, however, by explaining that the contract had been paid in advance. The story of this project also features a race against the clock for delivery. To make the tight schedule, even Barth Jacobsen had to work in the yard. In fact, the whole Barth Jacobsen family spent Easter of 1977 in Amsterdam. While his wife and children enjoyed the spring sunshine, Barth Jacobsen crawled around on all fours between compressors and turbines, installing signal inputs into thrusters, running wires and configuring computers. The ship was ready for delivery by late autumn of the same year, and the DP personnel that worked in the yard were invited on a trip. As *Capalonga*, heavily loaded with turbines and other equipment on deck, drifted out into the channel, the white tablecloths and fine Italian food and wine all came out.[43]

COMING UP WITH SOMETHING NEW

Although the story behind the *Capalonga* contract may have been overstated by the storyteller, it provides insight into how things operated in this early phase. There was a constant search for customers and business, with or without Qvenild's sanction. Although he managed to stop the Odd Berg contract, the Milan saga showed that he either couldn't or wouldn't oversee all the details. Some people describe the culture at KV after 1975 as both complex and out of control. The historian Knut Øyangen, who wrote a post-war history on KV, is critical and notes that Qvenild was «the right man at the wrong time».

Qvenild was more concerned about long-term results than short-term revenue.[44] Another perspective, and one that the former KV boss pointed out, was that during the 1970s KV was an innovation hub that spawned a number of projects and products that later became major commercial successes. In that respect Qvenild is right, and the Dynpos project is just one of these examples.

However, the extent to which this was down to good planning and administration is debatable. The reorganisation of KV into divisions in 1973 required comprehensive coordination between the various division managers and some projects were left to their own devices. This often resulted in blown out budgets, which were paid for by other projects or came out of the state coffers. This paradoxical image of KV – with outward confidence belying its lack of internal control – benefited the DP initiative. For Dynpos personnel, being highly independent was certainly an advantage in those crucial early years.

Bjørn Barth Jacobsen and Thor Skoland played important roles. While Barth Jacobsen had unconventional methods, Skoland showed great technical knowledge and the ability to execute. Nils Willy Gulhaugen, who was responsible for the finances in the turbulent first years, says about Barth Jacobsen: «He was broad-minded, crazy and impossible to pigeonhole. I think one of the main things he contributed was to get us to dare. He showed us the possibilities. He talked about seeking forgiveness rather than permission.» This provides insight into an important aspect of the corporate culture during this period. It was a time of taking chances and breaking rules. Barth Jacobsen sought forgiveness more often than he asked for permission. He also had his other sides. In May 1977, when Sverre Corneliussen had conducted a continuous two-month session on *Seaway Eagle*, Barth Jacobsen delivered a bouquet of flowers to Corneliussen's wife. An attached note contained a brief greeting and an apology for the fact that her husband would not be coming home this Friday night, either.[45]

While management sought new projects, someone had to do the development work and implement what was sold. The basic knowledge and equipment were in place, but a great deal had to be invented, developed or customised. Sales usually occurred before development started, and long before a system was ready for installation. In the early years, intense testing and experimentation was conducted in the factory at Kongsberg and on ships. Such testing was challenging and time consuming. Barth Jacobsen was barely involved in these tasks; it was Skoland, in cooperation with hardware personnel, who ruled this domain. While the families of the employees often felt that their fathers and husbands were working long days, the staff members tended to describe this period as more of an adventure.

THE IMPORTANT CUSTOMERS

Oil industry conferences and exhibitions in Norway and abroad provided ideal events for Albatross to show off its products. In 1976, having already attended ONS, Albatross was to participate in the Offshore Technology Conference (OTC) in Houston. As in Stavanger, Jacobsen and Skoland were the representatives. However, at this point they had nothing to show, so the KV workshop made a Dynpos system out of veneer, which was covered with plastic wrap and had a sonar display from Simrad mounted on the front. Before departing, Barth Jacobsen bought 500 brass locks and packed them with the wooden box. At OTC, Barth Jacobsen's DP 'dummy' was known as the 'The Wooden Albatross' and Honeywell staff surely got a laugh out of such primitive marketing. The brass locks on the other hand were a success, for who wouldn't want a nice lock? In any case, the boss was, according to his colleagues, mainly interested in a girl at the next booth.[46] The stories that were told about Barth Jacobsen say something about how outrageous things sometimes got, but fortunately, also how well they ended up. More importantly, they demonstrate that in

In 1978 Albatross delivered DP systems on three sand barges for a project in Dubai. A large dredging vessel was to trench a 'corridor' in to what would serve as the port for the United Arab Emirates. The barges were to shuttle between the dredger and the dumping grounds offshore. Loading was performed without tying up to the mother ship, and the task would have been near impossible without dynamic positioning. The barges were equipped with ADP501 systems and Artemis position reference systems. The illustration is from the 1982 brochure 'Dynamic Positioning Systems'.

entrepreneurial cultures, a common repertoire of stories is often established, which is critical in bringing employees together.

Another incident that shows the vagaries and improvisations that characterised Albatross personnel took place in 1977. Barth Jacobsen was in Amsterdam along with several others from the department to negotiate the delivery of three

ADP501 MkII systems to Costain & Blankenfort. The shipowner had contracted three sand barges for a large dredging project in connection with the development of the port of Dubai. A large dredger was to dig a channel some 20 kilometres long and 200 metres wide. The three barges were used to dispose of the dredged sand. The Sand barges, *GC 306*, *GC 307* and *GC 308*, were hinged at the top so that the bottom could open up and release the sand. Near land, the vessels had to move forward in sync with the mother ship. When one was full of sand, it transited to deeper waters where it dumped the sand, during which time the next barge took its place. The operation required precise coordination of the position held by the mother ship and barges at all times, and would not have been possible without the use of DP plants supplied by Albatross.[47]

At the meeting in Amsterdam, Barth Jacobsen was brimming with knowledge of The Netherlands and pretended to come from South Africa, explaining his somewhat strange accent. He also had a folder packed with slides for the project. To break the ice he intentionally dropped the slides all over the floor so that the Albatross salesmen and company representatives had to pick them up. After several hours of wrangling on prices and delivery, Albatross won the contract.[48]

A meeting with Stolt-Nielsen was scheduled for the next day in Sandefjord, so the Kongsberg team rushed to Amsterdam Airport Schiphol, only to see the last return flight taking off. Once again Barth Jacobsen led the way and ordered a private jet, but, due to the airspace over Norway being closed for the evening, it had to land in Skagen, Denmark. The group slept on the plane and then took off for Sandefjord in the morning, arriving in time for their meeting. On return to Kongsberg though, the astronomical bill somewhat dampened the mood, and Barth Jacobsen was once again forced to humble himself in Qvenild's office.[49]

However, a reward came in autumn 1977. Qvenild reported to the Board that Albatross was the Petroleum Division's top priority. There was a rapid increase in sales, and contracts had been won on a variety of installations and vessel types. Furthermore, Albatross showed its ability to win contracts abroad. *Capalonga* had delivered strong revenue, and payment for the sand barge work in Dubai was imminent, with installation and service on the barges' DP systems worth NOK 9 million, or NOK 37 million in 2014 inflation-adjusted terms. From then on, orders surged and the team expanded quickly. New employees were mostly young people, and many came from Balchen's institute in Trondheim. According to management, in 1981 the average age of staff was just 32.[50]

RATHER FORGIVENESS THAN PERMISSION

The Dynpos project started as a comprehensive technology partnership with a broad Norwegian industrial and research basis. The project wasn't exactly greeted with enthusiasm at KV, but slipped almost imperceptibly into place in a free corner of Building 11. It wasn't until the first contract was signed in November 1975 that planning and evaluation of possible DP designs started to take place. The result exceeded all expectations, and by the 1980s, it was no longer an ugly duckling, but a gleaming white albatross. By then, Albatross delivered over 80 percent of the world's DP systems.

What happened can only be interpreted as a great success, which might be explained as follows: Albatross DP systems were developed in a way that was very different to international competitors. The new systems had to have a simple user interface and be able to withstand the harsh conditions of the North Sea. The technology was the basis on which this daring attempt succeeded. The KS500 computer was good enough, but not particularly advanced. The key element, rather, was that it combined a simple user interface and advanced software solutions. With both Kalman filter, the DP functionality was in itself an innovation.

Although the most elegant software solutions proved difficult to implement in the beginning, their reputation formed an unbeatable sales argument. Customers preferred to have two Kalman filters and pay extra for it. It was said that it was pure magic, and this wasn't far from the truth. As computers advanced, it became possible implement the solution to its full potential.

This bold DP initiative had been conceived under the broad wings of Qvenild. KV represented quality, soundness and a guarantee of delivery. KV also had the hardware, people and experience with machinery and fire control systems, which would prove to be invaluable. But Albatross was something more. Those who drove the DP initiative came from outside. Balchen's young, ambitious cybernetics experts, possessing a new type of knowledge, were encouraged in their unbridled ways. When Bjørn Barth Jacobsen unleashed the initiative, it was a journey like no other KV had seen. Therefore, seeking forgiveness became more important than asking permission. During this period, where so much was in flux, there was room to make mistakes as long as everything worked out right and the customer was happy.

5

DP ON BOARD ALL VESSELS

IN NOVEMBER 1977, one month after the Italian *Capalonga* was launched, the Albatross team received a somewhat different assignment. The Ekofisk oilfield had been in operation since 1971, and until 1975, oil was being transported ashore by shuttle tankers, after which time an oil pipeline was put into operation to Teesside in England. This method of transportation to Norway had not yet been introduced, and now gas was going to be transported by pipeline on the seabed to Emden in Germany.[1]

The pipeline from Ekofisk to Emden measured a total of 437 kilometres in length, so this was no minor undertaking. Until that time, it was customary to have the oil and gas pipelines lie exposed in a trench on the seabed. On a sandy bottom, the pipeline would gradually be covered, however in clay the pipelines were left with no form of protection, which caused complications over time. Bottom nets, seines and anchors would get caught up in the pipelines, and in some cases, the pipelines were even broken in two. The authorities in the North Sea nations therefore demanded that all cables and pipelines on the seabed were to be buried. In order to carry out this task, the operators needed vessels to cover the pipelines with gravel. This type of operation not only represented a new phase in the use of dynamic positioning in the North Sea, but also posed a new set of challenges. Not only would DP be used to keep a vessel stationary, but now the system would have to follow a set track or programmed route on the seabed. Pipe laying was only one of the new challenges to be met by Albatross. Other marine operations were also being introduced. From the delivery of just a few DP systems a year, there was suddenly a need for many, and along with the development of the concept came new demands for both the system and the employees.

SEAWAY SANDPIPER

Covering pipelines on the seabed was not entirely effortless. Due to sand being volatile, special barges were used to dump gravel over the pipelines to keep them in place, but the load did not always land exactly where it should. Furthermore, the gravel was spread over a vast area, resulting in the need to use more gravel than necessary. Here, Stolt-Nielsen saw a huge potential for improving efficiency. Once again, the shipowner found another use for Albatross DP-systems. The idea was to drop the gravel from a flexible tube that could be positioned along the pipeline on the seabed with the help of an unmanned submarine (ROV) that followed the track. This solution appealed to both the operator Phillips and the pipeline company Norpipe, and Stolt-Nielsen was thus awarded the contract.[2]

Seaway Sandpiper was the first ship equipped with so-called 'auto-track' functionality. The DP system enabled the ship to follow a pipeline track defined by straight lines between geographical points. In order to assist with positioning, the deposit chute under the ship was also equipped with a thruster, allowing the nozzle to be moved sideways as needed. The operation was monitored by a remotely operated under water vehicle (ROV) to ensure that the pipeline was sufficiently covered with gravel. Illustration: KM.

Prior to work commencing, Stolt-Nielsen was given an urgent task. Before they would allow production on Ekofisk to commence, the Danish authorities demanded that pipelines be covered temporarily with sandbags before loading the gravel, and this operation was once again to be handled by Stolt-Nielsen vessels. A number of Haugesund housewives were hired to fill bags with sand at the docks. These bags were then loaded on board the *Seaway Eagle* and transported to the Danish sector. A diver was hoisted down to where the pipeline to Emden passed through. Sitting astride the pipeline, he received load after load of sandbags lowered down in a net, which the diver then opened and emptied. With this method, more than 700,000 sandbags were used to cover nine-kilometres of pipeline in the Danish sector during the course of two months. This urgent mission cost Phillips USD 18 per sandbag, a huge sum, but for the company, it was important to get started.[3]

As planned, in 1978 Stolt-Nielsen purchased a bulk tanker and retrofitted it as a specialised vessel for covering pipelines on the seabed, renaming it *Seaway Sandpiper*. Part of the retrofitting process involved the installation of a tailor-made ADP502 system that controlled the vessel's four azimuth thrusters. In addition, the ADP502 system included an auto-tracking programme that made it possible to plan both the route the vessel should follow, and the speed it should maintain. *Seaway Sandpiper* was also equipped with a fall pipe reaching down to the seabed for discharging gravel, with thrusters mounted at the outlet. Even if the nozzle could be moved over the seabed, the vessel had to also follow the pipe. Therefore, to get accurate positions, several different reference systems were used, such as Artemis, Syledis, Puls 8 and later HPR. Syledis was a position reference system operating via UHF-band radio waves. A vessel using Syledis was equipped with a transmitter sending coded signals to at least three beacons, each placed at a fixed point. Depending on how much time the coded signals used, the position could be calculated quite accurately. Sydledis was produced in France and was used in the offshore industry in the North Sea from 1980 up until 1995, when the reference system was replaced by GPS. Puls 8 operated more or less on the same principles as Syledis.[4]

Seaway Sandpiper became Albatross's eighth delivery, with further similar deliveries to come. One year later, Albatross sold an ADP503 system to *Flexiservice II*, a vessel whose purpose was not to load gravel onto the seabed, but to lay pipelines.[5] However, the DP system was based on the same principle as for the *Seaway Sandpiper*. In 1981, the cable laying vessel *Skagerrak*, owned and operated by Standard Telefon og Kabelfabrikk (STK) and Norges Vassdrags- og Eketrisitesvesen (NVE), was equipped with a DP system featuring an auto-tracking programme to operate on a pre-defined route.[6] With the introduction of these vessels and the respective operations they were required to perform, dynamic positioning proved to be both useful and necessary in a new and important business segment.

SUPPLY VESSELS

By 1981, Albatross had installed around 30 DP systems, consisting of eight ADP501, three ADP502, eleven AD503 and eight of the newest DP models, i.e. the ADP311 which was installed for the first time in 1979. The timing was not coincidental; that year there were deliveries of several series of similar supply ships that did not necessarily require redundancy, but rather a DP which enabled them to transport equipment and food to installations in the North Sea, thus opening up further areas of operation for dynamic positioning. Up until 1978, Albatross had delivered several installations to diving vessels, but from then on, supply vessels became increasingly significant.[7]

Albatross' first DP systems for supply vessels were delivered to Norwegian limited partnerships, administered by Parley Augustsson Management (PAM). In 1978, PAM ordered four DP systems for supply vessels, and acquired an option for the purchase of ten more in the years to come. Each delivery had a price tag of NOK 3.2 million (USD 460 000).

At 2014 NOK values, this would be over NOK 12 million per installation. Even though shipbroker Bjørn Bendigtsen, who had started his own company, was to have a fifth of the total proceeds, the contracts were extremely lucrative and once again a substantial amount of money was deposited via Albatross into KV's diminishing coffers.[8]

After PAM, shipowners like Farstad, Østensjø, Viking Supply and Austevoll Management followed suite, adding to Albatross's ever-growing reference list. When the major American shipping company Edison Chouest Offshore ordered DP systems for a number of their vessels, the first American shipping company to do so, this was a clear indication that Albatross had become a significant player in the DP market for supply vessels.

At first, supply vessels were equipped with ADP501 from KV. However, when a new DP model, ADP311, was launched in 1979, it became a kind of DP standard for many supply vessels. The new feature of ADP311, which appeared similar to ADP501, was that the KS500 computer was integrated in the actual DP console. Another innovation was the so-called «plug-in» connectors at the bottom of the console, which made both installation and service much simpler

The ADP311 was a more compact DP system than the ADP500 series, with all electronics now collected in the console. The photo shows Odd Inge Tangen performing trouble-shooting on the KS500 computer. Photo: KM.

than before. Most types of position reference systems could be directly linked to the ADP311 console. The position could also be read from small alphanumeric displays on the DP desk. The basic ADP311 was not delivered with its own display, but was ordered as an extra feature by most customers.[9]

Using DP systems onboard supply vessels presented both customers and suppliers with a challenge. GPS had not yet become available and there were limits as to which position reference systems could be used. The vessels were advised to use HPR, taut wire and microwave systems such as Artemis. Whereas taut wire could only be used when the vessel was stationary, the other position reference systems relied on the field or position where the DP vessel was to operate being equipped for this purpose. Despite the limitations these position reference systems had, the ADP311 was a good option for the fleet of DP vessels operating in the North Sea. This system was installed in a series of similar vessels, with almost identical features, which in turn allowed Albatross to achieve efficiency through standardization. A total of 44 ADP311 systems were delivered before being phased out.[10]

The introduction of class requirements for vessels with DP systems contributed to the standardisation of deliveries from Albatross. «Classification» is a private and voluntary system ensuring that a vessel, during its construction or operation phase, abides by a set of security requirements posed by a classification society such as Det Norske Veritas (DNV).[11] Since no class requirements for vessels with DP systems had yet been established, each individual delivery was tailor-made, which seems to have suited Albatross perfectly in the beginning. However, this changed quickly. DNV's first DP class DYNPOS, was introduced in 1979, after which each vessel with a DP system onboard could be certified under this class.[12]

Now that companies could relate to class requirements, the list of specifications for the DP system also became a kind of «blueprint» as to how a system should be put together and which functions it should have. Beyond the specified requirements, everyone was free to choose additional features. And since certification was voluntary, in principle, the situation did not change dramatically. To a certain degree, the introduction of class requirements entailed that the systems were becoming standardised, and negotiations between customer and supplier were increasingly being replaced by adjustments to regulations. For Albatross, this also meant that a standard of sorts had been established that occasionally led to shipowners ordering more powerful and more expensive equipment than previously. However, having class requirements could, in some cases, mean losing valuable input from customers when developing the systems. Although the customers related more and more to class specifications, the DP people still generally managed to maintain a close dialogue with shipowners. Over time, having class requirements contributed to a gradual move from tailor-made solutions to off-the-shelf products using the DNV standard.[13]

While the market for supply vessels was opening up for Albatross, things were beginning to get somewhat strained for management. Bjørn Barth Jacobsen evaluated the situation and in 1979, after having given all his time and energy to developing the remarkable DP concept, stepped down from his role as CEO and assumed new assignments. The first was in KV and the next was outside the company.[14] Head of the Petroleum Division, Rolf Qvenild, commented on these changes in a humorous, yet respectful, way: «Bjørn has been brought to the gas station to be filled up and is ready to take on major new assignments.» The gas station referred to the company's central staff, where Barth Jacobsen became head of a new rationalisation project.[15] For a short period, Thor Skoland continued as CEO, but then he also moved on to other KV departments before setting up for himself.

DRILLING OPERATIONS IN THE NORTH

At the end of the 70s, Albatross delivered dynamic positioning systems to diving vessels and supply vessels shuttling back and forth between land bases and platforms in the North Sea. In the North Sea, Albatross's most important market, the drill rigs could still be placed or anchored directly on the seabed due to shallower waters, so it was further north in the Barents Sea where DP for drilling operations first became valid.

In 1980, Albatross signed a contract with the Soviet import company Sudo-import for delivery of redundant positioning equipment to the three drillships *Valentin Shashin*, *Viktor Muravlenko* and *Mikhail Mirchink*, being constructed at the Finnish Rauma – Repola shipyard.[16] The vessels were operated by the Soviet oil company Morneftegaz, and the contract was signed in fierce competition with arch rival Honeywell. Rolf Qvenild argues that these contracts played a significant role in the dethroning of Honeywell from the top of the DP royalty, and thus represented an important symbolic victory for Albatross and Kongsberg Våpenfabrikk.[17]

This new customer segment presented other challenges than service vessels. The main challenge for a drill ship is ensuring that the riser isn't exposed to unnecessary wear and tear by keeping the lower riser angle within set tolerances. The riser tube runs from the ship's derrick and down to the BOP at the seabed. In addition, the lower riser angle must be kept within a given limit in order to carry

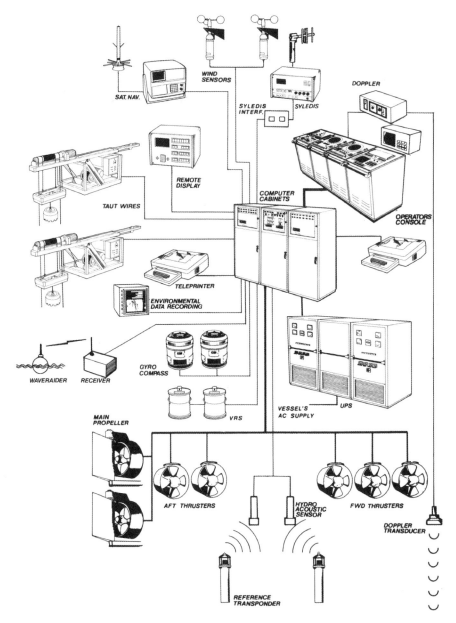

The Russian drillships delivered in the early 1980s were well-equipped with positioning systems: Simrad HPR 205, Albatross taut wire, the radio navigation system Syledis, and satellite navigation. The satellite receiver Magnavox was inadequate as a reference system, since satellite coverage was still sparse. Accuracy was modest and position fixes were received at best a few times an hour. Since vessels could be exposed to pack ice, a system was devised to allow the use of taut wire inside the ship, through the moon pool. Raising and lowering of the wire was done manually, using winches, which could prove to be quite strenuous. Illustration: KM.

out an emergency disconnection in case of severe problems, or otherwise damage the wellhead. Here the leeway in the radius was five percent of the ocean depth. For example, when drilling at 100 metres, the ship will still have five metres of leeway before the situation becomes critical. The three drillships were equipped for drilling in the Barents Sea to a depth of 450 metres, with a maximum leeway of just over 20 metres. In these waters, the weather conditions can be harsh, so the question was, how would it be possible to drill for oil and gas?

The advantage of a drillship as opposed to a rig is that they are faster and easier to manoeuver. In the Barents Sea, this is a tremendous advantage, as ice masses can move quickly in this region. The ships were designed for drilling 7,000 ft deep holes. Pulling the drill string up from such a hole would easily take over ten hours, so these three vessels were constructed in a way that would enable disconnecting the drill string and evacuating the drill hole quickly in the event of a storm or accumulation of ice. They could then return to the same position and resume drilling once the weather became more favourable.[18]

These harsh conditions also posed special requirements for DP equipment. The vessels were therefore equipped with a so-called ADP503 D. The D indicated that the system was specifically developed for drilling operations in the Arctic region. These tough conditions also demanded that position reference systems be tailor-made. In addition to HPR and Syledis radio navigation, Magnavox was also installed – a first generation satellite system.

Magnavox monitored the position hourly, and during the intervals it used a so-called «dead reckoning» from the Doppler speed log. This satellite navigation quickly proved to be of little use for DP purposes.[19] The vessels should also use taut wire, but because of ice condition and freezing risks, there was a danger that the traditional equipment would not function. Albatross therefore developed a special version operated through the vessel's moon pool, whereby the sensor head was submerged in water to increase accuracy and avoid freezing.[20] The first unit was installed at Christmas time in 1981, and the last two in May and September 1982.[21] Thereafter, the ships were commissioned for oil exploration in the Barents Sea.[22]

DELIVERY AND MAINTENANCE

All deliveries started with a sale. However, it was not common practice for customers to approach Kongsberg and buy a system that they had chosen in advance. Rather, the sales people approached the customers, who had been nurtured over time. Also, it was not just a question of which DP system a customer should have. The systems were complex and could be delivered in different versions with different types of position sensors and equipment.[23] There were numerous factors a customer had to take into account.

At first, the customers were the shipowners, and few of them had much experience with dynamic positioning. This was still something new and a little mysterious, and the Albatross sales people knew how to take advantage of this lack of knowledge. They even contributed to mystifying the systems themselves, not least the Kalman filter. Once the decision was made and the contract signed, there were still several factors to take into account before the deal was done. This is when the project team in Kongsberg stepped in.

Knut Lagim, project manager in the 1980s, said that the sales people did not always just sell products from the catalogue; on some occasions they may have also sold products that were not yet developed. It was therefore important to get these manufactured. Albatross was an easy-going organisation with solution-oriented employees who wanted to satisfy their customers' needs. At the same time, there was a certain leeway in the contracts, and the customers did not always get what they had originally envisaged. It was therefore up to the project team to ensure that customers were nevertheless satisfied.[24]

While class requirements and standardisation to a certain degree drove customers and suppliers apart, there were other factors that created close relations and exchange of information, ideas and knowledge between these parties. For those involved in the projects, it was not just about delivering according to the specifications of the contract; in many cases they also had to train the customers. This led to close contact between the project team and the customers, and resulted in strong personal relationships. Through this trust and openness that had now been established, the Albatross engineers felt that they could be open about any difficulties that arose. The customers saw that the project team took responsibility, and they were confident that matters would be sorted in the end.

Through this close contact, the Albatross developers soon learned a great deal about practical seamanship, which later proved useful when developing the DP systems. Also, as the strong relationship grew between the group and their customers, they became more involved earlier in the planning processes, which provided a perfect opportunity to get valuable feedback on existing products, and at the same time gather input for the development of new ones. When Albatross was so keen to live «for, with and by» their customers, they understood that this would be mutually beneficial to both parties. Demanding customers were good customers, and this over time provided Albatross with a competitive advantage.[25]

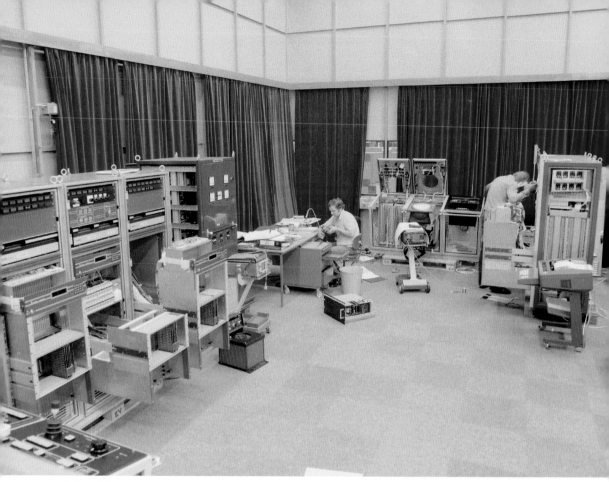

Before delivery to the shipyard, equipment had to be hooked up and tested at the factory in a Factory Acceptance Test (FAT). In the early days only hardware was tested, but eventually more complete testing was implemented, with real systems interfaced to simulators taking the place of the actual ship. The image from 1979 shows testing of an ADP503 installation. Photo: Mediafoto.

The equipment was assembled in Kongsberg, first at the weapons factory by the river Lågen, but as business grew, these facilities became too cramped. In 1981 they moved Albatross into the old ski factory in the centre of Kongsberg. Although much of the functionality lay in the software, there was a need for adapting the systems to each vessel. To start with, this required considerable rewriting of the programs, but over time, this became increasingly simplified through modularisation.[26] At that time there was no discussion about using simulators to test DP systems; everything had to be done in the field and a lot of the testing took place at sea after passing a FAT test (Factory Acceptance Test). This entailed checking that the hardware was in accordance with the specifications in the contract.[27] Not until the FAT test was approved could the equipment be installed on board the vessel, after which it was adjusted and then

A collection of customised manuals delivered to *Seaway Swan* in 1979. All technical drawings and illustrations were done by hand. Photo: Mediafoto.

put on sea trials. In the early 1980s, this often took place outside Kristiansand where the conditions were favourable for testing positioning systems with HPR, taut wire and Artemis. Once the factory had passed the CAT test (Customer Acceptance Test) at sea, and the client was satisfied, the DP system was ready for use.[28] It was also common practice for a service engineer to stay on board for a period of time after the system was approved.

In 1980 Albatross installed a DP system on the diving vessel *Stena Constructor* which was assisting a gas platform operating off the coast of New Zealand».[29] The company wanted to have a service engineer available on board to ensure that the DP system functioned at all times. This was the first time Albatross delivered a system to a vessel that would operate in such distant waters. It says something about the willingness to meet customer needs that they sent Oddvar Rusten, who was a service engineer at that time, over to the vessel for an entire year.[30]

TRAINING AND DOCUMENTATION

In order for DP operators to handle the systems in the best possible way without having to call for assistance from Albatross each time problems arose, detailed

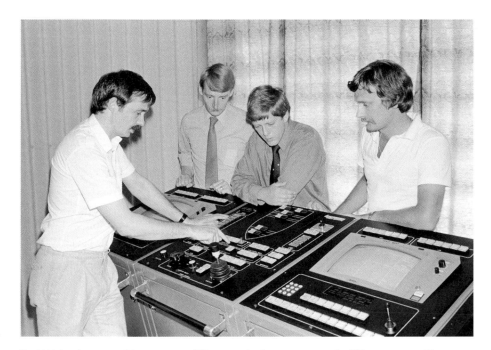

Roald Holstad was one of the pioneers in DP training, both as an instructor for DP operators, and for service technicians. Here Holstad instructs eager participants on how to operate the ADP systems. This photo, from 1983, was taken at KV's training centre in Kongsberg. Photo: Mediafoto.

user manuals were produced. The Documentation Department at Albatross designed custom-made manuals for each system. As the consoles in the ADP500 series were green, the manuals of course had to be green too. All the illustrations were drawn by hand, and Letraset characters were inserted manually for specific symbols and fonts, which proved most time-consuming. At first, it took about 300 hours to make one folder, but over time, the use of word processing programs and being able to reuse stored text made it possible to reduce this time significantly. In most cases, the documentation was in English, as was the text on the console, buttons and screens. Then Albatross started selling DP systems to the Soviet Union and had to translate all this into Russian.[31]

Using an advanced DP system requires more than just good manuals. The developers at Albatross therefore put a great deal of effort into creating user interfaces that were easy to understand and apply, for example through the «one button – one function» principle. Not least, it was critical that not only operators, but also the electricians, who would be maintaining the systems, had sufficient knowledge. Therefore, Albatross moved quickly to establish a course and training centre in Kongsberg.

The training of DP personnel took place with the first deliveries in the 1970s. To begin with, this was the responsibility of the sales department, and service engineers were brought in to demonstrate the systems. The first courses in the 1980s took place in a villa by Norcontrol's department at Eiken in Horten and were run by Rune Mellum. Relatively soon after, they saw a need for a more formal set-up for the training of DP operators, and Albatross contacted both the Norwegian Maritime Authority (NMA) and the Norwegian Petroleum Directorate (NPD). Being the dominant player in the DP market, it was natural to take advantage of the expertise that Albatross had gained within this relatively new technology. Together, these parties developed a programme that consisted of a five-day course followed by practical exercises on a DP-equipped vessel and a more advanced course where operators were trained in a simulator. For this course, Albatross developed a logbook for DP operators that was later used by both NMA and the Nautical Institute (NI) as a basis for the first DP certificates, a signed document proving that one could use a DP system at a certain level.[32]

The courses introduced people from different departments. For example, Roald Holstad was from the service department, while Terje Dølplass' background was from the Defence Division. After a while, Bjørn Engen, Morten Gunnerud and Jan Wikheim were employed as instructors. The course programme expanded when Holstad started maintenance courses for personnel from the diving vessel *Saipem Ragno Due*. Soon there was no longer room for all the activities in Horten, and a training centre was established at the former Saga Hotel Storgata 2 in Kongsberg in January 1982. The Data Division and Gas Turbine Division occupied much of the building already and the Training Department was therefore given offices and classrooms on the fourth floor, while the DP systems that were used for teaching purposes were placed on the first floor, which today is a restaurant. For the first couple of years, Kongsberg offered an operator course and a refresher course for ADP503 and 311. Later, however, the offer was extended to also include ADP100 and APM3000.[33]

Gradually, dynamic positioning was also introduced into the programme at maritime colleges. In 1983, Albatross installed an ADP503 simulator at the college in Haugesund, and two years later, a similar one at Lowestoft College on the British North Sea coast just east of Norwich. These simulators were developed by Norcontrol's department in Horten. The lectures at the maritime colleges had basically nothing to do with Albatross, but those who were educated there had a good opportunity to become familiar with the equipment. As Albatross expanded into new markets, more training centres were set up around the world to accommodate the training requirements of customers where they were located.[34]

THE CUSTOMERS WERE ALWAYS RIGHT

Although the equipment was tested and approved, and the crew well trained, there were occasions when the systems did not work or were inaccurate. The contracts could include service agreements, but errors occurred regardless. The service people were on call at all hours. In one example, *Seaway Swan* undertook an unscheduled but very serious manoeuver on the night of 27 September 1978. At midnight, the rig started to «live its own life» and swung into the platform it was serving. Only a quick intervention of the DP operator on board prevented the collision from being more than just a little «nudge». It's a serious business when vessels in the North Sea bump into each other, and the matter was investigated and reported to the KV board, but the cause was not found. Apparently, there was a tug with a line attached to the rig to ensure that it did not collide with the platform alongside. The internal report indicated that the tug's mooring line had been slackened, but the conclusion was not clear. In theory it could have been the fault of the DP system, but nothing pointed in that direction.[35] Although this was an isolated incident, it shows that the computers used and the software controlling them, had to be adapted and further developed. The parts were not simply «off the shelf» products to be used without further ado. There were many possible sources of error that could cause a computer to stop functioning. Memory chips could also be unreliable. One batch had a «hiccup» one or more times during a 24-hour cycle resulting in system failure.[36] In addition, a small bug was discovered in the software. An example from the early years was that if no wind was recorded whatsoever during a three-hour period, the system started to ignore the wind factor altogether. The opposite also happened, i.e. that the system «detected» artificial wind, leading the DP system onboard *Seaway Eagle* once to suddenly 'detect' a hurricane in Horten harbour and 'go crazy'[37].

The first installations were seen by many as pure madness. Eldar Mathisen, a key figure during this period, says: «I am one of few who knew exactly how close we were to this going wrong. For the first 18 months, I was the only one who could implement the systems. The customers became increasingly concerned. Without our solid industrial base, it would have gone wrong.»[38] What Mathisen was referring to, was the possibility to take full advantage of the KV system's capabilities.[39] Albatross therefore established a hotline that customers could call 24/7 for assistance. If the problems could not be solved by phone, a service engineer was sent out to fix it, which meant that you had no excuse if you were otherwise busy or on vacation.[40]

From the very start, it was a part of Albatross's culture to be uncompromising when it came to meeting the needs of the customers. The systems were adapted

Time is money in the offshore business, as oil companies can stop payment when a vessel is out of service. Vast resources are therefore used to transport both spare parts and service personnel to the vessels. Chartering small aircraft for this purpose was not uncommon. In this 1979 photo, a crate with spare parts, delivered by courier from Kongsberg, is loaded on a plane by Egil Settli at the Fornebu airport. Photo: Mediafoto.

to the extent possible and service was to be provided immediately.[41] Of course customers were followed up closely, but in the very beginning it was basically just Jacob Stolt-Nielsen. In 1977, when there was a failure onboard *Seaway Swan*, Eldar Mathisen got a call from the shipowner demanding that he come to Oslo Airport Fornebu right away. Mathisen was at home in Kongsberg at the time, but did not hesitate. He rented a sea-plane, which had its home base on the river passing through Kongsberg, and landed at the Fornebu sea-plane harbour just one hour later. When he ran up to the departure hall at the airport, he found a raging Stolt-Nielsen waiting for him. Mathisen was reproached in public, but it did not take long before a solution was proposed and the good cooperation between the two parties resumed.[42]

Odd Inge Tangen had a similar experience. He was hired in May 1979 and in July, right in the middle of the holiday season, the DP installation on board *Seaway Swan* came to a grinding halt and a service engineer was summoned immediately. As Tangen was the only one available, he had no other option but to go. Stolt-Nielsen had chartered a small plane to meet Tangen at the tiny airport in Notodden. Because he was new and had almost no experience with this kind of mission, Tangen had to get some 'basic training' first. So while Einar Christiansen drove, Sverre Corneliussen held a crash course for Tangen in the back seat. This was the first and only time a serviceman had ever received a DP course at 100 km/h on a winding road between Kongsberg and Notodden.

Upon reaching Notodden, Tangen boarded the plane immediately and flew to Stavanger where a helicopter was waiting. Tangen arrived at the *Seaway Swan* 19.00 that evening and was told to eat before being set to work. He carried on until 15.00 the next day when he finally had to take a break to catch up on sleep. Arne Iversen, a colleague with broader experience, was on board another vessel nearby and came to the rescue later that evening. During the night they managed to locate the error, and the rig was back in service. Back then, the rig had a 'rate' of GBP 55,000 per day, equivalent to around NOK 600,000. Stolt-Nielsen had barely three weeks left on his contract, so he did not dare to send both of them back to shore, and Tangen remained on board for an additional three weeks until the contract was completed.[43]

This story just goes to show that it could be a tough lesson being out on a service mission. Service engineers often had sole responsibility for getting a system up and running again, and they could not go home before this was done. Roar Inge Alfheim remembers how they could often be out in the North Sea for three to six weeks at a time in order to carry out repair work. The only tools they had to help them were the so-called 'patch card' and briefcases with all the software printed out on thick stacks of paper. PCs and cell phones did not exist at that time. If service engineers wanted to contact their colleagues in Kongsberg, they had to communicate over Rogaland Radio. As this was an open line, they needed to communicate in code so that the customers and competitors could not understand what they were talking about.[44]

Making changes was a laborious and time-consuming process. The software was originally written in Fortran on a Nord-1 machine in Kongsberg. KS500 was useless for that purpose.[45] Therefore, it was compiled to machine code and placed in the DP system using cassette tapes. It was not easy to go into the DP's computer and make changes directly. The Nord-1 machine and KS500 machine in the vessel's DP system did not speak the same language, and there were a considerable number of nautical miles of open sea between the two. The instructions therefore needed to be translated on board. When the service

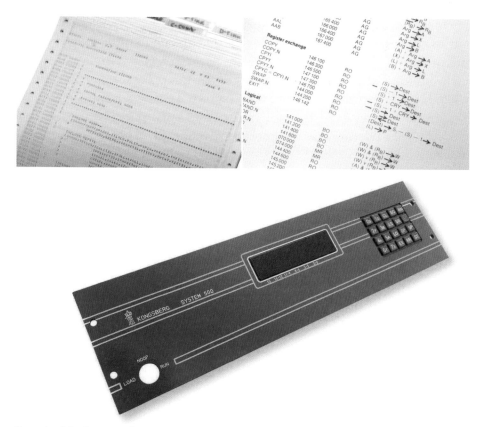

Example of the Fortran code (left). When a programming error was discovered, a printout of the computer program was needed in order to locate the fault and determine where in the computer's memory the
instructions were stored. To correct the error, the computer code was printed out in a series of cryptic octal
numerals (Base-8 number system) and manually decoded using a so-called 'patch card' (right) showing
octal code and the corresponding decipherable assembly code. When the assembly code was sorted out
on paper, the patch card was again used, this time to translate back into octal ciphers. The computer panel
was used to change the instructions in the computer itself (bottom). Finally the entire computer program
was dumped onto a cassette. The process was demanding, time-consuming, and risky, making experience
invaluable. Photo: Mediafoto.

engineers corrected errors in the program code, or 'patch', they had to first find
the lines of code that needed to be changed in the printouts, and then write new
instructions which were then to be translated from Fortran to assembler code,
which in turn had to be translated into machine code (octal coded numbers) by
using a patch card. The new program code was then transferred, or 'dumped'
onto a tape and read into the computer using a Tandberg tape recorder. This
procedure applied to the first Albatross systems with a KS500 machine, i.e.
ADP500 and ADP311 series.[46]

In addition to the service department in Kongsberg, Albatross had Parts and Service centres in all major areas where vessels with Albatross DP onboard were operating. In 1983, there were four such sites: Aberdeen for the UK sector of the North Sea, Dubai for the Middle East, Singapore for the Far East and New Plymouth in New Zealand.[47] In the 1980s, communication possibilities were much more limited than they are today, and much of the responsibility was left to the individual service engineer. In some cases, where the time factor was especially critical, two service engineers were sent out so that they could work around the clock in shifts. However, as the communication network developed over time, it became easier to draw upon assistance from shore.[48]

DP TECHNOLOGY BECOMES INDISPENSABLE

DP systems gradually expanded their spectrum of functions. At first, it was all about keeping vessel in place, but then came a growing need for the DP system to conduct other functions such as align itself with an object, follow a pipeline or a pre-determined route. It was crucial therefore that the technology behind the first Albatross DP systems ran smoothly in order to survive tough competition from major international companies. But a smart technological invention was simply not enough. In order for dynamic positioning to be more than just a good idea and an innovation in the market, it required a larger apparatus to not only solve technical challenges, but also handle all aspects from marketing and sales, training and customer support. Albatross succeeded with this. The combination of outstanding technical expertise, a flair for the market and the ability to follow up customers, proved a good recipe for success. Customers would also have to be willing to pay a price that provided adequate earnings.

The other cornerstone of this inspirational initiative was precisely this: the relationship to customers. Once shipowner Jacob Stolt-Nielsen ordered the first DP system, the project could take on a serious start. With the next contract, the Dynpos project gained momentum and could continue. However, it was not until several others became enthusiastic and wanted to have the same type of DP system that this became such a success. It was essential to have an uncompromising and innovative research environment. Equally important were the 'hungry' and determined technology-savvy sales people, who followed up the customers very closely. During this period, Albatross developed a unique relationship with their customers, a relationship which they have managed to maintain.

6

THE X-FACTOR

IN 1980 ALBATROSS had been running for five years as the modest Dynpos project in KV's petroleum division. A lot had happened during these years, organisationally, as well as technically, and on the market.

The new decade saw a reorganising of KV, and Albatross was placed in the newly formed maritime division as of January 1 1980. The maritime division encompassed the radio and electronics company Robertson Radio-Elektro in Egersund, producers of communications equipment and autopilots for vessels, the marine automation systems company Norcontrol in Horten, and KV's navigation department in Bergen. The latter supplied electronic navigational equipment for fishing vessels and the merchant fleet on licence from the British company Decca. At this point Albatross was marketing three DP systems: ADP501, ADP503 and ADP311. ADP502 had been phased out. The last of these was installed just days after the new division was formed.[1]

When the Dynpos group received its first order, Honeywell was the dominant supplier to the global DP market. In 1980 Albatross secured all orders for DP systems worldwide, thereby assuming the lead position. At the close of that year over half of all installed DP systems in the world were delivered by Albatross. This was remarkable, given the fact they had only been on the market for five years.[2]

The way to the top had been fast. Albatross had taken an offensive position and now there was a lot to defend, but still much left to win. How could Albatross protect and strengthen those traits that had brought them this far, and what should they do to continue growing and become even stronger?

A UNIQUE COMPANY CULTURE

The Albatross pioneers were an unconventional and hard-working crew, with a strong team spirit and a near fanatical focus on their customers. They were in many ways a strongly homogenous group. Most were engineers, and mostly men.[3] An overview of employees from 1983 showed that 15 percent were female, working for the most part in support roles like secretary, administration, switchboard, or in the canteen. A few did drafting or worked with technical documentation. The average age for the entire organisation was just over 30 years. The director had turned 30 in 1981, the chief financial officer was three years younger, and the head of sales just four years older.[4] The company culture greatly resembled the student lifestyle they had left only years earlier, where the boundaries between working, playing and partying were not always clear. In many ways they were rebels within the KV system. But as long as Albatross was making good money, the KV management was satisfied.[5]

Bjørn Barth Jacobsen has described the contrast to the rest of the organisation in this way: «We turned everything upside down. We let people do what they wanted. It was all based on the assumption that they were intelligent people with common sense.»[6] This thinking was anchored in the tenets of American management theorist Douglas McGregor of the Sloan School of Management at the Massachusetts Institute of Technology (MIT) and his Theory X and Theory Y.[7] Based on studies of companies in the US, McGregor described how management's theoretical assumptions influenced and characterised an organisation. Theory X is based on the premise that people are basically lazy, irresponsible and averse to work, and therefore require guidance, instruction, and controlling. This in turn demands a hierarchal structure with restricted areas of responsibility. Theory Y subscribes to the philosophy that employees enjoy working and are capable of self-motivation and control, and that encouragement and support are enough to obtain their maximum effort.

In Albatross, Theory Y was king. Employees were shown trust and given great freedom, and they were in turn motivated by interesting and challenging tasks. Management and staff compared Albatross with KV, with its formal management hierarchy and military inspired chain of command. KV's company culture more closely resembled Theory X.[8]

Albatross had its own internal newsletter, Albatross Highlights, which supported and strengthened the company culture, and kept employees informed on everything from new projects and contracts, to more everyday things like employee football matches and entertaining stories. Management had its own column called «His Masters Voice». One year before summer holidays,

The company newsletter 'Albatross Highlights' was launched in 1978 as a double-sided information sheet in A5 format. The flyer was published at irregular intervals and covered everything from the triumphs of the company football team to sales performance. The director had a regular column called 'His Masters Voice'. The format was changed in 1985 to an eight-page magazine.

employees were told that: «Even an Albatross has to land in order to rest.» The comparison was clear between the employees and the bird, even though the bird makes landfall only every other year to nest. The proclamation to the staff was as much a description of the work culture as an exhortation to hard work. «Working at Albatross is a lifestyle. Our journey toward new goals obligates each and every one of us to view Albatross as something more than a traditional workplace.»[9]

In 1980 Albatross was composed of 60 employees. The next year they would grow by 14. Then came the explosion. By the end of 1982, 135 people were employed in Albatross.[10] The rapid increase in numbers meant that there were many who had to be brought up and assimilated into the Albatross culture. The success of the group depended not only on quality technical solutions. Much was also due to the culture, in particular how they related to their customers. This culture was essential to preserve and promote. To do that, a more systematic cultural assimilation was needed.

With strong growth came also the need for a more structured organisation. This was about maturing and a need for order, and a more business-like attitude, rather than streamlining and conforming to the rest of KV. The group had been extremely successful in a very short time, and Albatross management realised the need to ensure that the values that had brought them to where they were could be preserved: energy, simplicity, tempo, and creativity.

To begin with, it meant enhancing the culture that had evolved, but also external models and pivotal impulses figured in. SAS CEO Janne Carlzon in Sweden had garnered much attention with his admonition to «tear down the pyramids.» His way of thinking about organisations served as inspiration to Albatross management. Another important source of inspiration was Klaus Dahl from Wilson Learning, hired in to hold classes for the staff.[11] At the same time, Kongsberg Våpenfabrikk (KV) was put forward as a contrast, something the Albatross employees did not want to be.[12] Here was both something to strive for, and something to avoid, often a good starting point for building a clear company culture and a strong group identity.

The cultural work was connected to the group's growth, but it also coincided with a change of leadership. Bjørn Barth Jacobsen had been a clear driving force in building the Albatross identity in the early years. He was followed by Thor Skoland. In 1980 Nils Willy Gulhaugen was appointed as new director. He held a degree in economics, and had been part of the KV system since 1975. When he joined the Albatross team in 1978 as director of marketing, his orders from KV director Qvenild were clear: «Bjørn Barth Jacobsen jumps in with both feet, but you make sure to mind legal issues, and the books.»[13]

The change in leadership meant not just a new man at the helm, but a change of style. Barth Jacobsen had been an expressive and unorthodox manager. Now a more introverted individual sat in the boss's chair. Gulhaugen was described as an inspirational leader, but more of a thinker than Barth Jacobsen had been. Head of finance Torfinn Kildal was often called upon to assume the more extroverted duties required of top management.[14] From the early 1980s this duo would be responsible for landmark work on the culture of Albatross. The group had its own distinct culture, and the employees had acknowledged that this culture was a key factor in the group's success. For that reason it was necessary to define the foundation of the group's values and make it infectious, in order to pass it on to new employees. This cultural foundation was given the name «Theory Albatross». Through a meticulously directed programme, the Albatross ideology was imprinted on the staff. One of them later commented that, «We were brainwashed to become individuals with a common goal, and we loved it!»[15]

From 'The Albatross Theory'. Here the guru impresses group values on the young 'albatross': strong customer orientation and personal responsibility, with loyalty to common goals.

THEORY ALBATROSS

'Theory Albatross' was presented to employees in 1981 in the form of a little red book. The pamphlet, printed on thick paper in A4 format, featured an Albatross hovering over the group's vision: «We help people improve their position».[16] The book was only 14 pages, and sparingly written. The message was essentially conveyed through simple illustrations. The story followed a young person seeking advice from an older, bearded figure referred to as «guru». The guru was the bearer of culture, and represented the company. It's fairly obvious that the intention was to get the younger employees to identify themselves with the young figure in the story.

On the first page we see the young upstart standing before the guru. The terrain is steep, and we can picture that the youngster has scaled a mountain to seek wisdom and learn the «meaning of life». The dialogue runs thus: «Tell me guru … What is the mission of an albatross.» The answer is clear, yet laden with double meaning: «It is to help people improve their position.»[17] The primary mission of Albatross was to deliver equipment that would keep vessels in position, but another, even more important mission, was to help customers

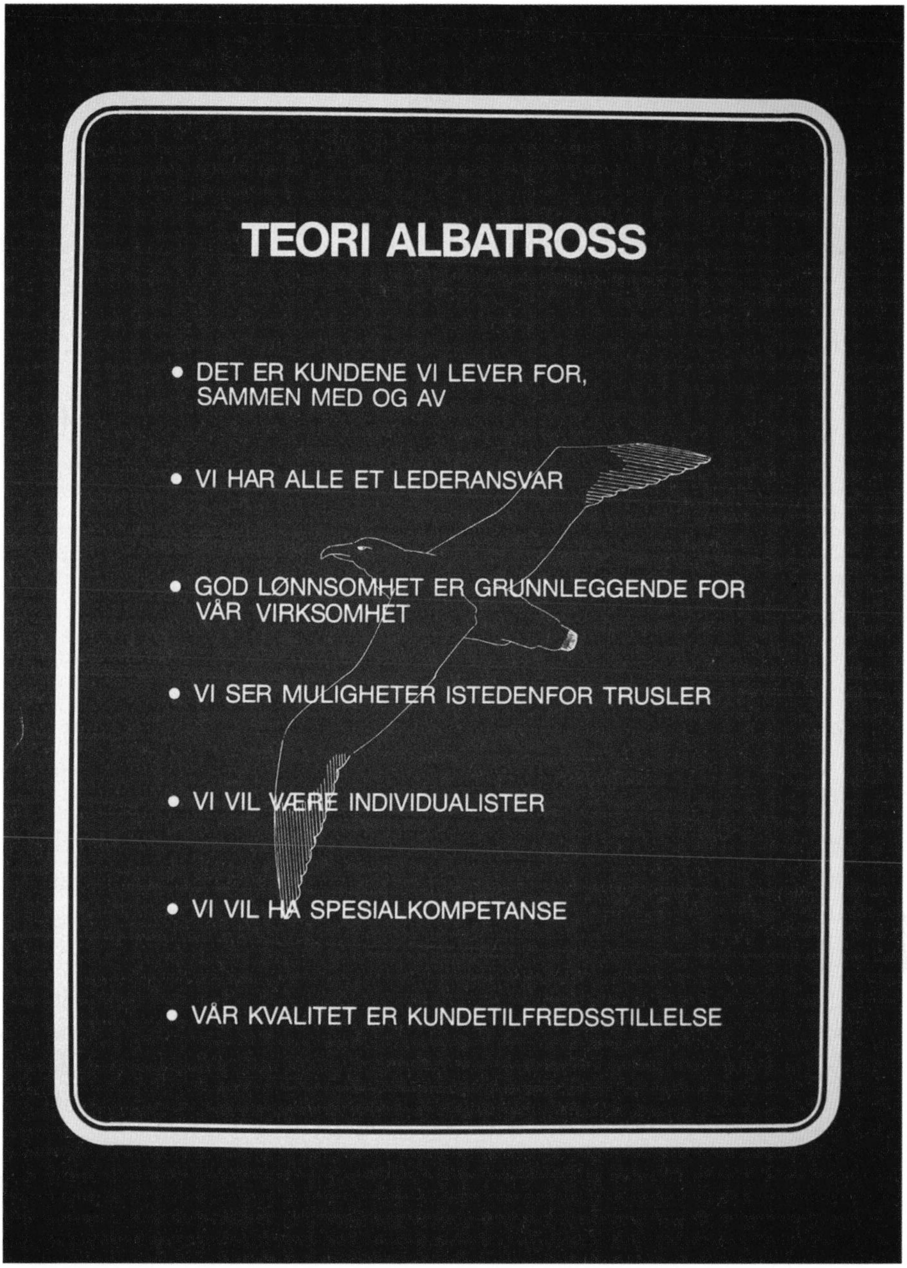

TEORI ALBATROSS

- DET ER KUNDENE VI LEVER FOR, SAMMEN MED OG AV

- VI HAR ALLE ET LEDERANSVAR

- GOD LØNNSOMHET ER GRUNNLEGGENDE FOR VÅR VIRKSOMHET

- VI SER MULIGHETER ISTEDENFOR TRUSLER

- VI VIL VÆRE INDIVIDUALISTER

- VI VIL HA SPESIALKOMPETANSE

- VÅR KVALITET ER KUNDETILFREDSSTILLELSE

Albatross's 'tablet of stone' with the seven commandments for success. The simple slogan-like visions and values hang on the walls and resonate through the Carpus head office building in Kongsberg. The company is still loyal to the philosophy that was chiselled out during the early years. When talking to employees, it doesn't take long before they point out that they live 'for, with and by' the customer, and that their goal is to help customers improve their position. Photo: Mediafoto.

Company philosophy using the cut-and-paste method. Drawings in 'The Albatross Theory' were lifted from a small pamphlet featuring the cartoon character Ziggy by Tom Wilson. In some cases passages were copied directly.

improve their market position. In other words, the guru was talking not just about coordinates, but cash.

Theory Albatross referred to both the group and the individual – «an albatross» and «Albatross». This was expressed explicitly on the last page of the pamphlet by emphasising that «friendliness, acceptance and helpfulness are the key traits of a true albatross».[18] Employees were not only employed by Albatross. They should also become «albatrosses». Eliminating the dividing line between the group and the individual signalled the clear intent of maintaining and strengthening the team spirit that originated back when the group was made up of a handful of believers. At the same time it expressed the intention that employees should identify with the group – and not with the KV corporation.

So what was «an albatross»? It was made clear that «thinking things to death» did no good. The important thing was to be on the hunt for new ideas and opportunities. There would always be time to fix mistakes. Albatrosses should look to the future and not «rest on their laurels.»[19] In an extension of this call to action, responsibility was also emphasised. Each individual was obligated to seize opportunity, but also to help shape an environment with room for improving and exploiting new ideas. While individual freedom was essential, the collective good was the highest priority.

While the first part of «Albatross's little red book» dealt with strengthening and enhancing the employees' creative potential, the next was dedicated to the philosophy surrounding customer relations». The guru instructs: «We live for, together with and by our customers.»[20] This almost fanatical dedication and close attention to the customer might well be the key to Albatross's strong market position. Customer orientation was also clear in the vision. The group's success was dependent on helping others improve their position. If the albatrosses couldn't keep the customer satisfied, the whole «foundation of their life» would crumble.[21] Phrases like «trust» and the importance of creating «two winners» were employed. This was illustrated by a drawing of the youngster proclaiming: «I help people improve their position!»[22] The message had reached home. It had become internalised.

This introduced a new section of the booklet with guidelines on how to preserve this inner culture. Key words were loyalty and respect: loyalty to the common goal, in the sense that employees were responsible for raising issues that could hinder the «attainment of group goals», and respect for colleagues and individuality that entailed a responsibility to create an «environment that encourages everyone to dare to share their resources».[23] The guru expresses this philosophy in the following way: «I want my people to be like wild ducks, but even wild ducks fly in formation.»[24] The phrase was based on a famous statement by the legendary IBM chief Thomas J. Watson jr., who in turn had been inspired by the Danish philosopher Søren Kierkegaard, and was perhaps better suited for ducks than albatross. The point was in any case clear. Albatross wanted people who sought out opportunity, and they would fly farther and faster, like migratory birds, if they flew in formation. Everyone enjoyed a great deal of freedom, but for the group to fly in formation, it was expected that they all work «loyally toward the group's mission and goals.»[25] And what was the goal? It was not just about enhancing the customer's position, but also about making money. To bring this point home, demand for profitability was to «colour every decision» made in the workplace. This was illustrated in a humorous way by the youngster holding a flower and exclaiming: «It is better to be rich and healthy than poor and filthy», and who could disagree?[26]

There are many thick books on leadership philosophy and company culture. This little booklet was as far from an academic endeavour as it could be, but it achieved the desired effect. The booklet did not make the culture, but it provided a means for structuring that culture and making it transferrable to new generations of Albatross employees. This facilitation was helped along by several factors. It was clearly important that the albatrosses were a homogenous group, relatively young, and relatively few. Nor did it hurt that business was going well. Success seemed to confirm that they were getting things right. At the same time, Albatross was in opposition to KV, and that strengthened the group identity. That made it important to hammer out a philosophy of what Albatross *was*, while making it equally clear what they were *not*. «Inside the fence» became a clear catchphrase for the rest of KV. The fence was more than the physical barrier surrounding Kongsberg Våpenfabrikk at Numedalslågen. For the people of Albatross it also became a symbol of cultural differences.

INSIDE AND OUTSIDE THE FENCE

The mildly anarchistic attitude that prevailed in Albatross stood in contrast to the stodgy and traditional culture in KV. The contrasts could at times be glaring. The Albatrosses saw themselves as something special, and were also seen as such by many KV employees. They began sporting t-shirts with the Albatross logo, and if there was call for celebration, management and employees alike were prone to throw parties in the office when the work was done. These celebrations were not always looked kindly upon. Qvenild was on one occasion sought out by then union leader Roar Flåthen, who informed him that «enough was enough». Qvenild listened to the union boss, but allowed the albatrosses to carry on.[27] Management had insight enough to let the albatrosses fly, and if they could manage that, they would not have their wings clipped.

Kongsberg Våpenfabrikk was, after all, not just stodgy. The management could be feisty as well. KV consisted of many weighty divisions, but there was still room for a rambunctious Albatross. Experimentation was allowed. In this way KV proved to be a great place to grow up. But it did demand some «guerrilla tactics» from Albatross, as Qvenild put it. They were more prone to ask for forgiveness than permission.[28] KV stood for solidarity and seriousness, while the Albatross gang brought in a new dynamic, and a dedication to the customer.

Many have noted the significance of a few personalities in the making of the Albatross culture. Nonetheless, it is important to remember that many of these had come from the KV system. Other factors also came into play. Their working methods can also be seen in light of the various markets they served. While KV produced largely for the military, Albatross catered for shipowners. The differences between these two groups of customers were profound. Shipowners could be flamboyant characters, and this applied in particular to Albatross' first customer, Jacob Stolt-Nielsen. They operated in markets flush with cash and where quick decisions were made. On the other hand, quick decision making was not a typical trait of the military.

Albatross's management troika in 1986. From left: Torfinn Kildal (Finance director), Nils Willy Gulhaugen (Managing director) and Svein Thorsen (Marketing director). From Albatross, Annual Report 1986.

As with KV, the majority of Albatross employees were engineers. Nonetheless, it has been pointed out that Albatross was driven by financial criteria more so than KV, which was seen as being motivated mostly by technology.[29] Here lies a perception of Albatross as orienting itself to market possibilities, while KV concerned itself with developing technologies. Kongsberg Våpenfabrikk was criticised for not paying sufficient attention to markets and profitability, and for a lack of international business experience and marketing expertise.[30] The same could not be said of Albatross. Put literally, Albatross never shot a bear before the skin was sold, while KV was inclined to follow the traditional moral of this old saying.

The difference between the two can perhaps be explained by the fact that KV had engineers in top management positions, while Albatross had economists. Two of the three in management, managing director Gulhaugen and chief of finance Kildal, were business economists. The third, head of sales Svein Thorsen, was an engineer, but it was as a salesman at Albatross he made his mark. The same applied to Bjørn Barth Jacobsen, the first managing director.[31] This coloured the organisation and was responsible for their market orientation and strong devotion to the customer.

Svein Thorsen has gone so far as to say that the technology didn't matter as much as the applications and the customers.[32] Perhaps no surprise that such a statement would come from a former sales manager. Regardless, the ranking of priorities seems rather pointless. Without the technical solutions, Albatross would have neither applications nor customers, and without applications or customers, the business would not have survived. Albatross's strength lay in the combination of good technical solutions and highly intensive sales efforts – and both of those require a strong customer orientation. The one would not have been possible without the other.

Many technological innovations never achieve commercial success, or at least not in such a short time as the Albatross DP. The Kalman filter was a technical solution exclusive to Albatross. Still they needed someone who could convince the customer that the filter was necessary, and that it made ADP systems far better than competing systems. Albatross had sales people who could manage this, but they had to earn the right to be right. They managed to sell not just machines with various technical specifications, but also something that could not be described with words, numbers or figures. They were selling trust and security, together with something intangible, something with a hint of magic – and the magic was found in the Kalman filter. For this reason the filter became important, not just for keeping customer's vessels in position, but for Albatross's own position.

Albatross had an understanding of their market and a sales organisation that many companies, not just KV, could be envious of.

STORM CLOUDS ON THE HORIZON

Around Easter time in 1983, director Nils Willy Gulhaugen sent out a memo with the title «The Albatross group's alternatives and strategies for avoiding economic crisis in 1985».[33] It had been seven years since the first DP contract was signed, and Gulhaugen feared an imminent seven-year crisis. He could see several signs that the first seven flush years could be followed by seven lean ones if Albatross failed to position itself prudently.

Thus far Albatross had experienced steady growth in orders. Since the first installation in 1977, the group had delivered around 60 DP systems. Growth had been strong and stable. The best year to date had been 1982, with 16 deliveries.[34] All the same, Gulhaugen cautioned against undue optimism. He was not counting on growth to speak of in the coming years.[35] Based on the price of oil it wasn't hard to share in his pessimism. Albatross's customers were oil companies, or shipowners who sold their services to the oil companies. High oil prices generated expectations and activity in the oil sector, while low prices led to reduced activity.

When the first DP contract was signed in 1975, the price of crude oil was around USD 11.50 a barrel. The 1979 revolution in Iran, one of the world's biggest oil producers, pushed oil prices up. By 1980 prices had tripled, reaching a high of USD 37 a barrel. This was a major factor in Albatross's strong growth. The company was equally as dependent on high oil prices as a farmer is on good weather. The early 1980s saw an oil industry flush with dollars, and activity. When Gulhaugen expressed his concern, the price of oil was on its way down and had reached USD 30 a barrel. This coloured his reflections.[36] The way he saw it, potential for growth in the North Sea home market was on its way to being exhausted. That meant looking to more distant markets, but development in these markets too would depend on the price of oil. Simply looking to new markets would not suffice. Albatross would also have to develop their portfolio of products. The DP systems had been a success so far. Profit margins had been spectacular in the beginning, but were beginning to tighten up, not least due to a sharp increase in the number of employees without concurrent growth in orders.[37]

The sum of these developments caused Gulhaugen to see dark clouds on the horizon, and he feared that Albatross would dip into crisis as early as 1985.[38] If this was to be avoided, there were two possible alternatives: layoffs or expansion. Based on The Albatross Theory, and the maxim that Albatross should always be «on the hunt», it came as no surprise that Gulhaugen chose the latter. This demanded both closer evaluation of the organisation, and stronger focus on product development and international markets.

FIRST THE NORTH SEA, THEN THE WORLD

The North Sea was Albatross's home market. This was where the first customers operated, and where the company had its strongest advantage, with closer geographical proximity to installations and ports than its competitors. Albatross also had the advantage of proximity to many of the operators, and the shipowners serving them. These were the venues for technological innovation. For that reason it was important to maintain and strengthen their dominance in the region.[39] Controlling the North Sea gave them a platform for success in other regions. It was the region with highest priority and the one that provided most of their revenue. In the early 1980s Albatross began to gain access to other markets as well.[40]

If they were to maintain their dominant position in the North Sea, it would not be enough to simply dispatch sales teams from Kongsberg.[41] Albatross had

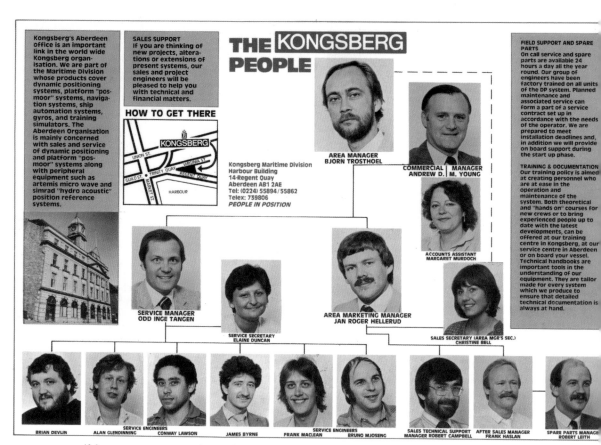

Kongsberg's Aberdeen office is an important link in the world wide Kongsberg organisation. We are part of the Maritime Division whose products cover dynamic positioning systems, platform "posmoor" systems, navigation systems, ship automation systems, gyros, and training simulators. The Aberdeen Organisation is mainly concerned with sales and service of dynamic positioning and platform "posmoor" systems along with peripheral equipment such as artemis micro wave and simrad "hydro acoustic" position reference systems.

SALES SUPPORT
If you are thinking of new projects, alterations or extensions of present systems, our sales and project engineers will be pleased to help you with technical and financial matters.

HOW TO GET THERE

KONGSBERG
UNION ST.
VIRGINIA ST.
GUILD ST. TRINITY QUAY REGENT QUAY
MARKET ST.
HARBOUR

Kongsberg Maritime Division
Harbour Building
14-Regent Quay
Aberdeen AB1 2AE
Tel: (0224) 55894 / 55862
Telex: 739806
PEOPLE IN POSITION

FIELD SUPPORT AND SPARE PARTS
On call service and spare parts are available 24 hours a day all the year round. Our group of engineers have been factory trained on all units of the DP system. Planned maintenance and associated service can form a part of a service contract set up in accordance with the needs of the operator. We are prepared to meet installation deadlines and, in addition we will provide on board support during the start up phase.

TRAINING & DOCUMENTATION
Our training policy is aimed at creating personnel who are at ease in the operation and maintenance of the system. Both theoretical and "hands on" courses for new crews or to bring experienced people up to date with the latest developments, can be offered at our training centre in Kongsberg, at our service centre in Aberdeen or on board your vessel. Technical handbooks are important tools in the understanding of our equipment. They are tailor made for every system which we produce to ensure that detailed technical documentation is always at hand.

THE KONGSBERG PEOPLE

AREA MANAGER
BJORN TROSTHOEL

COMMERCIAL | MANAGER
ANDREW D. | M. YOUNG

ACCOUNTS ASSISTANT
MARGARET MURDOCH

SERVICE MANAGER
ODD INGE TANGEN

SERVICE SECRETARY
ELAINE DUNCAN

AREA MARKETING MANAGER
JAN ROGER HELLERUD

SALES SECRETARY (AREA MGR'S SEC.)
CHRISTINE BELL

BRIAN DEVLIN

SERVICE ENGINEERS
ALAN GLENDINNING   CONWAY LAWSON

JAMES BYRNE

SERVICE ENGINEERS
FRANK MACLEAN   BRUNO MJOSENG

SALES TECHNICAL SUPPORT
MANAGER ROBERT CAMPBELL

AFTER SALES MANAGER
FRANK HASLAN

SPARE PARTS MANAGER
ROBERT LEITH

If they were to maintain and strengthen their dominant position in the North Sea, sending salespeople out in into the world from Kongsberg would not suffice. The sales staff had to be where the customers were. The sales and service office in Aberdeen was the first of a growing string of branch offices. The office was established in 1980, growing to 16 in 1983. Shown here is a brochure from around 1983.

to be present with sales and service where the customers were. The Aberdeen office was opened in 1982 and would be the first of a series of offices abroad. Bjørn Trosthoel was central in building up the office, and recalls that the sales strategy did not primarily consist of trade fairs and glossy advertisements, but more «footwork». He made sure they were up to date when a vessel made port. The offices were quayside, and when a ship arrived, he would go down to the docks and strike up a conversation with the skipper on the bridge. In this way he eventually became a part of the community. The contacts he made here gave him in-depth understanding of which equipment the crew needed. At the same time it gave him the opportunity to introduce Albatross systems to potential customers.[42] The office expanded rapidly, to 16 employees in 1983.[43] In the beginning they were organised under KV's Maidenhead office, but in 1986 they became a subsidiary of Albatross, as Kongsberg Albatross Offshore Services Ltd.⁴⁴

The USA and the fields in the Gulf of Mexico were outside Albatross's reach in the beginning. This was Honeywell territory. Kongsberg viewed this market as conservative and restrictive in its thinking. The sales force did however manage to break through, and in 1982 the first contract was signed, with ODECO, for an ADP503 and an ADP311 on the drilling rig *Ocean Alliance*.⁴⁵ The Gulf of Mexico was not just of interest as a market in itself. Many of the biggest US technology companies were engaged here. If Albatross could get in with them, it could mean a ticket to other regions where they operated. But in the early 1980s Albatross was just getting started in the Gulf, though they had ambitions to establish a presence and adapt to the market.⁴⁶

Albatross had already established itself in the Far East, with three systems in operation off Mumbai. With that they could virtually claim a DP monopoly in India. This new market was not big, but it was growing. In the early 1980s a «bridgehead» was established in Singapore, in order to serve the Asian market. In the beginning the office was manned only by Pål Rønning, who ran a pure sales establishment.⁴⁷ He was joined in 1984 by Tor Erik Sørensen and Finn Søberg, and they would go on to build up a substantial operation with many employees.⁴⁸ They had started small, renting an office that happened to be numbered 503 – and what better number for an Albatross sales office?⁴⁹

The former Soviet Union was another important market in the early years. As mentioned earlier, the first contract with the Soviet import company Sudo-import was signed back in the autumn of 1978. It wasn't just good products and clever salesmen that contributed to Albatross's strong position in Norway's neighbour to the east, though. International politics also came into play. This was the cold war era, and technology export to Eastern Block countries was strictly regulated by the so-called COCOM rules.⁵⁰ While Honeywell was hindered by the American authorities, the Norwegian ambassador kept a warm dialogue on cooperation in the north going with the Soviets.⁵¹

But the Soviet Union was no easy market to operate in. Export restrictions meant that DP systems had to be modified. Sensitive components in computers were exchanged.⁵² And the systems had to be maintained, not always an easy or convenient task for service crews. Border crossings were strictly regulated and negotiating one could prove to be a job in itself. Albatross managed to secure an agreement for passage of replacement parts and service personnel through the Kirkenes border crossing.⁵³ For the most part this solution worked well. On one occasion, though, it got a little too exciting. Two service engineers from Albatross suddenly found themselves on the wrong side of the border. Soviet president Leonid Brezhnev had passed away on November 10, 1982. International tensions mounted. Borders were sealed and placed on alert. By coincidence Albatross's 24 year-old service engineer Einar Gleditsch jr. and his colleague of the same age Knut Martinsen found themselves on the drillship *Viktor Marvlenko* in the neutral zone of the Barents Sea.[54] It was not standard procedure to send two inexperienced engineers on such a demanding assignment, but as no one else was available they suddenly became old and qualified enough. They were sent east to Murmansk through Moscow with ten-day visas in their pockets.

The day after the ship left Murmansk, the two were awakened by sirens to a state of emergency due to Brezhnev's death. The assignment was becoming more eventful and dramatic than the pair had anticipated. In addition to the countless hours of trouble-shooting and repairs, they were obligated to take part in transporting 150 fully armed soldiers to the Soviet Union's atomic testing facility in Novaya Zemlya. The faults were located and repaired, but new problems turned up and they were obliged to keep working. The assignment dragged on. When they were finally given their passports back, with permission to return home, they had been in the Barents Sea for more than five weeks – a fairly long stay on ten-day visas. Put mildly, it could not have been easy to be young and lacking in experience on a ship far out in the Barents Sea, under exceptionally tense circumstances, in heavy weather and with little food, homesick and with limited communications with home, and a crew that for the most part spoke only Russian. When they eventually did return home, they were rewarded with a three-week trip to Rio de Janeiro. Such an extended service trip also made a nice contribution to their wages.

During the first half of the 1980s, the Albatross logo could be found on board an increasing number of vessels, and steadily further afield from the factory at the land bound city by the river Numedalslågen. The sales team was expanding as Albatross captured new markets, and sales offices were opened in ever more parts of the world. With the growing globalisation, marketing staff began to refer to the «octopus» model, where the head, and brain, resided in Kongsberg, and steered the arms reaching out into the world. The arms would serve to pick up impulses on developments in the various markets.[55] To claim that it actually worked this way in the early 1980s would be an exaggeration, but it was this model Albatross management strived for, and the direction it has continued in since. The need to establish outposts around the world arose partly in response to the opening for exploration in new areas, but mainly due to a restructuring of the shipbuilding industry. More and more of the world's tonnage was being built in East Asia. Many shipowners still had their head offices in Europe and North America, but the trend was moving toward the yards taking more control over the outfitting of ships. This was an important reason for Albatross to be in locations where decisions were being made. The years ahead would see this trend strengthened even further.[56]

Albatross stationed their own personnel at these new posts, but they also established close relationships to agents. Parts of the marketing apparatus were formally organised through KV's marketing bodies: Kongsberg UK Ltd. in the UK, Kongsberg Asia Pty. in Singapore, and Kongsberg Inc. in the USA. Albatross retained full operative and economic control over these units. The company had expanded beyond its North Sea home market. By the mid-80s, Japan and South Korea were the fastest growing new markets.[57] Albatross was growing not just by conquering new markets, but because they had developed new technologies.

POSITION MOORING

Drilling activity on the Norwegian Continental Shelf (NCS) had increased dramatically during the 1970s. Norwegian yards had proven their ability to exploit the opportunities provided by discoveries in the North Sea. Akers mek. Verksted in Oslo was one good example. Their semi-submersible H3 rigs were some of the most popular on the NCS. Up to 1980, 28 such rigs had been built.[58] These employed an anchoring system consisting of 10 to 12 robust anchor chains, dimensioned for the so-called 10-year weather phenomenon, or the maximum levels for waves, wind, and current that could be expected in the course of a ten-year period. These calculations would soon prove to be insufficient. Such conditions occurred nearly every winter, and it became obvious that the dimensions would have to be adjusted accordingly. Frequent anchor chain breakage sent a clear message that something had to be done.

A major public project to develop new mooring regulations was initiated in 1980. Led by K. Magnus Havig of the Norwegian Maritime Authority (NMA), the project enlisted both research institutions and the supplier industry. The maritime research institute MARINTEK in Trondheim became a key partner. The institute had many years' experience with mooring calculations, in addition to solid competence in simulating the behaviour of anchored rigs in various weather conditions, and in the event of one or more broken anchor lines. Albatross was also involved in the project.[59]

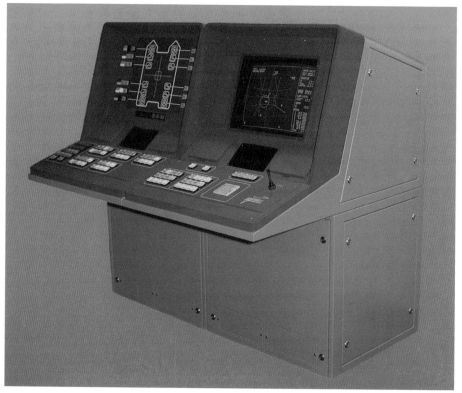

The Albatross Position Mooring System (APM). The image is of the operator console, taken from the first sales brochure in 1984.

In 1984 the NMA published new regulations with heightened requirements for anchored drilling rigs. The new principles were also adopted into DNV's new POSMOOR standards. Rig owners could become compliant in two ways. They could choose to use more winches and anchor lines, or install thrusters with control systems. The system would have to be able to determine when an anchor line broke and compensate by use of thrusters. This was often the least expensive and most flexible solution. Investing in such systems was relatively reasonable compared to the expense of meeting requirements through expanded mooring capacity.

All rigs operating on the NCS were required to have approvals from the Norwegian Authorities. This created new demand in the market and paved the way for new systems solutions. For Albatross the most important thing was that the new rules provided systematic application of mooring analysis, and that thrusters were approved for mitigation of the effect of waves, wind and current.

Albatross Position Mooring System — **APM**

APM sales brochure from 1984.

Operatively speaking this meant the need for a support system to assist the crew in safe operations. The newest rigs were also equipped with thrusters, not at the level of DP-vessels, but sufficient for manoeuvring. These thrusters could also be used during drilling operations to relieve stress on anchor lines. This was the starting point for Albatross' work on developing a system that could utilise DP functionality to handle or assist in anchoring. The original name for the system was Platform Data System (PDS), but the marketing department feared this could be associated with administrative data management rather than an operative system. The name was therefore changed to APM3000, which stood for Albatross Position Mooring.[60] Product development ran nearly parallel to the development of the new mooring regulations, and was in a way a prerequisite for the regulations turning out the way they did.

Development work commenced in 1981, which was before the new regulations were in place. As with development of the first DP systems, Albatross chose to divide work between one team in Kongsberg and one in Trondheim. And again this time the Albatross team worked with machine and systems software, as well as operator communications, while the SINTEF researchers handled algorithms for analysis and steering. Ingvald Løvdal was the lead man

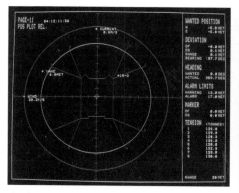
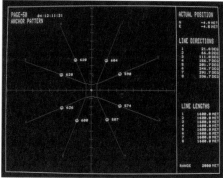

Anchor lines have a catenary profile in the water and meet the seabed at a certain distance from the rig, depending on tension and water depth. It is important to ensure that the touch down point is sufficiently far from the anchor so as not to cause lifting. Screen shots from an APM3000 show the mooring pattern and where each line is calculated to hit the seabed, the position of the rig, and observed tension and line length. Shown here from a 1988 brochure.

in Kongsberg, while activities in Trondheim were coordinated by Nils Albert Jenssen.

When Jenssen had finished writing the program code for the first DP system, he took his doctorate in cybernetics at NTH in 1981. His thesis, *Estimation and Control in Dynamic Positioning of Vessels*, was the first Norwegian thesis in dynamic positioning.[61] When Albatross began developing new systems, it made little sense to have much of their key competence in a research institution 400 km to the north. Jenssen therefore joined Albatross in 1982.

After Jenssen moved to Kongsberg he ran the algorithm work from there. From that point on, Albatross developed monitoring and steering algorithms in-house. In addition the group worked closely with MARINTEK on vessel simulation and mooring calculations. Simulator software was developed in the research institute in Trondheim, while the systems software and online elements were developed in Kongsberg. Thruster-assisted anchoring was completely new. Developers cooperated closely with captain Odd Nergård Skaug of Ross Drilling during development, in order to get to know the needs of their future end users and be able to develop functionality and tailor the system accordingly. Solutions turned out to be very complex, though, and perhaps more advanced than was absolutely necessary.[62]

The APM3000 had two main advantages. The one was an online system that monitored motion and line tension and provided thruster assistance as needed. The other was a built-in simulator that the operator could use to try out the effects of changing weather conditions, use of thrusters, or simulated line

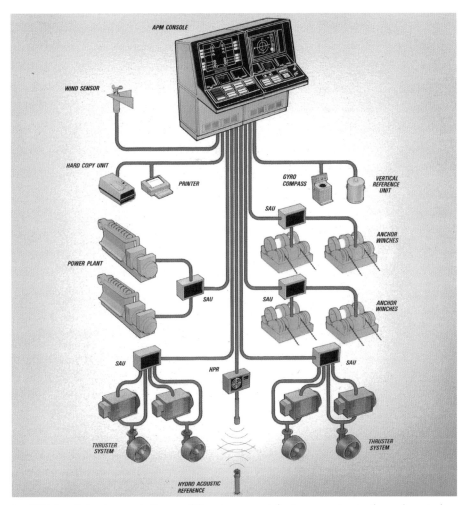

APM CONSOLE

WIND SENSOR

HARD COPY UNIT

PRINTER

GYRO COMPASS

VERTICAL REFERENCE UNIT

SAU

ANCHOR WINCHES

POWER PLANT

SAU

SAU

ANCHOR WINCHES

SAU

HPR

SAU

THRUSTER SYSTEM

THRUSTER SYSTEM

HYDRO ACOUSTIC REFERENCE

An APM installation is very similar to a DP system, except for its connection to the anchor winches. Readings from the winches (tension and line length) are used in the mathematical model that describes the rig's movements. This information is necessary in order to adjust the winches to achieve optimum tension distribution between the lines. Winches are not controlled by the APM system, however. In order to simplify interfaces, separate Signal Acquisition Units (SAU) are connected to the thrusters, winches and power systems on board.

breakage. The online was based on the same thinking as the DP system, with a mathematical model of the rig in a Kalman filter. The APM model also contained a mathematical description of the effect of mooring lines on the rig. This model was also employed by the simulator, which for the purpose of simulation also got additional calculations of the effect of waves. Since the mooring lines provided the primary station keeping, there was no need for redundancy in the

The first APM system was installed and tested on board the semi-submersible drill rig *Ross Isle* in 1983. The illustration is from the 1988 brochure 'Positioning and Control systems'. The rig was the first constructed following the Norwegian Maritime Authority's stiffened requirements in response to a series of anchor chain breaks on drilling rigs in the North Sea. DNV followed up with their own set of Posmoor rules. In order to qualify for POSMOOR ATA class, a rig had to have a system that monitored both anchor line tension and vessel movements, and automatically compensated for line breakage using thrusters should it occur. The system also had to carry out automatic consequence analysis to warn if a possible break could lead to excess transient movement or more line breaks. Ross Isle was the first vessel equipped with such a system.

APM system itself. In fact the mooring system and the APM were two systems for the same function, namely rig positioning. The APM system and thrusters could be used to mitigate rig movement caused by waves and wind gusts.[63]

Line breakage detection was a central functionality in the system. Based on readings from the winches and registration of the rigs movements, it could detect and report line breakage, also reporting which line had broken. In the event of a break, the system automatically activated thruster compensation for the broken line. This meant that the operator could add the rig's thruster capacity to the NMA-stipulated anchor line strength. This feature allowed them to operate in harsher weather than they could have without such a system. Another key feature was consequence analysis. Here the system simulated breaks in all lines, one at a time, and determined whether transient movement as a result of the breaks would bring the rig too far out of position, or whether remaining anchor lines would be overstressed.

Software development for Albatross was done on Nord machines manufactured by Norsk Data. Based on positive experience, these were also considered for use in the APM system. But here the reaction from KV management was unequivocal. Albatross would use KV's own KS500 machines, the same that were used in the ADP systems. The computer division was bleeding red, and procuring equipment from outside the company was out of the question.[64] KV was against buying anything from a third party that they could produce themselves, even though it might be cheaper to buy from a supplier. Albatross did on occasion defy KV management, but they were not allowed to reject the KS500 – yet.

Even though Albatross was still at the core of the new system, not all components in the cabinet were identical to the ADP machines. The practice of routing all process signals directly to the main computer had been discontinued. Now Signal Acquisition Units (SAU) were placed at each unit to be controlled. Signals were collected in-situ and sent on to the main unit. This made it quicker and easier to install the systems. Testing time was also reduced, and troubleshooting was easier. This configuration was given the name «distributed I/O». The SAU units were supplied by Norcontrol in Horten, which, like Albatross, was part of KV's Maritime division. This was the first time Albatross had engaged industrial designers to design a console. The ADP consoles had been developed by Kongsberg engineers, with sharp angles and smooth steel surfaces. Now the product developers were looking to come up with something more refined.[65]

The first APM system was sold in March of 1982 to Ross Drilling, part of the Sandefjord-based shipper Rosshavet.[66] The unit was to be installed on the drilling platform *Ross Isle*. Work was delayed, though, when the rig ran aground outside Sandefjord while being towed from Framnæs Mekaniske Værksted for sea trials. Two thrusters were knocked off the hull, and the platform had to be towed to Rotterdam for repairs. As a result, delivery to Rosshavet was delayed.[67] This was a blessing in disguise for Albatross, as the APM system was not yet ready for delivery. The delay allowed the project team to make their deadline on *Ross Isle*. The rig was delivered to the shipowner with the hardware at the end of March 1983, and six months later the software was in place and the system was operative.[68]

The following years would see APM systems installed on several rigs, among them *Dyvi Stena* (Stena Drilling, 1983), *Polar Pioneer* (Polar Frontier Drilling, 1984), *Deep Sea Bergen* (Odfjell, 1985) and *Dyvi Alpha* (Dyvi Offshore, 1986).[69] Some of the rigs were also fitted with a DP system, allowing them to perform both anchored and dynamically positioned operations. The two systems were in principle independent of each other, but they shared sensors and reference systems wherever technically feasible. The first with this combined solution was Smedvig's *West Vision* platform, and *Norjarl* from Nordenfjeldske, both delivered in the summer of 1985.[70]

Several generations of PM systems have been launched since that time. In 1996 ADP was replaced by the SDP series, and a new position mooring system was developed simultaneously, Simrad Position Mooring (SPM). This system featured a Windows user interface and was a more modern version of its predecessor. It was later upgraded to a new and more powerful version in 2003. Fourth-generation PM technology was unveiled in 2006, under the name K-Pos PM.

A «CUCKOO» IN THE KV NEST

KV director Rolf Qvenild described Albatross as the «cuckoo» in the KV nest.[71] Albatross employees also recognised themselves in that characterisation.[72] In many ways it is a fitting description, but in others it can be misleading. The expression is commonly used to describe a freeloader, one who thrives at the expense of those who have helped them along. Albatross was not that kind of cuckoo. From the moment the group began turning a profit it contributed significantly to KV's bottom line. The characterisation is more fitting as an analogy to the cuckoo that lays its egg in another's nest, and to the young bird that grows bigger than those hatched from the mother's own eggs. In that way, calling Albatross a cuckoo may be defensible. In many ways, Albatross was an «odd bird» in the weapons factory.

The unique Albatross culture, with its clear anarchistic traits, great freedom granted to the individual, and extreme customer orientation, had proven to be a good recipe for success. In the early 1980s this culture was passed on and refined by Theory Albatross. Parallel to cultivation on the home front, much was being done to build up the culture abroad.

KV management gave the albatrosses free reign in their working methods. But when it came to technology, they had to tow the line. They could get away with a lot, but they could not escape the KS500. The «cuckoo» had grown up. Was the nest getting too small?

7

FLYING SOLO

ALBATROSS EXPERIENCED REMARKABLE growth in the early 1980s. With 150 employees, the group had resembled a medium-sized Norwegian company. Taking the unorthodox Albatross culture into consideration, where being different from Kongsberg Våpenfabrikk (KV) was part of the mantra, it comes as no surprise that many began to regard Albatross as a more independent entity.

Albatross management described competition on the market in the autumn of 1983 as 'considerably intensified', particularly for small DP systems. This was not due to new competitors, but to the fact that Albatross's technological advantage was being eroded by Honeywell and GEC.[1] If Albatross was to maintain its leading position, the technology would have to be upgraded. KV's computer no longer provided any competitive advantage. Quite the contrary: it was becoming a liability. Albatross was at a crossroads, technologically and organisationally. Kongsberg Våpenfabrikk and KV technology were no longer the obvious choice.

TECHNOLOGICAL INDEPENDENCE – SBC1000

DP systems were not exploiting the full potential of the Kalman filter. The KS500's capacity was too limited for this.[2] The machine was also expensive. KV management was nonetheless adamant that buying equipment from Norsk Data or other suppliers was out of the question as long as KV had its own computer. Management insisted that all DP systems were to be delivered with KV machines. The issue was exacerbated by the development of the APM3000. Despite the restriction, developers at Albatross began to look around for alternative solutions. Computer technology was developing rapidly, and new and

When Vidar Solli joined Albatross in 1982, he was involved in tailoring DP systems to customer needs, as were the other engineers. His real interest, though, was in microprocessor technology. When a new interface to the Syledis reference system for the KS500 was to be developed, Solli proposed making a general microprocessor-based module that could also be used for new applications as needed. The result was the GPI100 module that became the springboard for further application of microprocessor technology in Albatross. Photo: *Laagendalsposten.*

powerful microprocessors made it possible to build smaller computers that could perform tasks previously requiring larger machines. Size was going down while performance was going up. With the launch of IBM's 5150-PC with Intel's 8088 processor in 1981, computers had become an off-the-shelf commodity. Purchasing a new personal computer for use in dynamic positioning was in any case not an option due to their lack of reliability.

In the spring of 1983, electronics engineer Vidar Solli joined Albatross. He had recently completed his thesis on microprocessor controlled systems at the Department of Engineering Cybernetics at NTH. To him, ADP's operator consoles with large, independent computer cabinets appeared archaic.[3] But it was no small task for a new hire to gain support for a proposal to move DP systems over to a new platform. Still, employees were allowed to pursue their ideas and use money on their own projects. Albatross had a flat structure permeated with creativity at that time. The attitude, at least among employees, was that the money was there to be spent. If they weren't used in Albatross, they would simply disappear in the «KV pit».[4] Over in KV, a group in the Computer division was already underway developing a successor to the KS500, named KS900. Production of computers under the direction of Albatross, however, was not part of KV management's plan. Computer engineer Ingolv Olsen has described Albatross's development work as «a kind of 'civil disobedience'».[5]

The key principle that the Albatross engineers were working by was a DP system run on multiple parallel computers. By splitting up tasks, cheaper and smaller machines could be used. Processor technology, with Intel's x86 in the lead, was developing at breakneck speed. Increased capacity and decreasing costs made this an attractive option.[6] In reality there were only two producers to choose from when it came to microprocessor technology for large systems in the early 1980s: Intel and Motorola. Solli and his development team had formed a favourable opinion of Intel processors during their studies. Based on this, they chose microprocessors and peripheral circuitry from Intel. The machine under development in KV was based on Motorola technology.[7]

Implementation of microprocessor technology proceeded rapidly in Albatross, but in stages. The first step was a general I/O unit called GPI100. This was later used as the new interface for reference and panel systems.[8] Development of this type of unit laid the foundation for the next step. In 1983 Albatross engineers began work on a machine to replace the KS500. With this, there were now two competing and parallel development projects being run in KV.

The Albatross group had begun to investigate a new communications platform called Ethernet. This made it possible to connect multiple units in a single network instead of using dedicated cables between them. Could it be possible to create a flexible system where the number of computers could be varied depending on the nature of the job to be performed, and where these machines communicated through Ethernet? Perhaps a redundant network could also be used to enhance reliability? Despite resistance, the group got the go-ahead from Albatross management, and a development project was started that produced a new computer in 1984. The machine was built around Intel's 80186 processor and was no bigger than a standard double European circuit board (204 x 155,5 mm).[9] At this size, there was no longer a need for a large cabinet to house computers in DP systems.

The new machine was tailor-made to perform the tasks required of a DP system, and featured a simple and reliable architecture. Since there was room for all components on one circuit board, it was named the SBC1000 (Single Board Computer). Albatross's use of funds to develop their own microprocessor-based computer, at the same time as KV was using large sums of money developing their next-generation machine, was not exactly applauded by KV management. As the computer neared completion the development team got the message that director Qvenild and top management were to pay a visit to see the result.

The Albatross team had gotten word that the KS900 group had managed to get their system to display a ticking clock. This they had to top. In true Albatross spirit, they worked night and day to come up with something to impress KV

The SBC1000 was not the most advanced computer of its day, but it was extremely compact. It was based on Intel's 80186 processor, a compact version of the better-known 8086 processor, and featured many of the support circuits integrated into the processor itself. The most expensive PCs of that time had Intel 80286 processors inside. Photo: Mediafoto.

management. When the day of the visit arrived, a tired but proud team clad in Albatross t-shirts presented a computer that ran a real-time operative system with multiple processors sending signals to each other.

«The computer coup» was successful.[10] Albatross had been forbidden to procure Nord machines for their APM system. With an in-house and purpose-built machine that worked, KV management dropped their requirement that Albatross continue using KS machines. KV's time as a producer of computers had come to an end. The new SBC machine would be the brain in second-generation Albatross systems.

The SBC1000 is often referred to as if there were only one type of machine on all installations. This is only partly true. In all, 15 variations were produced, even though this number eventually stabilised at around three or four. Albatross exploited the advantage of having their own tailor-made computer. It was a simple task for the engineers to customise the equipment to meet customer requirements, and deliver what they called an «as built» version of the system.[11]

With the new processor technology also came the need for a new graphics card. The SBG1000 (Single Board Graphics) was developed to fill this need.[12]

The Albatross engineers were leading on with several different solutions. They may not have been the first to use Ethernet as a communications protocol, but they were certainly early adopters. Components were often in the early stages of development with no track record. This could present certain challenges, some of which Intel could offer no solution for. One such problem was with the numerical co-processor. The Albatross team even found a solution that they passed on to Intel, who later shared it with other customers. This brought the project to the attention of the inner circles in Silicon Valley.[13]

ADP100

Albatross launched the ADP100 in the autumn of 1983, signalling the start of a new product line of compact DPs. The system was a supplement to the older generation of DPs, the ADP503 and ADP311, and not a replacement. Compared with its predecessor, the new system was both simpler and cheaper. The ADP100 was the first DP system with SBC1000. In addition to three such computers, it was equipped with the new SBG1000 graphics card. The new computer was in fact not fully developed on the launch of ADP100, but not a great deal of work remained.[14]

User-friendliness was important, and during development great emphasis was placed on making the user interface as simple and intuitive as possible. As with its predecessor, the ADP100 was based on the principle of «one button, one function», and information was presented to the operator graphically on a colour screen.[15] In keeping with the ideal of simplicity and low price, the system was built to receive signals from a single positioning reference system. An optional second system could be installed, but was not included in the standard package.[16]

The computers were not the only new feature of the ADP100. New development tools and software were also included. The choice of architecture meant that Albatross was «married to Intel» as one of the development team put it. This meant that chips from the Silicon Valley giant were not the only products taken into use, but also development tools, compilers and the real-time operating system RMX.[17] Programs for the previous generation of systems were in large part written using the programming language Fortran. On the ADP100 all code was rewritten to C.[18] In the older DP systems using the KS500 computer, software was stored on cassette tapes. This was also changed. The SBC

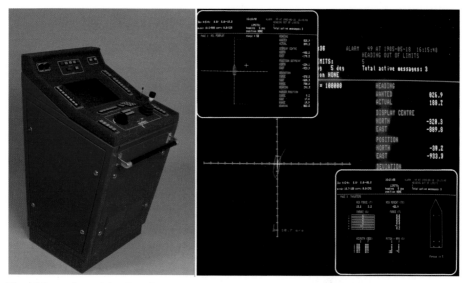

The ADP100 inherited the idea of 'one button – one function' from its forerunners, but had simpler and less expensive buttons and a new computer (GPI100) for reading signals from the buttons. The system featured a colour screen like the ADP311 and the newest version of the ADP503 (MkII), but utilised a newly developed graphical interface unit (SBG1000). Earlier systems used an alphanumeric screen for operator interaction and alarm display, while the ADP100 used the main screen. Only three screen images were available: 'pos plot' (true and relative motion) and a thruster image.

machines did not need an input medium since the code was stored in EPROM (Erasable Programmable Read Only Memory). In the successor, the SBC2000, released in 1987, this memory was replaced by a hard drive storage unit.[19]

As in the present, it happened that development projects were delayed, calling for creative solutions. Well before the system was completed the marketing department had concluded that the ADP100 should be presented at a major international exhibition. As opening day approached, it became apparent that the system would not be finished in time. The date could of course not be changed, so good advice was at a premium. The solution was as simple as it was brilliant – and perhaps a bit provocative to some. Instead of displaying the finished product, the Albatross sales team placed the shell of an ADP100 in front of a wall, with a KS500 machine on the other side. Naturally the cabinet of the new computer could not be opened – for reasons of confidentiality, of course.[20]

Sales of the new ADP100 started promisingly. Shortly following the launch in November of 1983, the first system was sold. The following summer it was installed on the marine geological exploration vessel *Ocean Surveyor*, owned

Rune Skyrudsmoen tests an ADP100 system. Compared to the ADP311, the new system was highly compact and user-friendly. Photo: Mediafoto.

by the unlimited company Ocean Survey, through J.K. Lindberg in Harstad.[21] The first sea trial, though, was anything but a success. The champagne brought along to celebrate the successful installation had to be put aside. Instead the crew set to work troubleshooting and trying to get the system to function properly. It proved to be easier to get a machine to work in the lab than to rig up a complete DP system with new technology while at sea. The problems were eventually solved, though, and the system performed satisfactorily.

During the course of 1984 Albatross sold eight ADP100 installations.[22] Contracts were later signed for another 30 such systems. The last of these was installed in 1989.[23] Many of these compact systems were installed on shuttle tankers, a new DP market for Albatross in the early 1980s.

SHUTTLE TANKERS

In the North Sea, the most important market for Albatross, diving vessels and supply ships was the primary users of DP. By the summer of 1980 Albatross

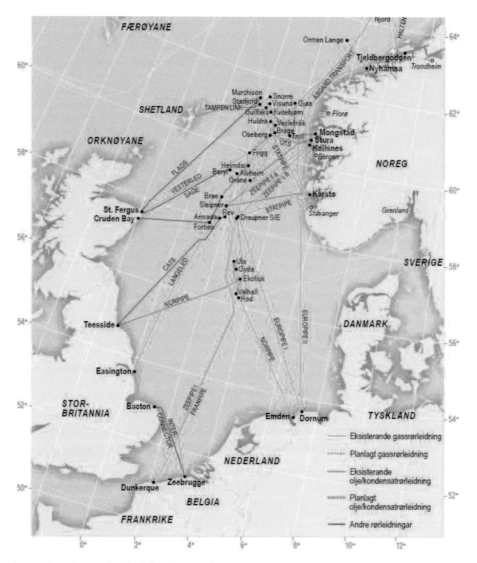

Large oil pipelines in the North Sea. From the Norwegian Petroleum Directorate, 2010.

had installed DP on around twenty each of these types of vessels, in addition to one cable layer and three drilling rigs.[24]

The North Sea would eventually open up for more applications of DP technology. Oil and gas couldn't simply be pumped to the surface, it also had to be brought to land. As early as 1971, Parliament had decreed that oil and gas from the Norwegian Continental Shelf (NCS) should be brought ashore in Norway.

However, there was one particularly large, or rather deep, problem with this principle. Between the major oil fields and the Norwegian mainland runs the Norwegian Trench, with depths up to 370 metres. Laying pipe required the assistance of divers, and here were depths more than twice what was possible to dive in at that time. The solution for Ekofisk was to run a pipeline to the UK, and later, a gas pipeline to Germany. History repeated itself for the Frigg field in the mid 1970s, when a pipeline was laid to the UK.[25]

1974 saw the discovery of large oil and gas deposits on Statfjord. Again several landing alternatives were considered. The difference from previous field developments was that the Norwegian state now had dominant ownership through Statoil. This increased Norwegian influence significantly. Statoil's transport study reviewed several alternatives for landing, both a pipeline to the mainland, and loading to ships on site from buoys, so-called offshore loading or shuttle tankers. Economic calculations showed the latter option to be considerably less expensive, convincing Statoil and operator Mobil to opt for this solution.

In 1976 the companies received temporary approval to develop Statfjord with a loading tower where tankers could moor and offload oil, but the Norwegian parliament demanded a new evaluation of the pipeline option that would land at Sotra. When this was presented in 1979, it proved to be fully NOK 6 billion more expensive than offloading. The companies therefore sought exemption from the Norwegian landing rule, and they received government approval in May of 1980.[26] The temporary solutions thereby became permanent. By that time offloading was already in full swing. The first oil from Statfjord was handled by shipowner Einar Rasmussen's *Polytraveller* in December of 1979. Sister ships *Polytrader* and *Polyviking* were later put into service transporting the oil.[27] The decision to transport oil from Statfjord using tankers, and not a pipeline, opened a new chapter in Norwegian shipping. At the same time, the need for effective and safe loading systems presented good opportunities for the Norwegian supplier industry – including Albatross.

In the beginning ordinary tankers were tied up to the loading buoy during loading. This solution led to heavy wear on equipment, in addition to adding a significant safety risk. Buoy offloading hadn't been going on for more than eight months when an explosive fire broke out on the *Polytraveller*, in August 1980. The incident was triggered by a break in the mooring line between the Statfjord A buoy and the tanker. As a result oil flooded the deck and was ignited by sparks from the chain at the end of the broken line. The nearly fully-loaded ship received only minor damage, but the captain and first mate were seriously

The tanker Polytraveller loading from the Gullfaks B offshore loading buoy. Photo: Øyvind Hagen / Statoil / Norsk Oljemuseum.

injured. The captain died from his injuries shortly after. Only a month and a half later another accident occurred. This time *Polytrader* was involved. Here again, the mooring line was the cause of the problem, but this time the pumps were shut down and the oil hose disconnected without any leakage.[28]

Buoy offloading was proving to be a risky business, and the search was on for safer and more reliable solutions. Could fitting the tankers with DP equipment solve the problem? If Albatross could find a good solution, offloading could turn into a new market segment for them. It was no easy task to get a DP system to work in harmony with the taught mooring lines forward on the ship, though, and this could lead to unstable positioning. The challenge was known from diving operations, where slack reserve anchor lines were used in addition to DP when the vessel was operating in close proximity to a fixed installation.[29] Based on theoretical studies and practical experience from other vessel types, Kongsberg engineers developed a special solution for shuttle tankers that performed well. Once again the technology team from NTH contributed in developing new concepts.[30]

The tankers were essentially manoeuvred manually, and kept in position by constant speed of the propeller, to keep tension on the mooring lines as even as possible. This was a very stressful task for those manning the helm. A DP system would allow automation of this task, and the operation would be not only safer and more precise, but also less stressful for the operator. By delegating positioning to a DP system, the ships were less dependent on the mooring lines. These could instead serve to offer added security in the event of a DP system failure. In turn the life of mooring lines would be extended considerably. Use of DP could thereby contribute to cutting costs.[31]

Albatross sold their first DP system to a shuttle tanker in November of 1980. The tanker *Wilnora* was owned by shipper Anders Wilhelmsen, and was chartered to the Statfjord field. It was fitted with an ADP311 with an Artemis reference system that monitored the distance between antennae on the ship and the loading buoy using radio signals. Since the mooring lines were viewed as sufficient backup in the event of a DP failure, no redundant DP system was required.[32] Albatross got the next three DP contracts for shuttle tankers in May of 1984. These were the two Rasmussen tankers that had been involved in the 1980 accidents, *Polytraveller* and *Polytrader*, and their sister ship *Polyviking*. In the meantime the ADP100 had come on the market, and would dominate the offloading market in the years to come.[33]

Control algorithms were steadily being improved and specialised for various types of loading buoys. Developments in DP systems steering philosophy were also introduced. Offloading did not require holding a fixed position as long as the distance between the ship's bow and the buoy was constant, making it possible to employ the «weather vane principle». This meant that it was only necessary to control the ship's distance and heading in relation to the buoy. The forces of weather would move the ship sideways, keeping it in the right position. The weather vane principle requires one or more tunnel thrusters in the bow and the stern, supported by the rudder as needed. The main propeller with variable pitch blades would be used primarily to maintain distance.[34] Employing this principle of DP also had consequences for tanker design. Offloading with DP became a great success. Up to 1990 Albatross delivered 10 ADP100 systems to tankers for several shipowners.[35]

Tandem loading. *Åsgard A* and the tanker *Navion Scandia*. Photo: KM.

In time other types of buoys came into use. In addition to the original «Single-Point Mooring» method, extremely costly with its floating tower, came new and cheaper methods. The UKOLS concept (Ugland Kongsberg Offshore Loading System) was installed on the Statfjord field in 1987. This represented significant cost savings thanks to a floating submerged loading buoy. The weather vane principle was employed in DP systems here as well, ensuring that the bow of the tanker was kept at a specific distance from where the loading hose was connected on the seabed. Since the loading system had no mooring lines, the tanker was completely dependent on a DP system.[36]

When Floating Production, Storage and Offloading systems (FPSO) hit the market, a new challenge arose. These systems employed tandem loading, where a tanker was hooked up to the stern of the FPSO by a hose. The FPSO itself was anchored by means of a swivel with anchor lines fixed so that the vessel could rotate like a weather vane. This allowed both vessels to find their own headings. When oil was pumped from one vessel to another, both altered their behaviour. The FPSO became gradually lighter, and increasingly effected by wind, while the tanker became heavier, and more effected by currents and waves. To counter this effect an additional functionality was developed for DP that allowed the tanker to stay aligned with the FPSO. As with the original loading buoys, a line was used between the vessels to secure the loading hose. The biggest safety risk was collision between the vessels, and there the line was not much help.[37]

Various concepts for offshore loading. From left, loading from a tower with safety line (Single Point Mooring, SPM), loading from a submerged buoy with no lines (UKOLS), Submerged Turret Loading (STL) and tandem offloading from an FPSO. For the STL solution, the DP is normally only used during attach and release. With other concepts, a DP system is essential in keeping the ship towards the weather.

The ADP100 units installed on most shuttle tankers in the 1980s did not have redundancy. If the DP system should fail for some reason, the skipper had to rely on the mooring line, which was the only available backup system. In 1991 Albatross installed the first redundant DP system, for the Haugesund shipowner Knutsen OAS, on the *Marie Knutsen*. By then the ADP100 had been relieved by a new generation of DP. Eventually most shuttle tankers were fitted with redundant DP systems.

The most complex offloading systems are Submerged Turret Loading (STL), and were taken into use for the first time on the Heidrun field in 1995. This system employs a submerged loading buoy that is pulled into the tanker itself. The STL system functions as an anchoring system as well. This is a costly solution, but with many safety advantages, and allows the tanker to maintain position without consuming energy under normal weather conditions. The DP system is used only during hook-up and release and in bad weather.

Measured in number of units, the offloading market has never been big. Of all DP units delivered by Kongsberg, offshore loading represents only a small percentage. The company has from the start been virtually the sole suppler to the shuttle tanker fleet. When all units were tallied in 2009, they had delivered 70 of 72 units worldwide.[38]

STAYING ON TRACK

The alternative to buoy offloading was laying a pipeline to the mainland. As previously mentioned, this was not a viable option for Statfjord, as the Norwegian Trench was too deep for diving. In other areas, however, pipelines were a highly attractive solution. Ekofisk and Frigg oil and gas was transported to UK soil via pipeline. Pipe-laying vessels up to that point operated pretty much as before, using anchors. By winching the mooring lines in and out manually they pulled themselves forward along the pre-set track. Attempts were made

Allseas was a pioneer within DP pipelaying. Their ship *Lorelay* was the first vessel to lay offshore pipelines of large dimensions without the use of anchor lines. In this type of operation, it is essential that the DP system and the pipelaying equipment do not work against each other. In the worst case this could lead to instability that could damage the pipe. Photo: Havenfoto, Henk van Kooten.

to semi-automate the winching, where an operator could use a joystick to coordinate multiple winches, but this method never proved fully satisfactory. This was clearly a new market for dynamic positioning systems. As opposed to the challenges facing diving vessels, this task required not staying put, but staying on track. Albatross had already implemented much of this functionality in its DP system for specialty vessels used to cover pipelines and lay cable.

The most common method of pipelaying was so-called S-laying, named for the shape of the pipe during the laying operation. In the summer of 1985 Albatross got its first contract for a DP system on a pipe-laying vessel for the Dutch company Allseas. Laying oil or gas pipelines on the seabed is a demanding operation requiring extreme precision. In addition to the challenges of placing the pipe in its proper position without damaging it, there was the risk of damaging existing pipelines and infrastructure with the anchors. The vessel *Lorelay* would have to operate with tight margins of error and high levels of precision, effectiveness, and safety. A single mistake could be very costly, so the ship was fitted with a redundant ADP503 unit combined with an ADP311 reserve system. The *Lorelay* represented a new generation of pipelaying vessels, and was the first to employ DP.[39]

One primary challenge was that the so-called tensioner system that served to support the pipe also restricted the ship's movement. DP and the tensioner system could work against each other if not corrected. Another challenge was that the vessel had to be held still while new segments of pipe were being welded. When welding was completed the ship needed to be advanced as quickly as possible before the next length of pipe was welded into place. This became more difficult as water depth decreased. In deep water the so-called J-configuration could be employed, allowing the vessel to move forward more or less continuously at even speed, without having to use too much force to keep the pipe taut. This method proved easier to handle for DP systems than the S-method.[40]

As subsea wellheads became more common, a new need arose for local pipe-laying on the fields. The so-called Reel system was generally used to perform this task, with the pipe coiled on a large spool and straightened out on board before being lowered into the sea. The Reel method worked well with both flexible pipe and cable. DP was well suited to this task, allowing the vessel to move forward evenly and precisely along the desired track.

CHANGE OF POSITION

The new systems sold well. Albatross sold DP systems for NOK 74 million in 1980, and for NOK 86 million the following year. Developments in the next decade would be formidable, with revenues growing from NOK 141 million in 1982, to 169 million the year after. The solid results reflected not only a growing product portfolio, but also that DP had been introduced to new market segments, while Albatross had grown into new geographical markets. Profit was good, amounting to around NOK 10 million annually.[41] Albatross was becoming a medium-large Norwegian company. This influenced the thinking of the albatrosses. No longer were they content to be «outside the fence». Now they wanted to be a separate, independent company. Outside the factory walls things were happening that made this solution seem ever more feasible. What was referred to a «rightist wind» had blown the Norwegian Labour Party out of office, and in the autumn of 1981 Prime Minister Kåre Willoch formed a conservative administration. This introduced a new mindset, which would come to dominate industrial politics. The consequences of this shift would come to affect both Kongsberg Våpenfabrikk, and eventually Albatross.

KV was in many ways the incarnation of Labour's industrial politics in the post-war period, favouring large, state-owned entities. The new Norwegian administration, by contrast, promised liberalisation, deregulation and independent, democratic ownership. A clear sign of change came in 1982 when two board members were replaced mid-term by Johan H. Andresen and Hans E. Sundt from the right-wing business community. The following year Andresen would take over Labour Nestor Jens Chr. Hauge's role as Vice-Chairman, and in 1985, he would take over former KV director Bjarne Hurlen's job as Chairman.[42] Rolf Qvenild, who took over as KV's Managing Director in November of 1978, would remain in the director's chair through all these changes.[43] By contrast to Hurlen, who had run the company with an iron hand for twenty years, Qvenild allowed units under his command more freedom.

Despite having delivered all DP systems sold globally in 1980, Albatross did not make up more than five percent of KV's total activities.[44] Seen in this light, the enterprise was of modest proportions, but the group distinguished itself from other KV units by succeeding not only with new technology, but by mastering the marketing side of the business. Earnings were also good. This was notable in a time where several of KV's businesses were struggling to make money. In the mid-1980s Albatross presented results at the same level as the Defence division, surpassed only by the Petroleum division.[45] From this perspective, Albatross was far from an insignificant part of KV.

Even though turnover and profit had grown nicely in the years since the first sale, Albatross was highly vulnerable. DP systems were expensive and the markets were limited. This made the business highly susceptible to economic crises. At the same time, potential for growth was great. As long as markets were expanding, the possibilities were significant. The Decca business was also going well. News was not so good for Robertson and Norcontrol, both of whom were struggling. This meant that the large new Maritime division established on January 1 1980 became a problem division right from the start, joining the Computer and Gas Turbine divisions in the doghouse.[46]

KV's management favoured the stability of state ownership and feared that the new government would open the door for partial privatisation.[47] This did not stop Qvenild from inviting private investors in on activities that were not at the core of KV's operation. In 1982 KV established the company Sys-Scan together with the Germany firm Messerschmitt-Bölkow-Blohm. The new company would develop a geographical information system for map publishers. This represented a break from the previous practice of establishing new business inside of the existing structure. So how would this affect Albatross? Strictly speaking, dynamic positioning was not a core activity either. This new development presented new opportunities, and towards the mid-1980s KV would come to loosen its hold on the Albatross group.

In 1983 KV appointed a separate Albatross board of directors, which would in many ways function as a traditional board in publicly traded company. KV director Qvenild chaired the board, taking with him several of KV's top management. With this Albatross began to take on the appearance of an independent company, but the group was still an integrated part of KV. As previously discussed, Albatross employees had long regarded themselves as an independent unit, using KV as the definition of what Albatross was *not*. The issue was not simply two distinct cultures. There were also other differentiating factors that would come to play a role in later negotiations.

On the one hand Albatross was facing major technical and market development challenges, and was transforming from a single-product company with success on the home market, to a multi-product enterprise dependent on a growing number of geographically distant markets. In addition they were in the process of fundamentally revising their basic technology.[48] Management had high growth ambitions, and they laid out aggressive strategies for meeting these goals.[49] However, this would require successful handling of a series of so-called 'strategic issues', among them what they called 'The welfare of personnel'.

THE WELFARE OF PERSONNEL

Management had a clear understanding of why Albatross had been so successful. A strategy memo explained in no uncertain terms: «The deciding factor in our success has been the human factor, not technology or capital.»[50] This statement might seem out of place in a company that sold highly advanced technical equipment with very low tolerance for error. The focus on human capital did not mean that the company had begun to rest on its technical laurels and was downplaying further development of DP systems. Albatross sought «excellence», and their ambition was to be a «market leader and trendsetter».[51] The technology had to work, but the group was not the only one capable of delivering good systems. The small, but significant difference lay in their devotion to their customers. Here, in the tight margins, lay the key to success.

In sales, no prizes are awarded for second or third place. There can be only one victor, and it was said that: «It's better to be one percent better than the competition in everything, than to be 100 percent better in one thing».[52] The desired position was to be «unique», and this meant in most cases having a good service concept and knowledge of the customer, and a high degree of influence on the market. In the company's growth spiral, human factors were more important than technical.

Personnel welfare was touted as «the most critical internal company issue».[53] In reality this meant policy for salaries, but that was not all. It also addressed company culture, keeping people motivated and encouraging extra effort. Management wanted freedom to select motivational measures that would spur employees to take on additional tasks and go the extra mile.[54] This often meant taking care of employees' families. Many albatrosses were young and had small children.[55] In the late 1980s the average age was 32. Finding day care in Kongsberg was not easy, so they determined to build their own day care centre. The Albatross company day care facility opened in the autumn of 1986.[56] This was a measure that allowed them to compete on the employment market. The offer of day care was seen as necessary if they were to attract the best people and at the same time create stronger bonds between employees and employer. According to the head of HR the day care centre gave employees one less worry, thereby increasing productivity.[57]

The company was especially interested in «getting new mothers back to work», offering a spot in day care in combination with the option of part-time work. This was before the time of paternity leave. In keeping with the flat organisational structure, day care spots were awarded on the basis of seniority and drawing lots. Applicants were treated equally, regardless of titles on business cards. The Norwegian daily Aftenposten called Albatross «the country's most kid-friendly company,» with its 50 day care spots divided among 150 employees.[58]

Workloads could be heavy and days could be long, and this could in turn be a burden for the families. Part of personnel welfare was sending flowers to the wives when their husbands were out on long business trips, or involved in projects with extensive periods of overtime. But flowers were not always highest on everyone's wish list. One employee recalls an episode where a representative from management showed up with flowers for the wife of one of the men putting in long overtime hours, and was told to go get her husband and bring him home instead.[59] It was not without reason that Albatross was sometimes referred to as «the divorce factory.»

Another employee recalled being stationed in Asia for an extended period with his wife at home when management decided that he needed new com-

Albatross's Christmas card from 1979. On this year Albatross management bought track suits for all employees. This provoked many in the KV system, and the goal of differentiating themselves and appearing as an independent group was reached with good measure. The case became the subject of much discussion on the streets of Kongsberg. Front row from left: Mabel Odden, Tove Britt Haugen, Mike Broadbridge, Vidar Djønne, Eva Beach, Paul Basset, Odd Inge Tangen, Stein Evje, Bob Campbell, Randi Wetterstad. Second row: Sverre Corneliussen, Ole Einar Garthus, Anne Lofthus. Third row: Jens Gjærevoll, Olav Sandbakk, Inger Marit Østerbø, Johan Rusaanes, unkown, Roald Holstad, Kristin Tingvall, Terje Hansen, Britt Groven, Eldar Mathisen, Hiton Cowie, Terje Løkling, Thor Skoland, Bjørn Haugen, Finn Søberg. Back row: Bjørn Trosthoel, Bjørn Barth Jacobsen, Vidar Guterud, Jan Roger Hellerud and Olav Ropstad.

pany stationary. This was clearly too important to send by mail and had to be delivered by courier. And what better solution than to send his wife as courier, especially when she could stay a few extra days?[60]

Despite some complaints, this aspect of the Albatross culture was tolerated by KV management.[61] When Albatross wanted to raise salaries and implement a more flexible and incentive-based wage system, corporate management had a harder time winning acceptance from the board.[62] The subject would come up repeatedly at board meetings. Albatross would be criticised for driving costs up in KV, while they themselves felt that they were lagging behind the other business units. There was a clear difference of opinion on the matter. Determining who was right depended on the way the numbers were viewed. On base pay, Albatross was not much different to KV. All the same, certain albatrosses earned relatively high wages. Service personnel could be required to spend

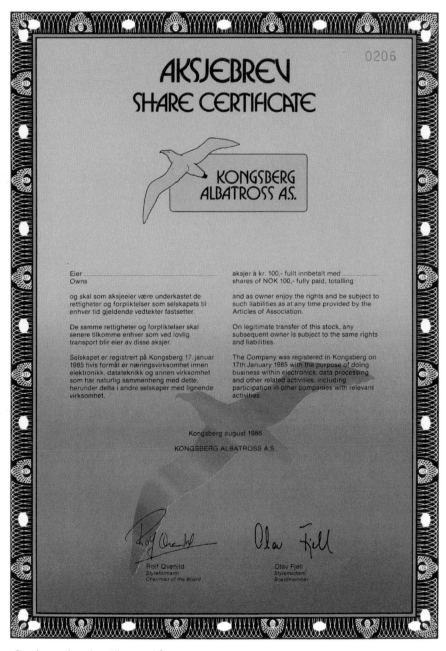

Certificate of stock in Albatross AS.

several weeks in a row on ships at sea, resulting in considerable overtime and other compensation. At Albatross, therefore, it was not top management who earned the most, but rather the service engineers.[63]

THE ALBATROSS DIVISION

Around Christmas of 1983, the KV board voted to dissolve the Maritime division and place the various units directly under corporate management as independent entities.[64] The changes took effect from the turn of the year. With that, Albatross became its own division, but it was still unclear whether management would grant the division the independence they sought.

In February 1984, Rolf-Erik Rolfsen, Executive Vice President in KV and a board member at Albatross, shared his thoughts with the board. He went straight to the point in an internal memo, posing the big question: «Albatross – quo vadis» – where are you going?[65] One could read into the question that KV management had already given up trying to run Albatross. In any case, Rolfsen had opened the door to reorganisation of the new division as an independent company.

There was considerable distance between Albatross management's visions and wishes for the future, and those of KV's board members. But Albatross management were not the only ones who were frustrated. Irritation was palpable among KV's top management as well. This frustration came to the fore in a 1984 memo with the telling title, «Albatross – problem or possibility?»

> Our recent experiences with Albatross can be seen as a symptom of our not leading, but being led. Albatross sets the pace and the agenda, and they are constantly on the offensive. Even if we should claim that they are «impossible to deal with,» we must conclude that we do not have full control of the situation. We have not resolved issues convincingly, nor have we taken the lead or shown the way forward.[66]

The Albatross culture was described as «vibrant, competent, and driven by a will to win». Questions were also being raised as to whether KV management had done a good enough job promoting entrepreneurship and nurturing successful ventures like Albatross.[67] KV management was clearly growing weary of the rebels of Albatross, but they were also willing to go far in search of a solution. The answer was a «simulated company model», where Albatross would not only have their own board, but would be allowed to manage their finances much as a limited company would.[68]

The proposal was put before the board on the 16th of May 1984. In addition to granting Albatross the freedom to regulate salaries and other initiatives on their own, the board also gave the green light for establishing a work group made up of representatives from the employees and management. The employees were also given representation on the board.[69] Albatross had delivered its first system on 17 May, just seven years earlier. Now they could celebrate Norway's Constitution Day content in the knowledge that they had the framework for greater freedom from the weapons factory. This was a critical step along the way towards becoming an independent entity. The next step would follow soon after.

When KV's next in command posed the question of the future of Albatross, he had clearly indicated that they would remain a division through 1985, after which alternatives could be considered.[70] With the new privileges granted by the board in May, it was only a question of when and how. With personnel welfare taken care of, it was time to address organisational matters.

ALBATROSS AS

Early in 1984, Albatross management had expressed a desire to «create an independent entity» and had presented a new company development concept to the board. The proposal entailed not only detaching the existing unit from the KV corporation, but also reorganising activities into new business areas. The first move would be to cull a small department from Albatross and merge it into the main structure of Norcontrol, forming a new navigation unit. The remainder of the enterprise would continue on as Albatross – Control Systems. In time the establishment of a new unit could be considered: Albatross – Instrumentation.[71] These units would be established as independent companies with employees taking shares. This development concept failed to win the board's support. They were, however, positive toward the proposal to combine parts of Albatross and Norcontrol to create a robust environment for offshore positioning.[72]

When Albatross management's proposal was considered by the board in May 1984, the plan had grown and was seen in connection with a total restructuring of the offshore business, developing Albatross in several stages.[73] The first stage would be to establish a navigation unit tied to the Albatross division. The offshore market tended toward consolidation of business segments, and management could see new market opportunities in exploiting Albatross's strong marketing apparatus to sell technologies in addition to DP systems.[74]

Establishing a new navigation unit was not the ultimate goal for Albatross management, though. When the unit was in place, Albatross was to be converted to a private limited company. And the vision did not stop there. Management also proposed a new company to be called 'Norway offshore electronics A/S'. It would encompass, in addition to Albatross, Simrad Subsea and Bird Technology.[75] In addition to dynamic positioning, the new company was to offer integrated navigation, position mooring, subsea positioning and underwater vehicles. The proposal was likely more of a vision than a concrete plan to be realised in the near future. The main idea was to include KV's navigation department. Independence as a listed company was the next order of business. The plan was actually not that far fetched, as the board did request that Albatross develop closer cooperation with Simrad and Bird.[76]

With summer vacation over, another matter rose to the top of the agenda. KV had developed a strategic plan for 1985–1989 where the various units were evaluated and categorised. Albatross was placed in the category «independent enterprises». These were the units deemed non-essential to KV's core business. The goal was to develop these businesses as shareholding companies using KV technology and competence in combination with external capital. This would reduce the capital burden on KV, while providing KV with additional income in the form of dividends.[77] In keeping with this strategy KV planned to divest a substantial portion of Albatross in the course of 1985.[78] In September of 1984 the corporate board approved the process to set up Albatross as a wholly KV-owned, listed subsidiary. This was to be the first step toward divestment.[79]

Kongsberg Albatross AS was formally established on 1 January 1985. The board, chaired by KV director Rolf Qvenild, included two representatives elected by the employees: Steinar Gregersen and Knut Lagim. The new company was to «market, develop and deliver offshore electronics and associated goods and services for use on offshore vessels and other floating structures».[80] The goal gave shape to an ambition of expanding into new territory. Albatross had become an independent enterprise, but the difference between existing as a separate division and a wholly owned KV subsidiary was perhaps not so great in practice. The formation of a new company nonetheless presented new opportunities and challenges.[81] As far as the surrounding world was concerned, the changes were minor. The new name, and the use of the KV and Albatross logos together, made the connection to KV clear. The umbilical cord was still clearly intact.[82]

A NEW BEAT

The new stock company had been formed on a solid foundation. The enterprise counted 150 employees and turnover had grown to NOK 162 million. The bottom line had also shown a positive development over the years, improving from NOK 3 to 14 million since 1980.[83] In 1985 the focus was on consolidating position in established markets and making inroads in new geographical areas.

The new form of company gave Albatross management significantly greater control over internal affairs. It didn't take long after their release before new personnel welfare policies were in place. At one of the first board meetings in the new company a bonus plan for all employees was adopted, encompassing 25 percent of profits exceeding the budgeted result. A sales commission of between 10 and 20 percent of base salary was also approved. The company was wholly owned by KV, but provisions were made for the employees to buy shares at reduced rates. With the bonus plans, it could have cost the company considerable money if the employees were also given the opportunity to buy reduced-price stock. For that reason the offer of shares was put on hold as long as the bonus plans were in effect.[84]

On the first of July 1985 the ship and simulator sections of Norcontrol were renamed Norcontrol Automation and Norcontrol Simulation respectively, and established as wholly owned subsidiaries of Albatross. Their purpose was to produce information and automation systems for ships, and sell navigation and engine room simulators to maritime schools.[85] With this Albatross achieved competency that allowed the company to expand its operations to cover a broader spectrum of automation systems for specialised vessels and rigs. With the addition of the two Horten-based companies, Albatross had become its own concern, with two subsidiaries and ownership in three other companies, including the electronics firm Bird Technology in Oslo.[86]

Both the APM3000 and the ADP100 were big successes. This gave rise to optimism, but also to concern for development activities.[87] Albatross had no dedicated development department. Development and delivery were grouped into one unit. This tight bond between development and delivery was good when tailor-made solutions were required, but when business picked up, deliveries got highest priority, and long-term development took a back seat. To counter this, the two units were separated into one technical, and one development department.

There was also talk of separating part of the company's development activities. The background for this was the interest that several units in KV were beginning to show for the SBC1000. In light of this there was discussion as to whether development of the computer should take place inside the company, or be organised in an independent entity with Albatross as owner. Parallel to this Albatross founded the industrial growth centre Konvekst together with KV and SysScan.[88] The centre was to serve as a resource that could offer support and competence to entrepreneurs who looking to form their own companies with ties to KV – not unlike what Albatross themselves had done. Albatross management envisioned that establishing a new company to carry on work with core Albatross technology would be a suitable task for the centre.[89] No concrete results came of these plans, however. Rather, computer development continued within Albatross.[90]

THE BIG PARTY

As the end of 1985 drew near, there was little evidence that Gulhaugen's «dooms-day prophecies» from two years earlier would be fulfilled, despite a slight economic downturn in 1984.[91] Stagnation was short-lived. In 1985 indicators were pointing up once more, and the company experienced sharp growth. Activity levels were described as «unusually high».[92] Projected year-end delivery levels were reached only halfway through the year. Its first year as a corporation was to be a successful one for Albatross. Orders were up by 20 percent, while revenues shot up from NOK 162 million to 234 million, close to a 40 percent increase. Profits more than doubled, from NOK 11.2 million to 22.9 million. The number of employees was also increasing, with 307 on the payroll, an increase of 167 from the previous year. 137 of these had come from Norcontrol, but the expansion was significant nonetheless.[93]

There were grounds for optimism on the technology side as well, with new systems selling well. In early autumn of 1985 the order situation was described as «very satisfactory».[94] With a strong bottom line and well-filled order books, prospects were bright as Albatross prepared for a gala ten-year anniversary celebration at the end of November. The company had over the course of these ten years grown from a small project in KV with an uncertain future and plenty of gumption, to an independent company with a dynamic culture and a skilled, hard-working staff, a strong financial situation and a solid technological base. With its dominance of global markets for DP systems, it was fair to say that Albatross was well positioned, and celebration was in order.

On 22 November 1985 it had been exactly 10 years since the signing of the *Seaway Swan* contract, and Albatross did not plan on letting this occasion pass unnoticed. At the end of the workday that Friday, a chartered train with

For the anniversary celebration on 22 November 1985, tables were set with a special-edition Figgjo porcelain dining set featuring the evening's menu. The borders were decorated with images of vessels from Albatross's past, as well as other historical images, like the KV logo from 1814, and Kongsberg Sølvverk's seal from 1624. Photo: Mediafoto.

Albatross banners on the sides awaited festive employees at Kongsberg station. Two hundred dressed up and jovial revellers were whisked off to Oslo and the ballroom of the Hotel Scandinavia. Tables were ornately decorated for the occasion, with specially ordered Figgjo porcelain printed with the evening's menu and a large, soaring Albatross. Around the edges were images of vessels in Albatross's history along with other features, including the KV logo from 1814 and the seal of the Kongsberg silver mines from 1624. On such a momentous occasion, history was being used for all it was worth.

During the course of the evening guests were treated with excellent service and entertained by a cabaret specially composed for the ten-year anniversary. No expense was spared.[95] The famous balladeer Trygve Hoff was engaged to write the manuscript, while employees took the various roles. There was no shortage of material for the show; the partygoers had experienced plenty over the course of the past ten years.

The evening was an occasion to look back, but also to look to the future. Many took the opportunity to raise a glass and address their peers. One of these was the KV director and chairman of the Albatross board. Rolf Qvenild chose to open with a slightly modified passage from Kahlil Gibran's *The Prophet*:

> KV may house the bodies, but not the souls of Albatross. For your souls dwell in the house of tomorrow which KV may not visit – not even in its dreams.
>
> KV may attempt to imitate you, but seek not to make an Albatross like KV. For life goes not backward, nor tarries with yesterday.
>
> KV is the bow from which Albatross as a living arrow is sent forth. The archer sees the mark upon the path of the infinite, and he draws the bow with his strength that the arrow may go swift and far.
>
> Albatrosses – let your sending from the archer's hand be for gladness, for even as he loves the arrow that flies, so does he love the bow that is stable.[96]

The arrow had been in the making for ten years. Now the bow was drawn. After looking back with satisfaction on a decade of accomplishments, Qvenild announced that he had proposed to the KV board that the weapons manufacturer release some of their Albatross holdings and bring in the employees and others as part owners. At the same time he promised that KV would always be a stakeholder in Albatross, and that the «family business» would be run in everyone's best interests.

When Qvenild introduced his *Prophet* paraphrase, he referred to Gulhaugen's earlier reading of the original text. Perhaps he also remembered the Albatross director's prophesy of dark times to come only a few years before. The first half of the 1980s had been marked by consolidation, growth, and independence. What would happen, then, when the arrow flew from the bow?

8

ANOTHER LEG TO STAND ON

THE ANNIVERSARY PARTY in autumn 1985 celebrated ten years of tremendous growth and progress. Less than a week after the event, Kongsberg Våpenfabrikk (KV) approved Qvenild's suggestion to reduce KV's ownership stake and grant employees shares in Albatross. The strategy implied employee ownership of five percent and a listing on the Oslo stock exchange.[1] This decision could be seen as the second step to Albatross becoming fully autonomous following its formation as a limited company. Seen from another perspective, it was clear that KV needed an injection of fresh capital.

The company's future ten-year scenario looked bright. DP systems were in demand and sold well and the number of installations increased each year – just like the profits. Game-changing technology was also being developed. No doubt, the inebriated, euphoric feeling invoked by the anniversary celebrations, the approval of shareholder positions, and a bright business horizon, had taken grip. However, a hangover was on its way, approaching quickly and fiercely.

THE HANGOVER

KV had invested heavily in major projects for several years. Unfortunately, these developments never became profit-making products but were rather a colossal financial drain. The company was now throwing good money after bad; exemplified by the jet motor and gas turbine projects. A large part of this business was debt financed and as the debt grew, it became increasingly difficult to repay. In 1985 the annual interest payment was NOK 160 million.[2] Only the defence contracts and oil-related business showed a plus.[3] The management therefore wished to realise asset gain through the partial sale of its offshore portfolio.

Albatross was viewed to be the business unit where reducing ownership control could be easily organised and financially attractive. The company had a great reputation and positive business growth. Business was booming. Qvenild envisioned a listing on the stock exchange during 1986 and KV selling between 60–70 percent of the company. He expected the sale to generate between NOK 120–200 million and profits of NOK 90–170 million.[4] The prospectus related to the sale of shares was ready in the summer of 1986.[5] But in the meantime, due to considerable change in market environments, the Board had serious doubts as to achieving satisfactory compensation for the true value of the company.[6] What had happened?

When Albatross signed its first contract in 1975 oil prices were at USD 10 per barrel. And though oil continued to rise for five years peaking at USD 36 per barrel, a market slump lowered prices to USD 27 per barrel in 1985. The downward spiral continued and oil prices plummeted to USD 14 per barrel in 1986.[7] This development was extremely unfortunate for a company with products targeted specifically for the oil industry.

The fall in the price of oil reduced the exploration activities of the oil companies, which in turn, cut back their orders from equipment and service sub-suppliers. Weak market demand pushed day rates even lower, which eventually halted a number of offshore activities, including the industry's newbuild programmes. Without new vessels entering the market, Albatross saw a dramatic decline in the installation of DP systems, its main income. Totally dependent on the offshore industry and exposed to the crashing oil price, Albatross witnessed a dramatic decline in its orders.[8]

As a first counterattack to increase volume and activity, Albatross intensified its aftersales efforts and broadened its range of products and functions. The creation of two wholly owned subsidiaries in the UK was part of the push to strengthen sales activities. Kongsberg Offshore Albatross Services Ltd in Aberdeen would drive service and after sales, and Kongsberg Albatross UK Ltd. in Maidenhead, London, would handle sales and marketing in the UK and the rest of Western Europe. The two companies employed a total of 18 people. Additionally, Albatross had taken over Kongsberg France looking to leverage opportunities in the French market through this branch office.[9]

Short-term strategy was set; the company would go the extra mile in every sales opportunity and penetrate new markets. Management wished to offset its weakened offshore business with future sales to the cruise, defence and process control industries.[10] Nevertheless, drastic consolidation measures had to be taken. The first subsidiary to be axed was Norcontrol Automation. The

In the spring of 1986, Albatross moved in to new and modern offices at Industritunet in Dyrmyrgata on the north side of Kongsberg. The new building, with its close to 270 inhabitants, was a joint project with the IT company Sysscan. Photo from the Simrad Albatross product catalogue, 1990.

company had been struggling for a long period and was described as a «disappointment».[11] 1985 year-end accounts showed a loss of NOK 1 million, of which tripled during the first quarter of 1986. The situation worsened during the next quarter.[12] Norcontrol Automation was a money drainer and Albatross, looking to pull out, sold the company later that autumn to Fønix Industries for NOK 1 million. The sale was a huge burden on the company's weakened financials. At year-end, Albatross posted a combined loss of NOK 17 million, driven by write-downs in capital stock and loans, and losses related to the sale of shares and other expenditures.[13]

Another post, though contributing to the weak results, had a positive impact. Cramped workspace in the old ski factory forced Albatross to use five different facilities around the city of Kongsberg and, needless to say, internal communication was suffering. In the spring of 1986 Albatross gathered all its employees under one roof, to a new building on Dyrmyr gata, located in city's north side Industritunet.[14] Despite a hike in office rent, the move significantly improved work conditions for the company's 180 employees, of which 134 were engineers and civil engineers.[15]

The new building, a joint project with SysScan – a data company springing out from KV, had office space from some 270 people. Kari Blegen, the secretary for Norway's Minister of Industry, officially opened the building on September 30, 1986.[16] Relocating to a new modern location was good reason to celebrate, otherwise there was little to get excited about on the business front.

KV IN CRISIS

The declining price of oil wasn't the only negative factor affecting Albatross. Problems compounded further as KV began to face its own financial challenges. Up to 1985, the mother company's difficult financial situation did not interfere with its activities. When Albatross ran into difficulty, KV, unfortunately, was not in the position to ride out the storm. They needed fresh capital and an owner with financial strength. Instead, KV transferred NOK 17 million of Albatross assets to its own account. Only NOK 1.9 million of the profits were channelled back into the business.[17]

While aiming to reduce its ownership stake in Albatross, KV also planned to raise fresh equity through a new share offering. In the summer of 1986, the management decided that KV – following the sale of shares and new share subscription – would, at 54 percent, control the majority interest of Albatross.[18] However, it wasn't only the price of oil that was falling; the stock market was struggling as well. The banking boom often referred to as the 'yuppie era' was ebbing out. And it had become difficult to make a good return on the sale of private company stock. The board of Albatross began to seek other alternatives, including a possible merger with Simrad Subsea.[19]

The management at Albatross had already assessed the potential gains through collaboration with its long-term business partner, Simrad Subsea from Horten, Norway. This was primarily a supplier-customer relationship, with Simrad Subsea being a main supplier of position reference sensors. However, it was decided that rather than merge, the companies would form a tighter alliance, focusing on specific markets and projects in selected business areas.[20] The merger plans were thus put on ice.[21]

The severity of Albatross's economic situation during the autumn of 1986 forced the company to change course to survive. Expenditures and the number of staff were excessive considering the shortfall of incoming business and revenue. Expenses had to be cut and during this period 30 people were let go.

In January 1987, Albatross launched its turnaround strategy, Target 90.[22] In short, the process focused on cost saving initiatives and the development of new investment areas to compensate the failing DP market. In 1987, every 'stone was turned' to cut NOK 20 million.[23] This meant, among other things, the removal of several fringe benefits and a freeze on annual salary increases. Not accustomed to squeezing the most out of every penny, Albatross had tightened the screws sharply.[24] During an interview with the Norwegian business monthly, Økonomisk Rapport, director Nils Willy Gulhaugen admitted that financial control in Albatross was too slack during the good times. He described the

Regjeringen foreslår KV-akkord

BRIT MYHRVOLD
HARALD FURRE

Regjeringen vil i dagens regjeringskonferanse gå inn for akkord for Kongsberg Våpenfabrikk. Akkorden vil koste Staten omkring 850 millioner kroner. Etter hva Aftenposten erfarer vil man gå inn for en tvungen akkord, da man regner med at en frivillig akkord ikke vil bli akseptert av de mange kreditorene. KVs flymotordivisjon vil trolig bli solgt til en gruppe av norske bedrifter.

handler om å gå inn i Kongsberg Våpenfabrikks flymotordivisjon vil trolig torsdag bekrefte at den fortsatt er interessert. Men en endelig avklaring vil neppe foreligge før ut i juni, får Aftenposten opplyst. Man diskuterer en eiersammensetning hvor de tre norske selskapene eventuelt skal ha 50—70 prosent av eierinteressene. Det ei meningen at KV selv skal ha 30 prosent, mens Pratt & Whitney eventuelt kan komme inn med 10—15 prosent.

Den norske gruppen som vurderer å gå inn i flymotordivisjonen består av Ludvig G. Braathens Rederi, Aker Norcem og Helikopter Service. Adm. direktør Gerhard

Kongsberg Våpenfabrikk had long been struggling with losses. Late in the autumn of 1986 it became clear that the company could no longer service its debt. The government was not willing to inject capital to float the company, and proposed an abandonment of rights in the spring of 1987. This signalled the end of 173-years of industrial history. Facsimile from *Aftenposten* 21 May 1987.

situation as follows: «Before it was 'laissez-faire' but now there is total control on all spending.»[25]

In addition to proactive cost-saving initiatives, management had an aggressive strategy to offset the current crisis. Albatross's short-term results were completely dependent on its offshore activities. Faced with very poor prospects in this market segment and a clear stagnation in market demand and products, Albatross decided, in addition to continued marketing and high level product development, to launch two new business areas: Cruise and Navy.[26]

The marketing department wanted a more aggressive crisis strategy than just savings and cutting costs. They wanted to expand out of the crisis by intensifying sales activities. They received no support, which fuelled the resignation of the marketing director, Svein Thorsen, who, together with key personnel from the sales and other departments, founded a new sales company called Alba International.[27] Albatross lost skilled and experienced sales executives and co-workers.[28] However, the sales department, despite the lack of business, proved to be robust enough. The exodus of staff had little effect. [29]

If Albatross had problems, they were nothing compared to the mother company. By late autumn 1986, it became clear that Kongsberg Våpenfabrikk could not service its debts, which were now larger than the value of the company. In reality, KV was bankrupt.

The conservative government was unwilling to provide fresh share capital to save the state-owned enterprise. On the November 21, the Ministry of Industry established a new board with Karl Glad as Chairman. In January 1987, the board agreed to sell all company assets except the defence activities. With that, the big question about how many Albatross shares should be sold became irrelevant. Now, everything was to be sold.[30]

ALBATROSS FOR SALE

A lot had happened in just one short year since Qvenild envisioned selling 60 to 70 percent of Albatross for some NOK 120 to 200 million. At that time, the market pointed upwards and Albatross was earning good money. But when KV prepared its financial report for 1986, the bottom line was in the red for the very first time. Within the course of the year, the company's positive 1985 profits and group contributions of NOK 1.9 million and 17 million, respectively, had fallen to minus NOK 17 million with zero group contribution. However, in contrast to the company's annual financial results, DP activities were better than expected.

Albatross posted a positive result of NOK 27 million for the year before extraordinary items. The sale of Norcontrol Automation and Bird Technology stood for the bulk the company's negative results.[31]

Even though the business was profitable, the future order book posed some challenges.[32] The number of orders fell from 20 in 1985 to 11 in 1986. Fortunately, some of these orders were quite large and even though sales were just one-third that of the previous year, Albatross sustained its business, posting only a five percent revenue loss in 1986. The order book didn't generate any optimism, though. The start of 1987 wasn't good, and the reserve of contracts began to diminish.[33]

Albatross no longer resembled the money machine that it once was. The sale of shares would be far less lucrative than previously estimated by the KV director. At the onset of 1987, Albatross started the process of selling its shares. Though several companies were contacted, interest was minimal. Some were only interested in Norcontrol Simulation.[34] Employees in KV's automotive division had purchased their workplace and subsequently established Kongsberg

Automotive.[35]A couple of entities within Albatross thought about doing the same, but never came so far as to make an offer.[36]

With only minimal market interest in the shares, and only those belonging to Norcontrol Simulation, KV chose to sell the two companies separately. Simrad Subsea was the only company to bid for Albatross shares. And on 29 April 1987, a contract was signed between Simrad Subsea, Kongsberg Våpenfabrikk and Kongsberg Albatross and its employees. Simrad Subsea purchased Albatross's DP activities and trademark for NOK 20 million and used a further NOK 9 million to buy out minority shareholders.[37] The significantly higher price paid for employee shares was due to an earlier price guarantee given by KV. All in all, Simrad paid NOK 29.4 million for Albatross. Seen against the backdrop of good company results a couple of years back, the purchase price was a steal, but at that time, in the spring of 1987, it was all the market would give. As of 30 April 1987, Simrad Subsea owned Albatross.[38]

A lot happened during the acquisition period, not only in the company but also in the forefront of technology.

ANOTHER LEG TO STAND ON

The oil price decline and subsequent market fall was an important lesson for Albatross. Being a world champion with a market-leading position within dynamic positioning means little if there is no prize to gain. Steps needed to be taken to hedge the company against vulnerable, single market swings. Albatross needed more legs to stand on. And like the development of the first DP system, the research environment of Trondheim stepped in with some new impulses.

The chief architect behind what would become Albatross's new leg was Steinar Sælid. As mentioned previously, he was instrumental in the development of the control and Kalman filter algorithms for the first Albatross DP system. Prior to that, he had completed a doctorate in process control, and his next important contribution to Albatross's core technology would stem from this discipline.[39]

To understand the beginnings of this development it is necessary to step back a few years in time. In the early 1980s, Sælid collaborated with colleagues from the Department of Engineering Cybernetics in a project to develop a system able to simulate the most important Distributed Control Systems, DCS.[40] Though the goal was to develop an instructional simulator, Sælid began to toy with the idea of developing a Norwegian DCS.[41]

At this time, one of the main DCS suppliers was Honeywell, formerly a well-known competitor in the DP market, alongside Foxboro and Siemens.

In Sælid's view, Albatross was the perfect platform to realise his ideas. Not only did the company operate in a market that needed a control system, it had all the expertise in development, marketing and sales to bring his ideas into reality. During the early 1980s Albatross earned good money and was willing to invest in project development. Involved in the first DP project, Sælid had a number of good contacts inside Albatross, several of whom were close friends from their student days at the Department of Engineering Cybernetics. One of these was Terje Løkling, the leader of software development who, in 1975, completed his graduate thesis on the Dynpos project.[42] Sælid rang him to discuss the idea of working together again and, in 1983, Løkling left NTH to join Albatross.[43]

Meanwhile, the offshore market was experiencing an increasing demand for systems able to manage onboard processes other than just positioning. As operational complexity continued to increase, so did the number of onboard systems to control specific assignments. This created a demand for a central management system designed to integrate a variety of specialised onboard systems through a common interface. Faced with these challenges, offshore operators and shipowners began to look for suppliers with a wider range of technology to reduce the number of suppliers of electronic equipment on each vessel. This development favoured fewer but larger suppliers with comprehensive system expertise.

This was both a threat and an opportunity for Albatross. Supplying just one of several onboard systems was no longer adequate. The company had to deliver ship automation systems in order to maintain their position as a market-leading DP supplier. When clients began to demand more comprehensive technology packages, it became obvious that they favoured suppliers offering a complete automation system. Supplying a total package was far more expensive than a DP system, but allowed for bundling a number of systems from the same supplier. It was not given that Albatross's position as a market-leading DP supplier would weigh heavily in a competitive tender. But on the other hand, its position in the DP market was pivotal to securing new vessel automation contracts.

Albatross management feared that a flat DP market would seriously impair the company's market position.[44] They realised that the best way to meet this challenge was to extend their product reach and become a «total supplier of comprehensive electronic instrumentation and control systems for ships and rigs.»[45] In March 1983, Gulhaugen pointed to integrated systems as the future growth business area.[46]

Once positioned in Kongsberg, Sælid wanted to investigate the feasibility of developing an automation system and quickly initiated a pilot project supported by past knowledge gained in Trondheim, and current Kongsberg technology. What happened wasn't that different from when Albatross developed its first DP system, but it wasn't clear that Albatross should develop this system on its own. Fearing that system development was too large, risky and financially demanding for the company, the sales and marketing divisions preferred to acquire a control system already on the market. This was strongly opposed by a very competent engineering department who wished to develop a system within the company. The discussion reflected the underlying, basic conceptions of business development as market or technology-driven.[47]

The conclusion was swift. This was worth pursuing. Sælid received financing and free hands to develop the project. Faced by limited spare office capacity at Albatross, he had a small team, but was allowed to secure additional resources and reinforced his team with past academic acquaintances from Trondheim, including Nils Albert Jennsen, an earlier colleague from the first DP project. All in all, it was enough to kick off the development project in 1983.

AIM – ALBATROSS INTEGRATED MULTIFUNCTION SYSTEM

The research project gave Sælid and his team a solid understanding about control systems on the market. These were neither flexible nor user friendly. In typical Albatross fashion, where user friendliness was all-important, the team chose to base its system on object-oriented technology, thus making it easy to develop and maintain. The aim was to develop a system-architecture with «modularity, flexibility and extensibility».[48] It had to be possible to implement different levels of redundancy and operational safety, with each system set up and documented swiftly and without error. This required the user interface to be so simple that an operator could configure the graphics by dragging predefined function blocks onto the display, giving them values and then connecting everything together into a system flowchart. Additionally, the system should also offer high-level control blocks to represent, for example, pumps, valves or motor controllers. Even a prototype touchscreen was created during the development phase, though the realisation of such a high-tech user interface would take a couple of decades.[49]

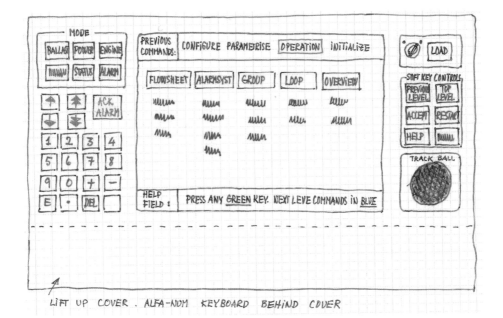

LIFT UP COVER. ALFA-NUM KEYBOARD BEHIND COVER

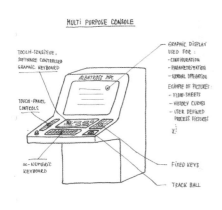

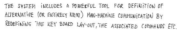

The new control technology was to be applied to all process control systems. This gave rise to the need for a multi-functional console that could be configured to any need. The sketches are Steinar Sælid's first versions from 1982. The console would feature a large colour monitor and a handful of standard buttons, with a user-friendly, programmable touch-screen (middle). The eventual solution was a standard colour monitor with a set of controls that corresponded to the menu on the main screen (right).

AIM 1000 FOR PROCESS CONTROL INDUSTRY **AIM 1000 FOR PROCESS CONTROL INDUSTRY**

AIM 1000 FOR LARGE AND SMALL PROCESSES
AIM 1000 uses the same modules for both large and small systems. A large system just has more modules. A small system can therefore be gradually expanded into a large system by buying more modules as the need arises.

ONE OR MORE SEGMENTS
AIM 1000 can be configured such that all process and operator stations are directly connected to the same data net. With very large systems, or for the purpose of data security, AIM 1000 can be divided up into separate segments where each segment handles one part of the process.
Communication between the stations connected to the different segments takes place via net bridges and a supervisory data net.
The data nets can either be single or double. With a double net the system automatically switches over to the alternative net if one of them fails.

FLEXIBILITY AND EASE OF USE
AIM 1000 is designed for flexibility and ease of use. The user can configure his preferred system by drawing a system flowchart on a screen. Changes to the system can be made in the same way. At an ordinary operator console the user can delete, change or add functions and I/O channels by means of the system's powerful on-line editor.

DISTRIBUTED DATA BASE
In AIM 1000, all data concerning a specific function is stored in the process station where that function is realized. Such data include parameters, variables, alarm data, graphic data, trend data, etc. This implies:
• That duplication of data is avoided.
• The operator stations are independent of the process because they do not store process data. Picture elements and alarm lists are examples of data types whose storage is distributed among the process stations and which are sent to the requesting operator station when it calls up a particular picture or alarm list.

ONE SYSTEM — MANY FUNCTIONS
Many systems are designed specifically for analogue control, servo control and monitoring, or for logic operations and sequencing (Programmable Logic Systems — PLS). AIM 1000 is designed to efficiently perform all such tasks in one and the same system. AIM 1000 can handle:
• Data acquisition, monitoring and traditional PID control.
• Adaptive control and complex multi-variable control.
• Digital control, interlocking functions, and supervisory functions.
• Complex batch control and composition management functions where digital and analogue modules are connected in complex sequences.
• The system is especially suited for the implementation of simulation functions such that the consequences of intervention in the process can be tested before they are performed.

AIM introduced several new technologies. At the time, existing systems used so-called 'token ring' communication between various stations. A 'token' was comparable to a relay baton. Whoever held the baton, was entitled to transmit data while the others waited for their turn. When data transmission was completed, the baton was passed on. The problem was that the baton could be dropped, and then had to be picked up again. This caused confusion in data transference. Ethernet had no such weaknesses, and was cheaper to install. AIM also possessed a unique online configuration system that enabled expansion and modification of the control system during normal operations. This was made possible by the system's distributed and modular design. The image shows a principle design scheme of the system, and its most important selling points, as they appeared in the AIM1000 brochure from 1987.

Scalability and modularisation was to be the basic principle for hardware, and regardless of the system's size, the same modules were to be used. The main difference between a small or large system was the number of modules, of which could be further expanded by adding new units as needed.[50] The age of large central computers was past, and distributed systems, consisting of several interconnected single board computers, had become the standard.

A decision to use the newly developed SBC1000 was made. One of its features was the use of two Ethernet ports for communicating. Choosing Ethernet was something new to automation systems, the decision was highly controversial and the object of considerable scepticism. The key advantage was its ability to connect multiple devices via a shared network instead of connecting each peripheral device to a central computer through dedicated cables. The downside was that Ethernet was new with no wide-scale industrial use. It was commonly accepted that Ethernet could not be used in process control applications since its protocol could not guarantee signals reaching the correct system component in correct order. In order to convince clients otherwise, Albatross presented its own calculations showing that the probability of communication failure due to Ethernet was less than the system units being struck by lightning. Not all were convinced, but in due time even competitors agreed. Today, Ethernet has become an industry standard.[51]

In 1984, the development team developed a concept for a distributed process control system. The system was called the Albatross PCDA-system (Process Control and Data Acquisition), and was highly innovative in several ways. Not only was the use of Ethernet new to existing PCDA systems, the implementation of functions commonly found in advanced CAD (computer aided design) systems was novel as well. These features significantly reduced the time needed to design, configure and document new systems.[52]

Project development progressed well, and in 1985 the project team presented a functional prototype. Looking to take the project to the next level and become a commercial product, Albatross engaged additional staff and significantly stepped up its activities. All possibilities were analysed. Norcontrol Automation, a subsidiary of Albatross at this time, had its own automation system. Would it make sense to implement Albatross technology into this system or develop something totally new? Or should Albatross merge KV's petroleum division's SCADA system (Supervisory Control and Data Acquisition) into a common system?[53] After calculating overall costs, these plans were shelved, mainly due to astronomical costs.[54] The solution, therefore, was to continue with the new project and to develop it into a proprietary system to be sold as a total system solution for rigs and ships, a so-called Vessel Management System.[55] The new system was named Albatross Integrated Multifunction System, later shortened to AIM.

The decision to develop their own system became easier after Albatross suffered bitter losses on two major tenders in England to competitor GEC. Honeywell had lost its pole position, but it was becoming increasingly more difficult to outperform GEC.[56] There were several reasons why Albatross lost these contracts. First, GEC had a strong position in its domestic market – the Brits preferred to buy from a British company. Secondly, GEC, unlike Albatross, could provide the total equipment package.[57] The Kalman filter had been a strong competitive advantage when Albatross achieved market leadership, but the systems to which it was applied were highly specialised, unsuitable to handle the tasks increasingly demanded by offshore operators. These systems were not designed to regulate large and complex processes. Perhaps it was time to expand the range of products?

In good Albatross spirit, one didn't wait to 'sell the skin before the bear was shot'.[58] And despite the project being still at blueprint level, Sælid, Løkling and a sales executive travelled to The Netherlands to promote the system. AIM was mainly a composition of ideas and sketches, thus the ability to preform and ad-lib with 'real-time chalkboard design' were important talents when explaining technical details and system characteristics to the potential client.[59] Although the presentation did not result in sales, these 'stunts' were an important impetus to system development. By bouncing ideas off those who knew the needs, the development team tweaked their thoughts about how the system should work – a practise not unusual at Albatross. Clients and potential clients were often used in product development and the actualisation of ideas. As Sælid put it, Albatross was good at selling «paper tigers».[60]

In August 1985, Albatross solid its first system, though it was still developing and testing operator and process stations and I/O units. The Italian offshore contractor Micoperi needed a system to manage its semisubmersible multipurpose platform *Micoperi 7000,* the world's largest crane vessel. The contract came at a very critical time. The project was financially strained and the development team needed a sale to back further development.[61] In addition to an ADP503 and APM3000, *Micoperi 7000* was equipped with the project's new AIM based load and stability calculator. The ADP311 system was later installed on board.[62]

The load calculator, with three SBC1000's, was installed in May 1986 and functioned well.[63] Despite a very cautious start, it now looked as though this initiative had a future. In late 1986 Albatross signed a significantly larger contract for the delivery of a control system to *Scarabeo 5*, a drill platform owned by the Italian company Saipem.

The project had a price tag of over NOK 50 million.[64] However, due to yard delays, this system would not be the second to be completed. Another was in the pipeline.

ALBATROSS GOES ASHORE

There are differences between keeping a vessel stationary and managing an industrial process, but in principle there are many similarities. First, you need to know your exact position, or status. Then this status must be compared with the desired status, and finally, adjustments must be made to close the gap between the actual and desired status. There is, however, a principle difference between dynamic positioning and process control. While the DP system's relatively few inputs (measurements) and outputs (thrusters) demand advanced mathematics and difficult computations, an automation system has many inputs and outputs, which demand simple math and easy calculations.

Since AIM worked equally well in the land-based process industry as it did offshore, commercially speaking, it wasn't as sensitive to the changing oil prices as a DP system. And in the midst of falling oil prices and a pending offshore market collapse, the system came along when Albatross needed it most.

In the autumn of 1986, Albatross discussed its strategy for land-based activities.[65] Even though the company possessed expertise and technology, and had a culture that embraced new challenges, there was no guarantee of success. A new investment demanded sufficient resources, not readily available at this time. Also, activities would have to be streamlined to make room for a new business area. There would be no heavy investments at first. Albatross would proceed with caution.[66] To accommodate the expansion of its core business, Albatross revised its vision to: «Albatross will be the preferred international problem solver and supplier of automation and process control.»[67]

Prior to making determined inroads into land-based industry, Albatross began to sound out the market. One project it deemed promising was Norsk Leca. In addition to it fitting KV's technology abilities, the project was scalable and part of a larger «Automation in Process Industry» program being conducted by the Royal Norwegian Council for Scientific and Industrial Research (NTNF). This meant that the project would entail not only a standard delivery, but research and development as well.

On 19 February 1987, the front-page of Laagendalsposten, the City of Kongsberg's local newspaper, stated that Albatross had gone ashore.[68] The company had signed a NOK 3 million contract with Norsk Leca for the delivery of a control and monitoring system for its production plant in Rælingen, just outside of Oslo.[69] Though land-based process industry fell outside its core business, Albatross had a tradition of taking on new challenges. And, it paid off. When Albatross gained its strong foothold in DP offshore, the market was in an early stage of development. There were few competitors, and none with dynamic positioning as their core business area. But this land-based venture was a different story. A large number of competitors had proven track records and extensive experience within industrial automation; Albatross prepared itself to battle major companies like Honeywell, Siemens, ASEA, Valment, Foxboro, General Electric and GEC. The Leca contract was won in strong competition with ASEA, which later became part of ABB after merging with Brown, Boveri & Cie in 1988.[70]

The timing for a major breakthrough in the process industry couldn't have been better. Prospects in the offshore market were dim; the process industry was less exposed to fluctuating oil prices, so there was good money to be made. But the new venture would face tremendous challenges. The established players were loath to let new competition into the market, and they not only had the technology, expertise and market contacts, but the financial strength to undercut Albatross.

Albatross had nothing more to offer than «a prototype and a stack of papers» when it signed the Leca contract.[71] Sales executives were familiar with aggressive marketing based on enthusiasm and good ideas. It wouldn't be the first time they relied on Kongsberg technologists to deliver what had been sold. The technical aspects of the system were of course important to Leca, but again Albatross had the significant advantage of their customer service and responsiveness in competition with other suppliers.[72]

The AIM system managed and controlled the entire production process. The process fed natural clay through a pipe into a kiln, with the clay eventually emerging as Leca balls. The system controlled the volume and quality of clay, controlled the kiln to ensure correct pore size, and performed quality control on the finished product. The main goal was to ensure optimisation of the coal used to fuel the kiln and to achieve the lowest possible product failure ratio. The whole process, from beginning to end, required some 1,500 measurements.[73]

In late autumn 1986, The Albatross group travelled to Rælingen to finalise system installation. The hardware was already in place with three process stations in the electrical room and two operator stations in the control room. Commissioning was successful but not without some hiccups. At the peak, 12 Albatross developers were on site to correct errors. On one occasion, they discovered an unresponsive start button. The error was quickly resolved. As a redundant system, AIM ensured that the process was not interrupted even if one signal disappeared. In this particular case, several hundred metres of parallel yellow Ethernet cables had been used to link the various system entities. The source of the problem was more elementary than feared. A forklift had driven over the parallel cables, causing breaks in both lines. The advantage of a redundant system is considerably compromised if all the eggs are put in one basket, and the basket is dropped.[74]

The Leca factory was the AIM system's baptism by fire.[75] The ideas that Sælid and others from NTH had worked with during the early 1980s, and

From the commissioning of the automation system at Norsk Leca. From left, Gorm Johansen, Terje Løkling, Even Askestad, Steinar Sælid and Ola Tjelmeland. Photo: Steinar Sælid's private archives.

which had been matured for half a decade at Kongsberg, contributed greatly to the company's commercial stability. But after time, the drive to sell land-based systems dwindled out. Albatrosses were truly in their element while at sea, home to their market and contacts. A small competitor on land, they were world champions at sea. As oil prices and the complexity of operations increased, Albatross turned its focus once again to the vast ocean. Several AIM land-based systems had been sold, to domestic factories including Nycomed, Saugbrugsforeningen, Union Brug and Titan, but the bulk of deliveries were installed on ships and offshore rigs.

AIM was important for several reasons. First, it created business activity in another industry during an offshore market standstill and a withering order book. Secondly, it increased the breadth of Albatross's product range, giving the company more legs to stand on. Last, but not least, AIM became a viable solution to the rising offshore demand for a system able to integrate the various onboard subsystems. As the oil market revived, Albatross was perfectly positioned for growth, able to use land-based system references to win new clients.

A NEW MARKET AT SEA

In May 1988, Albatross completed delivery of the large contract for Saipem, one and a half years after the contract had been signed. *Scarabeo 5,* a semisubmersible rig, was packed with Albatross technology.[76] The system network consisted of a dozen operator stations and over 50 SBC1000 computers. AIM controlled all ship-based technical processes, such as machinery, electrical power systems, ballast and bilge systems and auxiliary systems.[77] Additional installations included an ADP703, ADP100 and APM3000.

This particular delivery encountered several challenges. A relatively new and unfinished system, AIM was not functioning properly and several problems needed to be resolved. Additionally, AIM should communicate with other systems on board, and Albatross used considerable amounts of time with the shipyards resolving several communications challenges. Further, the development team lacked experience regarding the total scope of delivery. The challenges were not just of a technical nature. The rig was built and equipped at Fincantieri, a shipyard in Genoa, Italy. It was to be the yard's last rig project and shipyard workers had, evidently, no hurry to finish it. During commissioning, they discovered, among other things, that the signal cables to the control system were severed. This, understandably, did not enhance the pace of the project.[78]

Saipem was an old friend of Albatross and had ordered its first DP system already in 1979.[79] The company was an important partner in the development of AIM. When Micoperi declared bankruptcy in 1991, Saipem purchased *Micoperi 7000,* rechristening her *Saipem 7000.* Saipem still owns the first two vessels, though the AIM system has been upgraded several times.[80]

DP systems were Albatross's biggest source of income when the 1980s came to an end. But a new offshore-based market was approaching, of which, would eventually be a greater source of income than dynamic positioning. The oil industry's demand for floating production platforms had increased significantly. These offshore units demanded robust equipment and represented challenges very similar to those on board ships. Increasing onboard complexity demanded a multifunctional system able to handle and integrate several processes into one unified system, and AIM was up to the task. In addition to managing

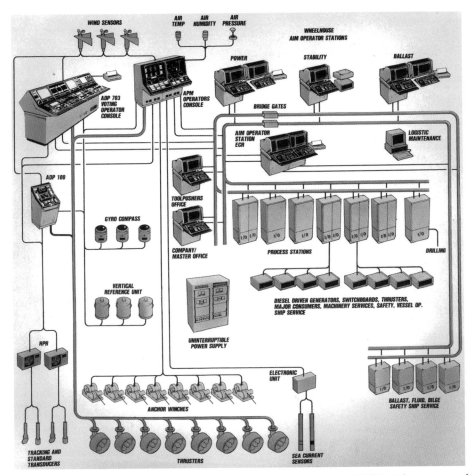

Scarabeo 5 was equipped with the first Albatross Vessel Management system (AVM1000), consisting of ADP703, APM3000 and AIM automation. The project would sound the starting gun of a marathon that would lead to integrated automation solutions for modern drilling vessels, and more. Automation systems handled all ship technical operations. Engine control was managed by means of multiple inter-connected PLCs (Programmable Logic Controllers) delivered by the yards, while the generator systems were handled by dedicated GCUs (Generator Control Units) from Norcontrol. Compared to the level of integration in modern systems, the *Scarabeo 5* installation was merely a combination of three different systems. Whenever exchange of information was required, standard serial lines were employed.

oil and gas production involving pumps and drilling equipment, AIM could monitor and control a wide range of tasks, including positioning, monitoring and control of the machine room, ballast and auxiliary systems like lubrication and fuel supply, and various security systems.[81]

Albatross had gradually built up a large customer network and a solid position in the offshore market. Now, for the time being, the sales staff would

Saipem was a ground-breaker, willing to invest in new technologies, and a strong partner for Albatross for many years. The first collaboration was on an ADP503-system for the diving ship *Ragno Due* in 1979. The image shows project manager Sergio Polito (right) and Mauro Brambilla behind a model of *Scarabeo 5*. From Kongsberg Albatross annual report 1986.

venture into new and relatively unknown terrain. Facing major oil companies and a lack of experience in this field, would the sales team succeed in selling automation technology equally as well as they did to shipowners? The low oil price didn't boost marketing efforts and sales encountered a rather slow start. But as oil prices rose, oil companies became more and more willing to invest.

Albatross signed a further AIM contract in the autumn of 1987. This time it was coupled with an APM3000 and installed on the semisubmersible platform *Drillmar 1*, owned by a drilling company of the same name. The following year, Albatross won an integrated process control contract with Saga Petroleum for its platform *Snorre*, a Tension Leg Platform (TLP), that is, a floating installation permanently moored by tension cables linked to seabed anchors. This particular system featured special ballast and pump control applications, which in addition to keeping the platform stable, simultaneously monitored mooring conditions.[82]

In October 1989, the company had reason to celebrate. Competing heavily with multinational companies, Albatross had managed to win its first contract with Statoil, the state-owned oil company. Statoil operated several fields. The biggest of them was Statfjord, where the company conducted its oil and gas production operations from three platforms: *Statfjord A*, *Statfjord B* and *Statfjord C*.

Safety is critical in the offshore industry. Statoil felt that these platforms posed a safety risk, as parts of the surveillance process were being conducted from local control rooms. Management decided to upgrade the platforms with a system that not only monitored and controlled all oil and gas treatment processes, but that was directly linked to Statoil's computer systems on shore. By increasing the degree of automation, the company would improve the safety of its offshore platforms and ensure the effective operational and maintenance tasks.[83]

The Leca contract, at NOK 3 million, was peanuts compared to the record-breaking NOK 35-40 million contract for the three Statfjord platforms. This contract was strategic, and Albatross did not beat the competition on quality or price alone. Choosing Albatross was Statoil's opportunity to make itself less dependent on Siemens, a major supplier. System implementation began on the *Statfjord A* platform in 1991. The Statfjord platforms were large, fixed gravity Condeep platforms, and thus did not require positioning equipment. Albatross's new, holistic monitoring system consisted of 60 SBC computers, of which received and processed signals from some 3,300 measuring points. The last unit was finished in 1993.[84]

The record was short lived. In December 1991, Albatross won a major automation system contract with Conoco for *Heidrun*, a TLP positioned on the Heidrun field off the coast of Trøndelag in Norway.[85] At NOK 80 million, it was the company's largest single contract to date. The assignment included the delivery and installation of a computer system to manage the production of petroleum and the platform's safety system.[86] The contract was strategically significant for Albatross. It demanded several solutions highly applicable to the oil industry's future focus, that is, the development of smaller fields, many of these in the North Sea. This industrial segment favoured floating and mobile production vessels, a vessel niche totally in line with Albatross's expertise.[87]

In time, Albatross landed significant automation system contracts for several oil platforms. After *Heidrun* came *Norne* in 1995 and *Åsgard* in 1996, both in the NOK 100 million price range.

Simrad Albatross was now gaining a foothold in a market quite different to the DP market. DP was on the verge of becoming an off-the-shelf product and as product volumes increased, the systems became highly streamlined and

In December of 1991 Albatross won the competition to deliver automation systems to Conoco's jack-up platform *Heidrun*, serving the Heidrun field off the Trøndelag coast. The contract was for NOK 80 million, and the company's largest to date. The assignment was to deliver and install a solution to control oil and gas production, and safety systems, on the platform. Photo: KM photo archive.

efficient. With AIM and vessel automation, there was a much higher demand for tailored solutions. In many cases this was nothing new for Albatross, which had from the very beginning cooperated with clients to deliver tailor-made systems. Oil companies now wanted to interact with the fewest possible suppliers to make this process as simple as possible.[88] The result of this was a significant increase in the total scope of each order – and, as well, in the total price.

Measured in the number of units sold per year, DP systems have always outperformed process control systems. The latter, however, have provided considerably higher revenue per system sale. In 1993, total income from sales of process control systems exceeded DP for the first time. They would fall behind again, but would later regain the lead that they have held since the new millennium.[89] However, the importance of DP is far greater than its sales statistics would indicate. It is the most critical element in larger systems deliveries, and, as explained by Torfinn Kildal, has carried the other systems «on its back». [90]

In principle, there is no difference between the systems installed in factories on land and those at sea. AIM is an extremely flexible and scalable system able to manage a large number of signals. In practice, however, there are certain configuration differences. While process control systems on land manage a specific production control process, the offshore installations integrate several subsystems including DP and PM systems.[91]

AIM was also the basis for the Albatross Vessel Management System (AVM). Both employed the same principles, but AIM was used primarily within oil and gas, while AVM was applied chiefly to maritime automation. AVM was modular and designed for flexible integration with DP systems. It could be expanded to handle all critical monitoring and control operations on board. Typical applications were thruster- and propulsion control and power management, as well as monitoring and control of the engine room and cargo.[92]

GROWTH THROUGH CRISIS

For Albatross, the hangover after the anniversary party was excruciating. A dramatic fall in the price of oil turned steady growth years into lean years, with declining sales and red bottom line figures. KV's problems didn't help the situation. In deep financial difficulty, it was technically bankrupt by late autumn of 1986. In the spring of 1987, the lifeline to Kongsberg Våpenfabrikk was severed for good. From then on, Albatross was part of Simrad Subsea in Horten, Norway. This, no doubt, wasn't completely what the Albatrosses had envisioned when they first planned their flight towards total independence from KV. Though it looked rather dark in 1987, there were signs that gave hope for better times. The groundwork for new growth was in motion before the crisis came. The value of the multifunctional system, AIM, was far more than its contribution to expanding Simard Albatross's product portfolio. As the complexity of installations and the enormous need for computing power grew, AIM became a catalyst in the development of new hardware, especially the SBC computer.[93] It would also further impact the DP systems.

AIM operator stations with mimicking image employed during ballasting operations on a drilling rig. AIM provided multiple types of images: flow charts, instrument group (like checkerboard), trends and parameter images. The most commonly used images were flow charts showing processes (mimicking) and signal flow (logical control). By clicking on symbols representing process elements (such as pumps, valves, or motors) and control objects (such as PID controllers), the operator could access a menu with options for controlling a given element. The flow chart was difficult to compose, but allowed for great flexibility. It provided many layers of information, and could easily be adapted to user needs. Photo: Mediafoto.

The crisis was a powerful wake-up call. A company with only one product was clearly vulnerable, especially in a volatile industry like oil and gas.

9

NEW WAVES

THE WORLD HAD been turned upside down. The sub-supplier of hydroacoustic positioning sensors was now the owner of the main supplier of DP systems. Both Albatross and Simrad Subsea had long benefited from their cooperation, building up a strong market position in the maritime electronics field. Long before they became separate companies, the two shared a common goal in the *Seaway Eagle* project, where their very existence was dependent on the success of the first DP delivery.[1] Since then, most of Albatross' DP systems had been delivered with hydroacoustic position sensors from Simrad.

When Albatross was sold, the company wasn't only in the process of developing AIM, but was also preparing to rejuvenate its DP systems by introducing a new generation of technology. This was a period of change, not just in terms of ownership, but also relating to technology and business culture. Although Albatross and Simrad were similar in many ways, there were also fundamental differences in the ways the companies operated. Both the change of ownership and the shift to a new generation of technology entailed major challenges.

TWO CULTURES

Simrad Subsea was established in 1981 as a result of a restructuring of Simrad. After a period of significant economic problems, the leadership took comprehensive measures to get the business back on its feet. In the first instance this meant that parts of the business were separated off, with the remaining units divided into their own individual companies.[2] Simrad Subsea was built around the portion of the offshore division that focused on underwater navigation. This solution worked well and the downturn was soon turned into an upswing.

Added to this, Simrad Subsea received significant sums following on from the company's IPO in 1982. This gave the firm a solid financial platform and the freedom to acquire businesses of the order of Albatross.[3]

Although the companies had a shared history, they had two different corporate cultures that would need to be homogenised. In his book *God På Bunnen* (Good At The Bottom) Knut Sogner describes Simrad as a company with a strong focus on profitability. With this in mind, its goal was to realign Albatross so that the company could begin to return a profit again, not to make it an integral part of Simrad.[4] Albatross enjoyed a degree of independence on this premise. Organisationally, it was a solution that wasn't so different from the one Albatross staff were used to from their time with KV. The difference lay in the form, not the formal operation. While the previous owner had been focused on engineering and technology, the new owner was largely concerned with financial matters. Initially, this difference stayed at management level and didn't really impact upon the daily activities further down the organisation. Both Simrad Subsea and Albatross were engineering firms with a high proportion of engineers amongst their employees. The attitudes that characterised the people in both Kongsberg and Horten were not so different. Rolf Arne Klepaker, who was one of Simrad's engineers, and later became Director of Simrad Subsea, has stated that they were convinced that «there was nothing that could stop us». This sense of self-assurance was reminiscent of the attitude that prevailed in Albatross. However, Klepaker added that his people were not as «disruptive» as those at Albatross.[5]

Albatross and Simrad didn't just have a different technology base, they were also located in separate cities that were an hour's drive from one another. It was therefore decided early on that they would continue as two separate business units. As a result, Albatross was organised as an independent limited company and renamed as Simrad Albatross, while Simrad Subsea changed its name to Simrad. The other Horten business (Marine and Subsea) took over the Simrad Subsea name.

Both Simrad Subsea and Albatross were companies with high profiles. In the media they had been portrayed as modern successful businesses, albeit in their own ways. Albatross had received publicity because of its management philosophy and Nils Willy Gulhaugen was, in many ways, referred to as a management guru for people who wanted strong commitment and involvement from their employees.[6] Articles about Simrad Subsea portrayed a business where smart economists used the stock market as a tool for creating growth in a company in crisis. The architect behind Simrad's successful IPO, economist Harald Ellefsen, was soon to become a star in the Norwegian financial world.

When Simrad had serious liquidity problems in the early 1980s, the company had to implement clean-up measures and rebuilding processes with strict and centralised financial management plans to get the company back on its feet. This helped Simrad Subsea maintain control over its costs.[7] Albatross had enjoyed a long history of strong profit margins, leading to a culture where it was not considered as necessary to keep tight control on expenses.[8] There was, for example, no one that reacted if employees added their parking fines into their travel expenses.[9] It had been fine as long as the business performed, but with the economic problems that came in the wake of the fall in oil prices, such spending became problematic. This worried Simrad's management, and after the acquisition, Albatross was subject to a more sober economic regime. The 'yuppy' period had come to an end.

Albatross had a corporate culture with great personal freedom and a high degree of delegation of responsibility to the employees. In Simrad the Albatross people met a leader who involved himself heavily in all parts of the business, and who wanted to have a say in both the detailed economic and technical issues. For some of the employees in Kongsberg, Kåre Hansen's leadership style was a source of major frustration. Hansen was an engineer and, amongst other things, had been head of Simrad's HPR development. In 1981, when Simrad Subsea was founded, he assumed the role of CEO.

People who had been accustomed to the freedom of taking decisions themselves now experienced a loss of power and influence over their own work assignments. However, others have described the shift as unproblematic and life under the new owners as «business as usual».[10] Even though the changes after the shift in ownership were experienced differently in different parts of the organisation, the transition from Gulhaugen's 'inspirational leadership' to Hansen's style of 'micromanagement' led to some friction between the Simrad environment in Horten and the Albatross group in Kongsberg. Simrad had been little brother in the relationship between the two companies, but now the relationship was turned upside down. Many found it difficult to be acquired by a former supplier.[11]

In addition, Albatross had an element of rebellion embodied in its corporate culture. Previously its employees had defined themselves as different compared to KV, and had used considerable time and energy to acquire their autonomy and freedom. This, together with very good financial results, led to a strong corporate culture that was characterised by creativity, self-awareness, pride and a strong esprit de corps. Steinar Sælid has characterised it as follows:

Albatross in the 1980s was a unique environment for creative people, spearheaded by company director, and the man who inspired that environment, Nils Willy Gulhaugen. The culture was very self-conscious in a positive sense. There was nothing you couldn't do. People often operated in 'easy conflict' with corporate management. (...) Albatross also had a unique environment for marketing and sales. It was a pack of smiling wolves with Svein Thorsen at its head. It could be stressful for a developer when one of the super salespeople came home with contracts worth tens of millions before the products were even finished. (...) The atmosphere at Albatross was made up of money, boldness, a willingness to invest, technical knowledge, skilled marketers, unlimited confidence, and a portion of madness.[12]

Shortly after its independence from the weapons factory, Albatross again fell under a 'foreign' regime. It's possible that parts of its culture of opposition were transferred into the new company. The new owner, which had ambitions to make Simrad into a strong brand in marine electronics, was not particularly enthusiastic about this 'cult of Albatross'.[13] Simrad CEO Hansen was often irritated by the perception that the Albatrosses were difficult to lead. While employees working with DP were proud of the high-flying Albatross, Hansen just saw an overgrown seagull, with qualities he wanted to extinguish through the 'Simradification' of the company.[14]

Albatross had been very conscious of building its brand. The drawing of an albatross in flight was recognised as a clear brand identity. To begin with, there were no major changes, with the Albatross name living on in Simrad Albatross. However, in 1989 the name disappeared from the company's overseas offices and, after a while, the bird also disappeared from the logo, replaced by Simrad's blue wave. Both the albatross and the Simrad wave were used during the transitional phase, but it didn't last long.[15] When Simrad was reorganised in 1995, and the operations in Kongsberg became part of Simrad's offshore division, the Albatross name disappeared completely. Many of those who had helped to build up Albatross were pained by this move and continued to use the Albatross name in their everyday speech. Even when the name had been officially out of use for some time, it could still be found hidden in the software.

It was not just the albatross that was gone, several of those who had been central to the development of the company also disappeared. This was a process that started before the company even changed hands, as orders dried up in tandem with the fall in oil prices. In personal terms, the realignment was a painful

After Albatross became part of Simrad, marketing became more uniform, even though the subsidiaries had their own marketing departments. Personal relationships between salesmen from Kongsberg and Horten had been established long before the acquisition. These then were reinforced and salesmen often performed as a team. The photo shows (from left) Morten Berntsen (HPR), Bjarne Skaar Nilsen and Bjørn Trosthoel (DP) on one of the many bus trips the salesmen took to market new products. Photo: Mediafoto.

one for Gulhaugen.[16] Criticism of his management style and resistance from the staff paved the way for his resignation as CEO just before Christmas, 1987. After a brief period in the executive management team he left the business, leaving CFO Torfinn Kildal to assume the leadership role. Kildal was now the only one from the trio that led Albatross remaining in the company. Although many experienced the time after the acquisition as turbulent, the situation eventually resolved itself. In addition to the fact that the two cultures adapted to one another, there was also the bonus of a new injection of projects and revenues.

A NEW TECHNOLOGICAL GENERATION – ADP703

In the mid-1980s, nearly ten years after its launch, the ADP500 generation was ripe for replacement. ADP501 and ADP502 were already phased out, without having sold especially well. The last of the seven ADP501 units sold was installed in 1979, with work on the ADP502 concluding the year after, when the third system had been completed.[17] They were replaced by the ADP100 and ADP311. The latter, which arrived in 1979, was based on a KS500 computer. With the launch of the ADP100 in 1983, Albatross went over to a completely new hardware platform based on the proprietary SBC1000. The next in line was the ADP503. The system worked well and had been very stable, but was perceived as old-fashioned, from both an economical and technological standpoint. It was very expensive to produce and a solution with such a large, separate computer cabinet was both space consuming and cumbersome.[18] Efforts to develop a successor were conducted virtually in parallel with the development of AIM.

The redundancy in the ADP500 series was based on Dual Modular Redundancy (DMR) or the master-slave principle, as it was also called. As discussed in Chapter 4, this system was not very user friendly, especially due to the so-called AB difference-issue. Albatross therefore began to look for other ways to deal with redundancy, with an objective of making the system smaller, cheaper and smarter.

In 1985, Albatross decided to develop a new generation of DP, establishing a development team under the leadership of Sigmund Sundfør. As with the development of the APD500 systems, a research stay in the US would exert a major influence on the technical solutions. In 1982 and 1983 system engineer Sverre Corneliussen attended Carnegie Mellon University in Pittsburgh. There he studied fault tolerant system design, gaining valuable knowledge from, amongst other things, the system used in NASA space shuttles. In this system there was not only redundancy by duplication, as was customary in DP systems, but instead a total of five independent computers working in parallel. To select the control signal that was most accurate, the system utilised so-called majority voting. This solution provided the inspiration for the redundancy concept Albatross would base its new system on, Triple Modular Redundancy (TMR).[19] The hardware solution was based on three sets of SBC1000 machines, coupled together with a redundant Ethernet LAN. Two of the machine groups consisted of three computers, so-called triads, while the third had two. The smallest group took care of the user interface, with screens, panels, buttons and lights, while the two triads handled control tasks. The machines in one triad were connected to the position reference systems and sensors, which were also in triplicate, and calculated the position of the vessel. In addition, they calculated the corrections that had to be made to accommodate the operator's desired positioning. It was here that the vessel model and Kalman filter were used. The machines in the second triad were connected to the thrusters, propellers and rudders, and used signals from the first triad as a basis for thrust allocation to calculate and provide the right signals relating to power actuation and direction.[20]

ADP 703 voting
improves your position

The ADP703 was a «democratic system» based on majority voting, though this figure might give the impression of a hostile system, where the two victorious parties celebrate their victory over the loser. The image was used in marketing and provided a grass-roots understanding of the essence of 'triple voting'.

The machines in the triads were synchronised and worked in parallel with the same signal from the sensors and reference systems. The results of the calculations were then compared, and the majority, or the machine which gave the median, took the decision. Since all computers received the same input and started simultaneously, the AB difference-issue could be avoided.[21] This principle was also used to find and eliminate errors on the reference systems and sensors, and represented a small revolution in the world of DP software. The master-slave relationship was replaced by a system of reconciliation whereby the majority decided. It was also reflected in the name of the new system, which was christened the ADP703 Voting System.[22]

As with the design of the ADP100's console, Albatross again used professional designers, resulting in a design that was not only functional, but also award winning. In 1987, the Norwegian Design Council awarded Albatross 'Merket for god design' (Award for Industrial Design) for the ADP703. The company had used the British-born designer John R. Houghton and his Norwegian design firm Anglo Nordic Design for the project. In the jury's assessment, they stated, amongst other things, that ergonomic considerations were «very well looked after by this well thought through concept».[23]

Deep blue was retained as the principal colour scheme, but the console had also been given decorative green stripes. The most noticeable visual difference was the angled operation panel, with two surfaces, creating a 'desktop' working environment. The ADP500 and ADP311 Series had flat and gently sloping panels with screens and buttons, while the ADP100 introduced a small spine/

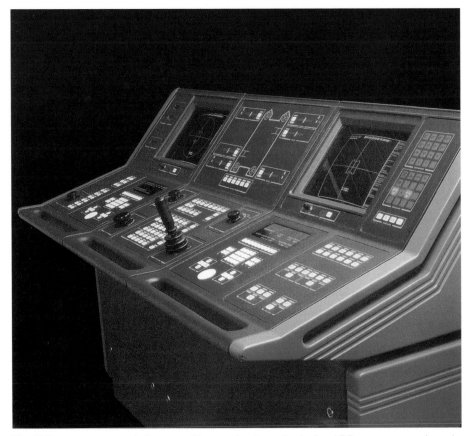

The ADP703 operator console from 1987. The console solution for the first ADP703 was extremely costly. One reason for this was the mid-section of the console. This section served all three of the redundancy units, and provided, in addition to buttons and indicator lights, a thruster mimic panel. Each button contained three switches, one for each computer, and three corresponding indicator lights. The thruster mimic panel was custom built for each delivery. The flank sections had separate graphic colour displays in addition to an alpha-numeric screen and buttons for user input. The image is from the 1990 Albatross brochure, 'Albatross – Positioning and Control Systems'.

break in the panel and a steeper angled screen. Nevertheless, the operator still had to look down to see the screen display. However, the ADP703 panel was far steeper, reducing the angle between the control portion and the display portion. This positioned the panel directly in front of the operator and made the whole solution both tidier and more user friendly.

This new DP system boasted several innovations. DP vessel operators are reliant on reliable systems that won't be knocked out by hardware or software errors, and this availability becomes more important the more expensive and dangerous operations are. The ADP703 offered triple redundancy and was therefore a very robust system. In addition it had something called 'hot repair', meaning that it was possible to replace a component while the system was running and thus increase safety and availability. In this way, it introduced the 'minimum voting age' when a new computer could be inserted to participate in the reconciliation process. The machine then had to acquire experience in the form of integrated values and time series data so that the outcome of the majority voting would be of optimal accuracy.[24]

On one occasion, however, the 'legal adult' status of the computers was not enough to ensure success. Thor Hukkelås, who was a key figure in software development for the ADP703, remembers a time where he was called out for a service assignment on a diving vessel that had drifted off course due to an error in its DP system. The rig had deployed divers and a diving bell, leading to some tense moments before the crew could regain control of the vessel and end the diving operations. The error appeared to be caused by someone taking a cable out of an operator station and utilising it for a screen in the diving control room. This screen was not earthed, causing the cable to work as an antenna and pick up noise. As a result, one of the three computers in the triad that gave signals to the thrusters stopped listening to the other two. Even though it was disengaged from the reconciliation process it still continued to send signals to the thrusters. Since these signals were not in line with those coming from the other two computers, the thrusters begun to behave in an uncoordinated manner. In the eyes of the service personnel, the fact that the machine had stopped listening, yet continued to talk was a clear sign of senility. They therefore came to the conclusion that the computers should also undergo a 'senility check'. Thankfully, everything turned out well for the divers involved in this dramatic incident.[25]

In February 1986, the first two ADP703 systems were sold to the Dutch shipowner Smit Tak. The semi-submersible rigs *Semi 1* and *Semi 2* were both equipped with ADP703, with a HPR from Simrad, and two taut wire positioning reference systems. The first unit was supplied in March, with the second arriving in December the following year.[26] Judged by its goal of successfully tackling the AB difference-issue, the ADP703 was certainly smarter than its predecessor the ADP503. The system also had an additional level of redundancy. But was it also smaller and cheaper?

The ADP703 was without doubt a more compact system than its predecessor. The ADP503 consisted of an operator console with four sections and a separate unit with three computer cabinets. The console was 1005 mm high, 1800 mm wide and 716 mm deep, while the cabinet component had comparable

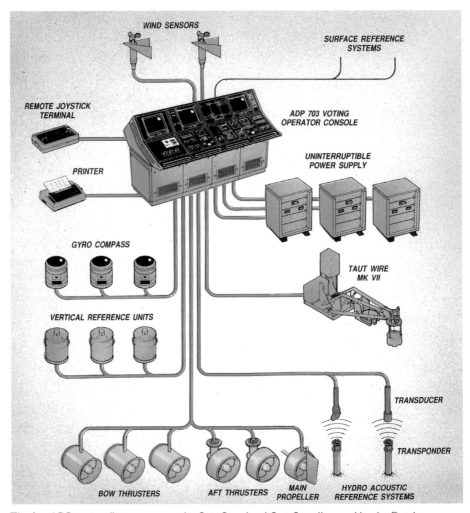

The first ADP703 installations were on the *Smit Semi I* and *Smit Semi II*, owned by the Dutch company Smit International. The drawing illustrates the actual system configuration. The vessels were equipped with Azimuth thrusters and two tunnel thrusters at 1250 kW each. This triple-redundant DP system contained three gyros and vertical reference sensors with majority-voting for error detection, and to determine which system to use for control. The vessel was equipped with double taut-wire, the latest Simrad HPR model, with tracking-transducer and Artemis position reference systems.

dimensions of 1805x2050x600 mm. Both the console and cabinet weighed 400 kg, making a total weight was 800 kg.[27] By comparison, the ADP703 was considerably smaller and a good deal lighter. Here everything was located in one compact unit, consisting of four sections with outer dimensions of 1300x2500x1068 mm and a weight of 650 kg.[28]

However, the system was still expensive.[29] A comparison of the prices of the systems Albatross sold at the time of the first ADP703 installation shows that customers were expected to pay more for it than the ADP503.[30] The two were actually sold in parallel for a short period.[31] In the spring of 1987 Simrad Albatross sold six different DP systems. The price of the basic configuration of the systems increased by roughly NOK 1 million for each step up in complexity. For example, the joystick system AJS cost some NOK 400 000, whereas purchasing an ADP100 would cost an extra NOK 1 million. For an additional million, customers could get the ADP311, while the APM3000 and ADP503 MKII stood, respectively, in the region of NOK 3 and 4 million kroner each. The top system, ADP703, commanded a price tag of over NOK 5 million.[32] However, this was only the basic equipment. In addition, there was a need for, amongst other things, reference systems. For a Simrad HPR309 the cost was NOK 1.2 million, while a taut wire cost about half that. Printers were not cheap at this time either, with customers expected to pay NOK 35,000 for a unit.[33]

Initially, the sales people had the freedom to fix prices in negotiations with customers. This was a huge advantage in the final stages of tight negotiations, where several suppliers were fighting for one contract. In such a scenario the sales person could avoid the delays incurred by calling the main office at Kongsberg to request permission to alter the price. Occasionally, the seller took too many liberties in this respect and had to beg for forgiveness when they came 'home'.[34] That said, there was a strong competitive instinct in the company, meaning it wasn't just important to win all the contracts, but also get the highest possible price.[35] Svein Thorsen revealed that on one occasion he sold a brand new system for about double the price that was originally intended. This meant both extra money in the bank and ample room to negotiate on subsequent system sales.[36]

Two days after the Simrad acquisition a new price catalogue was completed and tighter restraints were placed on the salespeople. Now they were told that all price reductions of over five percent had to be discussed with the marketing and sales manager and that discounts beyond this level would not be appreciated, although they were possible.[37]

A GROWING FAMILY

Service engineers reported mostly positive experiences with the ADP100 and SBC computer. They did, however, have one major problem: the so-called 'PROM hell'. Every time there needed to be a change in the software, big or small, a new PROM (Programmable Read-Only Memory) had to be created.

This had to be made in Kongsberg and then transported to the vessel and installed by a service engineer. It was both inefficient and costly. The ADP703 was therefore equipped with a 10 Mb hard drive and a 3.5-inch floppy disc drive, so that on board adaptations could be made more efficiently.[38]

After ADP703 was finished, the company's development engineers began planning an extended family of systems based on the same technology platform. They started by creating a system to replace ADP100 and thus make it possible to get rid of the PROM problem once and for all. The new development arrived in 1990 and was named ADP701. This DP solution was essentially a downscaled ADP703, streamlined into a single system with two SBCs. However, a new computer, the SBC2000, had been developed in-house since the last product launch and this was used in the new system. The SBC2000 was a further development of the SBC1000 and had its graphics system integrated on the circuit board. The computer program was read in the same manner as in the ADP703. The ADP100 had thus gained a successor that was both simpler and cheaper, and had more functionality. With this Albatross had freed itself from the 'PROM hell'.[39] The joystick system AJS700 was also launched simultaneously with ADP701.[40]

Initially, the product developers showed no interest in developing a dual system. Therefore, there were no ADP702. Instead there was a prevailing attitude that the ADP703 was so much better, and exactly what the customers needed. Nevertheless, the sales department still promoted the non-existent ADP702 in the catalogues. This was not the first time the sellers presented a non-existent product, operating under the assumption that if a system was sold it could then be developed and delivered.[41]

Simrad Albatross therefore lacked a modern double redundant system equivalent to the ADP503, and it proved to be just such a solution that the market demanded. Although the triple system was technically superior, most customers considered this level of redundancy to be extravagant and unnecessarily costly. This demand demonstrated the need to do something new with the ADP703. A plan was hatched to develop a new DP family with a single, a double and a triple system.[42]

The ADP703 had become expensive to produce and something had to be done to rein in costs. Amongst other features, the system included a so-called 'thruster mimicking panel' displaying the condition of the thrusters on a schematic vessel floorplan. As every vessel was different, the panels had to be created specifically for each delivery. This degree of customising was both costly and time consuming. In the new version of the ADP703 this expensive panel feature was removed, with the information instead shown on a computer screen.

The SBC3000 represented a considerable simplification of the system design. The computer had two processors. One handled all I/O: disk, network, serial lines and process connections. The other was an Intel 80386-based number cruncher with numerical co-processor. Photo: KM.

Calculating capacity was also emerging as a bottleneck. Intel's 80186 processor, as used in the SBC1000 and SBC2000, was becoming too slow for the more complex DP systems. At the outset, the computers had even less computing power than the KS500, but this was compensated for by the fact that more machines were used in the ADP100 and ADP703. Capacity problems in the new ADP generation could have been tackled by inserting even more machines, but instead the decision was taken to develop a more powerful computer.[43] Completed in 1990, this, the SBC3000, was based on Intel's 386 processor, which was the PC standard at the time.

The SBC3000 represented a major improvement in capacity. On paper it was ten times faster than its predecessor, but bottlenecks in internal communication capacity made it difficult to fully exploit this speed. However, this new, powerful machine meant that each of SBC1000-triads could be replaced by one SBC3000, simplifying the hardware in the ADP700 series. The first version of ADP703 had two triads plus two computers to handle the user

The new ADP703 operator console from 1992. This system was cheaper to produce and had dropped the physical thruster mimic panel. With the transition to the SBC3000, only three computers were needed, compared with eight in the original version. In addition, there were three colour monitors, one for each computer. The elimination of the alpha-numerical screens meant that the main screen took over. With the renewal came the ADP702 solution with double redundancy (two SBC3000s) and the single system ADP701 (one SBC3000). The image is taken from the 1993 brochure 'Simrad ADP703 Dynamic Positioning System'.

interface. In the new edition, these eight machines were now replaced by just three SBC3000s.[44]

The ADP series was launched in 1992, with the ADP701, ADP702 and ADP703. Once again Simrad Albatross and Houghton collected the Design Council's award for good design, although this time the accolade was not for the system, but for the 'Modular Dynamic Positioning Console'. The design had not changed significantly from the original ADP703, but was refined to have a more compact layout. The cosmetic decor was removed and the buttons and screens were tidied up. The thruster mimicking panel was also gone, with the information moved across to the screens. The jury emphasised that the console was flexible for adaptation and that it represented «a clean-up of a work environment that traditionally has had no organisation of the different instruments».[45]

The product catalogue had become considerably thicker in just a few years. In addition to the new ADP700 generation, Simrad Albatross also launched a thruster control system (ATC). In a further change, the company also sold AIM and AVM (Albatross Vessel Management).[46] The change in computers from the KS500 to SBC1000, with the later upgrades to SBC2000 and SBC3000, provided not only a technological boost, but also made the systems cheaper and easier to maintain.

There was another expense that could be cut. From the outset, functional testing of the units had incurred significant financial resources. When the project to improve the quality of ADP703 was launched in 1989 a new, highly ambitious goal to reduce hardware testing time to 40 hours was also introduced. At the time it was not uncommon to use between 300 and 400 hours to test out, and make the necessary alterations, in a redundant system. However, by the time of the release of the Autumn 1992 edition of corporate newsletter Tross'ern, the management could announce that this goal was reached, and congratulate the firm's employees. The testing of the last unit had started one afternoon and by the following morning everything was ready, without the need for anyone to work through the night. There were several factors leading to this improvement, including the product's redesign, a reorganisation of work tasks, and a change of subcontractor.[47]

After one and half decades, Albatross had also managed to reduce on-board testing time by around 90 percent. The accumulation of experience and a standardisation drive were significant factors in this, but investments in computer systems making it possible to conduct much of the testing in the factory facilities in Kongsberg was also key. While Albatross was still part of KV Group, the individual units were largely tailored from the system's basic functionality. In the absence of a simulator, they had to be tested at sea. This was both complicated and time consuming, and it was often difficult to acquire the necessary vessel data from the shipyards. The arrival of simulators, making it possible to conduct large parts of the testing before the systems were installed, was a real advance.[48] The savings meant that the company was able to maintain good profit margins, despite the fall in the prices of DP systems.[49]

ON THE OFFENSIVE

The economic downturn after the fall of oil prices was short-lived, as prices once again began to climb. In 1990, the barrel price stood at USD 10 higher than at its bottom level in 1986.[50] This rise meant oil companies increased their exploration activity and began to invest in new equipment, while upgrading old technology. This became a powerful catalyst for increased activity, both in

Terje Løkling was the first leader of the Albatross development department, and when the industrial division was established he became its first manager. From 1989 to 1992 he managed Simrad Albatross. Photo from 1987: Mediafoto.

the offshore market and at Industritunet in Kongsberg. Albatross's investment in developing technology meant that it had several new products to offer and, together with the upturn in the market, this led to growing revenues from the late 1980s onwards. In 1988, the accounts showed a loss of NOK 3 million. The following year there was a profit of just as much. In 1990, the annual report showed a further climb to a profit level of NOK 22 million. With this kind of financial performance, it wasn't too long before Simrad had recouped its investment. As the economy improved, it also appears that things began to settle into place after the post-acquisition transitional period.[51]

At the time Torfinn Kildal, a former albatross, had taken the top position at Simrad. He joined the group management team as head of Simrad Albatross and, after a tenure as CFO, he was promoted to CEO when Kåre Hansen moved to Hong Kong in 1989 to help build Simrad's position in the Pacific market. Terje Løkling succeeded Kildal as the head of Simrad Albatross.[52]

The positive figures in the accounts were not only a result of new technologies or greater activity in the markets Albatross already operated in. The company had also secured a foothold in a new market – one that would lead to closer collaboration between the Kongsberg and Horten facilities.

DEFENCE POSITIONING

In 1990, Simrad won a major contract worth NOK 350 million to equip nine mine hunting vessels and minesweepers that Kværner was building for the

Norwegian Navy.[53] Albatross also benefitted, as the contract included positioning equipment and tactical systems to keep the vessels at a safe distance from explosive devices. This was the first time Simrad Albatross had a customer from the defence industry.

The Navy proved to be a demanding client. The military character of the project, with the need for secrecy, meant that the business had to be organised into a separate 'closed' unit within the development department. There were also particularly high demands on the technological side, with equipment expected to withstand extremely harsh conditions, and as far as the positioning was concerned, any errors could literally blow up into a very serious incident. The contract was based on an overarching technical specification where many details were not clearly defined. The first year was therefore used to prepare specifications for the system as a whole, for the software, and for individual machine components. The work was carried out in close conjunction with Naval Command, and was reminiscent of the practice the development engineers had been used to throughout the first years. It led to Albatross receiving an additional order to develop new consoles. The end result was the design used in the new ADP700 family. There was also intense effort put into software development for the project, with approximately 500,000 lines of code written.[54]

The system was called MICOS, a shortened form of Mission Control System, and integrated four subsystems: navigation and dynamic positioning, surface surveillance, mine warfare, and sonar. In addition to Albatross' ADP701, the system featured equipment from Norcontrol, Simrad Subsea and the French company Thompson Sintra. It was here that the first ADP701 units were put to use.

In March 1992, the first mine hunting vessel, *Oksøy*, was delivered. Three and a half years later the work was concluded with the completion of the minesweeper *Glomma*.[55] All the hovercraft, measuring 55 metres long and 13.6 metres wide, were stationed at Haakonsvern in Bergen. Four of them were mine hunting vessels of the Oksøy class, while the other five were Alta class minesweepers.

MICOS was later registered as a trademark.[56] When the contract was signed, Simrad CEO Kildal did not hide the fact that it triggered «fierce optimism» in the company, noting that this was something they had worked towards for many years.[57] He hoped this would be the start of deliveries to other navies in other countries. However, this was not be, with orders restricted to just these nine systems.

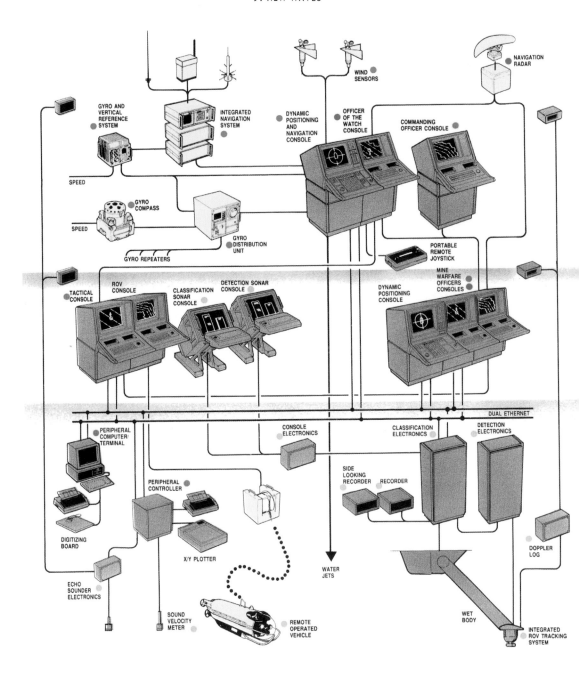

WIND SENSORS

NAVIGATION RADAR

GYRO AND VERTICAL REFERENCE SYSTEM

INTEGRATED NAVIGATION SYSTEM

DYNAMIC POSITIONING AND NAVIGATION CONSOLE

OFFICER OF THE WATCH CONSOLE

COMMANDING OFFICER CONSOLE

SPEED

GYRO COMPASS

SPEED

GYRO DISTRIBUTION UNIT

GYRO REPEATERS

PORTABLE REMOTE JOYSTICK

MINE WARFARE OFFICERS CONSOLES

TACTICAL CONSOLE

ROV CONSOLE

CLASSIFICATION SONAR CONSOLE

DETECTION SONAR CONSOLE

DYNAMIC POSITIONING CONSOLE

DUAL ETHERNET

PERIPHERAL COMPUTER/ TERMINAL

CONSOLE ELECTRONICS

CLASSIFICATION ELECTRONICS

DETECTION ELECTRONICS

PERIPHERAL CONTROLLER

SIDE LOOKING RECORDER

RECORDER

DIGITIZING BOARD

X/Y PLOTTER

WATER JETS

DOPPLER LOG

ECHO SOUNDER ELECTRONICS

SOUND VELOCITY METER

REMOTE OPERATED VEHICLE

WET BODY

INTEGRATED ROV TRACKING SYSTEM

The MICOS delivery was very big and comprised sonars for mine detection and classification, a tactical mine-hunting system, and DP. The Project was a collaboration between Simrad and Thompson Sintra. The DP system was unique, both in its operation and in its new functionality. Among other things, a special function to enable the vessel to circle at a constant distance around a suspected mine, enabling the classification system to identify the object as accurately as possible. The ADP701 system was controlled primarily from a dedicated console in the OPS room, which was hooked up to the main bridge systems. The illustration shows the system configuration. Photos show the operator console with (from left) the mine tactical console and the DP console in the OPS room and the mine hunter *Oksøy*. Photo: Mediafoto and KM.

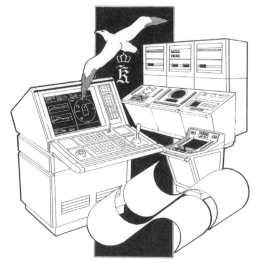

For a short period the Albatross logo and the Simrad wave were used together. This from an Albatross list of references.

FROM BIRD TO WAVES

At the end of 1992, the management at Simrad Albatross welcomed a new CEO. After four years in the role, Terje Løkling wanted to return to technology development and the head of development Steinar Gregersen replaced him in the New Year.[58] The Albatross logo was now replaced with Simrad's blue waves. This was mainly due to the fact that the management wanted a comprehensive, uniform profile for the company, but also illustrates the development the firm had undergone in recent years. It had also gone in waves, and now the company was riding on to new heights. There was much that gave reason for optimism.

It was not just the new multi-function AIM system that was a sales success, there was also a new momentum in DP system sales. In 1985, which was the peak year before the economic problems began, the firm's salespeople had signed 20 contracts. In 1987, the most difficult year, only five units had been sold. Throughout the following years, sales rose moderately, first to six in 1988, then to twelve the year after. By 1990 Albatross had passed the pre-crisis sales volume, with a record year showing a total of 30 new orders.

The good sales at the beginning of the 1990s were reflected in the company accounts. In 1985, Albatross had a turnover of NOK 233 million. Revenues then fell away, reaching a nadir in 1988. At that point they stood in the region of NOK 100 million, or over 40 percent lower than in their peak year prior to the downturn. It took until 1991 for the company to pass the pre-crisis revenue level, and after that point growth was spectacular. In 1992 the company registered sales of NOK 327 million, or almost NOK 100 million more than it achieved before the downturn began. The following year turnover increased by another NOK 100 million.

The company quickly climbed out of the red, but it wasn't until 1990 that it could again deliver a profit of above NOK 10 million. From 1989 to 1990 profits rose from NOK 3 million to NOK 22 million.[59] Over the next two years they climbed again to NOK 30 and 36 million. It's safe to say that Albatross had rebounded from the downturn, again becoming the 'money machine' it had once been. However, not everything was as before.

The changes following the acquisition manifested themselves in more ways than simply with a name change. The Simrad culture also began to affect the way the 'albatrosses' thought. The time for bold attitudes with regard to costs and loose financial management was definitely over.[60] Albatross itself had been an unconventional and slightly anarchic group, but was now on the way to being a disciplined and streamlined organisation. Now it was more common to ask for permission rather than forgiveness. A stricter regime had been established with a focus on keeping costs down. Through more sober spending, technology development and more efficient production and testing systems, Albatross managed to keep profit margins up, even though the price of DP systems went down.

In addition, the technology had become more streamlined, not just through a more elegant design, but also with the new ADP700 series, which included systems covering three levels of redundancy. Albatross also launched a new AIM system that opened up fresh market opportunities. Oil companies had started asking for systems that could handle the increasing complexity of on board automation. Customers were no longer simply shipowners, now oil companies were joining the client list.

Torfinn Kildal, who was CFO of Albatross during the acquisition in 1986, then CEO of both Simrad Albatross and Simrad, and later held the same position for Kongsberg Maritime, has stated that Albatross benefitted from its purchase by Simrad. It helped the firm get into a strategic industrial mindset that was «completely absent in the Kongsberg environment.»[61] Not everyone was equally delighted with the acquisition at the time. In the summer of 1992 the first edition of Albatross' new corporate newspaper was published. The name was shortly afterwards changed to Trosser'n, following a competition among employees. The new name had maritime mooring associations that applied to Albatross, but could also be interpreted in other ways – namely as an allusion to the company's rebellious nature.[62]

10

THE CORONATION

IN THE EARLY 1990s, the pieces began to fall into place for Simrad Albatross. The company had been through turbulent times with falling oil prices, weakening sales, terminations, and a change of owner. Now the upturn in the oil business and the offshore market gave them their brightest outlook in many years. A new generation of technology, together with new products, gave hope for growth and progress. Most indicators were pointing in the right direction.

Dynamic positioning, originally seen as something nearly magical, was now becoming obligatory for many maritime operations. At the same time the petroleum industry was operating in ever-deeper waters. These developments created a need for both new regulations and new technology that would carry DP into the new millennium.

Norway's maritime electronics industry was also in flux. In Kongsberg a new company was rising like the Phoenix from the ashes of Kongsberg Våpenfabrikk, and the ambition was to grow large. This would prove to have consequences for Simrad Albatross as well. There was much change afoot heading into the 21st century. The origin of these changes, however, lay several years back in time.

CONSOLIDATION ON LAND

Acquisition of Albatross in 1987 had proven to be good business for Simrad. In addition to hefty support of the bottom line, the company in Kongsberg contributed to a significantly broader technological platform, and the opening up of new market segments. And Simrad CEO Kåre Hansen had no plans to stop with this buy-up. Following two years in Asia he was back in Horten in 1991, and soon began to lay plans for solidifying and strengthening Simrad's

Robertson Radio-Elektro was founded by Thorleif Robertson in 1946. Their first products were based on modified American military surplus radios, marketed to the Norwegian fishing fleet. Their portfolio would later include auto-pilot equipment. Kongsberg Våpenfabrikk acquired the company in 1971, upon Thorleif Robertson's death. Since then the company has been bought and sold several times. It became a part of Simrad in 1993, and joined Kongsberg Maritime's Leisure Craft department following the NFT takeover in 1997. Robertson was in principle a production company, delivering various components to DP systems, among others PCs constructed with off-the-shelf parts, and control panel system for the SDP-family. From *Robertson 1946–1996 jubileumsskrift.*

position. The goal was to consolidate Norwegian maritime electronics and grow in export markets. The company had the wind at their backs, and their financial standing was strong. Management felt the time was right to grow through acquisition.[1]

In 1992 Simrad purchased the Osprey group, a producer of underwater cameras, and the following year they bought up Bentech Subsea and the Robertson group from the Bergen-based Bird Group. With that Simrad also gained control of Robertson Tritec in Egersund, producers of autopilots and navigation systems for the pleasure boat market.[2] The media touted the buy-up as the «long-awaited breakthrough in the necessary restructuring of the Norwegian maritime technology sector».[3] Simrad had not yet sated their appetite for acquisition, though, and two years later purchased the Shipmate group, producers of satellite navigational systems with chart plotters and VHF radios for the fishing and leisure craft markets.[4] The growing conglomerate of subsidiaries offered a significant opportunity for increased efficiency through consolidation into national organisations. In the US they were joined in Simrad Inc. and in the UK as Simrad Ltd. The same applied in Norway, where Simrad Albatross,

Simrad Subsea, Simrad Marine, Shipmate Norge and Bentech Subsea became Simrad Norge, as of 1 January 1995.[5] With that the Albatross name was retired, and the 'A' in the DP systems name officially stood for 'Advanced' and not 'Albatross'.

Simrad was not alone in their ambition of being the leading Norwegian supplier of marine electronics. Much had happened in Kongsberg since KV had been closed down in 1987. Even though the company had been dissolved, the enterprises were still in operation, though in different forms. Units producing for the civilian market, like Albatross, were sold off, while defence activities were restructured and continued within the newly established Norsk Forsvarsteknologi, NFT (Norwegian Defence Technology). Like its predecessor, NFT was wholly state-owned. They were to produce high-tech material for the Norwegian armed forces, but would also invest heavily in export markets.[6] It would not take long, though, before this business plan was changed dramatically. In 1989 the Berlin Wall came down, and two years later the Soviet Union was disbanded. The Cold War was over. This led to Norway, and a number of other countries, drastically reducing their military budgets. A positive development in many ways, but for a defence technology company, also a major threat. NFT desperately needed to find new business, and for that reason revised their strategy to embrace 'a balance between civilian and military markets'.[7]

It was no coincidence that maritime systems became a key sector for NFT. Kongsberg Våpenfabrikk had grown to become a major player on the market, and the competence still resided within the new company, and in the town of Kongsberg. Both Albatross and Norcontrol were former KV companies. In 1991 NFT began to make their move. First they bought up KonMap and Kongsberg Navigation.[8] The following year they assumed control over all Norcontrol shares. The acquisitions were followed by a reorganisation in the autumn of 1992, with Norcontrol at the core of the new business area Maritime Systems.[9] With this move, Simrad had assimilated a state-owned competitor that had also harboured ambitions of becoming a market leader in Norwegian maritime electronics.

Simrad had grown considerably through acquisitions, and held a steady course toward their goal of becoming a major Norwegian supplier within maritime electronics.[10] The problem lay in a weakening financial situation. Profit margins began to shrink in 1992, and the stock began to lose value.[11] At the same time NFT's financial position was improving. They were listed on the Oslo Stock Exchange in December of 1993, with 51 percent state owned and the remaining privately held shares.[12] With this new financial muscle, NFT

Transducer production demands extreme precision to achieve top-quality. The image is from the KM production unit on Strandpromenaden in Horten. Photo: KM.

became a heavyweight challenger to Simrad. In fact there was not much real competition between the two, since NFT primarily served the merchant fleet, while Simrad concentrated on the offshore market. Even if there had been a semblance of competition within automation between Norcontrol and what had been Albatross, the companies were more complementary than competitive in practice.

INTEGRATION AT SEA

The eagerness to acquire at Simrad and NFT was due not only to a desire to broaden product lines to guard against market fluctuations, or even to control profitable companies. In the beginning dynamic positioning and related technologies had been developed in relatively narrow niche markets. Now disparate technologies were converging, and the trend was toward ever-stronger integration.

The development of the AIM system and Albatross's contracts with the oil companies for offshore automation solutions, with several applications built into a single system, were examples of this. One could still focus on dynamic positioning and let others develop and produce supplemental systems for integration, but new players entering the market were presenting serious challenges. It was no longer enough to deliver stand-alone systems. In order to remain competitive, a supplier had to offer integrated systems capable of handling entire operations.

The Royal Norwegian Council for Scientific and Industrial Research (Norges Teknisk-Naturvitenskapelige Forskningsråd), NTNF, took the initiative for the so-called MITS program in 1991, to develop an IT standard for communication between various subsystems for navigation, positioning and surveillance.[13] The goal was to simplify integration of equipment from different suppliers. The idea was that the customer ought to be able to combine components from random MITS-compatible units to create a custom unit as needed.[14] The Research Council aimed to strengthen the collective Norwegian supplier industry by allowing the various players to collaborate rather than just compete with each other.

This industry-oriented philosophy pointed in the opposite direction from the one the main players were headed in. They were more interested in growth, through acquisition and other measures, in order to reach an ever-broader market segment. Not only Simrad and NFT were gearing up. Kværner had also thrown their hat in the vessel automation ring. Together with the research environments of MARINTEK and DNV, all these companies participated in the MITS project. Simrad's contribution was dynamic positioning.[15] The project was no great success, however, proving unable to deliver better systems integration or closer cooperation between the companies. It was an interesting endeavour nonetheless, as it underscored the trend toward more integrated systems, and showed that it was not yet clear whether this would come about through integration of systems from various companies, or from within a single company.

Albatross had out-competed Honeywell, a company that had initially supplied automation systems to factories on land. The close relations between Albatross and the shipowners, and their specialisation in technology for North Sea vessels, had given them a strong competitive advantage. Dynamic positioning was a stand-alone product then, focused on keeping a vessel stable in a certain position. With new platforms and production facilities and ever more complex maritime operations, new markets emerged for integrated systems to cover a broad spectrum of tasks. In this way the challenges of the 1990s began to resemble those facing dry land production facilities. AIM was a good example of the diminishing degree of difference between maritime and land-based automation. This development led to new competitors entering the market for maritime automation solutions. One of the largest and most formidable of these was the multinational conglomerate ABB, already a major supplier of automation systems to the process industry on land. In the early 1990, ABB had begun developing systems for dynamic positioning.[16]

A NEW CLASS OF UNDERSTANDING

With the trend toward more integration came the danger that DP would simply be absorbed by larger automation systems. Other trends, however, were heading in the opposite direction. DNV had been the first classification society to establish a separate class for DP-equipped vessels. Work had begun back in the 1970s but establishing concrete requirements had taken time. DNVs first DP class, DYNPOS, was unveiled in 1977, and the first ship to be classified was the Norwegian-owned Wilhelmsen ship *Tender Contest*.[17] Requirements established for this class were somewhat limited, though. There was no mention of vessel purpose or the size and quality of the propellers, hull or engines, to name a few shortcomings. DNV's Holger Røkeberg, a pioneer in the development of DP class, has rather bluntly asserted that one could get DYNPOS classification «with a mix-master on each corner» of a barge, as long as class requirements were met.[18]

Work to develop better-suited requirements led to the development of the ERN-number (Environmental Regularity Number). This gave an indication of a vessel's ability to maintain position in varying weather conditions, and the consequences of engine or propeller failure.[19] This method of calculation, devised by DNV in the late 1970s, set the standard and became an important sales argument in the shipowners' marketing of their vessels. Eventually all DP vessels seeking DNV class were required to have an ERN number indicating the vessel's ability to stay in position in a number of different failure scenarios. The number consisted of three digits from 0 to 99, and was arrived at by calculating the force of weather that the vessel was capable of withstanding with full thruster power. The basis for this was a table with wave and wind statistics based on measurements taken in the Norwegian Sea, and a fixed sea current load. The first cipher indicated the ability to hold position with all systems functioning, the next with the failure of the least effective thruster, and the third with the most effective thruster out of service.[20] If a shipowner hoped to get work for a DP vessel, the ERN number virtually had to be 99, 99, 99, or close. This was not a requirement, but market demand made it virtually the de facto standard.[21] DNV would later add a cipher addressing 'worst case single failure'.[22]

In time other societies like Lloyds Register of Shipping (LR) and American Bureau of Shipping (ABS) developed their own class notes for DP along the same lines as DNV. In the beginning, though, regulation of the industry through DP classification was largely a Norwegian phenomenon for vessels operating in the North Sea. In 1984 DNV and the Norwegian Maritime Authority began work to develop new and more comprehensive guidelines. The idea was that no DP operation could be performed if a failure could lead to unacceptable consequences. Based on a «better safe than sorry» principle, four categories of consequences were laid out, based on calculations of whether a vessel could maintain position in the event of failure of various DP system elements.[23]

Though this work began in Norway, there were many other contributors in the development of a new set of rules. Classification societies, national maritime authorities and various business interests were also involved. One of the most important was the DP Vessel Owner's Organisation (DPVOA), known today as the International Marine Contractors Association (IMCA). The goal was to lay the foundation for an international standard through the IMO (International Maritime Organization), the United Nations body for regulation of international shipping. Formulation of class requirements was also important for the Albatross team. They dealt with DNV on a daily basis and used this contact to influence the formation of rules in harmony with their own technology.[24]

The IMO ratified 'Guidelines for Vessels with Dynamic Positioning Systems' in 1994.[25] Initially these guidelines had been divided into four so-called consequence classes, spanning from the inconsequential to the catastrophic. In the IMO version the number of classes was reduced to three, and consequence classes were changed to equipment classes. The greater the consequence loss of position had, the stricter the requirement for DP system reliability. The equipment classes were defined based on 'worst case failure modes', or the single failure that would have the direst consequences. These three classes, DP1, DP2 and DP3, contained the following specifications:

- Equipment Class 1 had no redundancy. Loss of position may occur in the event of a single fault.

DNV Certificate for DP. Photo: Mediafoto.

- Equipment Class 2 had redundancy to the degree that no single fault in any active system would cause the entire active system to break down. Loss of position should not occur due to failure in any active component or system such as generators, thrusters, switchboards, remote controlled valves, and so on, but might occur in the event of failure of static components such as cables, pipes, manual valves, etc.
- Equipment Class 3 should in addition tolerate fire or flooding in a given zone without failure of the system. Loss of position should not occur due to any single failure, including loss of an entire fire zone, or flooding of a watertight compartment.[26]

The IMO regulations meant that equipment in Class 2 must have redundancy in all active components, including DP control systems. Components in a Class 3 system were additionally required to have a back up DP control system physically separate from the main system.[27] The vessel also had to have two engine rooms separated by compartment that could withstand smoke and open flame for up to one hour without the temperature exceeding 180° C.[28] While the old class requirements focused primarily on the control system, now there were requirements for redundancy at all points. This meant not only improved safety, but significantly increased cost as well. DP systems had also become more tightly integrated with the vessel's propulsion system, allowing the classes to provide a clearer picture of which level of safety a vessel could operate at.

The IMO equipment classes became a standard that the classification societies quickly embraced, developing their own classes for dynamically positioned vessels. For example, DNV's answer to IMO's new equipment classes 1, 2 and 3 were the categories DYNPOS-AUT, DYNPOS-AUTR and DYNPOS-AUTRO.[29]

The IMO standard clarified and expanded the understanding of the scope of a DP system. Prior to this it was common to use the term referring to the control system alone. Now all the elements under the control system were included in the definition. This meant that a DP system should be understood as a system consisting of three parts: the power system (normally diesel engines, generators and electric power distribution), the system of thrusters, and the DP control system with its sensors. In the jargon of the industry, however, it remained common to use the DP name when referring to the DP control system alone.

CONSEQUENCES AND SAFETY

The IMO regulations introduced the phrase 'equipment class' but made no mention of which classes were required for which conditions. It was left up to the shipowners, operators or national authorities to determine which class to use in a given situation. The oil companies did, however, demonstrate a preference for the highest standards. They sought to minimise the risk of losing money or reputation, and favoured standards that would simplify their orders. The same standards were promoted in requirements from the authorities on the Norwegian Continental Shelf (NCS).

Statutes issues by the Norwegian Maritime Authority (NMA) regulated the equipment classes to be used in various situations, based on consequences due to loss of position. Class 1 equipment was to be employed in operations where loss of position could lead to damage or pollution with minimal consequences. Class 2 was required where loss of position could cause personal injury, pollution, or damage with serious economic consequences. Class 3 was mandatory where loss of position could cause death, serious pollution, or damage with major economic consequences.[30]

The NMA did not produce detailed specifications for the various operations on the NCS, but they were clear that Class 3 equipment should be used in drilling and well service operations.[31] This meant that many shipowners equipped their vessels with Class 3 equipment in order to be able to compete for work in the North Sea. Requirements on DP systems were also influenced by NORSOK standards.[32] NORSOK was a result of collective efforts by the various players in the petroleum industry, the Norwegian industrial community and the authorities, in an attempt to reduce time and cost of building and operating installations on the NCS. The new industry standards superseded internal specifications of oil companies operating on the NCS, as well as many of the Norwegian Petroleum Directorate's own requirements. They also contributed to standardisation of the oil companies' requirements for DP systems.[33]

These new class requirements served to focus efforts on identifying the most critical failures. Assessment of effects of a system failure on a vessel's ability to maintain position could be done through a type of analysis called FMEA (Failure Mode and Effects Analysis), or during actual sea trials, and both methods were employed.[34] Together, the new standards and such tests contributed to improved safety. The vessel as a whole was regarded more systematically, not just the DP system. Nils Albert Jenssen has jokingly referred to the time prior to implementation of IMO standards as the 'cowboy culture inherited from the Americans,' when they joked that if a system was tested for longer than 10 minutes, it was over-tested.[35] Even though the number of installed DP systems virtually exploded following the ratification of IMO standards, the number of accidents remained consistently low.[36]

The trend towards ever more complex on-board systems continued unabated. One effect of the new class requirements was to preserve DP as a separate system, thereby reducing the risk of it being swallowed up as just another part of a larger automation system. Redundancy requirements on all system elements, and that the system remain operative even in case of fire or flooding, made integration of DP functionality into a complete automation system unreasonably complex and expensive. The trend towards ever-closer integration of the various bridge systems also continued at full strength. Classification requirements provided standards that made it easier for a customer to order a DP system, but also harder to alter it. The trend was toward more mass production and less customisation.

Many years had passed since Albatross salesmen sold system and functionality before they were fully developed. The time of extreme tailoring of systems for individual customers was definitely over. DP technology had come of age. The new standards meant less flexibility, but also more predictability.

A NEW TECHNOLOGICAL GENERATION – SDP

In 1994, the same year as IMO regulations were ratified, work was commenced on what would become Simrad Albatross's fourth generation DP system. The goal was not first and foremost to build a system around IMO rules. The new requirements had quickly become yesterday's news, and were already accommodated in the ADP700 series. Now there were other demands driving the development of a new DP system.

One of the main challenges lay in the system's user interface, which had become outdated and inflexible by comparison to competing systems. If Simrad wanted to maintain its market leading position, they would have to develop an interface based on modern graphics like Microsoft Windows or Unix Motif. Programmers favoured Unix. Other companies had already invested in this platform, but was it sufficiently geared to the future? The operating system Windows 3.1, the most likely alternative, was poorly equipped to handle the demands of a DP system. Microsoft had recently launched a promising NT version for the business market, but the question remained whether it would become a technology driver and thus emerge as the right choice for DP into the future.[37]

The new generation of DP systems was launched in 1996 under the name Simrad Dynamic Positioning, or SDP, and encompassed the SDP01, 11, 12, 21, 22, 31 and 32 models. The first cipher (0/1/2/3) indicated 'compact single', 'single', 'dual redundant', or 'triple redundant', while the second number indicated whether the DP system was stand-alone or integrated.

In addition the new systems featured a joystick, dubbed the SJS01 (Simrad Joystick System). Both this and SDP01 were replacements for the old Robertson products, ROBSTICK and ROBPOS, that had landed in the Simrad portfolio with the buyout of Robertson in Egersund in 1993.[38] These were now phased out. The new systems were developed jointly by departments in Egersund and Kongsberg, and combined the Egersund group's competence on less complex DP systems with the latest in Simrad technology. Production was located in Egersund. With the new SDP and SJS products, Simrad had a broad spectrum of offerings: from a simple joystick system for the low-end market, to the complex triple-redundant flagship models designed to handle the most complex and demanding jobs.

The new generation of DP was designed for simplified integration with other onboard systems. System developers had chosen a solution that resembled that used in the ADP500 series, but with a separate operator console and processing station. All the DP systems were developed in two versions. They could be installed as so-called stand-alone systems with a direct connection

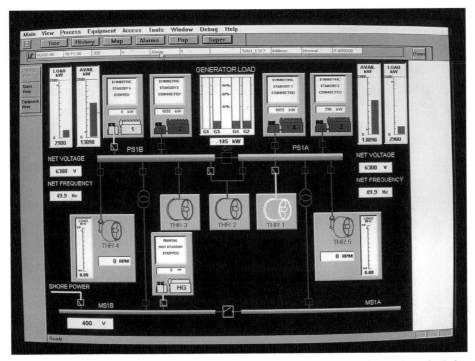

SVC (Simrad Vessel Control) was a distributed automation and monitoring system designed specifically for offshore vessels. SVC, STC and SDP systems were tightly integrated and based on common technology. This photo from 1997 shows a screen used to control the power plant on board, showing high voltage electrical switchboards with generator sets and thrusters, and low-voltage electrical distribution. Photo: KM.

from a central processing station to the sensors, reference systems, thrusters and other elements of the system. Alternatively they could be installed as integrated systems with network communications to distributed processing stations placed in the vicinity of peripheral units. The DP systems could also be combined with mooring systems through SPM (Simrad Position Mooring), an improved version of the older APM system. A thruster control system was also developed, the STC (Simrad Thruster Control).

The workhorse in the portfolio was the SVC (Simrad Vessel Control), a distributed automation and surveillance system based on AIM technology. DP and other Simrad systems, including thruster control and position mooring, could be integrated into a single unit and operated via a common user interface. The various Simrad systems were largely based on shared technology with many similar hardware components and software modules, and could communicate through a common data network. These features were particularly advantageous for integration.[39]

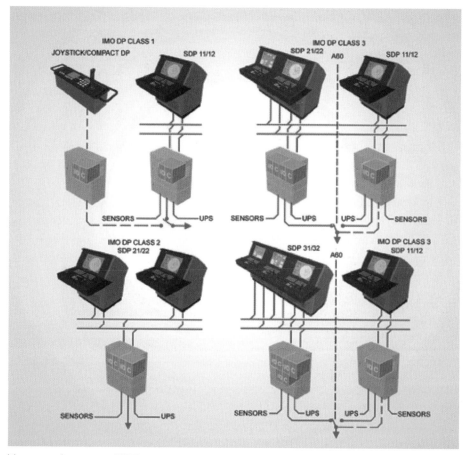

Various configurations of SDP systems to satisfy the requirements of different DP classes in IMO regulations.

Improved versions of the old HPR (Hydroacoustic Positioning Relays) were also available, as well as the Electronic Chart Display & Information System (ECDIS). These could be installed together with the DP systems, but they could also be delivered as separate products.[40] Development of these systems was done in-house, but Simrad also had agreements with other companies in order to be able to offer a wider range of technology packages to customers. One such collaborator was Seatex in Trondheim, developers of reference systems based on the satellite positioning system GPS (Global Positioning System).[41] The various systems were not merged, but rather developed and marketed as separate products. There had been changes since the launch of the previous generation of DP systems, though. For the first time, Simrad offered two versions of its DP systems: One stand-alone, and one that could be integrated into a larger system. This was indicative of the growing use of automation on board, requiring different systems to communicate and be integrated into a comprehensive on-board system. Parallel to this, the IMO redundancy requirements kept DP systems as separate units, and not merged into other systems. For this reason it was essential to develop an interface that allowed the systems to communicate with each other. This was part of the Research Council's ambition for the MITS project. The goal had been to strengthen the Norwegian supplier industry by developing a shared interface. Simrad was now doing just that, only on its own.

The new product line was well-suited to the new class requirements. A DP could be delivered in three basis versions: A simple system without redundancy; a double system with two parallel systems; and a triple system with triple modular redundancy and majority voting for all vital data. A triple redundancy system alone would not satisfy the strictest IMO requirements. This could be achieved with both double- and triple redundancy systems, if they were supplemented with an additional system isolated by a fireproof compartment that would also prevent flooding.[42]

The IMO rules were themselves no reason to develop or purchase a triple redundancy system. The key driver was risk of personal injury and environmental consequences, as well as monetary loss. Precision and reliability were not criteria. Many of Simrad's customers were in the oil and gas sector, though, where the saying 'time is money' means more than in most other sectors. It could easily pay to have the most secure DP system on board, since increased redundancy meant increased reliability and reduced down time due to systems failure. With its flexibility and modularity, the new SDP system was well equipped to improve both the safety and reliability of a vessel, and to protect personnel and the environment in keeping with the new class requirements.

A NEW TECHNOLOGY PLATFORM

In general appearance, there was not much to differentiate the new operator stations from the old. Both featured deep blue consoles with lighter side panels, and resembled each other in form. The big differences were found on the inside. Computers performing real-time calculations had been moved to separate cabinets, and two important and related innovations had been implemented. The one concerned the computers, the other software and user interface.

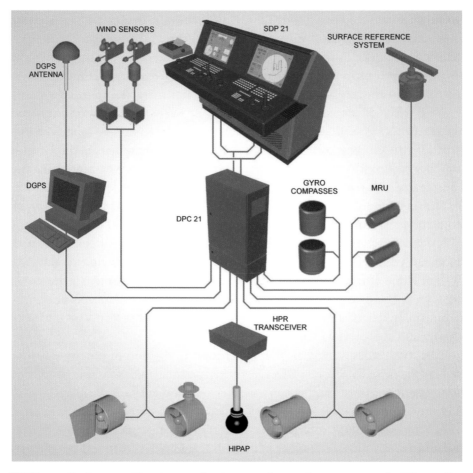

SDP System Configuration. Here the control and user interface is split into two units: the DP controller, responsible for position and heading control, and the operator station. Placing the DP controller in a separate cabinet made installation easier. It was simpler to connect field cables and could be placed in a more suitable room than on the bridge, for example, in an instrument room. With the new SBC400 computer the controller cabinet became more compact, making the SDP a more affordable solution than the ADP700 product line.

The ADP700-series featured an operator station based on an in-house developed processor and graphics card. At the time of its development, using PCs was not a viable option. Then in 1993, Microsoft introduced the Windows NT operating system. With this the PC became an interesting alternative to the homemade SBC as the brain in DP systems. Simrad's programmers took to the new operating system, and they began to plan and develop a PC-based operator station. The PCs themselves were deemed not reliable enough to drive the processing stations requiring real-time calculations. Here the SBC machines were preferred. This meant that the operator and processing stations were separated. The SDP series of operator stations were equipped with PCs running Windows NT.[43] The change in operating system also meant a transition from programming language C to the object-oriented C++.[44] This would also have consequences for the user interface.

In the ADP700 series, much of the interaction between the operator and the machine was through buttons, following the 'one button – one function' principle. In the new SDP series much of this functionality was moved into a Windows-based graphic interface. This allowed for simplification of the console design, and the operating station had a noticeably cleaner appearance. Buttons and lights were still used for certain functions, though. This was to keep operators from having to flip through several windows to access the most important functions in critical, high-stress situations. On the older systems each button had its own function, occupying a lot of space on the console. With the new Windows interface, large surface areas were freed up, making it possible to equip each console section with an identical set of buttons. A dual redundant system consisted of two identical console sections and it was up to the operator to select which one to use for commanding the DP system. The other section could be used to display information. Similarly the triple system had three console sections. This simplified construction greatly, as there was no longer a need for multiple computers to process the same button signal.[45]

Parallel to implementation of PCs and a new Windows-based graphic interface in the operator station, a successor to the SBC3000 was developed for the DP processing station. The old machine was replaced with an in-house SBC400 based on Intel's 960 RISC-processor, ten times faster than its predecessor, and at one fourth the cost.[46] The choice of two disparate computers established a clear division between real time control computation and user interface in the DP system. It also had consequences for the topology.[47] On the ADP700 series the operator console was connected directly to the sensors, positioners, and thrusters. In the new system, the processing unit was moved to its own cabinet with one, two or three SBC400s, depending on the degree of redundancy.

It wasn't long before the first system was sold. In January 1996 the partly Norwegian-owned cruise line Royal Caribbean Cruise Lines (RCCL) ordered two SDP11 systems, installed on the *Rhapsody of the Seas* and the *Vision of the Seas* in August of the following year.[48] In the Kongsberg annual report from 1996 it was noted with satisfaction that the product revamp «appeared to meet with approval on the market».[49] The SDP series became a solid success.[50] The last units were installed in 2007. The series had introduced several innovations, but not

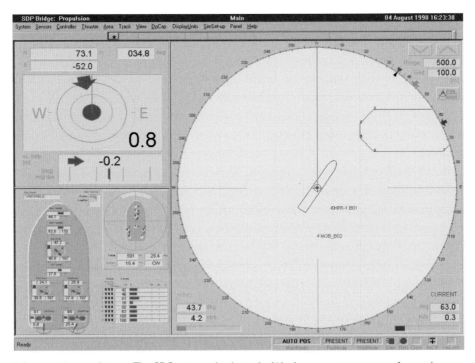

PCs created new solutions. The SDP system, thanks to the Windows operating system, featured a more modern look than previously. The screen was divided into three groups: The work area occupied two thirds of the right hand side of the screen, and the two remaining smaller areas monitored operation. The 'Troll-eye' in the upper left showed how well the vessel was »fine tuned into» the position. It turned out that this old idea, which was similar to that used in radio sets during the 1950s, was the most popular news for DP operators. The image is taken from an SDP operator manual from 1999. Photo: KM.

all of them influenced performance or safety. For the customers, the change of name alone, from ADP to SDP, replacing the A with an S, was largely viewed as a cosmetic change without practical consequences. It did, however, tell of significant changes at the supplier, as would the next name change, when the S was replaced with a K. The reason behind this change lay in events unfolding as the SDP series was being launched.

KONGSBERG MARITIME – THE CORONATION

As previously mentioned, both Simrad and Norwegian Defence Technology (NFT) harboured ambitions to become the leading Norwegian maritime electronics company in the early 1990s. Both were pursuing this strategy by expanding through acquisition. Simrad had long been the largest and strongest of the two. In 1996, however, the balance of power shifted.

While NFT had the wind in their sails, Simrad was entering stormy waters headlong. Even with rising turnover, the bottom line was taking a hit. In 1994 profits dropped by 40 percent, and the order book was thinning.[51] These developments were reflected on the stock market, where Simrad shares fell from NOK 120 to NOK 70 during 1994. The adversity continued into 1995, though to a lesser degree.[52] This drop in market value made Simrad an easy target for acquisition, and a buyer with cash to match their ambitions was waiting in the wings.

In May of 1995 a drama in two acts was staged, ending with the takeover of Simrad by its competitor from Kongsberg. The trigger was NFT's purchase of 17.44 percent of Simrad stock, making them the largest shareholder.[53] NFT's management confided that they had no further buy-up plans, and Simrad management confirmed their acceptance of the purchase.[54]

In the autumn of 1995 NFT determined to change their name to Kongsberg Gruppen (KOG, the Kongsberg group). The name change was partly in response to the company's expansion beyond the constraints of defence technology, and the Norsk Forsvarsteknologi name no longer invoked their full scope of activities. Another factor was that they aspired to a higher profile through the use of the Kongsberg name and the old KV crown in marketing their products. By taking back the name and logo, the company was also tracing its roots back to the industrial and technology concern that had operated on the banks of the river Numedalslågen since 1814.[55]

Despite assurances to the contrary, it soon became apparent that the Kongsberg Group had heftier ambitions than simply to be the largest single shareholder in Simrad. On 12 April 1996 the company bid NOK 120 a share for all Simrad stock. This was 30 to 40 percent over the trading rate for the previous year. The market responded favourably, and during the course of the day, KOG had acquired more than two-thirds of voting shares, thereby gaining effective control of Simrad.[56] In the year that followed they would up their holdings to 88.2 percent.[57] The remaining shares were acquired from the French company Thomson in April of 1997.[58]

Simrad's management was not informed of Kongsberg's plans for the buy-up. Though they tried to convince Simrad's leaders that their move was not hostile, that is precisely how it was perceived by many Simrad employees. If the mood was bleak in Horten, it was equally cheerful at Simrad in Kongsberg. The takeover stung Simrad director Kåre Hansen the hardest, and he would depart the company shortly after.[59] But for those working with DP in the Industritunet (the Kongsberg industrial park), especially those who had

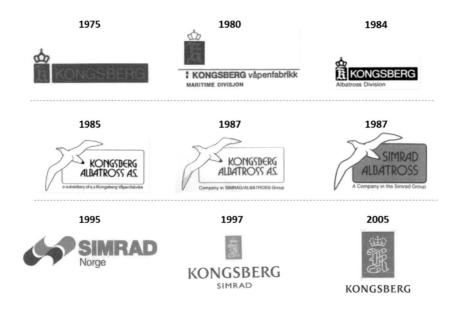

The DP business has been a part of several companies and departments. The illustration shows the different logos used throughout the years.

been involved since the Albatross days, the acquisition was seen as a kind of homecoming.[60]

The new company became operative from 1997 under the name Kongsberg Maritime. KOG had become a corporation with two strong divisions, the other being Kongsberg Defence & Aerospace AS.[61] These two units were similar in size, both in number of employees and turnover. With that the ambitions of management following the fall of the Berlin Wall in 1989 had been realised. The goal of striking a balance between civilian and military enterprises had been achieved.[62]

Kongsberg Maritime AS was founded as a wholly owned subsidiary of the Kongsberg Group, with four divisions, each organised as limited companies:

- Kongsberg Simrad in Kongsberg and Horten, in addition to several foreign subsidiaries, constituted the group's offshore interests. Main products were systems for dynamic positioning, vessel automation, process control and subsea technology.
- Kongsberg Norcontrol in Horten, suppliers of machinery control and navigation systems to deepwater shipping.
- Kongsberg Norcontrol Systems in Horten, suppliers of training simulators and systems for ship traffic surveillance.

Sea trial for *Seabex One* in 1981. The picture shows Steinar Gregersen (left) and Hans Jørgen Dyrnes. Gregersen had a long career with Albatross and was deeply involved in technical details as well as business matters and relationships with key customers. He headed Simrad Albatross from 1993 to 1998. Photo: Mediafoto.

- Simrad in Horten, Egersund and Støvring in Danmark, selling instrumentation to the fishing fleet and leisure craft industry, including fish locating devices. This encompassed sonar, echo sounders, trawler instrumentation, autopilots, and chart plotters.[63]

Several of these companies had their roots in Albatross, and for them, the KOG takeover meant that the process had come full circle. The same applied for the DP business, which once again was back in the state-owned Kongsberg fold. The corporation was no longer Kongsberg Våpenfabrikk, true enough, but the ties to the old munitions business were still strong. Reintroducing the old KV logo in a modern version was a clear homage to continuity.

The change of ownership did not greatly affect day-to-day affairs. For most, it was business as usual. The former Albatross group remained at their site in Industritunet in Kongsberg. Top management also had their offices here, even though head office was officially located in Horten. The Albatross name, though, had been dropped. The systems, sold up to that time adorned with the Simrad wave, could now show off the Kongsberg K, topped with a royal crown.

But the reorganising was not entirely trouble-free. Establishing Kongsberg Maritime with four subsidiaries was the first step in building the maritime business back into the Kongsberg Group. Toward the end of January 1998, the news broke that director Steinar Gregersen had resigned on the spot following a disagreement with the board.[64] Gregersen had been with the company since the slightly anarchistic Albatross days, and had occupied the boss's chair since 1993. Now he stood in opposition to integration with the Norcontrol companies, and what he deemed an excessively long chain of command and a heavy-handed bureaucracy.[65]

Gregersen's departure marked the end of an era with engineers in the driver's seat. With the exception of the two first years, the company had been managed by engineers during the entire Simrad period, starting with Terje Løkling in 1989, and continuing with Gregersen four years later. Now it was the economists' turn again. CFO Steinar Aabelvik was placed at the helm after Gregersen jumped ship, taking over as CEO in the autumn of 1998.[66]

11

FROM THE DEEP BLUE SEA
TO OUTER SPACE

IN THE YEARS before Simrad became part of the Kongsberg Group, the accounts for the Albatross business had shown annual turnover of approx. NOK 400 million. The change of ownership in 1996 marked the start of a period with formidable growth and strong results, with turnover doubling during the two first years of this period. 1999 saw turnover easily top NOK 1 billion for the first time. With NOK 184 million of this in profit, the purchase of Simrad could safely be said to have been a good investment for the new owners.[1]

Income on sales, that included DP systems, that was about 60 percent of Kongsberg Simrad's revenue in this period, also showed strong growth. Following a brief dip in 1995, sales increased sharply with the introduction of the new SDP system in 1996. During the last three years of the millennium revenue increased from NOK 250 to 646 million. Even though the DP-related share of turnover would decrease in the following years, dynamic positioning continued as the most profitable segment of the business.[2] The importance of DP for the company's economy was also greater than the bottom line showed. Because a DP order would often trigger sales of vessel automation and HPR, the DP systems served as a generator of new sales.

DP systems sales need to be seen in light of developments in the petroleum sector. The North Sea was still the dominant region for offshore investments, but the Gulf of Mexico was coming on strong, as were other regions, particularly offshore Brazil. Kongsberg Simrad established a service base in Rio de Janeiro in 1996 to strengthen their presence there.[3] Service bases were already established in Aberdeen, Houston, Singapore and Halifax.[4] With this, Kongsberg Simrad was now established in all the world's major offshore markets.

The company had learned that the oil and gas market could be extremely volatile, with big swings in both prices and activities, and this could have great consequences for DP systems sales. From a high of USD 20 per barrel in 1996, crude oil dropped to a low of USD 13 per barrel in 1998/99. This led to a more cautious approach from the customers toward new activities. The last time oil had dipped so low was in the mid 1980s, when Albatross got into serious financial difficulties. Many feared similar consequences this time around too.[5] Turnover had grown significantly for several years, but began to slow down in 1999. The following year sales fell off, and the final figures for 2000 showed a drop in sales of 15 percent.

NEW MARKET OPPORTUNITIES

The fall in oil prices did not lead to a radical shift in business activities. DP remained the top priority. But the weakened economy made it more diffi-cult to win new contracts, and the company was compelled to seek out new opportunities. The focus would be to offer cost-effective solutions that would be profitable for customers, even with low oil prices. Upgrades to existing equipment became a new priority. Since DP equipment from Kongsberg was installed on more than a thousand vessels, the potential was impressive.[6]

Over the years, close to 70 ADP503 installations had been sold. An upgrade to components from the SDP series was made available for these. The SDP521, as the new hybrid was called, still used the consoles and cabinets from the 1970s, filling them with components from the new series. Buttons and panels were replaced with the new and more user-friendly screen-based user interface.[7] Several ADP503 units were upgraded, including that on board the Russian drill ship *Valentin Shashin*, the seventh ADP503 ever sold, and thereby one of the oldest in operation.

Parallel to new approaches in the known market, the company was working to reduce dependence on the petroleum industry and strengthen investments in other areas.[8] One of these was the cruise market, where Kongsberg Simrad had some previous experience. This had its origins in the installation of an ADP701 unit on the *Grandeur of the Seas*, owned by Royal Caribbean Cruise Lines (RCCL). The following summer her sister ship, *Enchantment of the Seas,* received the same system. Eventually several other ships were equipped with the new SDP systems.[9] Another strong growth market was in cable-laying vessels.[10] Here Kongsberg Simrad further secured its already strong position as a supplier of positioning and control systems.

In 1996 Kongsberg Simrad signed a contract with Sea Launch for the delivery of two DP systems. The international consortium was established to launch rockets to put satellites in orbit from a floating platform on the equator in the Pacific. Kongsberg Simrad delivered DP systems for the launch platform *Ocean Odyssey* and the command ship *Sea Launch Commander*. Bruno Mjøseng (left), Kjell Erik Kvammen and Kenneth Wikerøy were at the launch site to test and adjust the system. During the launch, the rig's DP system was remotely operated from the command ship. The right image shows the rocket launch of a European communications satellite in September 2011. Photo: KM.

Another smaller, but more spectacular market, was offshore rocket launching. In 1996, Kongsberg Simrad signed a contract for delivery of two DP systems to Sea Launch.

This international consortium, with the Norwegian Kværner group as the major shareholder, had been established to send satellites into space using Russian Zenith rockets launched from a floating platform off Kiritimati (Christmas Island) in the Central Pacific Ocean. Launching from a base near the equator would provide optimal assistance from the earth's rotation to increase launch velocity. This reduced fuel costs, and made it possible to take on additional payload.[11]

Kongsberg Simrad delivered DP systems to the launch platform *Ocean Odyssey*, a converted drilling platform, and to the command ship *Sea Launch Commander*.[12] In principle these systems were similar to previous marine deliveries. One key difference was that, in addition to wind, current and waves, the platform system now had to compensate for the powerful rocket engine thrust.

The equipment was in place in the Pacific by 1999, and Kongsberg Simrad sent three service personnel to undertake the final adjustments and testing of the equipment. The vessels had their base in Long Beach, CA and the sea journey to the launch site took 12 days. For the service crew, accustomed to wintery conditions in the North Sea, it was an exotic assignment. Good weather throughout the trip did nothing to diminish the experience.[13]

The command ship and the launch platform both lay on DP, with a 12-metre gangway connecting them. This gave not only a clear visualisation of the accuracy of the DP systems, but also provided a unique reference system for positioning. By measuring length and angle of the gangway, and with a little help from Pythagoras, the Kongsberg engineers had a useful tool for measuring the relative position of the vessels.

Since the vessels lay on the equator, the service team had the possibility of testing the DP equipment on both northern and southern latitudes.[14] The first trial launch was in March of 1999, with everything functioning satisfactorily. The launch platform listed at no more than an acceptable 4.7 degrees during launch. With this successful result, Kongsberg Simrad had moved from the ocean deep, and into deep space.[15] Regular commercial launches commenced from the autumn of 1999, always with a service engineer from Kongsberg on board. As of the summer of 2014, 36 launces had been performed.[16]

By establishing themselves in several business segments, the company had reduced their exposure to swings in any single market. The most important challenge ahead would nonetheless lay not in reaching new heights in space, but new depths in the sea. A new deep-water market was opening up, with great potential for those who could provide good solutions to meet the challenges that lay further underwater.

WAY DOWN, AND WAY OUT

Toward the mid 1990s the oil and gas industry was moving into ever-deeper waters. When Albatross was founded in the mid 1970s, typical drilling depths could be around 100 metres. Twenty years on, depths were at 2000 metres, and sights were set as deep as 3000 metres. Activities were also moving to new geographical areas. The era of major field developments in the North Sea seemed to be drawing to a close. Towards the end of the 1990s, activity on the NCS was in decline, while in the oceans off West Africa and Brazil, and in the Gulf of Mexico, things were more stable.[17]

For operations in these areas, the oil companies were increasingly interested in simple, floating solutions. With greater depths it became virtually impossible to place platforms on the sea floor, and as depths increased even further, anchoring of platforms and ships using chains or steel wire ropes also disappeared as a viable option. The great depths also posed challenges for vessels employing DP. The biggest of these was obtaining sufficient position reference data.

Simrad's HPR system had been a core component of Albatross's DP systems from the start. Both the *Seaway Eagle* and the *Seaway Swan* were equipped with the HPR100. The system had been further developed, however, and by the mid 1990s the HPR400 family, with LBL and SSBL variations, had taken over.[18] With Simrad's purchase of Albatross, the DP and HPR activities had been more tightly coordinated. When Simrad Albatross and Simrad Subsea were merged into Simrad Norge AS in 1995, development of DP and HPR systems were coordinated by the same leadership.

Developments had long been pointing in the direction of greater precision in deep water, but in the 1990s greater precision at the heights was on the horizon. The starting point for this was what we know today as GPS, developed by the US military in the 1970s and 80s. The positioning system, known as NAVSTAR (Navigation System Using Timing and Ranging), consists of 24 satellites orbiting in a network around the earth, in order to provide global coverage. The first of these was launched in 1978, but it would take 16 years before the system would be operative with full satellite coverage.

Today GPS makes it possible to establish one's position with a high degree of precision. It was not that way to begin with. Back then the system was poorly suited to DP solutions due to lack of satellites. Dynamic positioning requires reference systems with 24-hour coverage, seven days a week. Continuous coverage became possible before the GPS system was complete, but since it was intended for military use, restrictions were put on precision for civilian use, so-called *selective availability*. This reduced precision by up to several tens of metres.

Access to satellite signals, and differential corrections by means of comparing position with known points on land, made GPS a viable reference system for DP from the mid 1990s. Using satellite signals alone it was only possible to achieve accuracy up to within 40–50 metres, but with land based corrective signals, so called DGPS (Differential GPS), accuracy could be improved by ten times or more.[19] With this combination the system was suitable for use in dynamic positioning. By orienting itself down to the sea floor and up to the satellites in space, and combining hydro acoustic systems with GPS, Kongsberg Simrad could achieve highly accurate position indication with its DP systems, with margins of error at under one metre.[20]

HIPAP

In addition to improving their HPR systems, Simrad engineers in Horten were also developing a new type of positioning system. In 1991 the company was well on its way toward launching the HPR400, better suited to deep-water operations than its predecessor. Statoil, however, one of the company's most important customers, was very clear that the new system was not good enough, and that there was a need for a positioning system substantially more accurate that those Simrad could deliver. The company considered this a threat to their leading market position, and the new demand sounded the starting gun in a race to develop the next technological leap forward.[21]

It was no small task the engineers had undertaken. No minor adjustment would do, in fact nothing less would suffice than an improvement in precision from one to one-tenth of a degree in measuring the direction to the transponders. This would not only require many hours of work from the development team. There was also a high degree of risk involved. Preliminary studies indicated that the system would place great demands on processing capacity and speed, and these were already pushing the limits of what was possible using available technology. In order to attain the desired precision, a transducer that would allow precision in all directions had to be designed. In order to avoid making such a high-precision system too large and costly, electronics would have to be drastically reduced in size.[22]

Costs estimates and risk analysis indicated that Simrad could not tackle the development project on its own. For Statoil, the need for higher precision was so pressing that the project was included in their supplier development program. The development contract was signed in 1992, and work could commence with full force.

Three years later, in 1995, HiPAP was launched. The name, which Simrad registered as a trademark, stood for High Precision Acoustic Positioning system. Even though it was a more complex system than he HPR, it proved easier to operate. Based on the SSBL principle, the system required only one transducer

The HiPAP sphere consists of many transducer elements and is covered with a thick red membrane to protect it against corrosion caused by seawater. Photo: KM.

under the vessel and one transponder on the sea floor. An LBL system would have required multiple subsea transponders, while an SBL system would need multiple transducers under the vessel.[23] With its characteristic signal red submersible ball with 241 senders and receivers, the new system could measure in all directions under water, providing a three-dimensional picture of the area below the vessel.

To begin with the HiPAP was specified for a range of 2000 metres, but tests showed that it functioned well within a radius of up to 2500 metres. With more powerful transponders the range could be increased to 3500 metres. This highly precise system provided extremely accurate measurements, three to five

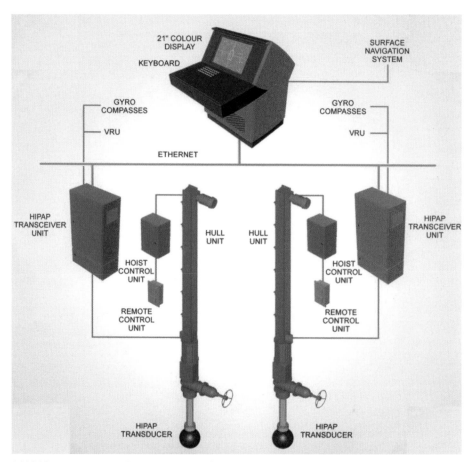

A HiPAP system consists of several elements. One sees, from bottom up, the HiPAP transducer (sphere) mounted on a hull unit. The transducer is lowered and hoisted by a remote-controlled motor. The hull unit also has a special valve to restrict seawater intake when the transducer is hoisted up into the vessel. The transducer sends signals to the transceiver (middle), which takes care of the primary signal processing. The final position is then calculated by the operator station (top). Photo: KM.

times more accurate than the most powerful HPR system.[24] The goal had been to develop a system capable of gauging the direction to a transponder within a tenth of a degree. Test results showed a margin of error of 0.087 degrees. This meant that the system could be used for operations requiring the highest degree of precision. Statoil was pleased, and soon deployed the system on construction of the gas pipeline from the Ormen Lange field to the processing plant at Aukra on Norway's northwest coast.[25]

HiPAP also helped improve the precision of DP systems. In 1995 the first DP system with HiPAP was installed on the Rieber-owned vessel *Polar Queen*.[26]

The system was later succeeded by a new generation, and is delivered today in four variations going under the model names 501, 451, 351 and 101. More than one thousand have been sold of the top of the line and best seller, the HiPAP 501.[27] In HiPAP 101, with its range of 10,000 metres, Kongsberg had developed a system designed for the greatest water depths. Much of the foundation for this type of deep-water solution was laid in an R&D project started around the same time as the HiPAP was launched.

THE DEEP WATER PROJECT

Drilling for oil in deep water requires a different type of vessel and different equipment than in shallow water. The complexity is in direct relation to water depth: the deeper the water, the greater and more complex the challenges. Keeping pace with ever-deeper operations therefore required improved safety and dependability for vessels operating in these waters. The company's DP systems were originally designed for vessels operating in the North Sea, in comparably shallow waters. The increasing depths that oil companies were beginning to drill at meant that conditions were pushing existing technology to its limits.

Kongsberg Simrad started its so-called Deep Water project in 1995 in response to these challenges, and to take advantage of the opportunities that lay in the deepest water. The goal was to improve safety and reliability in DP operations. This was to be achieved by improving existing technology and developing new systems with sufficient dependability to handle depths of up to 3000 metres.[28]

Based on experience from DP systems already in operation, efforts were concentrated around two themes: improving reference systems and their use, and developing support tools for the operators.[29] Most of the development work took place at Kongsberg Simrad, while work with satellite-based positioning was done at Seatex in Trondheim. Operating companies like Norsk Hydro, Statoil, Saga Petroleum, British Petroleum, Norske Shell and DSND Offshore were also present in the project's steering groups, along with Norwegian Petroleum Directorate and The Research Council of Norway.[30]

Reference systems had proven to be the Achille's heel of the DP systems, and the most frequent source of so-called 'incidents'. The problems were exacerbated as the oil companies moved into ever-deeper waters.[31] For Class 2 and Class 3 systems, at least three independent position reference systems were required.[32] In shallower water the choice was between DGPS, HPR, taut wire or microwave-based navigational systems. As activities moved into deeper waters, further from shore and fixed installations, several of these systems could no longer be used.

The 1998 Deepwater project report: «Reliability of DP Operation in Deep Water».

Microwave systems such as Artemis, previously used in Albatross systems, were no longer suitable. Taut wire had also been used, but was designed for shallow water and had many drawbacks in deep water.

Despite these restrictions, it was not impossible to obtain good references, even at great depth and far from land-based reference points. Several systems were considered as viable.[33] In addition to HiPAP, two systems were selected as particularly well suited for deep water operations, based on their ability to satisfy requirements for precision, availability, integrity and continuity.[34] The one was a combination of GPS and GLONASS, connected to a network of land-based reference stations, the so-called DGPS/DGLONASS system. GLONASS, the Russian equivalent to the American GPS system, did not have built-in accuracy restrictions. On the other hand, availability was inferior due to fewer satellites.[35]

The other reference system considered to be adequate was the hydro acoustic MULBL (Multi-User Long Base Line). Simrad had traditionally favoured SSBL, but in deep water the LBL principle was better suited due to a higher degree of accuracy. In deeper water, acoustic signals use more time to travel from the surface to seabed and back up again. This means a longer time gap between measurements, as long as five to eight seconds. Using MULBL technology, measurements could be taken virtually as often as desired. In addition, multiple vessels could use the same transponders simultaneously, establishing position in relation to a shared transponder network placed on the seabed.[36] An MULBL system of this type was developed in the Deep water project, and Kongsberg Simrad launched it on the market in 1998.[37]

With this technology, Kongsberg Simrad improved the degree of availability to the position reference systems in its DP deliveries. Calculations indicated that DGPS/DGLONASS could indicate position to within 0.5–3 metres, and that the system would be available virtually without interruption. A long-base system has the same degree of accuracy as DGPS regardless of water depth, while the precision of SBL and SSBL systems are compromised at increased depths.[38]

However, it was not possible to replace old systems with the new overnight. GPS signals for example had a tendency occasionally to indicate systematically drifting, while the DP systems were designed to handle random signal interference. Satellite-based systems provided more frequent measurements than the acoustic reference systems, resulting in a dominance of 'satellite voices'. This meant that systematic errors in the satellite systems could trick the DP system into thinking that the fault was with the acoustic systems. This issue was resolved by implementing a dramatically enhanced version of the Kalman filter.[39]

THE WORLD BECOMES ROUND

The first DP systems did not employ absolute geographic positions, but rather local references. This could mean, for example, calculating where a vessel was located in relation to a transponder on the seabed. Since distances were short, and the vessel operated within a defined area, the world could for all practical purposed be considered flat.[40] But if the vessel was to travel long distances, as was necessary when laying cable or pipe, the operation became at once more complicated. In any case it was no longer possible to position a vessel in relation to a single point of reference. Reference points would need to be geographical, also acknowledging that the world's surface is in fact curved.

The North Sea had been geographically mapped up into a UTM coordinate system. In the early 1980s a chain of radio navigation stations were installed around the North Sea that vessels could use in positioning. Syledis, as the system was known, also provided position information by UTM coordinates, with an accuracy of two to five metres.

UTM was based on land-based surveying, and was not particularly suited for marine navigation, where the compass was an important tool. A straight line on a UTM chart does not correspond to a straight line when navigating by the compass. When a vessel moved between two points, the DP screen showing the UTM position could indicate that it had followed a straight line between origin and destination. At the same time the position plotter on the vessel's chart system could indicate that it had followed a curved track between the two points. The DP system simply did not function the way the navigators were accustomed to and caused frustration and uncertainty. This situation was not made any better when GPS came into use.

The many complex navigational calculations began to require substantial computing capacity. Calculations also had to be incorporated into the Kalman filter, making it increasingly intricate. The 'simple' filter from 1976 had undergone a long evolution and was gradually adapted to a new reality. By the millennium shift it had been significantly altered in a mathematical perspective, even if its tasks were the same in principle. Robustness had also been improved. The Kalman filter was versatile, proving itself also to be capable of rounding off the earth's surface.

WELL POSITIONED

In addition to an improved method of calculating signals from the position sensors, new operator support tools were also developed for calculating a vessel's ability to stay on DP under various conditions (Online DP Capability Analysis) and to predict the vessel's movements in case of equipment failures (Motion Prediction). Capability analysis was an extension of the well-established consequence analysis required for all vessels with DP Class 2 and 3, and indicated operational margins in the vent of worsening weather. A so called RCA-system (Redundancy and Criticality Assessment) was also developed for continuous surveillance to ensure that the entire DP system, including power, thrusters, support systems, and DP control systems and their reference systems and sensors, were set up and functioning according to regulations. This function was in addition to existing software in the control system. The added functionality

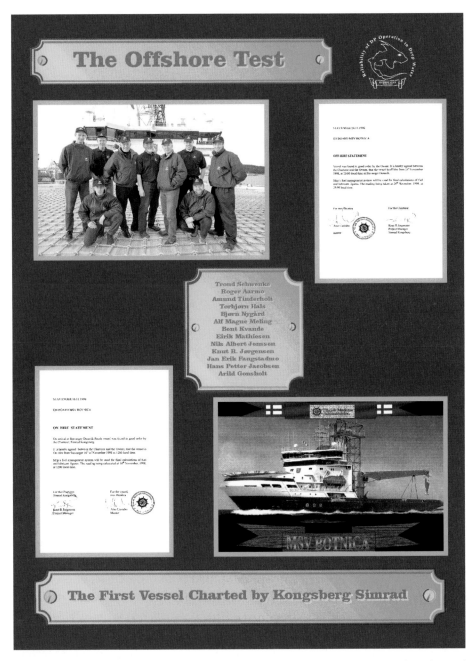

During the Deepwater project, Kongsberg Simrad chartered the combined icebreaker and supply vessel *Botnica* to test its newly developed technology. A special plaque was made to commemorate this occasion. «The Offshore Test – The First Vessel Chartered by Kongsberg Simrad». Photo: KM.

Though the software scope and complexity of DP has exploded since the creation of ADP503, new hardware components, reference systems and sensors continue to emerge. Algorithms still remain, but there is a steady progress and increasing evolution within methodology and user interface. Safety is perhaps the area with the greatest development. Software errors causing a DP system or maritime operation to stop, are unacceptable. Today, major resources go into software maintenance, focusing on strict change management and comprehensive testing prior to the release of new versions of software. The picture shows Finn Hegna, keystone to this particular field. Hegna started as service engineer and has experienced life onboard, but is now back 'home' in Kongsberg. Photo: KM.

allowed the operator to keep track of whether a ship had sufficient capacity in its engines, thrusters and other equipment to carry out operations under various conditions. RCA was an early warning system that indicated whether a vessel could experience difficulties in the event of equipment failure.[41]

The Deep Water project concluded in November of 1998 with testing of the newly developed technology on the combined icebreaker and research vessel *Botnica*.[42] This marked the first time the company was hired a ship to test new equipment. Previously the rule had been to perform testing on the first customer's vessel. A standard innovation process might be said to start with development, move on to testing, and end in sales. But in the early Albatross years, the process was often the opposite: first a sale, then development and testing, which were often carried out virtually in parallel. Thus development costs were incorporated into the price.[43] This time, several million NOK were spent to hire a ship.

Stricter requirements to DP systems as a result of deep-water operations were not a problem for Kongsberg Simrad, already a leader in the most advanced segment of the DP market. The Deep Water project further cemented this position, as well as contributing to renewal and advancement of Kongsberg

Seatex was established in 1984 by people from Continental Shelf Institute (IKU) in Trondheim. From left, Bjørn Fossum, Mathias Håndlykken, John Klepsvik and Hans Olav Thorsen. Photo: *Adresseavisen*.

Simrad's technology base. The new systems and functionality spawned by the project positioned the company well for their move into deeper waters.[44]

SEATEX

On 2 May 2000, restrictions on GPS systems were lifted, and precision improved dramatically for civilian operations. That same day the Kongsberg group put in a bid for Navia in Trondheim, taking over ownership later that autumn. Navia controlled two subsidiaries: Autronica, suppliers of maritime instrumentation, and Seatex, developer of systems for satellite positioning based on GPS.[45] The latter was no stranger to Kongsberg Simrad. The two had collaborated since the early 1990s, most recently on the Deep Water project.[46]

Seatex was established in 1984, a spinoff from the Continental Shelf Institute (IKU) in Trondheim, formed for the purpose of further developing and producing a seismic buoy. Seatex soon began to orient itself towards a broader market, and saw great potential in development of technological systems for navigation and seabed positioning.[47] In particular the satellite-based navigation system NAVSTAR GPS showed promise.

In the1980s GPS was still in the development and testing phases, and consisted of a small number of functioning satellites. Their orbits and the very limited constellation made it possible to use the GPS system only a few hours each day. Seatex's first product was the software Sea-Orbit, which calculated the hours of the day when coverage could be expected.

The first uses for Seatex's GPS products were to determine the position of drilling rigs being moved around the North Sea. Back then a navigation package had to be leased in order to determine one's position with acceptable accuracy. These packages were usually based on radio navigation systems like Argo, Syledis, Geoloc, Loran C and Hyperfix. Transit, the satellite-base forerunner of GPS, was also used. It was costly to lease such a navigation package, and operating the system required special training. The first rig move performed using software from Seatex was the 1985 maiden voyage of the *Polar Pioneer* rig, owned by the rig company Wilrig.

In order to achieve sufficient GPS accuracy, differential techniques had to be employed, essentially placing a reference receiver at a known location on land. As long as distances were not too great, the receiver on land would be subject to the same types of errors as the receiver on board. When the position of the reference receiver is known, these errors can be measured and sent on to the operator as corrections. This same technique has been improved on today,

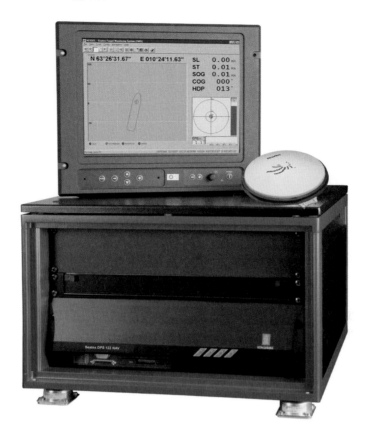

The DPS132 solution for GPS satellites with screen, satellite antenna, receiver and computer. Decimeter positioning accuracy is made possible through the use of correction signals. There are single and dual frequency receiver and system solutions that combine GPS and Russian Glonass satellites. Photo: KM.

and corrections are transferred automatically via satellite. During positioning of *Polar Pioneer*, the crew had to contact the operator of the reference station and have the correction values read aloud over the VHF. Then they had to run to the navigation computer, punch in the correction values, and hope that they remained on position. Another 10–15 minutes later, it was time once again to contact the reference station and repeat the process.

Even though Wilrig owned *Polar Pioneer*, Seatex got the assignment through KV Navigasjon, who had begun development of its own GPS technology. The software for rig positioning hadn't yet been completed, so Seatex got the job. Upon completion of the assignment, KV Navigasjon purchased a license for the Seatex software Seadiff. This would be the start of collaboration between the navigation communities in Kongsberg and Trondheim. KV Navigasjon

Seatex was a frontrunner of maritime AIS (Automatic Identification System) and delivered equipment to ships and the onshore infrastructure that collected and broadcasted ship positions. A satellite-based infrastructure was used to compensate for the limited range of ground stations. Making equipment for the aerospace industry is very demanding. Manufacturers must adhere to stricter requirements than those required by classification companies for the maritime sector. The picture shows Frode Storesund working on a PCB for an AIS transponder used in an ESA satellite. Photo: KM.

was sold when KV was wound down in 1987, and re-established as Kongsberg Navigation. Four years later the company would be acquired by Norsk Forsvarsteknologi (NFT).[48]

When Simrad Albatross won the major contract for DP systems for the Norwegian Navy's mine sweepers and mine hunters, the need for the Trondheim company's competence arose once again. MICOS was delivered with a DGPS from Seatex. This was an unusual solution, as access to the military application of GPS was a prerequisite. In addition it featured full integration with the radio navigation system Microfix. This was most likely the first military DGPS solution in the world.

When Seatex acquired Kongsberg Navigation in 1993, ties between the Kongsberg team and Seatex became even tighter. On the other hand, NFT received 15 perscent of shares in Seatex.[49] The enterprise was eventually moved from Kongsberg to Trondheim, and further development of positioning systems was based on Seatex's technology platform.

When the Kongsberg Group bought up Seatex in 2000, the company was organised under Kongsberg Simrad. With this move Kongsberg Simrad could

From the bridge of the cruise ship *Explorer of the Seas*. The vessel, owned and operated by Royal Caribbean International, was built in 1999 and accommodates 3,000 passengers. The picture shows an operational DP system. Photo: Mediafoto.

boast two strong in-house developmental environments for reference systems. Activities at Pirsenteret on the Trondheim fjord continued largely as before, but now under the name Kongsberg Seatex.

FROM PRECISION TO ECONOMY

As oil exploration moved into deeper waters in the US, Africa and Brazil, wells were commonly drilled in more than a thousand metres of water. This presented new challenges, but also certain advantages. Deeper water meant that greater deviances in position could be tolerated without the angle of the drill string becoming to extreme. While tolerances in the North Sea were down at just a few metres, they could be as much as 50 metres in deeper waters.[50]

The period approaching the millennium shift was also influenced by a growing awareness of environmental issues. This resulted, among other things, in cruise ship owners in the Caribbean meeting with increasing resistance from national authorities on use of anchoring. In 1997 an American cruise line was fined for damaging a coral reef with the ship's anchor. The sentence sent a clear message to the cruise industry: Find alternative ways to anchor up. This in turn opened a new door for Kongsberg Simrad's DP systems.[51]

As previously mentioned, the company's deliveries to the cruise industry had began back in the spring of 1994, when RCCL ordered an ADP701 system for one of its ships in the Vision class. The line later installed DP systems on several more of its ships, meaning they could anchor up with DP instead of conventionally.[52] Deviation of up to a few tens of metres was seldom an issue for these vessels, which did not have the same strict requirements for precision as, say, supply ships, where significant deviation from position could have catastrophic consequences when working close to an oil platform.

Drilling in ever-deeper waters, and stricter requirements on the cruise industry, both provided Kongsberg Simrad with new market opportunities. In particular deep-water activities resulted in several new contracts and contributed significantly to the strong growth that the company experienced from the mid 1990s. Another effect of these developments was to open up for new and different thinking on DP. Technological developments had been moving in the direction of higher precision systems. By this time, though, there was simply not much more to gain. But could there be anything to gain by reducing requirements on precision in order to save fuel? Kongsberg Simrad was already supplying DP systems to deep-water rigs and cruise ships. To keep a vessel on position using this technology meant that even the smallest deviation had to be corrected. This consumed substantial energy and was wearing on engines and thrusters. The cost of providing more accuracy than actually required was significant. With new applications that did not require the vessel to be held to pinpoint accuracy, might it be possible to save on fuel and reduce wear and tear? The growing environmental movement, together with the focus on greenhouse gasses and CO_2, provided additional motivation to develop a DP functionality that could contribute to reduced fuel consumption and more energy efficient vessels.

GreenDP

In 2001 Kongsberg Simrad launched a new DP product in answer to these new challenges. Its name was GreenDP, and it was marketed as a system that not only could provide dynamic positioning, but that was also friendly to the environment. At the same time the system was the result of an ambition to develop new products at a time when lower oil prices were stifling demand

The creation of a project logo often increased the enthusiasm around a given project. For internal use only, the logo was completely different from the established company logo and had a humorous touch. Such was the case in both the Deepwater and the GreenDP projects. Photo: KM.

for DP offshore. GreenDP led to DP being taken into use in a new area, geographical as well as practical.

Work on the new technology began in 1997. The challenge was to build a new system that could reduce fuel consumption significantly by allowing for larger margins of error in position keeping. The result was a solution that made it possible to position a vessel with an expanded area of operation. This demanded an improved mathematical model in order to be able to predict a vessel's drift, and a regulator that was optimised to control fuel consumption. The most important new feature was the system's ability to predict position much further forward in time than existing systems.[53]

The concept allowed the operator to choose the radius of a circle as the boundary within which the vessel should remain. Based on the mathematical model, the DP system would then calculate when the vessel would approach that boundary, and at the same time evaluate how to handle the situation in the best possible way, using the least possible fuel. By abandoning 'bull's-eye' positioning, the radius of the operations area was expanded and the time horizon extended considerably.

Instead of using real time measurements, the new approach was based on predictions of vessel movements using so-called non-linear model predictive control. In this way one could disregard small and short-term disturbances that would not bring the vessel outside its acceptable operative boundary. Thrusters could maintain even speed and avoid large power swings. This meant that peak loads could be reduced drastically compared with conventional dynamic positioning, while reducing wear on engines and thrusters. Maintaining even speed also requires less fuel than large and frequent variations. Using simulations it

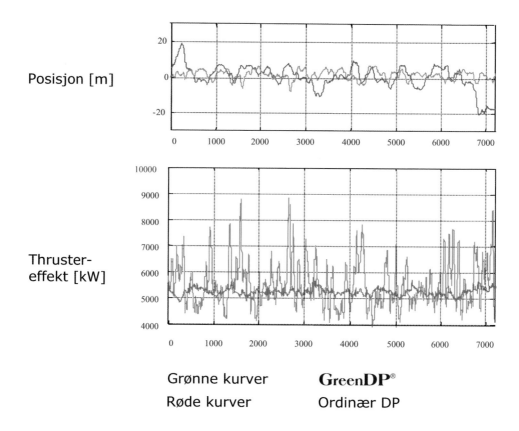

Posisjon [m]

Thruster-
effekt [kW]

| Grønne kurver | **GreenDP**® |
| Røde kurver | Ordinær DP |

The new methodology yielded substantial savings in fuel costs and wear and tear without significantly affecting the system's positioning abilities. From the GreenDP brochure (2001).

was calculated that the new system would provide up to 20 percent savings in fuel costs, with corresponding reductions in CO_2 emissions.[54]

The new algorithm was far more complex and demanding of computing power than the traditional control design commonly used in DP systems. As such its demands exceeded the capacity of the 'old' SBC400. The hardware teams were obliged to develop a new machine that was five times more powerful that its predecessor. The new SBC500, which would prove to be the last in-house developed model in the SBC series, was used as the DP controller in the new system. The operating station, like the new DP systems, was driven by a Windows NT computer. The topology was unchanged, employing the same consoles and cabinets. Because the systems were fully compatible, it was relatively simple to upgrade an SDP unit to GreenDP.[55] The new system was

The launch of GreenDP during the Nor-Shipping exhibition at Oslo in 2001. From left Torfinn Kildal and Steinar Aabelvik. Photo: KM.

not only 'green' inside, but green outside as well, very green, at least the version that was on display at Nor-Shipping in Oslo in the summer of 2001. The same went for the console pictured in the brochure used to market the system.[56] The consoles installed on board were still blue though, like the SDP systems, but they were no less environmentally friendly.

This technology development was a good fit for the Norwegian climate politics of the time. Kongsberg Simrad won support for development work through the Research Council's KLIMATEK program, with its stated goal of contributing to increased use of technology that could help reduce emissions of greenhouse gasses. As often before when new concepts were to be developed, R&D work was carried out in collaboration with SINTEF. Along the way, though, a number of key project personnel left to form Cybernetica, and work was completed within the new company. Kongsberg Simrad also benefited from cooperation with Norske Shell.[57]

GreenDP was launched in 2001, and was an immediate success. During the course of the launch year, 15 contracts for delivery of the new system were signed.[58] From that point on GreenDP became a standard option in the company's DP systems.

CARPUS – THE CIRCLE IS COMPLETED

The 1990s had been coloured by major shifts in the Norwegian maritime electronics industry, with much consolidation through acquisition. This structural change culminated in many ways with the purchase of Simrad by Kongsberg Group in 1996. The DP business became part of Kongsberg Maritime, which in turn became the new locomotive in Norwegian maritime electronics.

While the market experienced concentration, DP technology was undergoing integration. The oil and offshore business had begun to increase its demand for integrated systems. The AIM technology provided in this respect a solid platform for the company, and with the new SPD family, they also had a technology that was both flexible and compliant with class specifications and customer demands for integration on board. The IMO rules from 1994 had established a standard defining what a DP system should be, and soon became an important premise for the demands of class societies, the authorities, and customers. This had a stabilising effect on DP technology. The strict demands for redundancy in the new IMO standards meant that DP systems did not disappear into a larger automation system, but retained their independent technology, which was instead integrated into other onboard systems.

The oil industry was moving steadily further offshore and into deeper waters. This placed new demands on the DP, primarily on position reference systems. Through the Deep Water project, Kongsberg developed new knowledge and new technology that allowed for positioning of vessels with the aid of signals from both great depths and great heights with HiPAP and GPS. Development of dynamic positioning had begun with the goal of staying put, and had later evolved to encompass moving along a track. Now a system had been developed for staying within a defined area using as little energy as possible.

Throughout the late 1990s Kongsberg Simrad invested both time and resources in developing new technology and gaining access to new markets. This investment in development paid off, leading to impressive growth heading into the new millennium. In 1994 the company, then Simrad Albatross, had turnover of close to NOK 400 million. In 2001 it had grown to nearly NOK 1 billion. Sales of DP systems had during the same period more than doubled, to well over a half billion NOK.[59] 2001 was a very good year for Kongsberg Simrad.[60] The company had won contracts for delivery of integrated control and surveillance systems for two new drilling rigs with a total value of NOK 110 million. On top of this order from Santa Fe International in Dallas, came a large contract with Statoil for upgrading and replacing control and safety systems on the *Heidrun* platform.[61]

In September 2001, Kongsberg Maritime moved into new premises located in Kongsberg's industrial park area. The building is shaped like a hand with five fingers and is idyllically situated on the banks of the river Numedalslågen. Photo: Mediafoto.

But such growth does not come without growing pains, and it was not only turnover that was through the roof. The number of employees was skyrocketing too. The building at Industritunet had become too small, and the enterprise was spread out to three separate locations. There was a clear need for a new building to house all employees. On 17 September 2001 the goal was reached. 440 employees had their first day in a spanking new building in Kongsberg Næringspark.[62] With this they had come full circle. This was where the DP business had originated, as the tiny Dynpos project in Kongsberg Våpen-fabrikk back in 1975. Then it was all about getting 'outside the fence'. Now the question of the fence had been raised again. The conclusion seemed to be that they were now 'a part of the fence', in the industrial park with Kongsberg's defence business.[63]

The new building consisted of five large sections in white brick with large glass surfaces, connected by a glass-covered walkway. The structure was dubbed 'Carpus', from the Latin for wrist, referring to the shape of the building, with its five fingers spreading out towards the river Numedalslågen. In an anatomical perspective the most important function of the carpus is to enable 'effective positioning' of the hand. In this perspective one can say that the name was well chosen in more ways than one.[64] And not only the employees appreciated the new facility. Carpus was officially opened by the Minister of Oil Gunnar Berge on 22 October 2001. The same year it received Kongsberg County's award for architecture.[65]

Corporate head Jan Erik Korssjøen characterised the new headquarters on the banks of the Numedalslågen as an «extraordinary structure for extraordinary people».[66] No expense had been spared on the modern, 18,000 sqm facility. The standard was high, with a proper cafeteria, squash courts, and exercise room for the employees. The company was active in an employment market where competition for the best engineers was tough. Modern and functional premises were as such a way to make the workplace 'attractive and fun.' The twentieth century came to a close with the Norwegian technical weekly magazine Teknisk Ukeblad's readers voting 'Albatross's dynamic positioning' as the century's next- most impressive engineering feat in Norway.[67] In its new home, Kongsberg Simrad was well positioned to set its sights on new heights, and continue growing into the new century.

12

IN DEEP WATER

KONGSBERG MARITIME MOVED into the new millennium with great confidence. The company was well-managed and performing nicely, with a turnover in excess of NOK 1 billion and an established position as a leading global supplier of dynamic positioning solutions. There were several major contracts in the order books, inspiring genuine optimism throughout the whole organisation.

The headline *'Kongsberg to supply dynamic positioning to six American offshore vessels'* appeared in Teknisk Ukeblad (a Norwegian technology magazine) in 2001. KM had secured a new contract worth over NOK 27 million, with an option for a further three vessels. The ships, to be built in Singapore, were ordered by the US company Tidewater Marine.[1] Although the supplier of the DP systems was situated in Kongsberg, the company operated subsidiaries both in Asia and in the US. The completed ships would operate across the globe.

The article could also have explained how companies like KM, a supplier of state-of-the-art products, had to manoeuvre to position themselves in the race for customers. The chosen DP system was a Simrad Dynamic Positioning (SDP21), launched in 1996 and supplied to the market up until 2007. The system received its position referencing from a Kongsberg Simrad HPR, while navigation and collision avoidance systems on the bridge were provided by Norcontrol. This demonstrates that deliveries from Kongsberg increasingly came as 'packages', meaning there was an enhanced need not only for coordination between products and departments, but also for a unified corporate customer interface.

In the years immediately after the millennium, many Norwegian businesses experienced crises and declines in orders, while KM itself reported strong results. On the whole, the holding company Kongsberg Maritime – consisting of Kongsberg Simrad, Kongsberg Norcontrol and Simrad – fulfilled a large number of deliveries relating to process control, ship automation and dynamic positioning. Sometimes these were specialised, single orders, but often they were integrated full packages. A large part of the turnover came from KM's foreign offices and international subsidiaries. This showed that KM adapted to new needs, marine operations and locations and, as a result, became better equipped for the tasks that awaited in the decades ahead. One product stood out as an especially strong performer, namely DP, with over a hundred deliveries in 2002.[2]

However, the new millennium brought fresh challenges, with 'depth, distance and quantity' being of increasing significance. Gas and oil exploration and production was taking place at increasingly greater depths. The activities in the Gulf of Mexico moved from shallow areas to new and rich deposits in deeper water. Large petroleum finds were made off the coast of Brazil, situated under huge salt domes at depths of several thousand metres. As in the North Sea, small fields were also found far from land. In other locations, new technology meant that reservoirs that were seen as coming to the end of their life cycles could now be exploited for an extra few million barrels. All these factors indicated a need for floating or portable production equipment, which often entailed dynamic positioning.[3]

THE WORKHORSES OF THE OILFIELDS

Kongsberg Simrad had three main strategic business areas after 2000 (supply vessels or Offshore Service Vessels, construction vessels, and drilling vessels), each of which had its own individual profile and challenges. While DP deliveries for diving vessels and supply ships were key areas going into the 1990s, drilling vessel and FPSO (floating production and storage vessel) systems became essential post-2000. These deliveries were particularly significant because they were large and complex with various forms of monitoring and process control. At the same time, they were the most advanced DP-2 or DP-3 systems delivered. This shift from one business segment to another, from supply vessels to drilling vessels, is described in this chapter.

From 1978 onwards, the OSV segment was a significant market for Albatross. The first deliveries were for vessels operating in the North Sea, with the Gulf of Mexico also eventually developing into a strong market. Oil companies and offshore operators began operating globally from the 1990s, with West Africa, Southeast Asia and Brazil becoming common locations for these vessel types.[4]

Offshore service vessels are specialised for their tasks. This photo from 2013 shows newbuilding 129, the supply vessel *North Pomor*. The ship, designed by Skipsteknisk in Ålesund, built in Poland, equipped by Flekkefjord Elektro and Simek, is operated by Gulf Offshore. *North Pomor* is built for use in northern areas and is equipped with dynamic positioning from Kongsberg Maritime. Photo: Simek.

The main challenges for DP systems for the early OSVs were the limitations of available position reference systems. However, when GPS became a useful reference system, together with affordable, laser-based solutions for short distances, it became far easier for supply ships to perform DP operations without extensive preparations.[5] The expansion of the product line in the run-up to the millennium, with new offerings for vessel automation and remote control systems for propulsion and thrusters, provided a possibility to increase the scope of delivery for each vessel, including supply ships.

KM already had a system, the SDP01, with a more limited functional range, however it was cumbersome to use and lacked a graphical screen solution.[6] In 2004 the compact series cPos and cJoy were launched. The purpose of the new series was to provide a simple, affordable solution, with modest technical requirements, allowing Kongsberg to compete with companies that primarily sold on price. These solutions were also targeted at smaller vessels and for those where DP was a supplement to other instruments. The US market, which did not have the same requirements for DP as DNV and the North Sea, was also a clear target for the initiative.[7] Both cPos and cJoy had PC-based operator units

The cJoy terminal was used as an operator unit in small compact systems as well as for joystick manoeuvring at bridge wings, and as an independent joystick system as requested by class. In this picture, the device is situated on the bridge wing and linked to the vessel's regular DP system. Its location gives the operator an overview of the ship's side, an important function during manoeuvring in port and other DP-operations. Photo: Visual Garden.

and a simplified version of the control unit for thrusters, but otherwise had the same architecture as the SDP family. cPos was a compact DP control system with many limitations and greatly reduced functionality compared with the 'complete' systems, but nevertheless satisfied the requirements of IMO DP Class I.[8] cJoy was a joystick system with automatic heading as an additional option. This offered the opportunity to expand functionality to simple 'stationkeeping' based on position references from GPS.[9]

Around about the turn of the millennium there was also a growing awareness of safety issues relating to DP operations near drilling rigs and other offshore installations. Statistics showed a relatively high number of collisions between vessels and installations in the North Sea. As a result, supply ships were now required to have DP-2 systems. In addition to this tightening of the regulations, from amongst others the Norwegian Petroleum Safety Authority (Petroleumstilsynet), operating companies in the North Sea set requirements for work sharing and workstations on the bridge, while DNV followed up with new guidelines. Two operator positions were now required on the aft bridge. These were to be equipped so that one operator would be responsible for the actual DP operation, while the other took responsibility for the marine operations, loading and unloading activity.[10]

When designing an operator station, one must take into consideration the physical limitations of people and then best align these according to the tasks operators must perform. Mock-ups in cheaper materials are often used when trying out new ideas. Here, Bjørn Gjelstad (left) sits beside a styrofoam model of what later became the SMC system. When these systems were installed, it was evident that early prototypes had yielded results. The picture (right) was taken onboard the *Viking Energy* with KM's Nils Pedersen («DP Nils») as operator.

KM's position in the supply vessel market led to its involvement in early efforts to transform workplaces on the bridge according to the new guidelines, especially those on the aft bridge. When the SMC (Simrad Manoeuvring Control) system was launched at ONS (Offshore Northern Seas) in 2002, it was the first time the business had offered its integrated control system in consoles tailor made for this type of vessel. The concept was developed in cooperation with Eidesvik, and the first installations were made on the sister vessels *Viking Energy* and *Stril Poseidon* in 2003.

Supply ships could operate without DP. From the late 1970s several ship-owners began to use standalone DP systems for enhanced efficiency. In the other two market segments, construction vessels and drilling vessels, DP was increasingly bundled with other technologies, such as vessel automation, and promoted as part of 'packages' drawn up from KMs' extensive product portfolio.

NEW TASKS FOR CONSTRUCTION VESSELS

In November 2003, Kongsberg Maritime secured a delivery to the Prosafe-owned rig *Regalia*. The vessel was to have its electronic equipment upgraded before embarking on new assignments. *Regalia* first went to West Africa and then returned to the North Sea for assignments with Statoil. It was here that *Regalia* was charged with performing a variety of construction tasks on the Troll field, located in the 300 metre deep Norwegian Trench off the country's west coast.

This field is currently considered the most valuable petroleum reservoir on the Norwegian continental shelf and extends for over 700 km2. Production on this complex field is conducted from a concrete platform, a floating production vessel and over 100 subsea wellheads that pump up oil and gas. While the gas is sent by pipeline to Kollsnes, the oil is pumped through the pipeline systems Troll Oil Pipeline I and II for some 85 kilometres to Mongstad.[11]

Production from this type of complex field structure is now more common. That means more and different types of production units and many subsea installations tied together with pipelines. To build and maintain such installations, ships with heavy lifting capacity are required. A construction vessel may be a ship or a rig and is generally fitted with one or more large offshore cranes, alongside equipment to install cables and pipes, dependent on the specific tasks the vessel is equipped for. They have ROVs and often moon pools, where different modules can be hoisted in and out of the water. Divers were previously referred to as the North Sea's construction and infrastructure workers. They assisted in, amongst other tasks, pipelaying. Negotiating narrow passages or bridges over underwater canyons were just two examples of the assignments they had to perform. At this time, the pipelaying mostly concerned constructing large links to transport the oil or gas from petroleum fields to land. The pipelines laid from Ekofisk to Emden in Germany, and from Ekofisk to Teesside in England, provide typical examples. The character of this offshore construction work altered in the run-up to the millennium, however, as the addition of local pipelines and underwater units for production became increasingly commonplace.

Subsea fields are now the most common way to prepare reservoirs for production, a development that has employed a large fleet of construction vessels on assignments for subsea operations/wells (subsea installations). Maintenance tasks relating to wells and pipelines have also increased in tandem with their growing prevalence. A new breed of ship, the IMR (Inspection, Maintenance & Repair) is designed specifically to perform these types of operations. These DP vessels are, like the aforementioned construction vessels, specially equipped for their tasks.[12]

When the floating units, rigs or FPSOs that control underwater wells arrive at a field, they are first anchored and then connected to the wellheads. The various modules and subsea components on the seabed must be interconnected with pipes. Much of this work is performed with ROVs and the specialist cranes that construction vessels have on deck, rather than with divers working on the seafloor. For such operations construction vessels with dynamic positioning

DP has made possible very close, precise and safe manoeuvring around installations. This picture is an example of how a construction vessel can operate. Photo: Boskalis.

excel. This allows the operator to move the vessel precisely as they wish; in a controlled manner and in all three degrees of freedom.[13]

Another complex, important and commercially important industry innovation for KM was FPSO vessels, which grew in number after the turn of the century. Such vessels pump up oil that is then processed, meaning that water, stone and sand are separated from the oil. The oil is then stored temporarily in the vessel's enormous tanks, before being either sent ashore via pipelines, or loaded into shuttle tankers. The first FPSOs were introduced at the end of the 1980s and usually built for early production while permanent production facilities (e.g. a platform) were completed. Once this was in place, the FPSO would move to another field. However, this has altered from the end of the 1990s to the present day, with FPSOs now used as permanent production units, as they are at the Norne and Heidrun fields on the Norwegian Continental Shelf.

FPSOs met different needs than conventional platforms. Oil companies wanted to tap into reservoirs that were deep lying, small or had come towards

Delivered in 1986 to Golar Nor Offshore, *Petrojarl 1* was the first FPSO with DP equipment from Albatross. The FPSO was anchored from a turret and equipped with APM and ADP311, continually used to keep the ship towards the weather. *Petrojarl 1* was a trendsetter, a pioneer ship significantly influencing the development of FPSOs. Photo: KM.

the end of their life cycle. Furthermore, new technologies such as sidetrack drilling, advanced valve types and completion methods opened up possibilities of exploiting scattered fields and complex reservoir structures. It was advantageous to perform such operations with mobile, specialised vessels. The permanent FPSOs constructed by the oil companies were specially designed for the fields in which they would operate, while the units that undertook temporary assignments in various fields were often based on large converted tankers – providing a good alternative to scrapping for owners with vessels over 20 years old. The mobility of FPSOs is also an advantage, as vessels can be moved from field to field or withdrawn if an operating area is threatened by hurricanes or drifting ice.[14]

These specialised ships were still limited in number in the early 2000s and were not usually equipped with DP, although they often had automatic heading.[15] Various solutions to the issue of positioning eventually crystallised.

An FPSO could maintain its station with multiple mooring lines, or it could be anchored in a firm but rotatable point below the ship, creating a so-called

Drilling vessels are not only rigs. KM delivered its first DP systems to drilling vessels in the 1980s. In the foreground is *Discoverer Clear Leader*, Transocean's newer generation drillship. Photo: KM.

turret with pipelines (risers) and anchors lines to the bottom. A third possibility was maintaining position using DP. The last option, continuously holding position with DP-controlled thrusters, was the most operationally expensive and was not used if it could be avoided. However, DP was an option if the assignment was time sensitive or limited in duration, as the operating costs were small in relation to the mooring installation cost.

FPSOs often led to navigation, positioning and process control being placed in the same delivery package, a relationship that this type of vessel shared with the new, large deepwater drilling rigs. Such deliveries chimed with the long-term strategies of the KM management.

DRILLING IN DEEP WATER

«Nearly 50 drilling projects have been initiated and Kongsberg Maritime is involved in over 80 percent of these. The projects are important to us and are utilising the majority of Kongsberg Maritime's portfolio of products.» These were the words of KM CEO Torfinn Kildal when describing the main corpo-

A modern drilling vessel has a high degree of automation and demands a large control room with many stations and monitors. This vessel's engine and safety systems are being operated and monitored, as well as DP and various nautical functions such as radar and electronic charts. The navigation system is primarily used when the vessel moves under its own power from one location to another. Picture: *Discoverer Clear Leader*. Photo: KM.

rate achievements of 2006. «Never before has Kongsberg Maritime signed as many contracts for the delivery of dynamic positioning systems as in 2006. The majority of deliveries have been medium and large systems.»[16] The changes in the rig market were decisive in strengthening the position of the companies that were gathered under the KM umbrella post millennium. When the operators moved towards deeper water it was of real benefit that KM could supply DP-2 and DP-3 systems of recognised quality. Nevertheless, there was still no guarantee that KM would succeed in this market. In the United States there were suppliers with strong relationships to Houston that dominated this market until 1990. The breakthrough came in 1998 when KM secured contracts with two major drilling companies in Houston, namely Reading & Bates and Transocean, for the delivery of DP and vessel automation to a series of drilling vessels the firms planned to construct. This was followed by a new DP contract with Santa Fe International Corporation in Houston.[17]

The breakthrough in the rig market came after a prolonged period of relationship building. The strengthening of the office in Houston was also important, allowing for faster and easier communication channels with the drilling companies. KM salespeople initially experienced that Kongsberg Simrad DP was referred to as the 'diving DP'. However, as customers gained better knowledge of the systems and the systems themselves were better adapted to the drilling requirements, they were no longer seen as 'foreign elements', but well-suited for drilling vessels. This led to a growing trend that saw other vendors' systems scrapped in favour of KM's DPs. Many owners simply saw them as more modern systems.[18]

KM DP systems also secured berths on the drilling rigs in the North Sea. DP operated floating drilling units were seen as more suitable for tackling greater depths and smaller petroleum deposits. The giant *Stena Don,* which was used by Statoil in the Haltenbanken area, as well as elsewhere in the North Sea, was just one example of this.[19] «The cup runneth over», stated Dagens Næringsliv in 2005, in reference to the contracting frequency of the rig market.[20]

Norwegian contractors also signed drilling vessel contracts in the ongoing rig bonanza. A major player in the drilling vessel segment was the Norwegian shipowner John Fredriksen. Starting in 2005, he conducted a comprehensive expansion of his business. While the company Frontline earned good money from tankers, Seadrill focused on operating a fleet of jackup and semisubmersible drilling rigs, drillships and tender rigs. Seadrill expanded through the acquisition of well-known and established Norwegian companies such as Smedvig and Mosvold Drilling, but also by initiating a number of newbuild drilling vessels in Asia. When Fredriksen received delivery of the two huge deepwater rigs *West Eminence* and *West Phoenix* in 2008, it was Kongsberg Maritime that delivered the DP systems that would allow them to maintain position without anchoring.[21] *West Phoenix* began operations for Total on the Viktoria field in the Norwegian Sea, while *West Eminence* sailed directly to the Santos field offshore Brazil, where it commenced operations for Brazilian oil company Petrobras, commanding day rates of nearly USD 600,000. There it operated without anchoring, drilling into rich oil reservoirs at water depths of 2,400 metres.[22] In 2010, Seadrill had 28 drilling rigs on assignment, with a further 15 under construction. These contracts demonstrated that dynamic positioning no longer 'stood alone', but also led to sales in navigation, thruster control, fire and gas monitoring, and vessel automation. To be equipped to take this type of contract, it became necessary to further integrate the companies that had been gathered under the Kongsberg Maritime name.

KONGSBERG MARITIME BECOMES ONE

As indicated in the previous chapter, from 1997 Kongsberg Maritime consisted of four subsidiaries with different locations and product areas: Kongsberg Simrad in Kongsberg and Horten, delivering systems for positioning, vessel or process automation and subsea technology for the offshore market; Kongsberg Norcontrol in Horten, specialising in machinery control and navigation systems for commercial shipping; Kongsberg Norcontrol Systems in Horten, supplying training simulators and computer systems for vessel traffic management; and Simrad in both Horten and Egersund, producing instruments for fishing boats, yachts and other small vessels, alongside fish finding equipment such as sonar and echo sounders.

In 2000, KM acquired Navia AS and its subsidiary Seatex. In 2002, Seaflex was also incorporated into the group. The latter had been working with KM to develop a monitoring and decision support solution for risers, and its acquisition strengthened KM within the drilling vessel segment.

The goal of the acquisitions was to establish a powerful unit to satisfy an increasing customer demand, namely the delivery of dynamic positioning, navigation and automation from the same supplier.[23] To achieve this, the subsidiaries' activities had to be coordinated. 'Gathering strength', commented Teknisk Ukeblad in 2003, with reference to the new Kongsberg Maritime. The magazine interviewed group CEO Jan Erik Korssjøen, who voiced his concern that «... companies from Kongsberg Maritime compete with each other.» As Korssjøen saw it, the company's customer base was changing rapidly, while the subsidiaries often operated alone and, yes, sometimes competed with one another. The challenges lay primarily in the grey zone between Kongsberg Simrad and Kongsberg Norcontrol, where both companies delivered larger integrated automation and control systems.[24] Previously these two operated in different market segments, but now they often looked to the same customers.

The decision was taken to integrate the companies. This occurred in part through a major corporate values and branding exercise described in the next chapter. In addition, the management made several smaller organisational adjustments. In 2002, the subsidiary Kongsberg Simrad, excluding the part of the company focused on fisheries and leisure boating, was moved into a holding company owned by Kongsberg Group. The same then happened with Kongsberg Norcontrol and Kongsberg Norcontrol Systems. This created three legal entities in KM: Kongsberg Simrad (KS), Kongsberg Maritime Ship Systems (KMSS) and Simrad. In 2003, the first two were merged and given responsibility for navigation, vessel automation, process control and dynamic positioning for both the offshore market and commercial shipping. The significant change came when Kongsberg Maritime commenced operations as a company in 2005, with KS and KMSS merged into KM and ceasing to exist as separate firms. Simrad remained 'a Kongsberg company' for a little longer. The part of Simrad that was left after the DP related business was spun off retained the Simrad name, often being referred to as Simrad Yatching & Fishery.[25]

With offices in Horten, Egersund and Støvring in Denmark, Simrad supplied electronics and navigation equipment to fishing boats and yachts. The company faced fierce competition from international firms, and looked to strengthen its position with the acquisition of British business Brookes and Gatehouse (B&G) in 2003. B&G had a good reputation for delivering ship electronics to the high end of the leisure boat market. However, this attempt by the KM management to strengthen Simrad's position in the yachting and pleasure market ultimately failed, and in 2005 the leisure boat business of Simrad was sold to the Swedish investment firm Altor for NOK 586 million.

However, the part of Simrad that supplied echo sounders and sonars for the fishing fleet continued as a subsidiary of KM until 2007, when it was merged into the parent company. In 2007, a line was thus drawn under the organisational and legal part of the integration, and KM was consolidated as a single entity.[26] At the same time as the organisational work was in full flow, Kongsberg Maritime, and then the Kongsberg Group itself, received interest from eager suitors.

KONGSBERG MARITIME CHALLENGED BY ABB

A press release from ABB (Asea Brown Boveri) in early summer 2002 stated the following: «Kongsberg Simrad AS and ABB AS have signed a worldwide agreement on the marketing, sales and technology development relating to ships and offshore vessels. As part of the agreement, ABB's dynamic positioning will be transferred to Kongsberg Simrad.»[27] The background story to this release is extensive. In the late 1990s ABB entered the dynamic positioning market. ABB was a large corporation, originally formed in 1988 through a merger between Swedish ASEA (Allmänna Svenska Elektriska Aktiebolaget) and Swiss BBC (Brown Boveri & Cie). Headquartered in Zurich, Switzerland, with subdivisions spread out worldwide, the firm was a giant in relation to the Kongsberg Group, boasting over 100,000 employees, 2000 of which were based in Norway. The business worked with technology for energy supply and

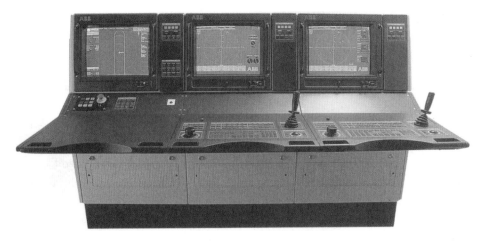

The *West Venture* was a flagship among ABB's DP system installations. Pictured here is the DP operator station. At first, it seemingly resembles KM's system. However, it was based on other ideas, especially the use of standard modules for process automation, used elsewhere in the ABB group. After KM acquired ABB's DP operations, their DP systems were replaced with systems from KM. The only ABB system still in use is that on board the *West Venture*. The picture is from the *ABB DP – Dynamic Positioning Systems* brochure, 2002.

automation, and Kongsberg Maritime and ABB had collaborated on services and deliveries for some years.

ABB had developed commercial DP systems since the 1990s. However, after the millennium, the groups' mutual movements into each other's product spheres – in that both KM and ABB delivered process control and sold DP systems – was seen as problematic. This meant the relationship between the companies became competitive.[28] Kongsberg's management initially viewed ABB's expansion into the DP market with concern, but in 2002 the company ceased deliveries of DP systems. This development was caused by major economic challenges the company experienced relating to both the general problems in the ship and rig market, a stock market in free fall after the millennium, and litigation concerning the use of asbestos. On a global basis, nearly 80 000 employees, or roughly 80 percent of its workforce, saw their contracts terminated. ABB subsequently refocused on the core areas of electrical and process automation.[29] One newspaper called the takeover a «successful polishing of the brand». Teknisk Ukeblad wrote: «So great has been the success, that one of the largest equipment suppliers, ABB, threw in the towel and decided to sell its operations in this area to Kongsberg Group, which consequently secured a market share totalling 80 percent.»[30]

In practice the agreement, which had to be approved by the Norwegian Competition Authority, meant that ABB would refrain from selling its own

DP and vessel automation systems for a five-year period. In addition, the giant group would also sell in KM's systems when negotiating specific contracts. When ABB secured a major contract with a Chinese shipyard in September 2003, Kongsberg received an order for several systems for vessel automation and dynamic positioning.[31] In the longer term the agreement meant that one of KM's competitors disappeared. Of perhaps more interest was the fact that ABB's DP people were transferred to KM, with a new DP development division being established in Billingstad, near Oslo. The KM management stated an ambition of developing a new generation of DP systems, with the best elements from both environments, namely Kongsberg's long experience and ABB's new DP approaches. The new division never succeeded and failed to fit into the KM system. Several of ABB's DP staff later switched to Rolls-Royce Marine, where they helped to develop DP systems for their new employer. This was hardly an optimal solution in the eyes of the KM management.[32]

NOT FOR SALE

In 2004 the Swedish financial conglomerate Nordic Capital made a bid for Kongsberg Maritime. The Swedes were willing to put NOK 3.3 billion on the table. The amount was half a billion more than KM was said to be worth on the stock market.[33] Financial observers described the offer as good and, according to the business press, it was a standard, normal bid. However, neither the staff nor management at Kongsberg Group shared this perception. When CEO Jan Erik Korssjøen and Chairman Christian Brinch came out against the sale, their main argument was that the best way to advance the company was to retain ownership of KM. The bonds between the civilian and military part of the company represented opportunities for good synergies within the Group. It was emphasised that both Kongsberg Defence & Aerospace (KDA) and KM worked with high technology for the monitoring and control of objects. Therefore, the units mutually benefited from the exchange of knowledge in these areas. The central argument was that since KM represented two-thirds of the company's value, the sale had to be approved by the General Assembly, where the government had a majority, namely 50.01 percent of the shares. It also meant that the sale would have to be raised in parliament.[34]

The Kongsberg Group board's decision was backed by the government, with Industry Minister Børge Brende spearheading the move. Brende stated that the offer was neither financially nor strategically interesting. His conclusion was that this exciting industry cluster should be secured and allowed to work in peace. Brende expressed that there were big things going on and that this technological environment should to be protected. Brende illustrated his stance by noting that: «Kongsberg currently has more employees in high-tech jobs than in its heyday of weapons manufacturing. Turnover is significantly higher, and the maritime division is a world leader in dynamic positioning.» While Brende was criticised by the financial market and labelled a «social democrat», dynamic positioning was elevated and portrayed as being symbolic of a world-class technology environment.[35] Due to the group management's resolute stance, in conjunction with the government's unquestionable support, KM remained part of the Kongsberg Group.

At the time when the offer came, Kongsberg Maritime had been consolidated as a well-integrated and successful Norwegian company with support from the government. There was opposition to the national 'family heirloom' being sold. Why should something so exciting and successful, with new products in the pipeline, healthy finances and thousands of employees, be privatised or sold out of the country? The proposed acquisition says something about both KM's special status and its apparently tight integration with the defence part of the company. For that reason KM could be considered as almost untouchable under the prevailing circumstances. The manner in which KM was locked into KOG shielded it from acquisition, as long as there was a political will to retain ownership of the expertise in Kongsberg and in Norway. This demonstrated that the dynamic of globalisation was therefore not without its limits and could be stopped by business models that apparently worked, and where politicians could still use their common sense.

In 1977, Albatross was a small and insignificant project in a market dominated by large international companies, including Honeywell. In 2005 the old Albatross, now under the name Kongsberg Maritime, was the most important player in the global DP market. Many of the old competitors however were still in the game. Honeywell's DP division was called Nautronix of Australia in 2005, but was later incorporated into marine division of L-3 Communication Holdings, and now a part of the Wärtsilä group. The British GEC (General Electric Company) had taken a path through Cegelec, Alstom and Converteam and was now part of the giant GE, in General Electric's 'Power Conversion' division. Both were strong contenders in the DP market. The changing constellations within Honeywell illustrates another point, maybe it wasn't always advantageous to be a small part of a giant corporation.

The same year that ABB gave up DP, KM met a competitor from within its own ranks. In 1992, Simrad had acquired Robertson Tritec, a DP-supplier in the low-end segment of the market. When the leisure boat/yachting division of Simrad in Egersund was sold out and the low-end DP team were to move to Kongsberg, several of the staff quit the department. It was seen as offhand treatment and was an important motivating factor for Jan Mikalsen, who was department manager of the local Egersund group, when he formed the competing DP company Marine Technologies (MT) in 2002. According to Stavanger Aftenblad, he was sick of the fact that most of the profits from Egersund went to Kongsberg, a situation not unlike that Albatross had complained of 20 years earlier.

Marine Technologies was established in the United States, rather than Norway. There the company was reportedly received with open arms by the largest supply shipping firm in the world, Edison Chouest Offshore, headquartered in Louisiana. The shipowner wanted to have full control of deliveries and service for the DP systems on board his ships, and thought that having MT as the sole supplier was a good solution. MT also secured another customer, Island Offshore, in which Edison Chouest Offshore admittedly had a major stake. In its first years MT's expertise was in the low-end segment of the market. After its establishment, the company has developed DP-2 systems, and is thus a competitor for KM, which supplies DP for all types of customers.[36]

Navis Engineering is also a challenger. Navis was established in St. Petersburg in Russia in 1992, initially focusing on the production of various control systems for ships. The firm launched its first DP system in 2000. In 2006 and 2007 the company delivered a number of DP-2 systems to Bourbon Offshore and has since built up its market position. Today they operate worldwide, delivering DP for all types of ships.[37] Since Navis has concentrated on the low price segment, the company has not posed any significant competitive threat for Kongsberg Maritime.[38]

A competitor of a slightly different nature was Rolls-Royce Marine, which came to Norway in 1998. Rolls-Royce (RR) was an established international giant that produced more than half of the Allied aircraft engines during World War II. After 1945 it ran more diversified engine production, but in 1973 came close to being declared bankrupt. That led to the main part of the company, Rolls-Royce Motors in the UK, being nationalised. The remainder was sold to Vickers, which itself sold out this part of its business to Volkswagen in 1998. Vickers used the profits from this to buy large parts of the Ulstein Group on the Møre coast of Norway. With this move, Vickers became the world leader in technology for the propulsion of ships. The following year Rolls-Royce acquired Vickers and, in doing so, received the Ulstein Group as part of the purchase. Rolls-Royce Marine (RRM) was created as a result.[39] The company supplied vessel design (UT) with associated equipment packages, power plants, propulsion, thrusters, and control systems. From 2005, RRM offered dynamic positioning as part of the equipment package. In reality, Rolls-Royce DP became a bonus feature of the broader outfitting packages.[40] RRM completed its DP-2 systems relatively early, while the development of DP-3 was more challenging. In 2014, Rolls-Royce received a DP-3 contract for two construction vessels for Farstad Shipping.[41]

The above examples show that KM's competitors utilised a variety of business models. The «old» established brands provide an on-going challenge. Honeywell, Nautronix, or Wärtisilä as it's now called, and General Electric's «Power Conversion» division are sleeping giants that may awaken and rush into the market again, something that happened in spring 2013. On 4 April 2013, when Dagens Næringsliv landed on desks in Carpus, KM people had the chance to read that GE had signed equipment contracts for drillships and semi rigs for a total value of over USD 600 million. A quote from Nordea noted: «(...) the Brazilian DP 3 market share exceeds 50 percent. This a slap in the face for Kongsberg Maritime's high quality DP domination, but they are still a supplier to key customers.»[42] The contract clearly demonstrated the changeable nature of the marine electronics market.

Within the DP segment there are various areas the companies compete on. Price and quality are obvious themes during any negotiation. However, it is also important for a company to be able to deliver a wide range of DP types to suit various applications.[43] Delivering DP in conjunction with a wide a range of other products, such as navigation, vessel automation and process control, has increased in importance. In addition, outstanding customer service and satisfaction are fundamentally important in an industry where predictability and quick response are vital. The availability of service worldwide is also key, as is its provision on a 24-hour basis. Good technologies perform poorly without continuous customer care.

TRAINING AND SIMULATORS

KM runs an extensive programme of training activity for DP operators. This takes place both at Kongsberg and at many of the company's field offices, representing an important and growing part of the firm's activities. Up until 2000, the training followed guidelines from the Norwegian Maritime Directorate (Sjøfartsdirektoratet or SD) or Nautical Institute (NI) in London. Today, it is largely the individual flag states that determine requirements for DP operators. Right from the time that the first rules were introduced, in 1984, there have been ongoing discussions and disagreements on various aspects of training and certification.

The discussions revolved around whether rules should be generic, regardless of which DP control system was being utilised, or whether they should be adapted to specific DP systems, vessel types and the operations concerned. This has been followed by discussions relating to practical experience, namely when training should take place, the number of hours required and how this DP practice should be performed. The last question has increasingly revolved around whether, and to what extent, simulator training can replace elements of practical, on board exercises.

The foundations for both the training and certification of personnel are built upon requirements from the International Convention on Standards of Training, Certification and Watchkeeping for Seafarers (STCW), which is the parent body for all certification of ship personnel. In 2012 STCW changed the rules for training and certification of DP personnel, positioning them as a 'B'

DP training has developed significantly. The regular classroom teaching style and practical exercises, in a designated training room and under instructor supervision, are partly history. Today, students also experience approximately the exact work environment on a DP bridge. They see the full picture, an extended view of the maritime environment including vessels and installations – a realistic picture of a working day at sea. Training has become more operation specific. A crew onboard a supply ship requires different skills than a drillship operator. Photo: KM.

Customers want extensive training in operations. Today's modern simulators provide an almost lifelike replication of instruments, vessels and the environment. This simulator is used by Maersk personnel for anchor handling operations training. Photo: KM.

element of the international rule framework, making them a recommendation. The recommendation covers vessel specific, system specific and operation specific training. It is then left up to each flag state to determine which standards of DP operator training should be followed.[44]

Dynamic positioning also became a mandatory element in the teaching portfolio at maritime colleges from the 1980s. The same schools were also among the first to adopt simulators for training. In 1983, the maritime college in Haugesund acquired a DP simulator from Albatross, and two years later a similar unit was delivered to Lowestoft College at Norwich in England. The systems had KS500 machines that simulated I/O signals to an ADP503 system. A similar simulator was later made for the APM3000. Demo programs to emulate simple operations for the ADP503, ADP311 and ADP100 were also created. Later models had simulation features built into the systems. The ADP700 Series, launched in 1987, boasted a 'training mode', while the SDP, from 1996, saw the training mode expanded to a fully-fledged simulator that was integrated into the DP system. SDP machines were delivered in two versions, one with a 'trainer' where wind, current and vessel draft could be entered, and one with a simulator giving control of all environmental parameters, where you also could make deliberate errors relating to measurement data and commands.[45] Producing these simulators for navigation and DP systems became a separate activity and business area for several companies under the KM umbrella.

Safety and cost control have become increasingly important for both the offshore industry and shipping. The Danish shipping company Maersk is a giant of the maritime industry. After a major accident in the 1980s, Maersk built up a wide range of courses for employees and is today viewed as a pioneer in this respect. At Maersk Training Centre (MTC) in Svendborg, Denmark 500 courses are held annually with over 9,000 participants. This naturally says something about the group's size, but also its emphasis on safety.

The importance of thorough safety training and realistic exercises was obvious to everyone within the sector in April 2007 when the anchor-handling vessel *Bourbon Dolphin* sank off Shetland during a routine mission to move the anchors for the *Transocean Rather* rig. The Accident Commission used the term 'system failure', to show that there were a number of different, and altogether catastrophic, failures that led to this tragic accident and the loss of several sailors' lives.[46] A year later, although not necessarily related to the accident, Maersk opened up its training offer for personnel outside the company. In relation to this, KM received an order for a simulator for anchor handling activities for rigs. When the simulator was shown at Offshore Northern Seas in Stavanger, it was said to be a comprehensive model, containing all the elements that had previously been sold individually.[47] The delivery was the start of an important and ongoing collaboration between Kongsberg Maritime and Maersk.[48]

Both the investment in training and the use of simulators for this purpose was emphasised in a speech when a new simulator for various types of offshore operations was unveiled at Ålesund University College in 2007. The simulator, delivered by KM, made it possible to train for various types of offshore operations – and particularly demanding bridge operations – where dynamic positioning was used. This equipment offered students the new feature of practicing operations in arctic regions and seas with ice floes.[49] Just two years later KM announced that their Polaris Dynamic Positioning simulator and Polaris Ships Bridge Simulator were the first units in the world with DNV Class A approval. Class A approval involved the use of both DP and manoeuvring in ice.[50] These two sales were followed up with a delivery to Haugesund Simulator Centre. This time it was KM itself, in cooperation with shipowners in the Haugesund district, which was responsible for the delivery.[51] The 'super simulator' could show visiualise scenarios with full 360 degrees sight and simulate complex offshore operations using DP.[52]

Teknisk Ukeblad featured a major story about KMs new simulator K-Sim in April 2014, reporting that it set a new standard for simulators focusing on ship navigation equipment. «The most critical and complex operations of an offshore vessel, for example drilling close to ice edges, can be done in the simulator, but not outside it.» In other words, simulators were the only option for the realistic training of DP operators when it came certain operations.

A NEW GENERATION OF TECHNOLOGY

By the time the compact cPos and cJoy systems were launched in 2004, KM engineers were already in the process of developing a new generation of DP systems. This work resulted in the launch of K-Pos in 2006, Kongsberg's sixth generation DP system. As with the SDP family, K-Pos was delivered in three variants depending on the type of redundancy: a single system with one computer for control and one operator station, a dual system with dual-redundant computers and two operator stations, and a triple redundant solution, system wise similar to the SDP family.

The control unit was based on the RCU501 (Remote Control Unit) and so-called RIO devices (Remote Input Output) for connection to the physical devices on board, such as the thrusters and sensors. Both RCU and RIO units were complete, encapsulated modules, which in principle could be mounted anywhere. Previously special electronics racks were required, as the connection between the computer and I/O modules was achieved with a parallel bus. These were made as a separate circuit board mounted in the rear of the rack, with contacts for each I/O card. In the new generation a serial bus solution was utilised, connecting the individual units in the system with a single cable, as you would with the standard USB connections used in today's PCs. The units were still located in a cabinet, but the interiors were simplified by the new solution, which provided easy rail mounting of the components.

K-Pos also changed the redundancy mindset. In both the ADP and SDP generations all I/O units were duplicated or triplicated, with an external switch that controlled which computer provided the thruster control signals. Such switches connected all output signals for the I/O module and were therefore a potential source of error, even if it was a technically simple, and therefore reliable, solution. K-Pos addressed this issue through segregation. Each thruster got its own I/O module and was connected to a RCU through a hub, similar to those currently used in PC networks. In redundant systems the communication channel between the RCU and RIO modules were also duplicated. If a single

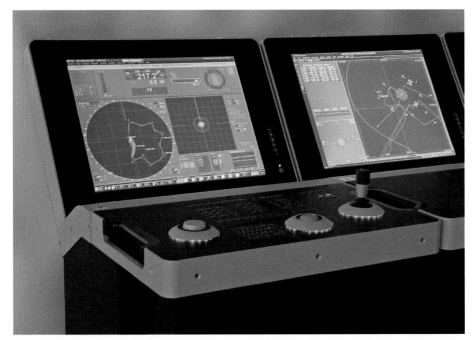

The K-Pos console reflects the high standards of KM. It should be elegant and the visual impression should create a «wow effect». Pictured here is a prototype from 2005 with flush-mounted displays, specially designed glass front, and LED lights under selected devices. Diode lights disappeared, however, by production start and glass screen fronts were removed from later models. Achieving acceptable production costs was the most important issue. Photo: KM.

component should fail, the error would only affect one thruster. Although K-Pos represented a step forward in technology, this generation had the same DP functionality as its predecessors.

A great deal had changed in terms of design too. While earlier generation consoles had been green or blue, the developers this time followed industrial design trends and chose black. Furthermore, the consoles had dedicated buttons grouped by function that were recessed and featured white outlines.[53] Hareide Design designed the consoles that became the standard for all KM's solutions.[54]

Although aesthetics had become more important in the design of new models, it was convenience and safety that still had precedence. As KM was no longer delivering 50 DP systems in the year, but 250, new challenges were emerging. An increasing number of DP systems had to be manufactured, assembled and tested in the shortest possible time. To meet the demand, the amount of work on each delivery had to be significantly reduced. While Albatross could, in the early years, spend months on each project, now that time-frame had diminished to weeks. One way to reduce the delivery time was to use standardised cabinets, rails and distributed modules. The 'RIO project' started in 1998 and resulted in the development of numerous distributed RIO and RCU modules with their own processors. As the modules could now be mounted serially, they could be placed anywhere.[55] The modules were designed in Kongsberg, but manufactured by subcontractors. They could be tested prior to assembly and snapped into place – a labour saving development. Although this production method admittedly limited opportunities for 'tailoring', the time used on assembly was significantly reduced.[56]

TESTING

The offshore sector is perilous. It is focused on great depths, high pressure and small margins of error. This also applies to dynamic positioning. Even by the time of KV's first delivery to *Seaway Eagle* in 1977, the DP system was subjected to extensive testing. This practice continued throughout the years to come, on all DP installations. After the millennium, most of the testing was conducted in the assembly halls at Kongsberg, in Singapore, Korea or China.

Testing takes place during the various stages of production, with a complete delivery test when the DP system is fully assembled. Representatives from the customer and classification society then visit the assembly location, regardless of whether it is in Kongsberg or abroad. If this so-called Factory Acceptance Test (FAT) is successful, the system is then transported to the shipyard.[57] There the cabinets, consoles and monitors are mounted, and the wires are run to the I/O equipment and power supplies. An engineer from Kongsberg commissions the system, ensuring that the cables are securely attached and the cabinet's contents are in order. The sensors, reference systems and all inputs are then checked.

A few days before the vessel sails, the engineers with responsibility for system software apply the finishing touches. After installation is completed, the DP system goes through a sea trial where, in particular, the thrusters are tested. The process finally reaches its conclusion with a Customer Acceptance Test (CAT) where the class company, customer and yards, and often the end customer, is present. After the CAT a Preliminary Safety Analysis (PSA) in run, which determines whether a 'Failure Mode and Effects Analysis Test' (FMEA) is performed. The manner in which this test is performed is dependent on the type of vessel in question, and whether it is a DP class 2 or 3 ship. The FMEA test involves the complete DP system and not just the DP control system. Class

KM ensures that each and every system is tested and reviewed before delivery to the customer. Yard employees work hard to get all the cables in place prior to equipment installation and connecting power and signals. This is how a bridge may look just six weeks before sea trials commence. In most cases, however, chaos becomes order at just the right time. Photo: KM.

companies such as ABS and DNV GL represent class, while an independent third party performs FMEA.[58] The need for a third party is due to the authorities' desire for safety to be central to all offshore operations.

However, much has changed since this regime for testing was established as the standard procedure. This is in part related to the development and variety of maritime electronics, as described above, with equipment becoming more software and less hardware based. Since software, unlike hardware, can be changed in a flash, and because software is more complicated to examine analytically, new ways to test it must be found. From the 1990s onwards, offshore vessels, particularly drilling rigs and ships, have become more complex, while also being equipped with increasingly more sophisticated systems for monitoring, measurement, process control, dynamic positioning, energy management, and drilling. One consequence of this is the prevalence of many, often interacting, computer systems. The programs for the various systems are frequently required to exchange data with one another.

Initially Kongsberg engineers were mainly taking care of onboard system commissioning. As volume and shipbuilding locations changed, KM established a global network to take care of these tasks. Here, employees at Kongsberg Maritime's subsidiary in Brazil undertake installation testing. Photo: KM.

Computer applications that previously functioned according to set specifications may produce errors when linked with other computer programs. There are several factors at play here: One is that software for different electronic systems may be tailored to specific tasks and not for interaction with other applications. Programs that work perfectly on their own may break down when operated in conjunction with other programs, and unforseen failure is always difficult to prepare for.[59] The origins of most problems can be eliminated through FMEA, but some are so specific, or so far outside trouble-shooting parameters, that they do not turn up until the systems are run simultaneously. Discovering an error in a system may not present any danger, but allowing the system to fail may. The outcome is dependent on human factors and the staff's approach to safety issues. Failure also represents a cost issue, and the further along in the delivery an error occurs, the more costly repairs will be.

Hardware-in-the loop testing (HIL-testing) was a solution to the complex systems and software challenges described above. This testing method was first employed in the aerospace and automobile industries, where the consequences of failure can easily be dramatic, or even deadly. The methodology proved so

From the test department in Kongsberg. From left: Orlando Zuleta Ortiz and Fredrik Johan Østheim. Photo: Tommy Normann.

effective that it quickly spread to other industries. Not unexpectedly, it was Statoil that first insisted on HIL testing of DP systems in Norway. Statoil's demand was picked up on by four NTNU professors, with Asgeir Sørensen in the lead. These four developed the first HIL testing system for DP, and in 2002 they founded Marine Cybernetics (MC) in order to offer HIL testing to the offshore market. The new company got off to a flying start when Statoil ordered HIL testing of 50 DP systems on ships they had operating on contract.[60]

HIL testing consists of hooking a DP control system up to a so-called HIL simulator that uses mathematical models to simulate the behavior of the actual vessel. The HIL simulator receives commands from the control system and sends back simulated measurement signals in real time. Connecting the control system to a virtual vessel allows for testing of any situation in a risk-free and controlled environment. Types of testing include functionality, integration, and problem spotting.[61]

Simulator-based testing is not a new phenomenon. All DP suppliers perform different types of tests as part of the delivery process, but the amount of testing was increased with MC's HIL. Not least, an objective third party could now perform standardised testing. DNV would later develop a voluntary supplemental class for HIL-tested control systems on ships, and took 70 percent ownership of MC in May of 2014.[62]

CONSOLIDATION

Kongsberg Maritime would meet their share of challenges in the new millennium. cPos allowed KM to compete in the low-price market, where class requirements and redundancy were seen as irrelevant. cJoy even became an IMO standard for DP requiring a simple backup system.

Another more important development concerned small reservoirs, complex geology and deep water. These challenges demanded greater use of underwater production units, and robust floating drilling and production vessels. KM's DP-2 and DP-3 systems, with the sixth generation Kongsberg K-Pos, were perfectly matched to these tasks, a fact borne out by the swelling order books.

These changes were also connected with yet another: Going into the 21st century, customers began to prefer ordering more products from a single supplier. Kongsberg Maritime's acquisition and consolidation of their various subsidiaries, requiring extensive and demanding integration processes, needs to be seen in this light.

When the daily paper Stavanger Aftenblad reported on the delivery of a drilling rig for Smedvig with a price tag of USD 550 million, they noted: «The rig is designed with twin drilling derricks and dynamic positioning, and is capable of drilling in up to 3000 metres of water».[63] In the vast media coverage of KM products, DP was the one most often mentioned. The share of DP deliveries was increasing year by year, but so were deliveries of KM's other systems. Still, DP did not 'disappear' in the rush. Even though the other systems were integrated into the Kongsberg Maritime 'family', and had become more standardised, there was no doubt that DP systems were still the driving force for the growing number of conglomerate deliveries that included navigation, vessel automation, and process control.

13

A GLOBAL BRAND

WHEN THE MANAGEMENT of Kongsberg Maritime looked back on the year 2006, the booming offshore market stood out as the main feature. Fully 60 percent of the company's orders had come from the offshore segment, with deliveries to drilling rigs making the strongest contribution to the bottom line. The 2006 annual report noted that 29 contracts had been signed for drill rigs with dynamic positioning. DP alone had brought in NOK 1.2 billion of KM's total orders of NOK 3 billion. Adding to this, many orders also included safety systems and vessel automation, GPS systems from Kongsberg Seatex, hydro acoustics from the Subsea division in Horten, and riser management systems from Kongsberg Seaflex.[1]

Kongsberg Maritime was in other words riding high on the income from sales of DP-2 and DP-3 systems to drilling vessels. On many vessels in the North Sea, but perhaps equally as much in the Gulf of Mexico, offshore Brazil, and West Africa, the new K-Pos consoles could be found on the bridge. Up until 2008 Kongsberg had delivered 2,100 DP systems in all. In 2008 alone, 350 new systems were installed around the world. DP emerged as the common denominator when global trends converged to generate income for Kongsberg Maritime. But the huge number of deliveries not only generated income – they also created challenges. Communication between subsidiaries, field offices and headquarters had to function seamlessly in order for information on contracts and service to keep flowing around the clock.

In the summer of 2010, Torfinn Kildal stepped down as managing director after having followed the Albatross adventure from its start in the 1980s.[2] His replacement was Geir Håøy, who was Executive Vice President of KM's Global Customer Support as well as involved in business in Singapore, China and South Korea.[3] Håøy's Asian experience was certainly no drawback for a KM manager at that time. During Kildal's turn at the KM helm, from 1999 to 2010, KM had gone from being a national unit with international success in the Kongsberg Group, to become a global concern with rapidly growing numbers of both contracts and employees abroad. In 2010 there were 3,100 employees at Kongsberg Maritime, 1,400 of whom worked abroad. Foreign offices and subsidiaries represented a significant portion of their revenue.

BUILDING THE BRAND

While 'tearing down the pyramids' had been the buzzword for many companies during the 1980s, building visible and recognisable brands became the new passion for many international concerns in the 1990s. In the spirit of the times, companies that wanted to succeed needed to appear as trustworthy, and with a clear and consistent relationship between product, company, and image.

Already in 2000, Kongsberg Group CEO Jan Erik Korssjøen had initiated profiling of the corporation that then consisted of two units: the holding company Kongsberg Maritime (KM) and the defence unit Kongsberg Defence & Aerospace (KDA). Even though KOG was the principal for the branding process, the main purpose was to integrate the KM subsidiaries Simrad, Kongsberg Simrad and Kongsberg Norcontrol. For that reason KM director Torfinn Kildal was assigned a central role in the branding initiative.[4]

Products from Kongsberg Simrad, Seatex, Seaflex, Simrad, Kongsberg Norcontrol and Kongsberg Norcontrol Systems were each unique and well known, but the customer was often unaware of their connection to Kongsberg Maritime. Kongsberg management had determined that Kongsberg Maritime would benefit from a clearer identity and a recognisable brand. This entailed highlighting the connection to KONGSBERG, the corporate brand name.

A corporate-wide format for presentations was devised, incorporating logo, colours and fonts. The profile was quickly implemented on the company web site, letterhead, envelopes and business cards. The modest beginnings of a branding process, perhaps most visible in the company newsletters, would soon come to encompass all aspects of the company's activities. Kunde & Co, a Copenhagen-based consulting company on the rise, was engaged to carry out a values and branding process for the Kongsberg Group. The Copenhagen outfit had built up a strong reputation in branding on assignments for major, high-profile companies. Their key task in a branding process was to help companies consolidate their profile under a unique and recognisable brand.[5] According to Kunde & Co, this identity needed to be cultivated from the inside.

On a more concrete level, the brand had to be built on three factors: How Kongsberg Group wished to be perceived; the market's perception of KOG; and KOG's own image of themselves. This would help identify a key goal for the branding process, by discovering what employees and customers thought of the company, its products and services. To this end a survey was launched canvassing both employees and customers.[6] KM's role figured prominently in the survey. How was this part of KOG perceived, and to what degree was the KM brand name associated with its subsidiaries? The results are generalisations and do not necessarily reflect the breadth and variety of the replies from employees, but the survey indicated that many employees felt that KM lacked a uniform image. The majority maintained that they had little or no knowledge of activities in other departments.[7] Customer replies made for more encouraging reading, with KM being almost exclusively the object of praise. Kongsberg Maritime was perceived as delivering as promised. Additionally, KM employees were not quitters, and they had 'guts'. Customers felt the company was upstanding, trustworthy, and innovative.[8] The customers' favourable impression of KM made for a good starting point in the branding process.[9]

Both the survey and the internal processes that would follow are noteworthy. The KONGSBERG brand appeared to have an established and credible presence. Because a brand does not build itself, and is never established once and for all, any internal friction was reason enough to stay on guard, and to continue the consolidation process. With the survey in hand, the management of KM and KOG initiated a dialog with the employees to devise a strategy for the future.

THE ALBATROSSES LEAVE THE NEST

The North Sea had long been the most important market for Albatross. In 1985, as much as two-thirds of their activity had been within the petroleum sector in the North Sea. The company had established itself early on, in 1982, with its first branch office in Aberdeen. Albatross management, though, had plans that reached beyond the North Sea.

The first DP-related activity in the US started in the oil capital of Houston, with Vidar Guterud as head of sales. From 1990 on, the balance of activity between the North Sea and the rest of the world would shift dramatically. Simrad Albatross experienced a major breakthrough on the US market, delivering an increasing number of DP systems to rigs and vessels operating in the Gulf of Mexico.

The first Asian foreign office was in Singapore in 1981. In the early years, Norcontrol was the most frequent visitor to the eastern yards, marketing navigation systems and machinery control for the merchant fleet. Later, Albatross would make inroads with its systems for dynamic positioning.[10] KV would eventually station representatives in proximity to the big Asian yards. This allowed the sales reps to establish good contacts in the Asian shipbuilding industry. The ties that were established to customers in Singapore, Busan in Korea, and Kobe in Japan, would be pivotal when shipbuilding took off again after the late 1980s slump.[11]

From 1990 on, Asian yards dominated construction of ships and rigs. And while newbuilding was concentrated in the east, the oil companies were shifting exploration and production activities to promising new provinces. Offshore activities were no longer restricted to the North Sea and the shallower waters of the Gulf of Mexico, but had moved into deeper Gulf water, and offshore Brazil and West Africa. Sales, production and service, and not least communication with subsidiaries and field offices, were reorganised accordingly. Sales activities were no longer limited to selected branch offices, or HQ in Kongsberg, but

As illustrated on the map, Kongsberg Gruppen and Kongsberg Maritime have a network of offices worldwide. The main locations for the maritime business are Norway, Korea, China, USA and Brazil. Photo: KM.

The collage shows the considerable span of both duties and cultures that belong under the KM umbrella. The people pictured here are from Korea, Singapore, China and Brazil. Photo: KM.

should be distributed throughout the world. Information on customers and potential sales alike needed to be exchanged between offices. The idea was for offices to share ownership of the bottom line, and reap the collective rewards.[12]

One aspect of KM's global enterprise was the dividing up of activities. Service was performed where operations were located, sales at the yards that built and fitted the vessels, and both sales and service wherever shipowners had their headquarters. A potential project at a yard in Singapore might have a Brazilian owner, an American consultant, and a Norwegian operator. This fractioning meant that Kongsberg Maritime's activities needed to be coordinated in new and different ways.

When KM first introduced the octopus model, it was precisely to meet these new challenges in the market. While technological advances and strategy development largely took place in Norway, steadily more sales, service and training was being carried out globally. This development had another consequence as well. While core competencies resided inn Norway, the more labour-intensive tasks were being carried out using resources close to the yards, with a proportionate increase in the use of local labour. KM allowed for parts of its business to be integrated into the economies of the host countries.[13] In many

Sister Seminar 2014

Kongsberg's portfolio of subsidiary companies gathers every second year to be updated on new products, discuss business and build personal contacts. Here sales, marketing, product management and delivery units are gathered. Personal relationships are nurtured to ensure that the company's 'octopus strategy' functions optimally. Photo: Mediafoto.

countries, such as Brazil, this was in fact a requirement in order to be able to do business. Up until 1995, the Kongsberg Group strategy was to operate as an international sales organisation. Later it became apparent that an increasing amount of value creation need to take place wherever offices were located, be it the Asia, Europe or the US.[14]

This geographic growth took place parallel to a major expansion of capacity for installation, service and training in the foreign offices. These offices dealt primarily with shipowners, contractors and yards, located in regions quite distant from the actual oil and gas activities. In 2006, 27 percent of employees were in foreign offices. Six years later, in 2012, the percentage had grown to 48.[15]

This model required the flow of information and communication to be improved. Gradually, systems were put in place for exchange of information between the offices and continents of the world. Today, employees working in Kongsberg are in touch with Asia in the morning, and the US in the afternoon. Sharing knowledge and taking action happens where and when it is required.[16] The importance of shared values and strategies, and the effective flow of information, is greater now than previously.

FROM KONGSBERG TO COPACABANA

It's a long way from Kongsberg to the beaches of Rio de Janeiro, and from the sunny beaches to the installations on the Peregrino field in the Campos basin. Major oil and gas resources were found off the Brazilian coast back in the 1970s. The discoveries were far from shore, in very deep water, and often sealed by a thick salt layer. Petroleo Brasileiro, or Petrobras, was initially the sole operator, but as the number of large discoveries grew, the Brazilians were pressed to invite large international companies to become involved in their petroleum industry. Petrobras went from being a strictly national oil company to one with international investors as well.[17] This change occurred against the backdrop of a major discovery in 2010, 180 km off Rio de Janeiro. Libra, as the field was named, was the biggest offshore discovery since 1976, when the giant Cantarell field was discovered in the Gulf of Mexico. The discovery of Libra would double Brazil's known oil reserves. On this news, Petrobras raised more than NOK 400 billion on the stock market, and Brazil became the world's tenth largest oil producing nation.[18] Developments in Brazil would in turn have a vast impact on the global offshore industry. First of all, Brazil had a relatively stable political and economic environment compared to countries like Iraq, Venezuela, or Mexico, who were deemed unreliable suppliers. This predictable climate made it attractive for foreign enterprises to invest and operate in Brazil. And as the reserves were located at extreme depths, and often with massive salt dome seals, new requirements arose for dimensioning of equipment. In addition, both floating production and subsea installations were in heavy use.

KM had a previous history of operations in the region. Bjørn Trosthoel had been in the Brazilian market since 1996 and played a central role in building up the regional office. Now increased activity prompted management to keep a closer eye on this market, and a Brazilian subsidiary was established in 2009, primarily to better handle the growing number of service orders. At this time there were more than 250 DP systems from KM on ships and rigs in service off the coast. In the years since 2005 alone, 150 new DP systems had been installed on vessels operating on the Brazilian fields.

In 2009, the market consisted primarily of shuttle tankers, FPSOs and supply ships. These vessels were equipped with both DP and automation systems. The authorities' strict regulation of the petroleum sector applied also to foreign companies with divisions or subsidiaries in the country. Those who wished to do business there were obliged to hire Brazilian nationals, or contribute in some way to the local or national economies.[19] Certain cases provided good reason to build up foreign offices. When a local parts warehouse was opened in

Building up the business in Brazil has taken place over a long period of time. In the early days, KM collaborated closely with state oil company Petrobras to gain entry into the market. It also created a training centre in Macae. The main activities in Brazil have centred around sales, servicing and training. When Kongsberg Maritime do Brasil was established in Rio in 2009, the training activity moved to the city. Today 100 people are employed by the company in Rio, servicing a fleet of over 400 DP vessels. Photo: KM.

Brazil, the main purpose was to simplify the time-consuming customs process. Brazil's bureaucracy was notorious, and something as simple as bringing parts into the country could take what seemed like forever. Brazil eventually became the primary market for DP, and thereby for Kongsberg Maritime. As recently as March 2014 it became known that KM had been selected to supply technology solutions for 10 pipe-laying vessels for Petrobras, with a total value of NOK 118 million. The equipment to be installed included dynamic positioning, position reference systems, thruster controls and vessel automation. These 146-metre long and 30-metre wide construction ships are to be used in laying flow lines and control cables at depths of up to 3,000 metres.[20]

IN THE MIDDLE KINGDOM

Early in 2010 a new rig arrived in Rio de Janeiro. *Sevan Driller* had been constructed at the Cosco Qidong yard in China, and was built and equipped for extreme conditions on the oil and gas fields off Brazil. According to its specifications, the rig was capable of drilling in waters of more than 3,000 metres, with storage space for the riser on board. Up to 15,000 tonnes could be stored on deck, considerably reducing the need for cargo handling during operation.

The enormous volume of the cylindrical construction meant that, in addition to being equipped with giant fuel tanks, it could also store up to 150,000 barrels of oil. The rig had double sidewalls and a double hull, making it less vulnerable to external damage. A DP-3 would keep the vessel in place during operations. Integrated into the DP system was a solution for riser management.

The giant *Sevan Driller* is just one of many ships and rigs built in China in recent years. Even though the country has a long history of shipbuilding, the industry did not really take off until the late 1990s, propelling China into the elite class of shipbuilding nations.

Pål Rønning and Finn Søberg visited China sporadically during the 1980s, following up construction of installations and shuttle tankers for the Norwegian owners Knudsen and Ugland, the only offshore-related projects in China up until the early 2000s.

In 2003 Kongsberg Maritime initiated collaboration with the merchant house of Hoi Tung. The agreement resulted in Kongsberg Maritime China Shanghai (KMCS) formally being located to Hong Kong. At the time Kongsberg Maritime employed 100 people in China, and the growing importance

KM's first base in China was established in the Pudong area of Shanghai in 2003. Eventually local offices were set up at the major shipyards in Dalian, Jingjuang and Guangzhou. The largest expansion came with the new 25,000 square metre factory in Zhenjiang. Today, Kongsberg Maritime has almost 700 employees in China. Photo: KM.

of China's shipbuilding industry was becoming apparent.[21] The collaboration generated close contact with the yards, and with suppliers of electrical equipment produced in China. Just as in Brazil, capable technicians and engineers were recruited and sent to Kongsberg for training and further education.[22]

The Chinese yards were known for having highly educated workers and low wages. Compared to the South Korean yards, known for their high degree of standardisation, the Chinese yards offered more tailor-made solutions.[23]

KM continued to establish new branch offices from 2005, and by 2008 they had four offices along the Chinese coast: Dalian northeast of Beijing; one at the New Times Shipyard in Jingjuang; the main office in Shanghai by the Jiangnan shipyard; and the last in Guangzhou.[24]

From 2010 on, KM installed between 150 and 200 DP systems each year. By 2011 the total number of KM employees in China had risen to 600. Service and support were expanding steadily.[25] 2011 would prove to be a turning point in many ways, with the establishment of a new factory for production and assembly of products manufactured in China. The 25,000 sqm facility was located in Zhenjiang, not far from Shanghai.[26] The build-up began to resemble that in Brazil, with KM becoming integrated into local production and activities, and employees hired from within the country.

STRONG GROWTH IN SOUTH KOREA

To embark on an enterprise on a new continent with a different climate and often completely different cultural codes could prove challenging. In South Korea, Albatross employed an agent to begin with. He was a former Hyundai employee and knew many of the customers, and he knew how best to handle negotiations with the yards. Negotiating sessions could be marathon, sometimes lasting for as many as 14 days in a row. First came discussions with the technical department or the projects group. Then the albatrosses were sent on to procurement. Finn Søberg recalls negotiations at the Daewoo yard in the 1980s taking place in a long corridor, in a glass enclosure without a ceiling. Procurement staff at the yard went from supplier to supplier, negotiating prices with all present. In order to avoid this method, the Albatross people often went straight to the shipowner. If the owner followed the salesman's proposal, the yard had little choice but to follow up.[27]

In the early 1980s, the same period when Søberg joined the company, Tor Erik Sørensen was hired on to handle sales in Japan and South-Korea. According to Sørensen, the hire was a coincidence. He was waiting for a flight in

Kongsberg Maritime has had offices in several locations in Korea, with the headquarters for merchant fleet operation in Seoul and offshore activities handled from Busan. In 2007 the local business was focused within a new office in Busan. In addition, local offices have been established at the largest shipyards to support building projects. In total, 230 people currently work for KM in Korea. Photo: KM.

the Stavanger airport at Sola when an unusual job ad in the paper caught his eye. It posed the question: 'Do you want to join us on our flight around the world?' The ad was an expression of the somewhat playful spirit that characterised Albatross at the time. Sørensen applied and was called in for an interview. It turned out to be a strongly personal and unusual session, in keeping with the tone of the ad. The interviewers must have liked what they heard, because Sørensen was hired into 'Sales', first in Norway and later covering Scandinavia. When management decided to begin exploring Asia, he was sent east. He was given primary responsibility for Japan and South Korea, where he made the rounds to the yards, established good contacts, and eventually won contracts. Throughout 1984 and 1985 he travelled between South Korea and Japan, which served as his home base. In the spring of 1985 he and his family moved to Kobe. He shared responsibility for Japan and South Korea with Odd Hansen up until 1987.

In the early 1980s there were still many yards that were not familiar with dynamic positioning. Japan in particular proved a challenging environment for marketing the systems, and a raft of illustrations were produced to convey the message. Another challenge was the signing of contracts. Sørensen was

33, and his counterpart, with a different view of age and status, doubted that Sørensen had the authority to sign a contract. A call was made to Kongsberg's management, who could assure the client that he did. Misunderstandings were as a rule resolved, and Sørensen established many solid contacts that the company benefitted from in later years.

The good start in Asia took a dramatic turn in 1986. Roy Larsen, who had been in Asia since the beginning of the 1980s, experienced the event first-hand. He was employed in the 'old' KV Maritime Division with responsibility for Norcontrol's navigation and machinery control systems, commuting between sales jobs in South Korea and the regional office in Singapore. After returning to Norway from Asia he held several management positions in sales and marketing. But before he got that far, he experienced one of the biggest crashes the industry has known. According to Larsen, 'everything' came to a screeching halt in the autumn of 1986. The events in Norway and in Kongsberg were mirrored in Asia, when the bottom fell out of the market. To consolidate their position, KV employees were brought together in Singapore. Some were sent home from 1987 on, while others stayed on to keep the business simmering on the back burner. Back home times were turbulent, with KV's sale of Albatross, Norcontrol Automation and Norcontrol Simulation. But under Simrad's management, activities would soon pick up again.[28]

Tor Erik Sørensen stayed in Singapore with responsibility for Japan and Korea until 1993, when he decided to return to Norway. As often seems to happen with those working in DP, he was contacted on his way home. Simrad director Kåre Hansen asked Sørensen if he could see to a couple of minor matters in Italy, since he was already on the road. This resulted in Sørensen getting responsibility for the operation in Genoa, and later Rome, together with Knut Bøe. It wasn't until 1996 that Sørensen would return to Norway. In the meantime Pål Rønning had assumed responsibility for marketing in India and the ASEAN countries. While Roy Larsen had witnessed a collapse, Pål Rønning, Finn Søberg and Tor Erik Sørensen were experiencing the start of the remarkable rise of Asia that began in the 1990s.

The South Korean yards became serious players in the shipbuilding business in the early 1970s, and South Korea was one the first countries where KV established a foothold. This situation would change with the new millennium. While China was competing in the lower price segment, South Korea's forté gradually became standardised ships of high technical quality. This shift meant that the relationship between the owners, the yard and KM had changed character. While the owners were the primary authority up until the 1990s, making key decisions on equipment and which suppliers to use, this authority gradually shifted to the yards. When the big South Korean yards implemented more standardisation in newbuilding projects, it became too expensive for owners to exchange equipment chosen by the yards. In such a situation, solid contacts and dialog with the yards were a necessity in order to maintain good sales results.[29]

In the period from 2003 to 2004, South Korean yards received fully 40 percent of all shipbuilding contracts in the world. The number of large, modern yards and the highly skilled work force made building in South Korean attractive for many shipowners. While China could still compete on price, South Korea emphasised standardisation and high quality. In 2005 South Korea passed Japan as the world's leading shipbuilding nation.[30]

Three major companies dominate modern shipbuilding in South Korea. These are Samsung Heavy Industries, Daewoo Shipbuilding and Marine Engineering and Hyundai Heavy Industries. Together they had a turnover of USD 20 billion in 2007.[31]

During the years to follow, Kongsberg would continue to develop the side of the company's strategy that emphasised creating value in customer home markets.

THE GLOBAL ECONOMY IN CRISIS

«The collapse of the global economy has led to increased activity in refitting and upgrading the existing fleet. Additionally, Kongsberg Maritime's systems are often installed late in the building process. These factors have contributed to a high level of activity for Kongsberg Maritime, with a relatively strong order book despite low newbuilding levels at the yards over the past two years.» Thus read KM management's summary of 2010.[32]

2008 signalled the start of a new crisis in the global economy, one that would affect both the merchant fleet and the offshore segment. Retrofitting suddenly gained new significance, with contracts covering the replacement of electronics on board. DP systems, as well as other marine electronics, require periodic replacement or renovation. In down times, when shipowners are sceptical to place new orders, the alternative is to upgrade or renovate existing ships. Thus retrofitting presented itself as a good alternative for shipowners in the economic doldrums that followed the crash of 2008.

One example of a retrofit was the *Offshore Stephaniturm*, owned by Offshore Works in Kuala Lumpur, scheduled for an upgrade in 2010. The ship had been

The oldest Kongsberg DP system still in use, perhaps the world's oldest, is located on board the supply ship *Seahorse Spirit*, owned by Defence Maritime Services in Australia. The ship was built in 1980, christened *Balder Hudson* and owned by Parly Augustsson. An ADP311 system was installed that same year and has been in continuous use ever since. There have been several attempts from KM's side to replace it, but the crew wouldn't hear of it as they're so pleased with the system. Photo: KM.

built in Germany back in 1978, and had been through one previous upgrade, and in 1994 an ADP702 and an HPR410 were installed. With the ship due for a new round of renovation, the DP systems were high on the list of equipment due for replacement. During the course of six weeks the Kongsberg crew removed the old DP system and installed a new one. The 'package' included, in addition to a new control system for the main engines, a thruster control system, remote rudder control and an alarm system for the engine room.[33] Soon Hoe Sim, who headed up the work, described the operation in the following glowing terms: «Kongsberg Maritime is just like a general hospital you know. We have doctors for everything. You just leave the vessel with us, and we will make it better ... we had a team that really went the extra mile to complete this.»[34]

Two years later Kongsberg Maritime carried out its biggest-ever retrofit project. The heavy-lift and pipe-laying vessel *Saipem 7000* received a full overhaul, not in South Korea or China, but in Stavanger and Rotterdam. Europe had begun to win back their share of the major fitting contracts. When *Micoperi 7000* and now *Saipem 7000* were fitted with DP in 1985, it was KV Albatross that got the job. Now the 'same' supplier was set to perform the *Saipem 7000* retrofit. This time around the 'Full Picture' consisted of thruster control, ballast control, engine room controls and dynamic positioning, all with the latest KM models. 60 cabinets and 35 consoles were installed on board, connected by 35,000 metres of cable. The system had to handle more than 10,000 I/O signals, in addition to maintaining position using the 12 motors and 12 thrusters that provided propulsion for the rig.[35]

THE DESIGNER CHAIR

The spectacular K-Master was launched in 2009, an improvement on Kongsberg Maritime's solution for the aft bridge on anchor handling and supply ships, situated in and around one or two operator chairs. The installation was an optimised system with nearly all functions of the ship's bridge, and automation and DP systems integrated into the chairs. There was one chair for ship handling, and another for marine operations, such as loading and unloading cargo. If necessary the operators could swap tasks without switching places. One of the key design elements behind 'the chair' was the so-called 80-20 principle, based on the observation that 20 percent of the functions were used 80 percent of the time.[36]

The idea of placing an operator station on the aft deck was not new, however. Most offshore supply vessels are controlled from the aft bridge during operations. Around the year 2000, this bridge was often impractical and difficult to operate. A growing number of incidents were being reported, especially during interaction between supply ships and platforms, where a high stress level was seen as the main cause of operator inattentiveness. A so-called Joint Industry Project (JIP) with DNV, Statoil and Hydro as key partners, was initiated to provide guidelines for organisation of the aft bridge and which equipment should be available there. This project resulted in a new safety class, NAUT-OSV, which led to two workstations with chairs being required on the aft bridge.

Before this rule took effect, Kongsberg Simrad launched its Simrad Maneuvering Control (SMC), in 2002.[37] This concept utilised a new way of arranging screens and service apparatus, borrowed from existing units like SDP, SVC and STC. In contrast to the trend of placing levers and other controls in the

Kongsberg Maritime reached the point where it had all the components needed for the aft bridge of an OSV, but lacked a 'complete solution' – this fired the starting gun for the K-Master chair project. The chair was designed around the tasks that were required to be performed, rather that what existing systems could offer. All controls that needed to be readily available were integrated into the chair, namely important buttons, thruster levers and joysticks. Functions less frequently used were placed on the touch screen. Photo: KM.

armrests, the choice was made to create dedicated side consoles that could be adjusted up, down and sideways to accommodate the operator. Additionally, the design made it possible for the operator to choose a sitting or standing position during operations. The intention was to create a more ergonomically correct workplace. The chair was horseshoe-shaped, with the screens facing the operator. The operator sat in a chair that could be moved back and forth, facing the aft deck. This provided good visibility and control during operations, for example when a supply ship had to be positioned very close to fixed installations or drilling rigs in order to load and unload cargo. The SMC would nonetheless be short-lived.[38] Seen from an ergonomic perspective the SMC was a success, but sales never took off. The solution was deemed too expensive, and the yards were able to create simpler solutions on their own, with nearly the same ergonomics.

The industry's call for a solution with the operating environment incorporated into the operator chair led KM to revive the ideas behind the launch of SMC. It became clear early on that this new operator chair was going to redefine perceptions of what such a chair should be, both with regard to functionality and appearance. Thor Hukkelås headed up the development of the K-Master, under the mantra of «simplification, integration, and multiple functionality, in an avant-garde kit».[39] These elements received unique treatment in the K-Master. The time had come for a total re-think. 'Truck seats' and old-fashioned design were definitely out. Professional industrial designers were recruited to give the chair a 'wow effect'. The chair was to be a workplace that would make operators proud of their jobs. This harkened back 30 years to when Bjørn Barth Jacobsen coerced the production department to install a large brass button for manual control of the DP system. The button cost several thousand kroner extra, with an image of an albatross engraved on top. Then as now, the 'wow effect', that little something extra set Albatross apart from the pack.[40]

A very special piece of furniture was emerging in the K-Master project, tailor-made to satisfy general ergonomic requirements, as well as new requirements for bridge design (NAUT-OSV). This gave the K-Master a unique 'look' that heightened the already high expectations for the product. The next task was to meet these expectations by developing a simplified user interface that included all sub-systems. The choice went to a concept known as 'split interaction', where touch screens in the armrests provided simplified user panels, and operational information could be observed on larger screens placed around the chair. The design template was still the 80-20 principle. For their efforts, Kongsberg and Hareide Design were awarded «Merket for god design» (award for industrial design) in 2010. The award was handed out at a formal ceremony during Designer Days in Oslo, arranged by the Norwegian Design Council.[41]

The K-Master was first and foremost intended for advanced supply and anchor handling vessels. The person in charge of loading, unloading or other operations, could focus specifically on activities taking place on deck. The strength of the K-Master concept came especially to the fore when DP and thruster control were delivered together with subsystems for navigation and automation. This was Kongsberg Maritime's plan for cementing its position as a supplier of sophisticated systems in the upper echelon of the market. When the K-Master was first presented, it went under the moniker of *integrated reality*.

The term refers to the way in which automation, surveillance and navigation systems had been interconnected, but it was also in keeping with the trend of the time in describing communication technology. This technology revolutionised not only the way operations were carried out, but also the way in which those carrying out operations perceived and participated in their tasks.

FOLLOW THE SUN

From the time Albatross delivered the first DP system to Jacob Stolt-Nielsen's canary yellow diving ships in 1977, the uncompromising rule had been to provide support whenever the customer required. The reputation that Albatross, and later Simrad Albatross, had established in the first decades didn't disappear over time, either. Rather, it came to be the core value of the DP team, and KM, in the years that followed. During the first years, when both computer technology and DP systems were less reliable, quick response from the service team was essential. KM's customers operated in a market segment where time was money – a lot of money. With day rates of more than NOK 1 million, it was not an option to let the vessels lay idle. Even though KM's service teams at offices around the globe were highly available, KM's service was drastically altered when the 'Follow the Sun' principle was launched in 2012.[42] Now customers everywhere, no matter what time of day or where the vessel was located, were assured of a response when they called for help.[43] Three high-tech support centres for Europe, Asia, and the Americas ensured 24-hour service.

When the employees come to work in the morning at the Customer Support Centre, the cutting-edge service base in Kongsberg, they log on to the virtual chat room, where they hook up with their colleagues in Singapore, who are about to head home for the day. Ongoing jobs are handed over from Singapore to Kongsberg. The same procedure is repeated when the lights go on at the KM centre in New Orleans, eight hours later. And so it goes with KM's customer service and support, around the clock.

Images of the three service centres call to mind the mission control room on a space launch. Personnel sit in a circle, surrounded by glass walls, screens, cameras and microphones. On the wall hangs a giant screen with clocks showing the time at various places around the world. Centre staff communicates with clients through video conferencing and digital sharing of programs and documents.[44]

The three centres handle around 1000 emails each day, and replies must be sent no more than eight working hours after receipt. There are many tele-

The Customer Support Centre at Kongsberg, which became fully operational in 2012, is one of three similar facilities located around the world. The other two are in Singapore and New Orleans. The service centres take turns to serve customers in eight-hour cycles, thus working around the clock. In this way, a customer can contact someone who can help solve their crew's problems at any time of the day. Staff at the centres can directly access vessel systems for the potential correction of minor errors. Photo: KM.

phone requests as well, and these are to be handled immediately, around the clock. One person at each centre handles inquiries and directs them to a staff member with the relevant expertise. In most cases, inquiries can be handled by staff at the centres. If the service team is remotely connected to the vessel through a data link, they can access the screen being used aboard the vessel, enabling real-time consultation and troubleshooting. The service engineers can also recommend basic adjustments to the system.[45] The three centres are equipped with dedicated rooms where service engineers can hook up directly to the vessel's own systems. In the event of more serious or complex issues, task forces are organised in offices dedicated to the specific case. As soon as the need for onsite repairs is identified, a service engineer or team is dispatched to the vessel.[46]

THE FULL PICTURE

When the first DP systems were delivered, a lone console was connected to the computer, thrusters, wind meter, and the hydroacoustic position sensors.

Full Picture Magazine, first published in 2004, has become a showcase for Kongsberg Maritime, where customers old and new can keep up to date with the latest developments in maritime electronics. The title refers to the company's product philosophy: the goal is to deliver the full spectrum of maritime products for modern ships. Photo: KM.

Additional marine electronics were supplied by other manufacturers. Heading into the 1990s, navigational instruments, process and vessel automation, and dynamic positioning were often delivered in the same package. The bundling didn't stop there, either. From 2000 even more instrumentation, like surveillance, measurement systems, and energy management were available in KM's portfolio. This meant that the customer, usually the yards, got offers of larger 'packages' from the same supplier. For KM, this meant that deliveries at greater volumes. An expanding portfolio also meant acquiring companies with the expertise they needed in order to supplement their own family of products. This strategic thinking, originating in the mid-1990s, was carried into the next century. One step toward this future vision was the value and brand process from 2003, led by Kunde & Co.

The branding process had varying consequences and effects: For customers, it was a confirmation that KM could deliver nearly all types of marine electronics for navigation, automation, and positioning. For management, it presented the opportunity to 'preach' coordination and integration. Among employees, the process was more about technical coordination, where user interfaces,

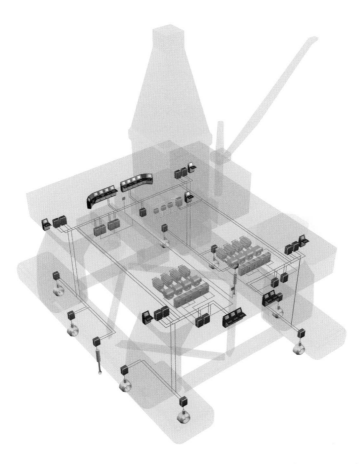

Kongsberg Maritime offered products for dynamic positioning, navigation, thruster control, vessel auto-mation, and process automation, as well as safety systems for process shutdown. KM realised that these systems constituted a whole – a complete proposition – that was not being fully utilised. When a vessel is considered as a whole, performance and safety can be improved. The slogan «Maximising performance by providing THE FULL PICTURE» encapsulated this and became of great importance for corporate strategies and the delivery of system solutions in the years that followed. Photo: KM.

documentation, and manuals were standardised using a common template and aesthetics. The common identity that emerged through these processes can be seen today in KM's HMI standards and graphical interfaces. In practice, standardisation means that an operator can move from one console for DP, to another for navigation, and still feel at home with KM.[47]

Another signal to employees and customers was the introduction of the phrase 'Full Picture'. The phrase was used publicly for the first time in 2004, when The Full Picture, a new customer magazine, was published. Not surprisingly, KM's

CEO Torfinn Kildal set the tone on the magazine's editorial page. He summed up the branding process, stating: «Uniting all our business units will enable us to utilise and share resources and information more openly and effectively. We will be able to offer you more in terms of service, products and all-round cooperation».[48] This weighty statement served both as a fitting conclusion to the branding project, and as the introduction of an important communication tool for the company in the years to come. In addition, the magazine launch highlighted what was in 2004 still an admirable vision, but one that would be realised in the decade ahead: a growing number of 'package deliveries'.

In December of 2012, petroleum production on the Skarv field commenced. An advanced FPSO, *Skarv*, was brought on line, operating as a combined processing plant and storage tank. *Skarv* was moored by its turret, to which the risers from the subsea installations were also fed. In order to reduce fatigue on the anchor lines that held the ship in place, five propellers, controlled by a combined DP and PM system from Kongsberg Maritime, would help keep the vessel headed into the wind.[49] In addition to DP, KM delivered safety, monitoring, information, and control systems. 200 cabinets, a host of servers, and 40 workstations were installed on board. The delivery included a system capable of handling more than 70,000 process signals simultaneously. The crew at Carpus, together with the yard in South Korea, had been at work on the ship for a total of six years. The system was assembled by a crew of 200 KM employees over the course of a full year. As project manager Per Hægstad put it, everything KM had in the way of products went onto the giant ship. Navigation systems were the exception, as the vessel was stationary for the entire service life. *Skarv* was a milestone for BP in Norway, and for KM it represented their biggest delivery to a single owner.[50]

POSITIONING FOR THE FUTURE?

The FPSO *Skarv* lies off the coast of Nordland municipality, in an area where wind and current converge to create dangerously volatile waves. At its worst, winds can reach speeds of 40 metres per second, with waves up to 30 metres high. Weather presents a challenge in other places as well. In the Gulf of Mexico, hurricanes can damage even the sturdiest of platforms. The impact of extreme weather and climate change has opened up new opportunities, but creates new challenges as well. If the Northwest Passage becomes truly navigable for much of the year, this would open the way for transportation of oil and gas between Europe and Asia. And if oil and gas exploration is allowed in the high north,

If oil and gas exploration and production moves to the polar regions, the offshore industry will be faced with completely new challenges regarding safety and environmental considerations. The cold, darkness and the fact that many operations would be far from land entail strict requirements for both people and equipment. Photo: Shell.

darkness, ice and the vast distances to nearest installations will present major challenges. Accidents could also have major environmental consequences.

The increased interest in the polar regions and the possibilities and challenges that lie in these areas were a major factor in Kongsberg Maritime's decision in 2009 to finance a professorial chair in marine cybernetics at NTNU in Trondheim. The chair is one of more than 20 in the Global Maritime Knowledge Hub initiative, with DNV GL, MARINTEK, and several of Norway's leading shipowners, equipment suppliers and shipyards joining KM as sponsors. This 'supercluster', as it was referred to in the media, raised over NOK 100 million to sponsor the 20 professors over five years. The donors' motivation is the creation of a knowledge cluster to encourage more interaction between industry players, while strengthening technical knowledge in the maritime sector.

The first of KM's two professorships went to Roger Skjetne, who is doing research and lecturing on dynamic positioning in Arctic waters.[51] Skjetne is unquestionably qualified for the position, with his education from the University of California at Santa Barbara and NTNUs Institute for technical cybernetics, and the company Marine Cybernetics, before taking the post in Trondheim.

In January of 2013, a few years after the hiring of professor Skjetne, the Norwegian business daily Dagens Næringsliv wrote about dynamic positioning that would allow a ship to «lock on to a point on the sea floor» and resist the forces of drifting ice. As previously mentioned, this was not a new notion, as KM had worked with Statoil, NTNU and the German research institute Hamburg Ship Model Basin (HSVA) to study a specialised DP system in their test tank. Tests were performed on a model of the concept drill ship for Statoil and Stena Drilling, the specially constructed arctic drilling ship *Stena DrillMax Ice*.[52] Just as the extreme depths in Brazilian waters presented great challenges for the oil companies and operators, the extremes of the high north are challenging the industry, including the Norwegian authorities, to find ways to produce petroleum in arctic waters. This is one of the areas where KM is beginning to accumulate expertise, but what the future will bring in this field remains to be seen.

Another example that illustrates how new technology stretches the limits of the possible, is the odd little HiLoad vessel from Remora. The company takes its name from the small parasitic fish that attach themselves to a shark, living off scraps from the host's mouth. HiLoad is basically a large L-shaped unit that can be manoeuvred alongside a ship and attach itself simultaneously to both the hull side and underneath. The 'vessel' has several coupling mechanisms that allow oil and gas to be transferred to other ships or to a terminal on land. Equipped with DP, the unit is manoeuvrable by means of three large thrusters. HiLoad functions as a mobile positioning system for the host ship, eliminating the need for a tugboat or on-board machines to keep on station. What this rather exotic solution illustrates, is just how adaptable KM's DP systems actually are. With HiLoad, conventional tankers can hook up to a production ship with the highest degree of precision.[53]

One piece in the future puzzle will undoubtedly be Kongsberg Information Management System (K-IMS), an all-new information platform developed for the offshore and maritime industries. The mission of K-IMS is to provide continuous data recording and exchange, both on board and ashore, through interactive web-based solutions. Access to this information makes a vessel's status, functions and operations more accessible than previously, enabling new ways of managing a ship, and providing more parties with access to information and monitoring of systems. The first K-IMS was installed in February of 2014 on the Royal Caribbean Cruises *Allure of the Seas*.[54]

Another enticing dream for the future is fish farming in deep water. The large density of fish farms along the Norwegian coast is increasingly linked to various environmental challenges, from the build-up of waste in pens to problems with lice. These problems can to some extent be mitigated by placing the

The HiLoad concept was conceived by Hitech Marine in Arendal in 2003, with the objective of reducing investment costs for shuttle tankers. The idea was to connect a remote controlled unmanned L-shaped 'thruster vehicle' to any tanker, making it possible to load oil from an FPSO as you would using a shuttle tanker with DP. The HiLoad was to stick to the tanker with a unique suction cup system and be controlled from the FPSO. The result was a complete, self-contained DP vessel with its own control room and operators. Photo: Remora.

pens in open waters. The large SalMar Group, an industrial salmon farming operation, has established a separate company, Ocean Farming, for developing open ocean fish farming. Planning commenced in 2012, and a model was tested at MARINTEK in 2013. The unit consists of a round steel frame that is 110 metres across and 67 metres high. Six horizontal spokes with floatation tanks underneath bind the unit together, allowing the structure to flex, with an operations room in the centre. Ocean Farming plan to anchor the first facilities in depths of 100 to 300 metres. In the same way as with semi-submersible drilling rigs, the facility will be attached to the bottom with six anchor chains. Since developers are striving for an oceangoing plant independent of auxiliary vessels, one likely scenario is using DP systems.

DP might also prove useful in what is called deep-water mining, or recovery of minerals from the ocean floor. The Canadian company Nautilus Minerals is planning world's first deep-water mining in the Bismarck Sea off Papua New Guinea, north of Australia. China, which is considered an upcoming superpower in this field, has stated that mining metals on the seabed will be underway by 2030. The great international interest has in turn led the EU Commissioner for Fisheries and Maritime Affairs, Maria Damanaki, to declare that Europe must use its advantages as modern maritime power to create new economic growth «with the ocean as the engine». At the EU's annual maritime conference, with over 1,000 in attendance, her message was that the sea and the coast would be central pillars of the EU's new blue-green *strategy*.[55] The Norwegian researcher Tom Heldal has hinted at mineral deposits along the mid-Atlantic ridge, in the sea between Norway and Greenland. In addition, researchers at the University of Bergen have identified minerals of interest in what has been called Loki's Castle, located at 2300 metres deep 300 km west of Bjørnøya.[56] Researchers will probably use AUVs (Autonomous Underwater Vehicle) or ROVs in mapping the seabed. These underwater vessels can capture very detailed images and high-resolution video of the seafloor, providing researchers with valuable information.[57]

KONGSBERG – RIGHT IN THE MIDDLE

«This contract is a milestone for Kongsberg Maritime, and one of the most comprehensive Full Picture contracts in Kongsberg Maritime's history.» This was the text on the Kongsberg Group website in 2014. Prompting this proud declaration was the contract for delivery and integration of all electrical, tele-communication and control systems for Petrofac's new *JSD 6000*, a deep-water

Zeppaloon is a small airship built by students at NTNU, formerly NTH. In 2014 the task of getting Zeppaloon to steer itself was assigned to six engineering students who had summer jobs at Kongsberg Maritime. Using dynamic positioning they enabled the ship to stand still in the air. The project stirred significant interest among students with regards to summer job hunting. From left: Jon-Arne Pedersen, Elias Bjørne, Stine Marie Hjetland, Bjørn Olav H. Eriksen, Kristoffer Gryte and Eivind Harris. Photo: *Finansavisen* / Silje Sundt Kvadsheim.

pipe-laying vessel to be built at the Shanghai Zhenhua Heavy Industry yard in China. The contract is valued at more than NOK 230 million.[58] Not only a major contract, the deal with one of the premier shipbuilders in China illustrates Kongsberg's steadily stronger position in Middle Kingdom.

Kongsberg Maritime underwent significant changes in the years before and after the start of the new millennium. One aspect of this change was the growing importance of regional offices and subsidiaries in Europe, Asia, the US, and Brazil, not only for sales and service, but also for the generation of new ideas and the strengthening of cultural diversity in the company. The presence of sales staff around the world for the last decades has had great significance. Building a presence, not just in sales and service, but in all links in the KM supply chain, was critical, perhaps even decisive, for how well Kongsberg Maritime would succeed out in the world.

Directing and coordinating this enterprise had only grown in importance. Information and knowledge needed to flow unhindered. Values and strategies had to be clear and present in order to avoid misunderstandings. And last, but not least, the organisation serving the customer had to be efficient and effective.

When a potential customer is considering a DP system, they are concerned with more than just specifications and price. Customer support and service, and confidence, are also key factors. Much of this is intangible, and related to overall brand perception. And yet a brand is not created once and for all. It must be developed and nurtured over time, and not least, it must be constantly maintained. The value of a brand is the sum of all the parts, not just those that go into making a DP system that keeps a vessel on station, but also those parts that help a customer to believe that the system is the best at what it does, now and into the future. Or to put it another way: A strong brand should help the customer to achieve the best possible position, both literally and figuratively. This message also had its roots in the company's history. «We help people improve their position», was the original slogan, indicating that Kongsberg Maritime and its forbears had been doing branding since the beginning. The news in 2014 was that the brand was no longer national but global, with all the accompanying demands. No longer only about price and quality, the brand now had to embrace a global presence, and respect.

14

THE JEWEL IN THE CROWN

IN THE COURSE of the hectic years from 1975 to 1977, Kongsberg Våpenfabrikk (KV) developed a Norwegian DP system, together with NTH/SINTEF, CMI and Simrad. KV's Dynpos project would soon take the name Albatross, and begin producing a series of DP systems: the ADP501, ADP502 and ADP503. With these DPs, KV managed to establish itself in a market dominated by the American Honeywell and British GEC. Three years later, Albatross had become the world DP leader.

Almost 40 years later, the news broke that Kongsberg Maritime had won a major contract with the Brazilian energy giant Petrobras, in competition with leading international companies. KM was to deliver technical solutions for close to NOK 118 million to ten new pipelaying vessels. That the company had maintained its hegemony in the market was equally as remarkable as the fact that they managed to outmanoeuvre Honeywell and GEC back in 1980.

Much has changed since the first DP system was activated aboard the *Seaway Eagle* on the 17th of May 1997. Stand-alone DP systems have been replaced by extensive integrated systems solutions. The green ADP501 consoles, with their buttons that required a heavy hand to activate, have given way to elegant black consoles that can be operated by the click of a mouse. And not just the technology has changed. The first DP systems were created in a project by a group of enthusiasts that often worked through the night in KV's Building 11. Now the advanced DP systems are developed in precisely planned processes in a world-class organisation. The soaring albatross that decorated the first systems has been replaced by the KONGSBERG 'K' topped by a crown.

On Saturday 8 November 2014 it was open day at Kongsberg Technology Park, with over 7,000 guests in attendance. Kongsberg Carpus was brimming with visitors, who, amongst other things, experienced an energetic physics show. The occasion also allowed for a tour of the 'follow the sun' facilities and a chance to try the latest offshore training simulators. Photo: KM.

SIX GENERATIONS OF DP SYSTEMS

Dynamic positioning has undergone dramatic changes in the years since 1977. The 400 kilo DP cabinets that had to be winched on board and lowered through a hole in the pilot house roof have been replaced by smaller, lighter modules that can be located various places on board. Ethernet, fast new processors, and alternative I/O solutions have made the computer architecture and organisation of the systems better suited to carrying out their assignments. Performance and reliability have been greatly improved. The ADP501 system from 1977 on *Seaway Eagle* bears little resemblance to the K-Pos system on board the towering *Sevan Driller* rig operating off the coast of Brazil.

The first ADP500 series was supplemented by a simpler ADP311 in 1979. Four years later, Albatross launched the APM3000. This was a new system that used DP functionality to support the anchoring system on a drilling rig, so-called position mooring. In the same year the ADP311 was replaced by the ADP100, with KV's KS500 computer being exchanged for Albatross's in-house developed SBC1000. This met with considerable resistance from KV's management, but the introduction of the SBC1000 proved to be an important technological step forward for Albatross, and laid the foundation for a new generation of technology, including the automation system AIM.

The next generation of DP was introduced with the launch of the triple redundant ADP703 in 1987. The principle of redundancy was altered, from master-slave to majority voting. Over the next five years the ADP701 and APD702 followed, giving the DP developers the option to offer single, double, or triple redundancy. This series of systems would receive several upgrades as well.

Over time the Albatross user interface began to appear outdated and inflexible compared to competing systems. Albatross, now owned by Simrad, determined to develop a new DP with an interface based on modern Windows graphics. In 1996 they launched a new generation SDP that employed Windows-based PCs for the operator stations, and a new in-house SBC400 to handle real-time processes in the processing station.

The sixth and latest generation of DP systems was rolled out in 2006. K-Pos was based on an RCU501 processor and so-called RIO units for interconnection of onboard elements like thrusters and sensors. These were complete, enclosed modules that could be installed virtually anywhere on board. At the same time a serial bus solution was introduced, allowing the connection of individual system units using a single cable. K-Pos also made it possible to change the redundancy principles of the system. Previous generation systems either duplicated or trebled the I/O units, using an external switch to steer which computer would relay commands to the thrusters. This switch, though it was a simple mechanism, was also a potential source of failure. The move to segregation meant that each thruster had its own I/O module and was connected to each RCU through a hub. In redundant systems, the communications channel through RCUs and the RIO modules was also duplicated. If a component failed, it would at worst affect only one thruster.

Position reference systems had also been improved, and new systems have been introduced. In the first years, taut wire, HPR100 and Artemis were the most frequently used, and covered most needs for DP operations. When satellite-based GPS systems became available, the conditions for positioning changed. It became easier to operate in deep water and far from land. In 1995, the HiPAP system was introduced. This was a leap forward from existing HPE systems. The first DP systems had position reference systems with accuracy to within five to ten metres. Today systems can operate with accuracy down to the decimetre.

The very first DP systems were used to keep diving ships on station while the divers worked on the sea floor. Today's systems can also help a pipe-laying

ALBATROSS

REFERENCE LIST 1

NAME OF VESSEL	ORDERED	DELIVERY	SYST.CONFIG.	VESSEL OWNER
SEAWAY SWAN **TREASURE SWAN**	Nov. 75	Dec. 77	**ADP 5031** Artemis Nav. radar Taut wire HPR 100	Stolt-Nielsen
SEAWAY EAGLE **DSV AFRODITE**	Nov. 76	April 77	**ADP 501** Artemis L. W. Taut wire MK II HPR 100	Stolt-Nielsen R.R. Spa Italy
SEAWAY HAWK **ABEILLE SUPPORTER**	Oct. 77	March 78	**ADP 501** Artemis HPR 309T/100	Stolt-Nielsen Societé Pro- gemar & Cie, Paris
CAPALONGA	Dec. 76	Oct. 77	**ADP 502** Artemis Nav. radar Taut wire	SSOS/Talassa

This is the first page in Albatross' reference list from 1984, showing all ships that the firm had delivered to up until that point. Details relating to delivery dates, company names and the type of DP system the ships were equipped with were also included. Photo: KM.

vessel move along a pre-programmed track, or follow another vessel or an ROV. A drilling vessel can stay on station while drilling for oil. If necessary, a cruise ship can remain on station near a corral reef or be guided to a berth. A vessel waiting on standby can be programmed to stay within a defined area in order to reduce fuel consumption. A tank ship or FPSO can be set up to follow the wind or current and counter strain on the loading buoy, or reduce stress on mooring lines keeping the vessel anchored in place.

Not only the function and application of DP systems have changed. Design has also undergone an evolution. High-resolution colour screens with touch-control functionality have replaced the unsophisticated monochrome Stansaab screens from 1977. The consoles from 1977 were green and developed in keeping with maritime tradition. Today industrial designers with interface and ergonomic expertise design the sleek consoles. Modern consoles compete with other products for design awards, and Kongsberg Maritime has won several prizes for good design.

With the Full Picture, deliveries have grown in scope and size. Shipowners and yards alike have seen the value of bundling several systems of the same make and with the same service apparatus. This means that Kongsberg Maritime now supplies solutions for more functions on a vessel than previously. This is perhaps most obvious in the comprehensive deliveries made to FPSOs and deep water drilling rigs where KM also delivers control of onboard power systems.

CANNOT LIVE BY TECHNOLOGY ALONE

Professor Jens G. Balchen was not a timid man. When he saw an opportunity, he seized it and went to work. He was a charismatic figure. He sowed ideas and set projects in motion. He had plenty of use for this enthusiasm in 1971, when he went before KV management with a new idea.

KV was a national industrial cornerstone supplying weapons to the Norwegian military, a state-owned company with a mission. The assignments it had to oversee, which came at any time, varied greatly. From 1960 on, one task was to be an industrial incubator for tech products in the development phase. This mission was modified somewhat in the 1970s. From 1972, KV was to strengthen the Norwegian industrial contribution in the offshore sector. This was a task they carried out together with state-owned Statoil.

When Balchen approached KV in 1971, they were not ready to handle his request, but when he returned some years later, things had changed. The North Sea offshore industry was starting to take off, and the multitude of possibilities in this sector were becoming apparent. Balchen's idea had gone from unfeasible to attractive, albeit with a limited market, but with good profit margins on each DP system delivered. To what degree dynamic positioning would win market shares in the North Sea remained to be seen. In 1975, the main task was to find a customer who would order a DP system.

While well-established Norwegian shipowners like Smedvig and Odfjell entered the drilling market, the shipper Stolt-Nielsen Seaways chose to concentrate on service and diving vessels. Jacob Stolt-Nielsen and his right-hand man Bjørn Bendigtsen were interested in trying something new. When they saw an opportunity to make inroads with Statoil on future jobs, new opportunities opened up. Dynpos head Bjørn Barth Jacobsen knocked on Bendigtsen's door, and the door swung open.

In other words, the Dynpos project was made possible by several coinciding factors and developments. It was conceived in the vortex of Balchen's business concept, KV's industrial mission, and the blossoming offshore market in the North Sea. When shipowner Stolt-Nielsen came on board, the stars aligned for a Norwegian DP system produced by KV.

FROM PROJECT TO ENTERPRISE

In the beginning, the project was a collaborative effort under KV's direction. While the CMI team simulated waves, wind and current, SINTEF's people wrote code for cybernetic algorithms. Simrad's engineers developed a hydroacoustic positioning system, while KV contributed the computers, consoles and the operative system KOS. KV was a solid enterprise capable of taking risks and handling both costs and legal discussions. Not least, they had the engineers with the competence and the resources to build a DP system. This was important for starting up the project, but not for its ultimate success. None of the partners had what it took on their own – but together they were effective. Bjørn Barth Jacobsen and Thor Skoland comprised the vital leadership team in the early years. Together they convinced employees that this was a project they could and would succeed with, and one that would make them world leaders in DP. Barth Jacobsen dealt with the customers while Skoland ensured progress in the project, seeing to it that specifications and deadlines were respected. Not everything the albatrosses did was to KV management's liking. Barth Jacobsen was often called in to KV boss Rolf Qvenild's office. As payments from the first orders began to trickle in to KV's coffers, forgiveness became easier to find. By contrast to many of KV's development projects, Albatross made money on their products. Engineers with a knack for sales were key from the beginning. Using a combination of strong technology, skilful sales and stellar service, they conquered the world DP market heading into the 1980s.

While challenging convention and authority made sense in the early years of DP development, it was not a good long-term strategy. Breaking the rules can clear the way for new ideas, but it is no way to ensure success in the long run. The continuation of this development story would therefore take another turn in the years to come.

MARITIME INDUSTRY

Albatross experienced a steady stream of deliveries and a growing number of employees during the 1980s. Those who followed after had not experienced the intense working environment and never-say-die attitude of the years prior to 1980. New manager Nils Willy Gulhaugen decided that if this entrepreneurial spirit and willingness to take chances were to be perpetuated, something had to be done. Training employees to be Albatrosses also involved professionalisation of the company, all the while highlighting the essential importance of customer relations.

Attention to, and close contact with customers, was critical in order for Albatross to be able to maintain its market position. If the Albatrosses couldn't manage to keep the customer satisfied, their lifeblood would ebb away, just as warned in the 'little red book' on The Albatross Theory, written for the first employees. The behavioural patterns of the early albatrosses, and the reputation it earned them, would determine the company's path to the future.

The price of oil nearly bottomed out in 1987, leading to reduced activity and dampened investor enthusiasm in the oil sector. Albatross, which had become a listed company, was hit hard by the crisis. It soon became apparent that KV was technically bankrupt, and that all activities not related to defence were to be cut. Albatross was sold to Simrad, and the change of ownership was tangible. While Gulhaugen had given employees great freedom and responsibility, Simrad CEO Kåre Hansen was a detail-oriented manager. This was the scenario as Albatross management lead the way toward professionalism, while the Simrad chief assumed responsibility for streamlining internal processes and industrialisation.

The period under Simrad management was determinate for continued investments in DP, and for the company establishing a stronger industrial foundation. Crisis was followed by growth, and the new IMO regulations for

DP ratified in 1994 contributed to this development. While DNV classification from 1979 had established the Albatross DP solution as the class standard, IMO's reworking of the rules for standardisation led to less 'tailor-making' of systems.

Early sales had often been seen as 'coups' on the market, but now a competent organisation, able to serve the customer in a professional manner, was being built up. Without this uncompromising attitude toward the customer, the situation could have easily been very different. Good relationships were established to Norwegian shipowners who were not only world leaders in their fields, but who also served as role models for their international competitors.

When markets first went international, and later global, the nature of contact between sales staff and shipowners changed. With the owner and the producer in one country, newbuilding in another, and sales and service in a third, many relationships were due to change. This became particularly obvious in the relationship to the Korean yards. Their move from tailor-made to standardisation meant that contact with the shipowners was replaced by dialog with the yards.

THE GLOBAL BRAND

In 1987, on the occasion of the opening of new offices at Industritunet in Kongsberg, management had a giant golden egg placed on a pedestal near the entrance. The egg now stands in the atrium of Kongsberg Maritime's head office Carpus, with a significantly less prominent placement than at Industritunet. The golden egg might serve as a reminder of the technology that started it all, but as in the fable, also a reminder to preserve the culture that gave life to the golden egg.

At the turn of the century, various maritime electronics technologies from KM's subsidiaries were on their way to becoming more tightly integrated. This would eventually have consequences for the companies behind these products. What were once virtually independent companies were transformed, moulded, and integrated through various organisational processes. The albatrosses, like their counterparts in Norcontrol, Simrad, Autronica, Seatex and others, were gathered under Kongsberg Maritime, a central part of the Kongsberg concern.

Integration of companies and technologies occurred simultaneously with a growth in the number of activities, field offices and subsidiaries abroad. KM's subsidiaries had been built up where activities were the most intense, thus aiding the company's communication with the customer. In this way the global brand, like the national, was built over time. The brand name had been

Many of the people who once helped make Albatross, Simrad and Norcontrol into leading businesses are currently employed in Kongsberg Maritime, an important division of the Kongsberg group. This photo shows KM employees gathered at Brunstad congress centre in Stokke in 2008. Such gatherings are an important means of conveying and preserving a sense of community in a company with branches, subsidiaries and offices throughout Norway and the wider world. Photo: KM.

cultivated and developed to reflect the characteristics and traditions of the host countries, whether it be production, service, or sales.

Both external and internal diversity had to be managed. With a diverse mix of people and activities to coordinate, management needed to project clear values, and the company needed to establish solid systems for communication. KM's 'Follow the Sun' service system was one good example of this.

SMARTER, SAFER, GREENER

The Petroleum industry is a key factor in the global economy. The price of oil is both a barometer for the global economic situation and a driver for development and change in global markets. But the capital economy has also had to make way for the green economy. The price of emissions has been established through carbon quotas that are growing in importance. Not least, the interest in so-called green solutions is ever more relevant. This applies to both energy and the environment.

For operators in the offshore business, thrusters are one of the biggest energy consumers, and it is important to pursue anything that can be done to reduce their energy consumption. Ships that use less energy, cost less to operate. Lower energy consumption also means fewer emissions, and with that, an improved environment. KM launched 'GreenDP' in 2001. Here was the solution to at least two interconnected challenges – profitability and reduced emissions – in a system that would help protect the environment.

Many would maintain that the age of oil is in decline. Investments are falling and discoveries getting ever smaller, at least in the North Sea. Many of today's and tomorrow's resources lie in deep water and are often complex and difficult to produce. More and more reservoirs are marginal, or soon drained. Exploitation of areas that have been previously unfeasible or under restrictions is becoming a pressing matter. Drillships specially designed and equipped for Arctic operations are being planned. In the same way that the deep waters off Brazil challenged equipment suppliers at the turn of the century, the polar regions present one of today's greatest technological challenges, and strongest drivers for development.

Offshore exploration and production in the polar regions demands thorough knowledge of the challenges that cold and ice represent. These types of complex and diversified operations place new requirements on the rigs and the equipment on board. When the boundaries for exploration and production of petroleum are expanded, new dangers and greater risks appear. Darker, colder operations far from shore place new demands on equipment. Falling reserves and new areas of production mean a need for more technologically advanced equipment. This means not only technological innovation, but also increased complexity in the methods used to locate and extract petroleum resources. It also means new and better methods of equipment testing.

With the demise of oil, it may be necessary to prepare for the new 'blue-green' ocean revolution that many are predicting. Finding new and more environmentally friendly methods of fish farming and mineral and biomaterial exploration will be critical in the years to come. Knowledge and technology from the offshore industry can certainly be put to use in other contexts. Production of food will only increase in importance, proportionate to the growth of the world's population. The similarities between sea farming and the offshore industry may quickly become more apparent than they seem today. The same could apply to extraction of minerals from the ocean floor. An FPSO hovering above a subsea installation may well prove to be the best way to harvest minerals from the deep.

THE DP ADVENTURE

DP technology has made an invaluable contribution to the Norwegian, and international, petroleum industry – but it doesn't stop there. DP technology in general, not only Kongsberg's, has been of critical importance for the Norwegian petroleum success story in the North Sea, and other regions around the globe. This segment, built on and around activities in Kongsberg, has grown into one of Norway's most vital and globally oriented industries, with vast ripple effects for other segments of the Norwegian maritime industry.

DP technology is essential for a number of different offshore operations, whether it be drilling, laying of cable and pipe, offloading, installation and maintenance of subsea equipment, operation of floating hotels, or loading and unloading of equipment and supplies. Without DP, many of these tasks would be either virtually impossible, highly expensive, or simply too risky to undertake.

Kongsberg did not invent dynamic positioning, but since 1980, the company called Albatross, today Kongsberg Maritime, has been the dominant supplier of DP systems in the world. Despite entering this business later than others, they have contributed significantly to the development of DP systems over the last 40 years.

It may seem paradoxical that such a small project in a traditional state-owned enterprise, based in a land-locked Norwegian town, could outperform major international corporations and achieve dominance in the global DP market – in only a few years. Equally improbable is the likelihood of this company maintaining their leading position into the present. The company has demonstrated the ability to position itself effectively over the years. This is first and foremost due to their ability to reinvent themselves and develop new technology for use in new applications, and adapt that technology to the needs of the customer.

A dynamic positioning system is much more than the sum of its technical parts. Kongsberg Maritime's success, and that of its forerunners, has in large part been made possible by the many people through the years who have also

In 1986 Albatross had moved into its own facility, Industritunet. Here we can see company employees gathered in front of Rolf Hansen's sculpture located at the building entrance. The sculpture was designed as a kind of totem pole with a golden egg on top. The totem is made of a piece of wood found in the river Numedalslågen and the blue colour symbolises association with the water. The gold egg, on the other hand, hints at knowledge and wisdom. This was, no doubt, a group who had great faith in their capabilities. Photo: Mediafoto.

had what it takes to get a system to function, from customer care and service, to sales and training. From the start of the Dynpos project and the Albatross years, a culture has been established with the attitude of living not just off, but also for and with the customer. In the same way that a DP system is designed to keep a vessel in position, those working in DP have made it their mission to help their customers achieve the best possible position. That same attitude has also helped keep Albatross, and Kongsberg Maritime, in the position that they enjoy today.

What began as the tiny Dynpos project at the Kongsberg Våpenfabrikk in the mid 1970s, and was near extinction when the first life-giving contract was signed on 22 November 1975, is today a large and vital enterprise. The significance of DP extends far beyond keeping a vessel in position. It has created jobs and income, and represents a technology that has generated revenue and activity on many fronts for the Kongsberg Group. Seen in this light, DP has truly become the shining jewel in the Kongsberg crown.

NOTES

NOTES TO CHAPTER 1

1 *The Bible, Jonah, Chapter 1, verses 4–6.*
2 *Verne 1895, quoted from Faÿ 1990: 181.*
3 Helix Energy Solutions: Helix 534. Well Intervention Vessel. Fact Sheet. *Discoverer 534* renamed *Helix 534* in 2012. www.helixesg.com/media/9382/hel_534_r4.pdf (10.07.14).
4 Wayne E. Griffith: «Witch». Report from *Discover 534*.
5 *Discoverer 534* had an AIM and ADP703 onboard. It was installed in May 1990. Simrad: Reference list Positioning & Control Systems. Issue 20: 47.
6 Kongsberg Maritime: *Annual report and sustainability report*: 22.
7 Kongsberg Maritime: *Annual report and sustainability report*: 9.
8 The description of the DP system based on Faÿ 1990; Morgan 1978; Kongsberg Simrad: Offshore and Ocean Survey products. February, 1998: «Mannen bak DP-eventyret» article in *Teknisk Ukeblad* 19/20 2013: 65–69 and Nils Albert Jenssen: «The modern DP vessel». Notes 07.08.14.
9 http://snl.no/Gamlebrofoss kraftverk.

NOTES TO CHAPTER 2

1 Bjørnstad 2009: 68.
2 Interview with Steinar Sælid 10.11.04; interview with Eldar Mathisen 13.10.04.
3 Bascom 1961.
4 Priest 2007: 86–87, 96–100.
5 Gurbachan Singh Virk: »Four decades of DP innovation at Transocean», Maritime Research Institute, Netherlands, http://www.marin.nl/web/Publications/Publication-items/Four-decades-of-DP-innovation-at-Transocean.htm (03.09.14).
6 Faÿ 1990: 7.
7 Faÿ 1990: 7–8; http://en.wikipedia.org/wiki/Walter_Munk (20.08.14).
8 Bjørnstad 2009: 64–65.
9 Bascom 1961.
10 http://www.nationalacademies.org/history/mohole/ (29.02.12); Shatto 2011.
11 Interview with Howard Shatto 04.10.13; Shatto 2011.
12 Interview with Howard Shatto 04.10.2013; Shatto 2011.

13 Interview with Howard Shatto 04.10.13; Bjørnstad 2009.

14 Shatto 2011.

15 Interview with Howard Shatto 04.10.13; Shatto 2011.

16 Morten Christian Swensson: «Praktisk prosess-regulering – PID-regulatoren» article in *Teknisk Ukeblad* 07.05.13.

17 Interview with Howard Shatto 04.10.13.

18 Kvaal 1992: 54–55; Sejersted 2002: 340.

19 Kvaal 1992; Sejersted 2002: 340.

20 Wiener 1948.

21 Kvaal 1992: 295; Breivik and Sand 2009: 101–125.

22 Kvaal 1992: 295.

23 Redmond and Smith 1986: 106–112.

24 Interview with Jens Glad Balchen 10.10.88.

25 Bergbreiter 2005: 7–10.

26 Bergbreiter 2005: 10–13.

27 Zachary 1999.

28 Brandt and Nordal 2010: 262–264.

29 Østby 1989: 81–88.

30 Østby 1989: 94.

31 Østby 1989: 144–149.

32 Østby 1989: 230–235.

33 Breivik and Sand 2009: 101–125.

34 Overbye 1989: 38; Dybing 1999: 70.

35 Nordal 2010: 111–112.

36 Breivik and Sand 2009: 101–125.

37 Overbye 1994: 152; Dybing 1999: 72. The computer built by Nordata – Norsk Data Elektronikk under the leadership of founders Lars Monrad-Krohn, Per Bjørge and Rolf Skår. These individuals had been involved in the development of FFIs SAM computer. Both the privately owned Nordata and the state owned KV wanted to drive the industrial production of computers.

38 Breivik and Sand 2009: 101–125.

39 Overbye 1994: 175; Nordal 2010: 113–115.

40 Bugos 2010: 133; Mindell 2008: 103.

41 Interview with Rudolf Kalman 20.01.14.

42 Minorsky 1922: 280–309.

43 Kalman 1960: 35–45.

44 Kalman and Bucy 1961: 95–108.

45 McGee and Schmidt 1985.

46 Skogen and Holme 2003: 4; Nordal 2010: 363.

47 Skogen and Holme 2003: 10; Nordal 2010.

48 Skogen and Holme 2003: 10; Nordal 2010.

49 Skogen and Holme 2003: 10.

50 Skogen and Holme 2003: 14–15.

51 Øyangen 2014: 204.

52 Skogen and Holme 2003: 10–17.

53 Rabben 2012; Godin 2006: 639–667.

54 Andersen 1994: 145–164.

55 Sejersted 2002: 335.

56 Wicken 1994.

57 Sejersted 2002: 341–342.

58 Høivold 2006: 154–161.

59 Myrvang 2014.

60 NOU 1989: 2 *Kongsberg Våpenfabrikk*: 15–16; Wicken 1988: 25–26.

61 NOU 1989: 2 *Kongsberg Våpenfabrikk*: 15–16.

62 Gulowsen 2000: 224–226.

63 Bjørnstad 2009: 66.

64 Steinar Sælid's private archive. Note written by Steinar Sælid, most probably in 1989.

65 www-odp.tamu.edu/public/life/index.html (25.11.13); http://www-odp.tamu.edu/glomar.html (01.10.14).

66 Morgan 1978: 4–6.

67 Interview with Howard Shatto 04.10.13.

68 http://en.wikipedia.org/wiki/Short_baseline_acoustic_positioning_system (20.08.14).

69 Dunham 1996.

70 Hammett 1974: 60–74.

71 Hammett 1974; Morgan 1978: 60–74.

72 Hammett 1974; Morgan 1978: 60–74; Leffler, Pattarozzi and Sterling 2003: 15–16.

73 The oil and energy department, http://www.regjeringen.no/nb/dep/oed/tema/olje_og_gass/norsk-oljehistorie-pa-5-minutter.html?id=440538 (01.10.14).

74 Sejersted 1999: 22–24; Furre 1993: 353–354; Tormodsgard 2014.

75 Brandt and Nordal 2010: 270–273.

NOTES TO CHAPTER 3

1 Faÿ 1990: 119.

2 Faÿ 1990: 119.

3 Faÿ 1990: 120.

4 Steinar Sælids archive: «Positioning of semi-submersible platforms», CMI, Bergen 30.06.73: 14.

5 Steinar Sælids archive: «Positioning of semi-submersible platforms», CMI, Bergen 30.06.73: 7.

6 Steinar Sælids archive: Minutes of meeting on the Continental shelf research: Dynamic Positioning: written by Gjert Lading 09.12.74.

7 Sælid 1976.

8 Asphjell and Børresen 2004: 60–63.

9 Balchen, Jenssen and Sælid 1976, 1981.

10 Jenssen 1974.

11 Sogner 1994: 64.

12 Sogner 1994: 65–70.

13 Sogner 1997: 78–81.

14 Sogner 1997: 81–92.

15 Interview with Rolf Klepaker and Karstein Westgård 21.09.12; Rolf Klepaker: Memo to technology meeting in Kongsberg: Hydroacoustic position reference system (HPR). 22.10.13.

16 NOU 2003: 5 *Pioneer Divers in the North Sea*.

17 NOU 2003: 5 *Pioneer Divers in the North Sea*.

18 Ilner 2009: 180.

19 Bjørnstad 2009: 50–60.

20 Interview with Bjørn Bendigtsen 29.05.14.

21 Interview with Bjørn Bendigtsen 29.05.14.

22 Interview with Bjørn Bendigtsen 29.05.14.

23 Interview with Bjørn Bendigtsen 29.05.14.

24 Steinar Sælids archive: Letter from KV to Jens G. Balchen 17.09.74, with appendix: «Dynamic Positioning Development Project» 13.09.74. Signed Bjørn Jahnsen.

25 Kongsberg national archives: Letter from Rolf Qvenild to the Fund for the Promotion of Research and Development Work in Industry, Kongsberg 10.11.75: 11.

26 Steinar Sælid: A description of the circumstances at the start of Kongsberg Våpenfabrikk's DP project.

27 Qvenilds archive: Minutes of meeting between NTH, CMI, Simrad og KV, written by Bjørn Jahnsen 30.09.74.

28 Qvenilds archive: Development project, Dynamic Positioning, minutes of the meeting between NTH, CMI, Simrad and KV 30.09.74.

29 Steinar Sælids archive: Notes written by Steinar Sælid in 1989; Appendix in letter to Jens G. Balchen from Bjørn Jahnsen, project manager at KV 17.09.74. Appendix title «Dynamic Position Development Project», dated 13.09.74.

30 Steinar Sælid's archives: Notes written by Steinar Sælid in 1989.

31 Rolf Qvenild's archive: Development project – Dynamic Positioning– minutes of meeting between NTH, CMI, Simrad and KV 30.09.74.

32 Ovenild's archive: Olav Berdal: «Competition Relationship Simrad – Norcontrol – KV» 19.06.75.

33 Trondheim municipal archive (Balchenarkivet): Ibb Høivolds draft to Norcontrol's history, undated, s. 87.

34 Rolf Qvenild's archive: Internal notes KV, signed by Odd Berdal 19.06.75.

35 Øyangen 2014: 201.

36 Sejersted 1999: 27.

37 Sejersted 1999: 26–28.

38 Bjørnstad 2009.

39 NOU 1989: 2 *Kongsberg Våpenfabrikk*: 104; «Petroleum division at Kongsberg Våpenfabrikk» Corporate magazine issue, 2 1975: 8–17.

40 Steinar Sælid's private archives: «Development project – Dynamic Positioning». Minutes from meeting 15.01.75 between SINTEF, SIMRAD, CMI and KV 17.01.75.

41 Steinar Sælid's archives: Minutes from meeting on Continental Shelf Research: Dynamic Positioning. Written by Gjert Lading 09.12.74.

42 Steinar Sælid's private archives: «Development Project – Dynamic Positioning». Memo from meeting 15.01.75 between SINTEF, SIMRAD, CMI and KV 17.01.75.

43 Steinar Sælid's private archives: Minutes from meeting of the Steering Committee NTNF's research, Dynamic Positioning, 07.03.75.

44 Rolf Qvenild's archive: Letter from KV to Seaway Offshore Services A/S, 11.09.75: 2. The letter was an offer for DP for *Seaway Heron*; Letter from Rolf Qvenild to Norcontrol 09.01.76: 2.

45 Interview with Thor Kjell Skoland 02.02.14.

46 NOU 1989: 2 *Kongsberg Våpenfabrikk*: 158.

47 NOU 1989: 2 *Kongsberg Våpenfabrikk*: 159.

48 Letter from chairman Bjarne Hurlen to shipowner Stolt-Nielsen 17.01.75; «Ubesvart tilbud om SPESIALBÅT!» article in newspaper *VG* 24.02.75.

49 Interview with Thor Kjell Skoland 08.02.14.

50 Interview with Thor Kjell Skoland 08.02.14.

51 Interview with Bjørn Barth Jacobsen 12.06.12.

52 Bjørnstad 2009: 101.

53 Interview with Thor Kjell Skoland 08.02.14.

54 Bjørnstad 2009: 84.

55 Qvenild's archive: Letter to Seaway Offshore Services with contract proposal for *Seaway Heron,* signed by Rolf Qvenild and Bjørn Barth Jacobsen 11.09.75.

56 Ilner 2009: 191–192.

NOTES TO CHAPTER 4

1 Bjørnstad 2009: 83; Simrad: Reference list Positioning & Control Systems. Issue 20: 1, estimated 1982.

2 Sverre Corneliussen's archive: Frode Galtung: «Dynamic positioning», status per 31.09.76, CMI-notat nr. 75148-7, 23.10.76.

3 Bjørnstad 2009: 84.

4 Technology meeting at Kongsberg 07.05.13: Cited from Ingolv Olsen: «HW benyttet i DP/AIM systemer».

5 Cited from Nils Albert Jenssen on specifications for KS500, without date; *KS 500 General Purpose Computers, Programmers instruction manual*, Kongsberg Defence 1975. http://vt100.net/kongsberg/ks500_prog_man.pdf (22.08.14).

6 Jenssen was with SINTEF until 1981 when he was hired by KV and moved to Kongsberg.

7 Interview with Nils Albert Jenssen 08.01.12 and Eldar Mathisen 13.10.04.

8 Bjørnstad 2009: 84.

9 Njølstad and Wicken 1997: 279–280.

10 Samuel Taylor Coleridge: «The Rime of the Ancient Mariner» in *Lyrical Ballads* 1798.

11 Rolf Qvenild's archive: Letter from Bjørn Jahnsen to Unn Kristin Daling 26.04.99; Bonde 1994: 47.

12 Report/brochure: *Kongsberg Dynamic Positioning System* 04.09.75.

13 Interview with Sverre Corneliussen 06.08.14.

14 Nils Albert Jenssen: «Input about computers», 06.01.14; Thor Hukkelås: On redundancy, ADP703 and the belief of the majority dictatorship. Undated citation [2013].

15 Cited from Nils Albert Jenssen about the specifications for KS500, undated.

16 Cited from Nils Albert Jenssen about the specifications for KS500, undated.

17 Nils Albert Jenssen: «Input about computers» 06.01.14.

18 Odd Inge Tangen: Memorandum from the years working in Albatross, e-mail 18.07.14.

19 The GPS system is a network consisting of at least 24 satellites orbiting the earth. The system is set up and operated by the US military. With GPS, it is possible for a receiver to determine its position with very high accuracy anywhere in the world under virtually all conditions. http://no.wikipedia.org/wiki/NAVSTAR_Global_Positioning_System (21.06.14).

20 Rolf Klepaker: Hydroacoustic Position Reference System (HPR), 22.10.13: 12–17.

21 Rolf Klepaker: Hydroacoustic Position Reference System (HPR), 22.10.13: 12–17.

22 Bjørnstad 2009: 107.

23 Bjørnstad 2009: 107.

24 SA. KV-A Letter from Bjørn Barth Jacobsen to KV's management (OS) 12.01.76.

25 SA. KV-A Letter from Bjørn Barth Jacobsen to KV's management (OS) 12.01.76.

26 SA. KV-A Letter from Bjørn Barth Jacobsen to KV's management (OS) 12.01.76.

27 SA. KV-A. Letter to KV's management: «The ODD Berg case», written by Bjørn Barth Jacobsen 18.01.76.

28 Interview with Steinar Sælid 03.12.12.

29 Balchen 1976.

30 Morgan 1978.

31 Balchen 1980.

32 Breivik and Sand 2009.

33 Interview with Morten Breivik 10.11.13.

34 Interview with Sverre Corneliussen 06.08.14.

35 Interview with Sverre Corneliussen 06.08.14.

36 Interview with Sverre Corneliussen 06.08.14.

37 Kongsberg oil division. Albatross 501 dynamic positioning. Sales brochure, undated; interview with Sverre Corneliussen 06.08.14.

38 *Albatross: Reference List: 1.* Undated.

39 *Albatross Reference List: 1.* Undated.

40 Interview with Bjørn Barth Jacobsen 28.08.12.

41 «These stories are true … and penned by Thor and Nils Willy», undated and anonymously written.

42 Nils Albert Jenssen, «Construction Vessels», cited 19.11.13; interview with Thor Kjell Skoland 09.02.14; *Kongsberg oil division: Albatross 502 dynamic positioning*, sales brochure, undated.

43 Interview with Bjørn Barth Jacobsen 28.08.12.

44 Øyangen 2014: 268.

45 Interview with Nils Willy Gulhaugen 29.10.12.

46 «These stories are true … and penned by Thor and Nils Willy», undated and anonymously written.

47 ADP Applications, Gulf – Cobla Split Barges, undated.

48 «These stories are true … and penned by Thor and Nils Willy», undated and anonymously written.

49 Interview with Bjørn Barth Jacobsen 28.08.12.

50 «Høyteknologi og suksess bak beskjedne fasader på skifabrikken» article in newspaper *Laagendalsposten* 06.11.91: 3.

NOTES TO CHAPTER 5

1 Culture Memories Ekofisk. Pipelines: http://www.kulturminne-ekofisk.no/mod-
ules/module_123/templates/ekofisk_publisher_template_category_2.asp?strPara
ms=8%233%231187l545%23&iCategoryId=651&iInfoId=0&iContentMenuRootI
d=1435&strMenuRootName=&iSelectedMenuItemId=1453&iMin=40&iMax=41
(31.01.14).

2 Ilner 2009: 195–196; «Dynamisk posisjoneringsanlegg fra KV» article in company
newsletter *Bedrifts-avisen* 2 1978: 9.

3 Per A. Loeken: «Engineered Backfilling on the 36» Ekofisk – Emden pipeline». OTC
3741. Offshore Technology Conference, Texas. 05.–08.05.80.

4 Simrad: Reference list Positioning & Control Systems. Issue 20: 6 and Kongsberg:
Dynamic positioning, estimated 1982.

5 Simrad: Reference list Positioning & Control Systems. Issue 20: 6 og Kongsberg:
Dynamic positioning, estimated 1982.

6 Simrad: Reference list Positioning & Control Systems. Issue 20: 9 og Kongsberg:
Dynamic positioning, estimated 1982.

7 In English one can either use the term Diving Support Vessels, Platform Supply
Vessels or Offshore Supply/Support Vessels. In this book, we mainly use the term
Supply Vessel.

8 SA. KV-A. Contract between PAM and KV on the delivery of DP systems for PAM
vessels was signed in September 1978.

9 SA. KV-A. Contract between PAM and KV in September 1978: You're A-Z of
Kongsberg ADP product brochure, undated.

10 Simrad: *Reference list Positioning & Control Systems.* Issue 20: 1. Undated.

11 http://www.regjeringen.no/nb/dep/jd/dok/nouer/2000/nou-2000-31/5/2/5.
html?id=362602 (06.10.14).

12 Det Norske Veritas: Dynamic Positioning. Brochure, undated.

13 Bjørnstad 2009: 119–123.

14 Interview with Bjørn Barth Jacobsen 28.08.12 and 12.06.12; Bjørnstad 2009: 115.

15 «These stories are true … and written by Thor [Skoland og Nils Willy Gulhau-
gen]»: 7. Undated.

16 Simrad Albatross: *Reference list Positioning & Control Systems.* Issue 20: 8 ; «Skipene
øremerket for Barentshavet», interview with Markus Lindholm, adm.dir. at Rauma-
Repola published in newspaper *VG* 26.10.81.

17 Interview with Rolf Qvenild 18.09.12.

18 «Skipene øremerket for Barentshavet», interview with Markus Lindholm, adm. dir.
at Rauma-Repola published in newspaper *VG* 26.10.81.

19 Nils Albert Jenssen: «The Drilling Market». Memo 01.10.13.

20 Simrad: Reference list Positioning & Control Systems. Issue 20: 9; Kongsberg:
Dynamic positioning. Undated, estimated 1982.

21 Simrad: *Reference list Positioning & Control Systems*. Issue 20: 8; «Skipene øremerket for Barentshavet», interview with Markus Lindholm, adm.dir. at Rauma-Repola published in national *VG* 26.10.81.

22 http://www.amngr.ru/index.php/en/about/history (13.11.14).

23 Kongsberg, Maritime Division: *Dynamic Positioning Systems* 1982.

24 Interview with Knut Lagim 12.11.13.

25 Interviews with Oddvar Rusten, Knut Lagim, Roar Inge Alfheim and Odd Inge Tangen 12.11.13.

26 Interview with Ole Gunnar Hvamb 12.11.13.

27 Kongsberg, Maritime Division: *Dynamic Positioning Systems*. 1982; interview with Kenneth Wikerøy 16.04.12.

28 Interview with Roar Inge Alfheim and Odd Inge Tangen 12.11.13.

29 Simrad: *Reference list Positioning & Control Systems*. Issue 20: 3.

30 Interview with Oddvar Rusten 12.11.13.

31 Interview with Galina Guran 12.11.13.

32 Interview with Bjørn Engen 12.11.13.

33 Kongsberg Maritime Division, *Dynamic Positioning Systems ADP 100,* 1983; interview with Bjørn Engen 12.11.13.

34 Simrad: Reference list Positioning & Control Systems. Issue 20: 16 and 36; David J. Bray: (Lowestoft College): «Effective Training of DP Operators», Dynamic Positioning Conference 12.–13.10.99.

35 SA. KV-A. Internal report for the KV board: Uncontrolled manoeuver of *Seaway Swan* 27.09.78 which resulted in collision with *Thistle Alpha* platform 09.10.78.

36 Interview with Eldar Mathisen 13.10.04 and Thor Kjell Skoland 09.02.14.

37 Interview with Eldar Mathisen 13.10.04 and Thor Kjell Skoland 09.02.14.

38 Interview with Eldar Mathisen 13.10.04.

39 SA. KV-A. Report to KV's board 14.03.78.

40 Conversation with Thor Hukkelås 07.05.13.

41 Bjørnstad 2009; «Tjene penge og have det skægt» article in *Berlinske Tidende* 26.11.86: 13; interview with Bjørn Barth Jacobsen 28.08.12.

42 Interview with Eldar Mathisen 13.09.04.

43 Odd Inge Tangen: Memo with experiences from my years as a service engineer in Albatross 18.07.14.

44 Interview with Roar Inge Alfheim 12.11.13.

45 Conversation with Nils Albert Jenssen 04.08.14.

46 Interview with Roar Inge Alfheim and Odd Inge Tangen 12.11.13.

47 Kongsberg, Maritime Division: *Dynamic Positioning Systems* 1982.

48 Interview with Ole Gunnar Hvamb 12.11.13.

NOTES TO CHAPTER 6

1 Simrad: *Reference list Positioning & Control Systems*. Issue 20: 6.

2 «The Kongsberg Group: Experts on Dynamic positioning. The group has delivered 42 of the 80 modern DP systems in use today» in *Scandinavian Oil-Gas Magazine* no. 7/8 1981: 70–71.

3   SA. KV-KOR. From Albatross board meeting, 1986, Prospect. Undated memo regarding sale of shares and capital expansion.

4   *Who's who and where in Albatross.* Assumed (1983).

5   Interview with Bjørn Barth Jacobsen 27.08.12, Nils Willy Gulhaugen 18.09.12, Rolf Qvenild 18.09.12 and Svein Thorsen 13.02.14.

6   Interview with Bjørn Barth Jacobsen 12.06.12.

7   McGregor 1968.

8   Interview with Bjørn Barth Jacobsen 27.08.12, Nils Willy Gulhaugen 18.09.12, Rolf Qvenild 18.09.12 and Svein Thorsen 13.02.14.

9   «His Masters Voice» article in *Albatross Highlights.* Undated

10 Kongsberg Albatross A/S: Project survey of people's development, ca. 1987. Figure 1.3.1

11 Interview with Nils Willy Gulhaugen 22.09.12 and Svein Thorsen 13.02.14.

12 Interview with Nils Willy Gulhaugen 22.09.12 and Torfinn Kildal 05.04.13.

13 Interview with Nils Willy Gulhaugen 22.09.12.

14 Bjørnstad 2009: 116.

15 Nils Albert Jenssen in Bjørnstad 2009: 117.

16 Albatross: «Leadership development» 82–83.

17 Albatross: «Leadership development» 82–83: unpaged.

18 Albatross: «Leadership development» 82–83: 14.

19 Albatross: «Leadership development» 82–83: 3.

20 Albatross: «Leadership development» 82–83: 8.

21 Albatross: «Leadership development» 82–83: 8.

22 Albatross: «Leadership development» 82–83: 9.

23 Albatross: «Leadership development» 82–83: 10.

24 Albatross: «Leadership development» 82–83: 11.

25 Albatross: «Leadership development» 82–83: 11.

26 Albatross: «Leadership development» 82–83: 12.

27 Interview with Rolf Qvenild 18.09.12.

28 Interview with Rolf Qvenild 18.09.12.

29 Interview with Rolf Qvenild 18.09.12 and Svein Thorsen 13.02.14.

30 NOU 1989: 2 *Kongsberg Våpenfabrikk*: 10.

31 Interviews with Rolf Qvenild 18.09.12, Nils Willy Gulhaugen 18.09.12 and Svein Thorsen 13.02.14.

32 Interview with Svein Thorsen 13.02.14.

33 SA.KV-A. «Albatross group alternatives/strategy for avoiding economic crisis». Memo. Nils Willy Gulhaugen til MS 17.03.83.

34 Simrad: Reference list Positioning & Control Systems. Issue 20.

35 SA.KV-A. «Albatross group alternatives/strategy for avoiding economic crisis». Memo. Nils Willy Gulhaugen til MS 17.03.83: 1.

36 BP: *BP Statistical Review of World Energy*, June 2013. Spot Crude Prices: 15 and Charts Bin (http://chartsbin.com/view/oau) (13.11.14).

37 Interview with Bjørn Barth Jacobsen 27.08.12 and Svein Thorsen 13.02.14.

38 SA.KV-A. «Albatross group alternatives/strategy for avoiding economic crisis». Memo. Nils Willy Gulhaugen for MS 17.03.83: 2.

39 SA. KV-KOR. Albatross board meetings 1983. Board minutes 29.09.83. Case 2: Strategic process, what, where and market strategy, undated case documentation for case 2 of board meeting 29.09.83.

40 SA. KV-KOR. Albatross board meeting. 1983. Board minutes 29.09.83. Case 2: Strategic process, what, where and market strategy, undated case documentation for case 2 of board meeting 29.09.83.

41 SA. KV-KOR. Albatross board meeting. 1983. Board minutes 29.09.83. Case 2: Strategic process, what, where and market strategy, undated case documentation for case 2 of board meeting 29.09.83.

42 Interview with Bjørn Trosthoel 12.11.13.

43 Albatross: *Who's who and where in Albatross.* 1983 and Kongsberg in position in Aberdeen. Undated brochure, 1983

44 Kongsberg Albatross A.S.: *Annual Report 1985*: 33.

45 Simrad: Reference list Positioning & Control Systems. Issue 20: 14 and Nils Albert Jenssen: «Drilling market». Memo. 01.10.13: 5.

46 SA. KV-KOR. Albatross board meetings. 1983. Board minutes 29.09.83. Case 2: Strategic process, what, where.

47 SA. KV-KOR. Albatross board meeting. 1983. Market strategy, undated case documents for case 2 for board meeting 29.09.83: 6.

48 Interview with Tor Erik Sørensen 06.06.12 and Finn Søberg 16.04.12 and 12.11.13.

49 Interview with Tor Erik Sørensen 06.06.12.

50 COCOM is the acronym for *Coordinating Committee for Multilateral Export Controls*, an organisation including NATO countries and other western supportive countries to hinder sales of sensitive technology to the East Bloc. Wicken 1988.

51 Interview with Rolf Qvenild and Thor Skoland 04.12.12.

52 Interview with Roy Larsen 14.02.14.

53 SA. KV-A. Marketing of KV's offshore products in East Europe. Letter from N.W. Gulhaugen to R.E. Rolfsen, 8.1.1985 og KV-KOR. Albatross board meetings. 1983. Board minutes 29.09.83. Case 2: Strategy process, what, why and market strategy, undated case documentation for board meeting 29.09.83: 7–8.

54 Interview with Einar Gleditsch jr. 06.08.14; Einar Gleditsch jr.: «Hostage on the Barents Sea», notes to the interview 06.08.14.

55 Interviews with Tor Erik Sørensen and Roy Larsen 06.06.12 and Bjørn Trosthoel 12.11.13.

56 Interviews with Tor Erik Sørensen 06.06.12, Bjørn Trosthoel 12.11.13 and Morten Stanger 06.08.14.

57 Kongsberg Albatross A.S.: *Annual Report 1985*: 10.

58 Kvaal, Moan, Moe and Wilhelmsen (ed.) 2003.

59 Review of APM at Kongsberg, Albatross Division: *Albatross Position Mooring System – APM*. Product brochure, 1983, Nils Albert Jenssen: «The Drilling Market». Memo. 01.10.13 and Nils Albert Jenssen: «Position Mooring system». Undated [2013].

60 Nils Albert Jenssen: «The Drilling Market». Memo. 01.10.03.

61 Jenssen 1981.

62 Nils Albert Jenssen: «The Drilling Market». Memo. 01.10.13.

63 Nils Albert Jenssen: «The Drilling Market». Memo. 01.10.13.

64 NOU 1989: 2. *Kongsberg Våpenfabrikk*: 153–159.

65 Kongsberg, Albatross Division: *Albatross Position Mooring System – APM*. Product brochure 1983 and Nils Albert Jenssen: «The Drilling Market». Memo. 01.10.13.

66 Simrad: Reference list Positioning & Control Systems. Issue 20:15.

67 «Drilling platform», Diary of Ross Isle's grounding, repair and delivery to Rosshavet. Excerpts from a workman's diary» in *Kaldnes Blink* no. 1, 1983: 20–22 and interview with Nils Albert Jenssen 07.10.14.

68 Interview with Øystein Andreassen 06.08.14.

69 Simrad: Reference list Positioning & Control Systems. Issue 20: 20–34.

70 Simrad: Reference list Positioning & Control Systems. Issue 20: 29 and 31.

71 Interview with Rolf Qvenild 18.09.12.

72 Interview with Sverre Corneliussen 06.08.14.

NOTES TO CHAPTER 7

1 SA. KV-KOR. Albatross board meetings, 1983. Albatross's board report (5) 1983. Memo from Nils Willy Gulhaugen. Board meeting papers, item 1, board meeting 29.09.83. Minutes of board meeting 29.09.83.

2 Interview with Steinar Sælid 03.12.12.

3 Vidar Solli: «The Development of a Single Board Computer». Undated notes [2013]. See also: Vidar Greiff Solli: *Mikroprosessorstyrt grafisk farvemonitor.* Thesis, NTH, 1980.

4 Ingolv Olsen: «HW used in DP/AIM systems». Undated notes [2013].

5 Ingolv Olsen: «HW used in DP/AIM systems». Undated notes [2013].

6 Ingolv Olsen: «HW used in DP/AIM systems». Undated notes [2013].

7 Vidar Solli: «The development of Albatross Single Board Computer». Undated notes [2013].

8 Vidar Solli: «The development of Albatross Single Board Computer». Undated notes [2013] and Ingolv Olsen: «HW used in DP/AIM systems». Undated notes [2013].

9 Vidar Solli: «The Development of a Single Board Computer». Undated notes [2013].

10 Vidar Solli: «The development of Albatross Single Board Computer». Undated notes [2013].

11 Amund Tinderholt: «The first years». Undated notes [2013]. Ingolv Olsen: «HW used in DP/AIM systems». Undated notes [2013].

12 Ingolv Olsen: «HW used in DP/AIM systems». Undated notes [2013]; Vidar Solli: «The Development of Albatross Single Board Computer». Undated notes [2013].

13 Vidar Solli: «The development of Albatross Single Board Computer». Undated notes [2013].

14 Kongsberg. Albatross Division: Dynamic Positioning System ADP 100: 2.

15 Kongsberg. Albatross Division: Dynamic Positioning System ADP 100: 3 and 5.

16 Kongsberg. Albatross Division: Dynamic Positioning System ADP 100: 4.

17 Vidar Solli: «The Development of Albatross Single Board Computer». Undated notes [2013].

18 Amund Tinderholt: «The first years». Undated notes [2013] and Vidar Solli: «The development of Albatross Single Board Computer». Undated notes [2013].

19 Ingolv Olsen: «HW used in DP/AIM systems». Undated notes [2013].

20 Vidar Solli: «The Development of Albatross Single Board Computer». Undated notes [2013].

21 Simrad: Reference list Positioning & Control Systems. Issue 20: 23.

22 SA. KV-KOR. Albatross board meetings. 1983. Albatross's board report (5) 1983. Notes from Nils Willy Gulhaugen. Notes for item 1, board meeting 29.09.83. Minutes and notes from Albatross board meetings, 29.09.83 and Simrad: Reference list Positioning & Control Systems. Issue 20.

23 Morten Breivik (Kongsberg): «Dynamic positioning and beyond ...». PPT-presentation 2.03.12; Simrad: Reference list Positioning & Control Systems. Issue 20.

24 Nils Albert Jenssen: «The Drilling Market». Memo 01.10.13: 3; Simrad: Reference list Positioning & Control Systems. Issue 20.

25 NOU 1972: 15. *Landing of petroleum*; NOU 1974: 40. *Pipelines in deep water*; Kristin Øye Gjerde and Gunleiv Hadland: «Bøyelasting eller oljerør?» article in http://nom.nb.no/OEkonomi-og-samfunn/Boeyelasting-eller-oljeroer (28.01.14).

26 Lindøe 2009: 9–17; S.tid.: 16.06.76.

27 Lindøe 2009: 37–41; Kristin Øye Gjerde and Gunleiv Hadland: «Bøyelasting eller oljerør?» article in http://nom.nb.no/OEkonomi-og-samfunn/Boeyelasting-eller-oljeroer (28.01.14); Nils Albert Jenssen: «Shuttle tankers». Memo 03.10.13.

28 Lindøe 2009: 115; Trude Meland: «Brann på Polytraveller» article in http://nom.nb.no/Feltet/Statfjord-A/Brann-paa-Polytraveller (28.01.14).

29 Nils Albert Jenssen: «Shuttle tankers». Memo 03.10.13.

30 See for example, Sørheim 1982.

31 Nils Albert Jenssen: «Shuttle tankers». Memo 03.10.13.

32 Simrad: Reference list Positioning & Control Systems. Issue, Simrad: Reference list Positioning & Control Systems. Issue 20: 10, Kongsberg: *Dynamic positioning*. Year unknown, estimated 1982]; Lindøe 2009: 97.

33 Simrad: Reference list Positioning & Control Systems. Issue 20: 25–26. See also: Statfjord Cultural History: Shuttle tanker operations at Statfjord (Film). http://www.nb.no/kulturminne-statfjord/nb/49819dd2a704c4fbb8d1a561ad9d06f9?index=22 (30.01.14).

34 Nils Albert Jenssen: «Shuttle tankers». Memo 03.10.13.

35 Simrad: Reference list Positioning & Control Systems. Issue 20; Nils Albert Jenssen: «Shuttle tankers». Memo 03.10.13.

36 Nils Albert Jenssen: «Shuttle tankers». Memo 03.10.13.

37 Nils Albert Jenssen: «Shuttle tankers». Memo 03.10.13.

38 Lindøe 2009: 97.

39 Simrad: Reference list Positioning & Control Systems. Issue 20: 34, Simrad: Albatross. Positioning and Control Systems. 1990: 76–77, Nils Albert Jenssen: «Construction vessels». Memo 19.11.13; http://www.allseas.com/uk/58/equipment/lorelay.html (31.01.14).

40 Nils Albert Jenssen: «Construction vessels». Memo 19.11.13.

41 Bjørnstad 2009: 306. Nominal kroner.

42 Øyangen 2014: 291–292.

43 NOU 1989: 2. *Kongsberg Våpenfabrikk*: 179.

44 «The Kongsberg Group: Experts on Dynamic positioning. The group has delivered 42 of the 80 modern DP systems in use today». *Scandinavian Oil-Gas Magazine*, no. 7/8 1981: 70–71; Øyangen 2014: 262.

45 NOU 1989: 2. *Kongsberg Våpenfabrikk*: 101–107, 137, 151 and 158.

46 Øyangen 2014: 262.

47 Bjørnstad 2009: 163.

48 SA. KV-KOR. Albatross board meetings. 1983. Item no. 2. Personnel welfare. Undated most likely notes for board meeting 22.12.1983. Item 3: Strategic issues.

49 SA. KV-KOR. Albatross board meetings. 1983. Item no. 2. Personnel welfare. Undated most likely notes for board meeting 22.12.1983. Item 3: Strategic issues.

50 SA. KV-KOR. Albatross board meeting. 1984. Undated and unsigned with no title: 5. The minutes of board meeting, 23.03.84, state that this is background information for item no. 5: Albatross – quo vadis?

51 SA. KV-KOR. Albatross board meetings. 1984. Undated and unsigned with no title: 7. The minutes of board meeting, 23.03.84, state that this is background information for item no. 5: Albatross – quo vadis?

52 SA. KV-KOR. Albatross board meetings. 1984. Undated and unsigned with no title: 7. The minutes of board meeting, 23.03.84, state that this is background information for item no. 5: Albatross – quo vadis?

53 SA. KV-KOR. Albatross board meetings. 1983. Report from Albatross board meeting 22.12.1983 – kl. 0900. Item 3: Strategic issues.

54 SA. KV-KOR. Albatross board meetings. 1983. Item no. 2. Personnel welfare. Undated, most likely notes for board meeting 22.12.83. Item 3: Strategic issues.

55 Albatross: *Who's who and where in Albatross,* 1983.

56 *Albatross Highlights*, September 1986: 1, 6–7 og «Kutter ut bedriftsbarnehagene» article in newspaper *Laagendalsposten* 19.01.05.

57 «Barnehaver til bedriftens beste» article in *Aftenposten* morning newspaper 06.10.89.

58 «Barnehaver til bedriftens beste» article in *Aftenposten* morning newspaper 06.10.89.

59 Vidar Solli: «The development of a Single Board Computer». Undated notes [2013].

60 Interview with Tor Erik Sørensen 06.06.12.

61 Interview with Rolf Qvenild 18.09.12.

62 SA. KV-KOR. Albatross board meetings. 1983. Item no. 2. Salary proposals for employees in Albatross, 14.12.83. Attachment no.1 regarding personnel welfare. Undated, most likely notes for board meeting 22.12.1983. Item 3: Strategic issues.

63 Interview with Nils Willy Gulhaugen 18.09.12 and Kenneth Wikerøy 13.02.14.

64 State archives, Kongsberg: Kongsberg Våpenfabrikk. Board. VII Board minutes 7. 1981–1985. Board meeting 13. Desember 1983. Item no. 4: Strategic lan 1984–86, part 2. Operational plans and budget for 1984: 672–674.

65 SA. KV-KOR. Albatross board meetings. 1984. Albatross – quo vadis? VADM: RER, 09.02.84.

66 SA.KV-A. Albatross – problem or possibility. Notes from F. Lund til AD, VADM, ØD, 22.03.84: 1.

67 SA.KV-A. Albatross – problem or possibility. Notes from Jan F. Lund til AD, VADM, ØD, 22.03.84: 3.

68   SA.KV-A. Albatross –problem or possibility. Notes from Jan F. Lund til AD, VADM, ØD, 22.3.84: 2.

69   SA. KV-KOR. Albatross board meetings. 1984. Minutes from Albatross board meeting 16.05.84. Item 5: Albatross personnel policy

70   SA. KV-KOR. Albatross board meetings. 1984. Albatross – quo vadis? VADM: RER, 09.02.84.

71   SA. KV-KOR. Albatross board meetings. 1984. Undated and unsigned with no title: 8 - 11. The minutes of board meeting, 23.03.84, state that this is background information for item no. 5: Albatross – quo vadis?

72   SA. KV-KOR. Albatross board meetings 1984. Report from Albatross board meeting 21.03.84. Item 5: Albatross – quo vadis?

73   SA. KV-KOR. Albatross board meetings. 1984. Report from Albatross board meeting 16.05.84. Item no. 4: Cooperation with Albatross – navigation.

74   SA. KV-KOR. Albatross board meetings. 1984. Cooperation with Albatross – navigation. Torfinn Kildal 09.05.84.

75   SA. KV-KOR. Albatross board meetings. 1984. Cooperation with Albatross – navigation. Torfinn Kildal 09.05.84.

76   SA. KV-KOR. Albatross board meetings. 1984. Report of Albatross board meeting. 16.05.84. Item no. 4: Cooperation with Albatross – navigation. Cooperation with Albatross – navigation. Torfinn Kildal 09.05.84.

77   Strategic planning, September 1983.

78   SA. KV-KOR. Albatross styremøter. 1984. Item no. 6 for board meeting 12.09.84: Establishing Albatross Ltd.; Øyangen 2014: 87–288.

79   State archives, Kongsberg: Kongsberg Våpenfabrikk. Board. VII Board minutes. 7. 1981–1985. Board meeting 12. September 1984. Item no. 6: Establishing Albatross as Ltd.719.

80   SA. KV-KOR. Albatross board meetings. 1985. Report from board meeting no. 1 Albatross A.S. 01.02.85. Item 2: KA's markets and tasks.

81   SA. KV-KOR. Albatross board meetings. 1985. Report from board meeting no. 1 Albatross A.S. 01.02.85. Item 2: KA's markets and tasks.

82   SA. KV-KOR. Albatross board meetings. 1984. Letter from corporate management, Rolf Qvenild to Albatross's management via Nils-Willy Gulhaugen 05.10.84

83   SA. KV-KOR. Albatross board meetings. 1984. Item no. 6 for board meeting 12.09.84: Establishing Albatross Ltd. Attachment 2: Albatross – performance overview. The result is after deducting interest on the capital KV had tied up in Albatross, Kongsberg Albatross A.S.: *Annual Report 1985*: 27; Bjørnstad 2009: 306

84   SA. KV-KOR. Albatross board meetings. 1985. Minutes of board meeting no. 3 Albatross A.S. 29.03.85. Item 4: Personnel matters.

85   SA. KV-KOR. Albatross board meetings. 1985. Minutes of board meeting no. 5 Albatross A.S. 27.06.85. Item 2: CEO's report and Kongsberg Albatross A.S.: *Annual Report 1985*: 2.

86   SA. KV-KOR. Albatross board meetings. 1985. Minutes of board meeting no. 5 Albatross A.S. 27.06.85. Item 5: Establishing NC/Automation and NC/Simulation, Norcontrol Automation. Undated notes and Kongsberg Albatross A.S.: *Annual Report 1985*: 31; Minutes from Albatross board meetings.

87 SA. KV-KOR. Albatross board meetings. 1985. Minutes of board meeting no. 5 Albatross A.S. 27.06.85. Item 2: Managing director's report and minutes from Albatross board meetings.

88 «KV, SysScan og Albatross med nytt vekstsenter: KONVEKST vil skape ny vekst i Kongsberg» article in *Laagendalsposten* 04.07.85; Øyangen 2014: 341.

89 SA. KV-KOR. Albatross board meetings. 1985. Minutes from board meetings no. 6 Albatross A.S. 02.09.85. Sak 5: Continuation of Albatross's base technology and notes for item 5: Continuing Albatross's base technology.

90 SA. KV-KOR. Albatross board meetings. 1985. Minutes from board meetings no. 6 Albatross A.S. 02.09.85. Item 5: Continuation of Albatross's base technology and notes for item 5: Continuing Albatross's base technology and SA. KV-KOR. Albatross board meetings. 1985. F10: OB: Technology cooperation KA-Group 28.05.85.

91 SA.KV-A. Albatross alternatives for avoiding economic crisis in 1985. Memo from Nils Willy Gulhaugen to MS 17.03.83.

92 SA. KV-KOR. Albatross board meetings. 1985. Minutes from board meetings no. 5, Albatross A.S. 27.06.85. Item 3: Economic status.

93 Kongsberg Albatross A.S.: *Annual Report 1985*: 3, 5–6 og 27. Profit before appropriations.

94 SA. KV-KOR. Albatross board meetings. 1985. Minutes from board meetings no. 6, Albatross A.S. 02.09.85. Item 2: CEO's report.

95 Interview with Nils Willy Gulhaugen 22.09.12.

96 SA. KV-KOR. Albatross board meetings. 1985. Rolf Qvenild: 10-year anniversary, Albatross 22.11.85.

NOTES TO CHAPTER 8

1 Statsarkivet (State Archives), Kongsberg: Kongsberg Våpenfabrikk. Board meeting. VII board minutes 7. 1981–1985. Board meeting 26.11.85. Case no. 6: Change of ownership in Kongsberg Albatross – Sale of shares to employees

2 NOU 1989: 2. *Kongsberg Våpenfabrikk*: 201.

3 NOU 1989: 2. *Kongsberg Våpenfabrikk*: 101–107, 137, 151 og 158.

4 SA. KV-KOR. Albatross board minutes. 1985. Change of ownership in Kongsberg Albatross – Sale of shares to employees. Case 6 board meeting 26.11.85. Notes to board members by R. Qvenild, 19. November 1985.

5 SA. KV-KOR. Albatross board meeting. 1986. Prospect. Undated notes in connection with the sale of shares and capital expansion.

6 SA. KV-KOR. Albatross board meetings. 1986. Minutes of board meeting no. 4/86 at Kongsberg Albatross 03.07.86. Case 3: Prospect Kongsberg Albatross A/S.

7 BP: Statistical Review of World Energy – Spot crude prices. (http://www.bp.com/liveassets/bp_internet/globalbp/globalbp_uk_english/reports_and_publications/statistical_energy_review_2008/STAGING/local_assets/downloads/pdf/oil_table_of_spot_crude_oil_prices_2008.pdf) (13.11.14).

8 Simrad: Reference list Positioning & Control Systems. Issue 20.

9 Both companies were established 1 January 1986. Kongsberg Albatross A.S.: *Annual*

Report 1986: 15 and SA. KV-KOR. Albatross board meetings. 1986. Prospect. Updated notes in connection to the sale of shares and capital expansion.

10 Kongsberg Albatross A.S.: *Annual Report 1986*: 21 and 24.

11 SA. KV-KOR. Albatross board meetings 1986. Minutes from the board meeting no. 4/86 in Kongsberg Albatross 03.07.86. Case 2: ADs orientation, financial status, expectations.

12 NOU 1989: 2. *Kongsberg Weapons*: 166.

13 Kongsberg Albatross A.S.: *Annual Report 1986*: 21 and 24.

14 Kongsberg Albatross A.S.: *Annual Report 1986*: 9.

15 SA. KV-KOR. Albatross board meetings. 1986. Prospect. Updated notes in connection with the sale of shares and capital expansion.

16 NTB: «Særegent industritun i Kongsberg» (Unique industry area in Kongsberg) 30.09.86.

17 Kongsberg Albatross A.S.: *Annual Report 1985*: 27 and 31.

18 SA. KV-KOR. Albatross board meetings. 1986. Prospect. Undated notes in connection with the sale of shares and capital increase.

19 SA. KV-KOR. Albatross board meetings. 1986. Minutes from board meeting no. 4 1986 in Kongsberg Albatross 03.07.86. Case 3: Prospect Kongsberg Albatross A/S.

20 SA. KV-KOR. Albatross board meetings. 1986. Simrad Subsea. Notes for board meeting no. 4 1986. Case 6: Cooperation SSS/KA.

21 SA. KV-KOR. Albatross board meetings. 1986. Minutes from board meeting no. 5/86 at Kongsberg Albatross A.S. 11.09.86. Case 4: Cooperation with Simrad Subsea A/S.

22 Kongsberg Albatross A.S.: *Annual Report 1986*: 19 and *Target '90*. Internal newsletter for Kongsberg Albatross A.S. no. 1 1987.

23 *Target '90*. Internal newsletter for Kongsberg Albatross no. 2 1987.

24 Interview with Steinar Sælid 03.12.12.

25 Interview with management in Albatross. «– Vi var for slappe!» article in the *Økonomisk Rapport* no. 14 1987: 57.

26 SA. KV-KOR. Albatross board meetings. 1986. Minutes from board meeting no. 6/86 at Kongsberg Albatross 23.10.86. Case 2: Budget 1987.

27 «Snuoperasjon Albatross: Magrere, men flygedyktig!» article in the Økonomisk Rapport no. 14 1987: 58.

28 Interview with Torfinn Kildal 05.04.13 and Svein Thorsen 13.02.14.

29 Interview with Torfinn Kildal 05.04.13 and Steinar Sælid 03.12.12.

30 NOU 1989: 2. *Kongsberg Våpenfabrikk*: 201; Øyangen 2014: 346.

31 Kongsberg Albatross A.S.: *Annual Report 1986*: 21.

32 Kongsberg Albatross A.S.: *Annual Report 1986*: 5.

33 Simrad: Reference list Positioning & Control Systems. Issue 20; Bjørnstad 2009: 306.

34 SA. KV-A. Albatross /NCS status report. 30.01.87. Market philosophy. Undated notes. Stamped 29 September 1983.

35 *NOU* 1989: 2. *Kongsberg Våpenfabrikk*: 43 and 103–104.

36 Interview with Steinar Sælid 03.12.12 and Svein Thorsen 13.02.14. See also Bjørnstad 2009: 175.

37 SA. KV-A. Agreement between Simrad Subsea («Simrad») and Kongsberg Weapons,

(KV) Kongsberg Albatross (Albatross) and Employees in Kongsberg Albatross, 29.04.87.

38 Simrad Subsea bought 30.04.87 Kongsberg Albatross. Attachement to: Kongsberg Albatross.: *Annual Report 1986*.

39 Sælid 1976.

40 Gotaas 1982.

41 Interview with Steinar Sælid 03.12.12; «Steinar Sælid: Sol(ar)kongen», interview in *Automatisering* (http://www.automatisering.org/default.asp?menu=6&id=6819) (12.12.12).

42 Løkling 1975.

43 Interview with Steinar Sælid 03.12.12; Sælid 1999: 88.

44 SA. KV-A. Nils Willy Gulhaugen: «Albatross-gruppen. Alternativer/strategi for å unngå økonomisk krise i 1985». Notes to MS 17.03.83.

45 SA. KV-A. Nils Willy Gulhaugen: «Albatross-gruppen. Alternativer/strategi for å unngå økonomisk krise i 1985». Notes to MS 17.03.83.

46 Terje Løkling quoted in Hatling 1990: 10.

47 Terje Løkling quoted in Hatling 1990: 10.

48 Steinar Sælids archives: «Kort beskrivelse av Albatross PCDA system». Undated notes. Estimated 1984/1985.

49 Interview with Steinar Sælid 03.12.12.

50 Kongsberg Albatross: *AIM 1000*. Updated brochure. Estimated 1986; Sælid 1999: 88; interview with Steinar Sælid 03.12.12.

51 Interview with Steinar Sælid 03.12.12; Sælid 1999: 89.

52 Steinar Sælids archives: «Kort beskrivelse av Albatross PCDA system». Undated notes. Estimated 1984/1985.

53 SCADA stands for Supervisory Control And Data Acquisition. KV's SCADA- technology was largely based on technology developed for monitoring nuclear plants, and was in collaboration between Siemens and the Department of Atomic Energy. KV contributed system expertise and was reponsibile for sales. Øyangen 2014: 324; SA. KV-KOR. Albatross board meetings. 1985. Minutes from board meeting. No. 3/85 at Kongsberg Albatross. Case 6: Cooperation Albatross – SCADA. O. Berdal: «STP 85 – discussion notes to form an offshore system group in core-KV. Notes 03.09.85.

54 Interview with Steinar Sælid 03.12.12 and SA. KV-KOR. Albatross board meetings. 1985. Minutes from board meeting. No. 3/85 at Kongsberg Albatross. Case 6: Cooperation Albatross – SCADA.

55 SA. KV-A. Nils Willy Gulhaugen: «Kongsberg Albatross. Noen tanker om bedriftens rolle i norsk næringsliv». Notes to Hurlen, 23.10.84.

56 Interview with Svein Thorsen in the group interview 04.12.12.

57 SA. KV-A. G.I. Buchanan: «Marketing evaluation and 'Post mortem': August/September 1985» 24.09.85.

58 SA. KV-KOR. Albatross board meetings. 1985. Minutes from board meeting no. 5/85 at Kongsberg Albatross A.S. case 2: Managing Director's Report.

59 Interview with Steinar Sælid 03.12.12; Sælid 1999: 90.

60 Steinar Sælid: Comments on technology collection in the DP book project, Kongsberg 07.05.13.

61 SA. KV-KOR. Albatross board meetings. 1985. Minutes from board meeting no. 6/85 at Kongsberg Albatross. Case 2: Managing Director's report; Interview with Steinar Sælid 03.12.12; Nils Albert Jenssen and Steinar Sælid: Contribution to DP book. DP algorithms and the first period. Undated notes [2013].

62 Simrad: Reference list Positioning & Control Systems. Issue 20: 36.

63 Simrad: *Albatross. Positioning and Control Systems* 1990: 96–97.

64 Kongsberg Albatross: *Annual Report 1985*: 3, 12 and 24, SA. KV-KOR. Albatross board meetings 1985. Minutes from board meeting. no 6/85 at Kongsberg Albatross. Case 2: Managing Director's report; interview with Steinar Sælid 03.12.12; Sælid 1999: 90.

65 Steinar Sælids archives: «Albatross On-shore strategi. Diskusjonsunderlag til møte 3/10.86» T.L. (Terje Løkling).

66 SA. KV-KOR. Albatross board meetings. 1986. Minutes from board meeting. no 4 1986 in Kongsberg Albatross. Case 2: Managing Director's orientation, financial status, expectations.

67 Kongsberg Albatross: *Annual Report 1986*: 11.

68 «Albatross går i land» in newspaper *Laagendalsposten* 19.02.87.

69 Sælid 1999: 90.

70 Sælid 1999: 90.

71 Sælid 1999: 90.

72 Kongsberg Albatross: *Annual Report 1986*: 18.

73 Kongsberg Albatross: *AIM1000*. Brochure, June, 1987: 10–11.

74 Interview with Steinar Sælid 03.12.12.

75 For a more thorough description see: Kongsberg Albatross: *AIM 1000*. Brochure, June 1987.

76 Kongsberg Albatross: *Annual Report 1985*: 3, 12 and 24, SA. KV-KOR. Albatross board meetings, 1985; Minutes from board meeting no. 6/85 at Kongsberg Albatross. Case 2: Managing Director's report; interview with Steinar Sælid 03.12.12; Sælid 1999: 90.

77 Kongsberg Albatross: *Annual Report 1985*: 3, 12 and 24; SA. KV-KOR. Albatross board meetings, 1985; Minutes from the board meeting no. 6/85 i Kongsberg Albatross. Case 2: Managing Director's report; interview with Steinar Sælid 03.12.12; Sælid 1999: 90.

78 Nils Albert Jenssen and Steinar Sælid: Contribution to DP book. DP algorithms and the first period. Undated notes [2013].

79 Kongsberg Albatross: *Annual Report 1986*: 17, SIMRAD. Brochure 1988 and Simrad: Reference list Positioning & Control Systems. Issue 20.

80 Nils Albert Jenssen and Steinar Sælid: Contribution to DP book. DP algorithms and the first period. Undated notes [2013].

81 Kongsberg Albatross: *AIM*. Brochure. Undated.

82 Simrad: Reference list Positioning & Control Systems. Issue 21: 10–11.

83 Odd Jan Lange, Information Manager, Statoil: NTB: Simrad Albatross outperforms multinational competitors. 02.10.89; Simrad: Reference list Positioning & Control Systems. Issue 21: 9–10.

84 NTB: Simrad Albatross outperforms multinational competitors. 02.10.89; Simrad: Reference list Positioning & Control Systems. Issue 21: 9–10.

85 NTB: «Heidrun contract to Simrad» 02.12.91.

86 «Heidrun – Norges råeste plattform» in *Computerworld* no. 1 1996.

87 «80 milliners kontrakt til Simrad» in newspaper *Dagens Næringsliv* 02.12.91.

88 Bjørnstad 2009: 241.

89 Bjørnstad 2009: 306.

90 Interview with Torfinn Kildal 05.04.13.

91 Kongsberg Albatross: *AIM 1000. Brochure1987; Kongsberg Albatross: AIM. Brochure.* Undated.

92 Simrad: *Albatross. Positioning and Control Systems,* 1990: 49–54; Simrad: *Simrad AVM. Vessel management.* Product Description 1994.

93 Ingolv Olsen: HW used in DP /AIM systems. Undated noted [2013]; Ingolv Olsen: Comments on technical collection in the DP project book, Kongsberg 07.05.13.

NOTES TO CHAPTER 9

1 Interview with Karstein Vestgård and Rolf Arne Klepaker 17.09.12.

2 The offshore division was reorganised into Simrad Naval, which focused on military sonars, and Simrad Subsea, concentrating on underwater navigation. The rest was grouped under Simrad Marine. Simrad Subsea acquired Simrad Marine in 1983.

3 Sogner 1997: 143–160.

4 Sogner 1997: 187–188.

5 Interview with Rolf Arne Klepaker 17.09.12.

6 See, for example, Poulsen 1987.

7 Interview with Karstein Vestgård 17.09.12.

8 Interview with Steinar Sælid 03.12.12 and Nils Albert Jenssen 04.12.12.

9 Interview with Steinar Sælid 03.12.12.

10 Interview with Nils Albert Jenssen 08.01.12, Kenneth Wikerøy 16.04.12 and Finn Søberg 16.04.12.

11 Interview with Torfinn Kildal 05.10.13 and with Karstein Vestgård 17.10.12.

12 Sælid 1999: 90–91.

13 Sogner 1997: 143–160.

14 Interview with Finn Søberg 16.04.12, Karstein Vestgård 17.10.12, Rolf Arne Klepaker 17.10.12, Steinar Sælid 03.12.12 and Nils Albert Jenssen 04.12.12.

15 See both logos in, for example, Simrad Albatross: *The Albatross KONMAP Mk II.* Brochure, April 1989.

16 Interview with the Albatross leaders. «Vi var for slappe» article in *Økonomisk Rapport* no. 14 1987: 57.

17 Simrad: *Reference list Positioning & Control Systems. Issue 20.*

18 Discussion with Nils Albert Jenssen 14.02.14.

19 Thor Hukkelås: «About Redundancy, ADP 703 and faith in the majority dictatorship». Undated notes [2013]; conversation with Nils Albert Jenssen 14.02.14.

20 Thor Hukkelås: «About Redundancy, ADP 703 and faith in the majority dictatorship». Undated notes [2013].

21 Thor Hukkelås: «About Redundancy, ADP 703 and faith in the majority dictatorship». Undated notes [2013]; conversation with Nils Albert Jenssen 14.02.14.

22 Kongsberg Albatross: ADP 703 Voting. Undated [1987].

23 Norwegian Design Council. Award for design excellence, industrial design. «Positioning and control system ADP 703». www.norskdesign.no

24 Thor Hukkelås: «About Redundancy, ADP 703 and faith in the majority dictatorship». Undated notes [2013]; Thor Hukkelås: Post on: Technology collection in the DP book project, Kongsberg 07.05.13.

25 Thor Hukkelås: «About Redundancy, ADP 703 and faith in the majority dictatorship». Undated notes [2013]; Thor Hukkelås: Post on: Technology collection in the DP book project, Kongsberg 07.05.13.

26 Simrad: *Reference list Positioning & Control Systems. Issue 20*: 39; Simrad Albatross: *Positioning and Control Systems* 1988: 74–75.

27 Simrad Albatross: *Positioning and Control Systems* 1988: 17.

28 Simrad Albatross: *Positioning and Control Systems* 1988: 23.

29 Conversation with Nils Albert Jenssen 14.02.14.

30 Kongsberg, Albatross Division: *Dynamic positioning Systems. ADP 503 MK II*. Undated.

31 Albatross: Pricelist. Offshore products. Positioning and Control Systems. Kongsberg 01.05.87: 13.

32 Albatross: Pricelist. Offshore products. Positioning and Control Systems. Kongsberg 01.05.87

33 Albatross: Pricelist. Offshore products. Positioning and Control Systems. Kongsberg 01.05.87.

34 Interview with Finn Søberg 16.04.12, Tor Erik Sørensen 06.06.12, Finn Søberg and Bjørn Trosthoel 12.11.13 and Svein Thorsen 13.02.14.

35 Interview with Thor Skoland 04.12.12 and Svein Thorsen 04.12.12 and 13.02.14.

36 Interview with Svein Thorsen 13.02.14.

37 Albatross: Pricelist. Offshore products. Positioning and Control Systems. Kongsberg 01.05.87.

38 Ingolv Olsen: «HW used in DP/AIM systems». Undated notes [2013]; conversation with Nils Albert Jenssen 14.02.14.

39 Simrad: Albatross. Positioning and Control Systems. 1990: 14–15, Simrad: *Reference list Positioning & Control Systems. Issue 20*: 47 and Ingolv Olsen: «HW used in DP/AIM systems». Undated note [2013]

40 Simrad: Albatross. Positioning and Control Systems. 1990: 14–15, Simrad: *Reference list Positioning & Control Systems. Issue 20*: 43.

41 Simrad: Albatross. Positioning and Control Systems. 1990: 16–17; conversation with Nils Albert Jenssen 02.07.14.

42 Conversation with Nils Albert Jenssen 14.02.14.

43 Ingolv Olsen: «HW used in DP/AIM systems». Undated notes [2013] and conversation with Nils Albert Jenssen 14.02.14.

44 Ingolv Olsen: «HW used in DP/AIM systems». Undated notes [2013].

45 Norwegian Design Council. Award for design excellence, Industrial design. www.norskdesign.no

46 Simrad: *Reference list Positioning & Control Systems. Issue 20*.

47 Terje Løkling: «Med fokus på kvalitet …» article in *Tross'ern*, no. 2, September 1992: 2.

48 Interview with Kenneth Wikerøy 16.04.12.

49 Bjørnstad 2009: 235 and 262.

50 BP: Statistical Review of World Energy – Spot crude prices. (http://www.bp.com/liveassets/bp_internet/globalbp/globalbp_uk_english/reports_and_publications/statistical_energy_review_2008/STAGING/local_assets/downloads/pdf/oil_table_of_spot_crude_oil_prices_2008.pdf). (13.11.14). Nominal dollars.

51 Bjørnstad 2009: 197 and 306.

52 Interview with Torfinn Kildal 05.04.13 and Terje Løkling 04.04.13; see also Sogner 1997: 186.

53 «Viktig Simradkontrakt» article in *Aftenposten*, morning edition 14.02.90.

54 Hans C. Helle: «Om livet på skyggesiden» article in *Tross'ern*. Corporate newspaper for Simrad Albatross no. 1, June 1992: 6–8.

55 Simrad: Reference list Positioning & Control Systems. Issue 20: 47–49. The nine ships were as follows (delivery times in brackets): *Oksøy* (March 1992), *Alta* (March 1993), *Karmøy* (September 1993), *Otra* (January 1994), *Måløy* (May 1994), *Rauma* (September 1994), *Hinnøy* (January 1995), *Orkla* (May 1995) and *Glomma* (September 1995).

56 Simrad: Simrad MICOSTM MCM – Control System. Product brochure. Undated.

57 «Viktig Simradkontrakt» article in *Aftenposten*, morning edition 14.02.90.

58 *Trosser'n* no. 3. December 1992: 2.

59 Bjørnstad 2009: 306. Nominal NOK.

60 Conversation with Roy Larsen 14.02.14.

61 Interview with Torfinn Kildal 05.04.13.

62 *Tross'ern* no. 1. June 1992.

NOTES TO CHAPTER 10

1 Sogner 1997: 205–206.

2 Simrad: *Annual Report 1992*: 6, Simrad: *Annual Report 1993*: 7; interview with Steinar Gregersen 04.04.13.

3 «Bird slaktes» article in newspaper *Dagens Næringsliv 06.02.93*.

4 Simrad: *Annual Report 1994*: 6.

5 Simrad: *Annual Report 1994*: 8 and Simrad Inside, no. 2 1994.

6 NFT: *Financial Statement 1988*: 1.

7 NFT: *Financial Statement 1990*: 8.

8 NFT: *Financial Statement 1991*: 8.

9 NFT: *Annual Report 1992*: 7, 36–38.

10 More about this in NFT's and Simrads financial statements and Sogner 1997: 205–206

11 Simrads financial statements

12 NFT: *Financial statement 1993*: 31.

13 MITS stands for Maritime Information Technology Standard.

14 The Royal Norwegian Council for Scientific and Industrial Research: *Financial statement 1992*: 12.

15 Sogner 1997: 208–209. NFT did not initially participate in the MITS project, but joined in 1992 with the purchase of Norcontrol, which had been in from the start.

16 Interview with Asgeir Sørensen 02.07.14.

17 Det Norske Veritas: Dynamic Positioning. DNV brochure.

18   «Breaking the Waves. Holger Røkeberg, a pioneer in the maritime industry» in *The Full Picture Magazine*, no. 1 2004: 26.

19   «Breaking the Waves. Holger Røkeberg, a pioneer in the maritime industry» in *The Full Picture Magazine*, no. 1 2004: 26.

20   DNV: *Rules for Classification of Ships*. Part 6, Chapter 7. Dynamic Positioning Systems. Ships. Newbuildings, Special Equipment and Systems Additional Class, January 2004: 21.

21   Björn von Ubisch: «Station Keeping Criteria for Dynamically Positioned Vessels». Dynamic Positioning Conference, Houston, 28.–30.09.04.

22   DNV: *Rules for classification of ships. Newbuildings. Special equipment and systems. Additional class. Part 6 chapter 7. Dynamic positioning systems*, January 2011: 37–38.

23   «Breaking the Waves. Holger Røkeberg, a pioneer in the maritime industry» in *The Full Picture Magazine*, no. 1 2004: 26 and Holger Røkeberg: «Presentation of DP Class 2 and Class 3.» Dynamic Positioning Conference, Houston 21.–22.10.97.

24   Interview with Knut Lagim 12.11.13.

25   International Maritime Organization: Guidelines for Vessels with Dynamic Positioning Systems.» Maritime Safety Committee (MSC) Circular 645, June 1994.

26   International Maritime Organization: «Guidelines for Vessels with Dynamic Positioning Systems». Maritime Safety Committee (MSC) Circular 645. June 1994: § 2.2. See also: IMO DP Classification (http://www.km.kongsberg.com/ks/web/nokbg0240.nsf/AllWeb/D9479D5DB35FCA01C1256A4C004A876E?OpenDocument) (10.06.13).

27   International Maritime Organization: «Guidelines for Vessels with Dynamic Positioning Systems». Maritime Safety Committee (MSC) Circular 645, June 1994: § 3.1.2.

28   International Maritime Organization: «Guidelines for Vessels with Dynamic Positioning Systems». Maritime Safety Committee (MSC) Circular 645, June 1994: § 3.2.4.

29   DNV: *Rules for classification of ships. Newbuildings. Special equipment and systems. Additional class. Part 6 chapter 7. Dynamic positioning systems*, January 2004: 5.

30   Holger Røkeberg: «Presentation of DP Class 2 and Class 3». Dynamic Positioning Conference, Houston, 21.–22.10.97: 3.

31   Holger Røkeberg: «Presentation of DP Class 2 and Class 3». Dynamic Positioning Conference, Houston, 21.–22.10.97: 7.

32   NORSOK refers to the competitive position of the NCS.

33   Nils Gundersen (2012, 21. November). Norsok. In *Store norske leksikon*. Gathered on 17. September 2014 from https://snl.no/Norsok.

34   Holger Røkeberg: «Presentation of DP Class 2 and Class 3». Dynamic Positioning Conference, Houston, 21.–22.10.97: 5–6.

35   Interview with Nils Albert Jenssen 19.01.12.

36   Interview with Nils Albert Jenssen 19.01.12.

37   Amund Tinderholt: «The First Years». Updated notes [2013].

38   Simrad: Reference list Positioning & Control Systems. Issue 21: 3–4 and Kongsberg Simrad: *Offshore and Ocean Survey products*, February, 1998: VC-8–VC15.

39   Simrad: Reference list Positioning & Control Systems. Issue 21: 3–4 and Kongsberg

Simrad: *Offshore and Ocean Survey products*, February, 1998: VC22–VC25.

40 Simrad: Reference list Positioning & Control Systems. Issue 21and Kongsberg Simrad: *Offshore and Ocean Survey products*, February, 1998.

41 «Finansnotiser» article in newspaper *Dagens Næringsliv* 03.08.94.

42 Kongsberg Simrad: *Offshore and Ocean Survey products*, February 1998: VC1, VC6–VC7.

43 Kongsberg Simrad: *Offshore and Ocean Survey products*, February 1998: G7.

44 Amund Tinderholt: Memo for technology gathering in DPBOK project, 07.05.13

45 Kongsberg Simrad: *Offshore and Ocean Survey products*, February 1998: G13; interview with Nils Albert Jenssen 30.09.14.

46 Kongsberg Simrad: *Offshore and Ocean Survey products*, February 1998: G9 and Ingolv Olsen: Memo for technology gathering in DPBOK-project, 07.05.13.

47 Amund Tinderholt: Memo for technology gathering in DPBOK project, 07.05.13

48 Simrad: Reference list Positioning & Control Systems. Issue 21: 14.

49 Kongsberg Gruppen: *Annual Report 1996:* 15.

50 Kongsberg Gruppen: *Annual Report 1998:* 36.

51 Simrad: *Annual Report 1994:* 6.

52 Simrad: *Annual Report 1994:* 23 and Simrad: *Annual Report 1995:* 23. See also Sogner 1997: 212–216.

53 Simrad: *Annual Report 1995:* 9; Kongsberg Gruppen: *Annual Report 1995*: 19.

54 «NFT kjøper større aksjepost i Simrad» article in newspaper *Aftenposten* 12.05.95.

55 Kongsberg Gruppen: *Annual Report 1995*: 6.

56 «Kongsberg tar over Simrad» article in newspaper *Aftenposten* 13.05.96.

57 Kongsberg Gruppen: *Annual Report 1996*: 14, 34.

58 Kongsberg Gruppen: *Annual Report 1997*: 5.

59 «Kongsberg tar over Simrad» article in newspaper *Aftenposten* 13.05.96; interview with Karstein Vestgård 17.09.12; *Pinget*. Company newsletter, Simrad Norge in Horten, no. 2, 1996; Sogner 1997: 205–206.

60 Interview with Nils Albert Jenssen and Rolf Arne Klepaker 26.06.13.

61 Kongsberg Gruppen: *Annual Report 1997*: 2–3, 15, 32.

62 Kongsberg Gruppen: *Annual Report 1997*: 4.

63 Kongsberg Gruppen: *Annual Report 1997*: 2–3.

64 «Simrad-sjefen gikk» article in *Dagens Næringsliv* 30.01.98.

65 Interview with Steinar Gregersen 14.04.13. Norcontrol: Board notes. Minutes from boardmeeting nr. 1 (extraordinary) at Kongsberg Simrad 26.01.98.

66 Kongsberg Gruppen: Press release: «Steinar Aabelvik to be new managing director in Kongsberg Simrad AS», 25.09.90.

NOTES TO CHAPTER 11

1 Bjørnstad 2009: 306. Nominal NOK.

2 Bjørnstad 2009: 306. Nominal NOK.

3 Kongsberg Gruppen: *Annual Report 1997*: 34.

4 Kongsberg Gruppen: *Annual Report 1996*: 44.

5 Kongsberg Gruppen: *Annual Report 1998*: 36–37.

6   Kongsberg Gruppen: *Annual Report 1998*: 37.
7   Kongsberg Simrad: SDP521. Data sheet.
8   Kongsberg Gruppen: *Annual Report 1999*: 42.
9   Simrad: Reference list Positioning & Control Systems. Issue 21.
10 Kongsberg Gruppen: *Annual Report 2000*: 50.
11 Interview with Kenneth Wikerøy 16.04.12 and 13.02.14.
12 Simrad: Reference list Positioning & Control Systems. Issue 21: 13. The platform was equipped with ADP702 and the command ship with ADP701.
13 Interview with Kenneth Wikerøy 13.02.14.
14 Interview with Kenneth Wikerøy 16.04.12 and 13.02.14.
15 Kongsberg Gruppen: *Annual Report 1999*: 43.
16 http://en.wikipedia.org/wiki/SeaLaunch (10.11.14).
17 Kongsberg Gruppen: *Annual Report 1999*: 42.
18 Kongsberg Simrad: *Offshore and Ocean Survey products*, February 1998: UI8. See also: Rolf Arne Klepaker. «Hydro Acoustic Position Reference system, (HPR)». Technical history, per 22. October 2013.
19 Simrad: *Albatross. Positioning and Control Systems* 1990: 30–37.
20 «Kunsten å ligge i ro», interview with Trygve Myrland and Ole Gunnar Hvamb in *Cicerone*, February 2002: 14.
21 Jan Erik Faugstadmo: «HiPAP Story». Kongsberg, 2013.
22 Jan Erik Faugstadmo: «HiPAP Story». Kongsberg 2013.
23 Rolf Arne Klepaker: «Hydro Acoustic Position Reference system (HPR)». Technical history, per 22. October 2013.
24 Lars Ove Strat and Jan Erik Faugstadmo: «Stabile og nøyaktige målinger med HiPAP» article in *Pinget*, no. 1 1997: 4–5; Kongsberg Simrad: *Offshore and Ocean Survey products*, February 1998: UI10–11; interview with Karstein Vestgård and Rolf Arne Klepaker 17.09.12.
25 Lars Ove Strat and Jan Erik Faugstadmo: «Stabile og nøyaktige målinger med HiPAP» article in *Pinget*, no. 1 1997: 4–5.
26 Simrad: Reference list Positioning & Control Systems. Issue 21: 19.
27 Kongsberg: *High Precision Acoustic Positioning – HiPAP* ®. Brochure, updated.
28 Kongsberg Gruppen: *Annual Report 1998*: 37; «Reliability of DP Operation in Deep Water». Project report 1998.
29 «Reliability of DP Operation in Deep Water». Project report, 1998: 2.
30 «Reliability of DP Operation in Deep Water». Project report, 1998.
31 «Reliability of DP Operation in Deep Water». Project report, 1998: 12.
32 «Reliability of DP Operation in Deep Water». Project report, 1998: 4.
33 «Reliability of DP Operation in Deep Water». Project report, 1998: 4–6.
34 «Reliability of DP Operation in Deep Water». Project report, 1998: 4–6.
35 «Reliability of DP Operation in Deep Water». Project report, 1998: 7–8.
36 «Reliability of DP Operation in Deep Water». Project report, 1998: 9–11.
37 Kongsberg Maritime: *MULBL*. Product brochure, 2004.
38 «Reliability of DP Operation in Deep Water». Project report, 1998: 6.
39 «Reliability of DP Operation in Deep Water». Project report, 1998: 12–13.
40 This sub chapter is based on notes (2014) by Nils Albert Jenssen: «Da jorden ble rund».

41 «Reliability of DP Operation in Deep Water». Project report, 1998: 16–19.

42 The test vessel had a fully integrated automation system on board, consisting of SDP22, SDP12, STC40, SVC40, SPS (ECDIS) and STC with the following reference systems: two HPR-HiPAP (combined SSBL and LBL and with multi-user functionality – MULBL), tow integrated GPS/GLONASS-systems and a Light Weight Taut Wire. «Reliability of DP Operation in Deep Water.» Project report, 1998: 19.

43 Interview with Kenneth Wikerøy 13.02.14.

44 Kongsberg Gruppen: *Annual Report 1998*: 37.

45 Kongsberg Gruppen: *Annual Report 2000*: 47; «Kongsberg tar kontroll» article in newspaper *Adresseavisen* 20.05.00; «Skal styres fra Horten» article in newspaper *Adresseavisen* 30.09.00.

46 Review of Seatex is based on Nils Albert Jenssen's «DP reference systems in Seatex» Undated notes [2014].

47 «Seatex-gründere ble millionærer», interview with Hans Olav Torsen in newspaper *Dagens Næringsliv* 05.07.95.

48 NFT: Årsmelding 1991: 8 and 39.

49 NFT: *Annual Report 1993*: 9; «NFT går inn i Seatex» article in newspaper *Dagens Næringsliv* 18.06.93.

50 «Kunsten å ligge i ro», interview with Trygve Myrland and Ole Gunnar Hvamb in *Cicerone*, February 2002: 15.

51 «Kongsberg Gruppen cruiser på miljøbølge» article in newspaper *Dagens Næringsliv* 08.07.97.

52 Simrad: Reference list Positioning & Control Systems. Issue 21.

53 Kongsberg Simrad: *GreenDP. A breaking technology saving the environment*; «Kunsten å ligge i ro», interview with Trygve Myrland and Ole Gunnar Hvamb i *Cicerone*, February 2002: 14–15.

54 Kongsberg Simrad: *GreenDP. A breaking technology saving the environment*; Ole Gunnar Hvamb: «A New Concept for Fuel Tight DP Control». Dynamic Positioning Conference 18.–19.09.01.

55 Kongsberg Simrad: *GreenDP. A breaking technology saving the environment*. 2001; Ingolv Olsen: memo to the tech conference in the DPBOK project), 7 May, 2013.

56 Kongsberg Simrad: *GreenDP. A breaking technology saving the environment*. 2001.

57 Kongsberg Simrad: *GreenDP. A breaking technology saving the environment*; «Kunsten å ligge i ro», interview with Trygve Myrland and Ole Gunnar Hvamb in *Cicerone*, February 2002: 15.

58 Kongsberg Gruppen: *Annual Report 2001*: 51.

59 Bjørnstad 2009: 306. Nominal kroner

60 Kongsberg Gruppen: *Annual Report 2001*: 51.

61 Kongsberg Gruppen: *Annual Report 2001*: 51.

62 Kongsberg Gruppen: *Annual Report 2001*: 51.

63 «Et bygg for ekstraordinære mennesker» article in newspaper *Laagendalsposten* 18.09.01.

64 http://en.wikipedia.org/wiki/Carpus

65 «Fjær i hatten for lokalt arkitektfirma» article in *Telen*, 05.12.01.

66 «Et bygg for ekstraordinære mennesker» article in newspaper *Laagendalsposten* 18.09.01.

67 «Århundrets norske ingeniørbragd. Stødig på alle hav» article in *Teknisk Ukeblad*, no. 33, 09.09.99.

NOTES TO CHAPTER 12

1   «Posisjonerer skip» article in *Teknisk Ukeblad* 19.04.01: 99.

2   Anders J. Steensen: «Kunnskap gir vinnere» article in *Teknisk Ukeblad* 19.09.02: 99; *Simrad reference list, Positioning and Control Systems, issue 20: 27–36.*

3   Bjørnstad 2009: 267.

4   Øystein Andreassen and Nils Albert Jenssen: «The OSV market», Memo 14.10.13: 1.

5   Øystein Andreassen and Nils Albert Jenssen: «The OSV market», Memo 14.10.13: 1–2.

6   Interview with Pål Corneliussen 24.01.12.

7   Minutes of board meeting 02/04 i Kongsberg Maritime 18.05.04.

8   http://www.km.kongsberg.com/ks/web/nokbg0397.nsf/AllWeb/18832C5DC078E A75C1256FC5002D9944/$file/177186c-low-res.pdf?OpenElement (10.09.14).

9   http://www.km.kongsberg.com/ks/web/nokbg0397.nsf/AllWeb/A724A780B26742 6AC1256FC5002E0D74/$file/177188d-low-res.pdf?OpenElement (10.09.14).

10 Øystein Andreassen and Nils Albert Jenssen: «The OSV market,» Memo 14.10.13: 2; NAUT-OSV (2003 – class notation from 2006).

11 *Store Norske Leksikon*, https://snl.no/Troll/petroleumsfelt, 20.10.14.

12 Nils Albert Jenssen: «Construction ships» 19.11.13.

13 http://www.dnv.no/tjenester/klassifikasjon/offshore/index.asp (21.09.14); Nils Albert Jenssen: «Construction ships» 19.11.13.

14 «Få mer ut av undervannsbrønner» article in *Teknisk Ukeblad* 27.10.05.

15 Cathexis Consultancy Services Ltd.: «Floating Production, Storage and Offloading (FPSO) Facilities» Presentation that describes the history, functions, use and types of FPSOs. Gathered from: http://www.energyclaims.net/assets/FPSO-Presentation. pdf (23.08.14).

16 Kongsberg – Annual report and sustainability report, 2006: 67

17 «Major contract to USA» article in *Teknisk Ukeblad* 05.07.01

18 Memo from Nils Albert Jenssen 15.10.14.

19 «Nordsjøens vagabond» article in *Teknisk Ukeblad* 24.10.02.

20 «Nå flyter det over» article in *Dagens Næringsliv* 07.09.05.

21 «Rigger for 15 mrd. bare i år» article in newspaper *Stavanger Aftenblad* 18.06.08.

22 «West Eminence' er endelig levert» article in *Teknisk Ukeblad, internett version*, 13.03.09.

23 Interview with Torfinn Kildal 07.05.13.

24 «Samler kreftene» article in *Teknisk Ukeblad* 12.06.03: 99.

25 «Samler kreftene» article in *Teknisk Ukeblad Magasin* 12.06.03: 99.

26 «Kongsberg Gruppen selger lystbåtvirksomheten» article in *Teknisk Ukeblad* 12.10.05; Minutes of board meeting 2 August, Kongsberg Maritime 20.02.07.

27 Kongsberg Simrad and ABB enter into market and technology cooperation – web version article: http://www04.abb.com/global/noabb/noabb069.nsf!Open-

Database&db=/global/noabb/noabb071.nsf&v=3195A&e=no&url=/global/
seitp/seitp202.nsf/0/E86A32F4F1389D4E85256BDD00252A9C!OpenDocument
(19.06.02).

28 Interview with Asgeir Sørensen 02.07.14.

29 Call to board meeting no. 1/01 in Kongsberg Simrad 15.05.01.

30 «Kunnskap gir vinnere» article in *Teknisk Ukeblad* 19.09.02: 99; «Jubel i Kongsberg»
article in newspaper *Dagens Næringsliv* 21.08.02: 26.

31 «Kinakontrakt» til 100 millioner» article in *Teknisk Ukeblad* 25.09.03.

32 Letter from the Competition Commission: About Kongsberg Simrad AS and ABB
AS – konkurranseloven § 3-9, jf. § 3-2 – dispensasjon til anbudssamarbeid (Vedtak
V2003-11) 17.02.03.

33 «Milliardbud på Kongsberg» article in newspaper *Aftenposten* 07.09.04: 12.; Bjørnstad 2009: 264.

34 Bjørnstad 2009: 264.

35 «Forsvarer nei til delsalg» article in newspaper *Dagens Næringsliv* 21.09.04: 20.

36 «Rogalendinger har satset med stor suksess i USA» article in newspaper *Stavanger
Aftenblad* 23.03.06: 35.

37 http://www.navisincontrol.com/company/history/ (28.08.14).

38 «Kongsberg Maritime får finsk konkurrent på dynamisk posisjonering» article in
Teknisk Ukeblad 11.11.13; http://www.navisincontrol.com/cooperation-with-aker-
arctic/#more-1817 (28.08.14).

39 Bjørnstad 2009: 257–258.

40 *Teknisk Ukeblad* 26.08.05.

41 «Rolls-Royce DP3. To Farstad subseafartøy blir de første med Rolls-Royce DP3-
system» article in *Teknisk Ukeblad* 29.01.14.

42 «Dette er et slag i ansiktet for Kongsberg» article in newspaper *Dagens Næringsliv,
web version,* 04.04.13; http://www.dn.no/nyheter/2013/04/04/-dette-er-et-slag-i-
ansiktet-for-kongsberg-maritime (28.08.14).

43 Bjørnstad 2009: 257–258.

44 Roald Holstad: «DP Training History»; interview with Roald Holstad 06.08.14.

45 Roald Holstad: «DP Training History (the Kongsberg view)».

46 Press release no. 35 2008 from the Ministry of Justice and Public Security 23.03.08.

47 «Bedre opplæring for skipsmannskaper» article in *Teknisk Ukeblad* 15.08.08.

48 «Simulating for safety» article in *The Full Picture Magazine* no. 3 2008: 34–35.

49 «Ulsteinkonsernet er 90 år» article in shipping magasine *Skipsrevyen* 20.04.07.

50 «Kongsberg Maritime DP Simulator becomes first to achieve Class A DNV Approval» article in *Skipsrevyen* 20.10.09.

51 «Haugesund kjøper KOG-simulator» article in newspaper *Laagendalsposten* 22.06.10.

52 «Kongsberg Maritime har simulatorsuksess» article in newspaper *Laagendalsposten*
30.11.10; «Skal bli enda bedre på simulatorer» article in *Laagendalsposten* 19.01.11;
«KOG-simulator til danskene også» article in *Laagendalsposten* 10.01.12.

53 Kongsberg: *Kongsberg K-Pos DP, Dynamic Positioning System,* 2006.

54 Interview with Øystein Andreassen 06.08.14; «A new bridge concept is born» article
in *The Full Picture Magazine* 01.01.05.

55 Ingolv Olsen: «HW benyttet i DP/AIM systemer» (HW used DP/AIM systems).

Undated notes [2013]; Ingolv Olsen: Contribution to tech gathering for DP book proejct, Kongsberg 07.05.13.

56 Interview with Pål Corneliussen 24.01.12.

57 Interview with Pål Corneliussen 24.01.12; interview with Morten Breivik 06.05.13.

58 Interview with Pål Corneliussen 24.01.12.

59 Øyvind Smogeli: «Fremtidens verifikasjon av kontrollsystemer for skip og offshore-fartøy» presentation at Maritime Technical Days 2013.

60 «Problemer også på norsk sokkel» article in the *Teknisk Ukeblad,* web version, 26.08.14. http://www.tu.no/it/2010/09/23/problem-ogsa-pa-norsk-sokkel (20.10.14); interview with Asgeir Sørensen 02.07.14.

61 Tor A. Johansen, Thor I. Fossen, Bjørnar Vik: «Hardware-in-the-loop Testing of DP systems», Marine Technology Society's Dynamic Positioning Conference, Houston, 15.11.05; Øyvind Smogeli: «Experiences from five years of DP software testing», Marine Technology Society›s Dynamic Positioning Conference, Houston, 13.11.05.

62 http://www.dnvgl.com/news-events/news/dnvgl-kristian-gerhard-jebsen-group-to-jointly-develop-marine-cybernetics.aspx (22.10.14).

63 «Kontrakt i Vest-Afrika» article in newspaper *Stavanger Aftenblad* 15.11.03.

NOTES TO CHAPTER 13

1 Kongsberg Gruppen: *Annual report and sustainability report 2006*: 26–27.

2 «Kildal slutter i Kongsberg Maritime» article in newspaper *Dagens Næringsliv* 03.07.10.

3 http://www.kongsberg.com/nb-no/kog/news/2010/september/1409_km_new_president/ (03.07.14).

4 «Spennende prosjekt i Kongsberg Maritime» article in *I fokus* – Corporate newsletter for Kongsberg Gruppen, May 2002; interview with Torfinn Kildal 07.05.13.

5 Kunde 2000; board meeting minutes no. 2 in 2002 at Kongsberg Maritime 19.04.02: 2.

6 «Spennende prosjekt i Kongsberg Maritime» article in *I fokus* – Corporate newsletter for Kongsberg Gruppen, May 2002; interview with Torfinn Kildal 07.05.13.

7 «Spennende prosjekt i Kongsberg Maritime» article in *I fokus* – Corporate newsletter for Kongsberg Gruppen, May 2002; interview with Torfinn Kildal.

8 «Spennende prosjekt i Kongsberg Maritime» in *I fokus* – Corporate newsletter for Kongsberg Gruppen, May 2002

9 Minutes of board meeting, no. 2 2002 i Kongsberg Maritime 19.04.02: 2.

10 Bjørnstad 2009: 250.

11 Letter with memo written by Roy Larsen, received 31.07.14.

12 Interview with Tor Erik Sørensen and Roy Larsen 06.06.12.

13 Interview with KMs president Geir Håøy under the title «Mester på maritimt» in *Automatisering og industridata* 24.05.11.

14 *Annual Report for Kongsberg 2008*: 14.

15 Kongsberg Gruppen: *Annual report and sustainability report 2006*: 70; Kongsberg Gruppen: *Annual report and sustainability report 2006*: 12 og 17.

16 Interview with Roy Larsen 14.02.14.

17 Kongsberg Gruppen: *Annual report and sustainability report 2006;* «Landet som redder verdens oljebehov» article in newspaper *Dagens Næringsliv* 23.10.13, updated 28.03.14, web version.

18 «Største oljefunn siden 1976» web based article in E24-http://e24.no/makro-og-politikk/stoerste-oljefunn-siden-1976/3882287 (05.03.14).

19 «The Heart of the matter» article in *The Full Picture Magazine*, no. 1 2010: 9–11.

20 http://www.km.kongsberg.com/ks/web/nokbg0238.nsf/AllWeb/ B35A4472F5FE18 E5C1257C9E00423C05?OpenDocument (09.04.14).

21 «Mester på maritimt» article in *Automatisering* no. 3 2011.

22 «A partner in China» article in *The Full Picture Magazine*, March 2008: 3–5.

23 «Jiang Shipyard, Shipbuilding in the Middle Kingdom» article in *The Full Picture Magazine*, January 2005: 17–18.

24 «A partner in China» article in *The Full Picture Magazine*, March 2008: 3–5.

25 «Mester på maritimt» article in *Automatisering* no. 3 2011.

26 «Norway promotes business peace with China» article in *Norwegian Solutions* 2012: 75–76.

27 Interview with Finn Søberg 16.04.12; interview with Morten Stanger 06.08.14.

28 Interview with Finn Søberg 16.04.12; interview with Tor Erik Sørensen and Roy Larsen 06.06.12.

29 Interview with Roy Larsen 14.02.14 and with Morten Stanger 06.08.14.

30 «HSD Engine: gearing up for more success» article in *The Full Picture Magazine* January 2005: 21–22.

31 «Frontier Spirit» article in *The Full Picture Magazine*, February 2008: 51–52.

32 Kongsberg Gruppen: *Annual Report 2010*: 9.

33 Simrad: *Reference List Positioning & Control Systems*, Issue 20.

34 «Offshore Works: An almost impossible task» article in *The Full Picture Magazine* January 2011: 55–57.

35 «Bridge and automation retrofit project completed on Saipem 7000 crane vessel», http://www.saltwaterpr.com/Story/Print.aspx?story=6061 (23.09.14).

36 «Fra informasjonsflom til oversikt» article in *Teknisk Ukeblad* 14.04.11: 55.

37 «SMC Kongsberg Simrad Maneuvering & Control System», Brochure, 2002; NAUT-OSV – as described: 7.

38 «Bedre sikt og bedre kontroll» article in *Teknisk Ukeblad Magasin* 03.10.02: 99.

39 Interview with Thor Hukkelås 13.06.12.

40 «Fra informasjonsflom til oversikt» article in *Teknisk Ukeblad* 14.04.11: 55.

41 «Maritime Design Day» article in *K-Magazine* 01.02.12: 23.

42 Interview with Torfinn Kildal 05.04.13; memo from technology meeting in Kongsberg 07.05.13; interview with Morten Breivik 07.05.13.

43 Global Customer Support Follows the Sun, Kongsberg Gruppen website, http://www.km.kongsberg.com/ks/web/nokbg0238.nsf/AllWeb/BE5B960C6278FF3EC 1257AC6004144AC?OpenDocument (30.11.12); http://www.km.kongsberg.com/ks/web/nokbg0238.nsf/AllWeb/96E1E2060B6955FCC1257B19004C99CC?OpenDocument (28.08.14).

44 Global Customer Support Follows the Sun, Kongsberg Gruppen website, http://www.km.kongsberg.com/ks/web/nokbg0238.nsf/AllWeb/BE5B960C6278FF3EC12

57AC6004144AC?OpenDocument (30.11.12); http://www.km.kongsberg.com/ks/web/nokbg0238.nsf/AllWeb/96E1E2060B6955FCC1257B19004C99CC?OpenDocument (28.08.14).

45   Global Customer Support Follows the Sun, Kongsberg Gruppen website, http://www.km.kongsberg.com/ks/web/nokbg0238.nsf/AllWeb/BE5B960C6278FF3EC1257AC6004144AC?OpenDocument (30.11.12); http://www.km.kongsberg.com/ks/web/nokbg0238.nsf/AllWeb/96E1E2060B6955FCC1257B19004C99CC?OpenDocument (28.08.14).

46   Global Customer Support Follows the Sun, Kongsberg Gruppen website, http://www.km.kongsberg.com/ks/web/nokbg0238.nsf/AllWeb/BE5B960C6278FF3EC1257AC6004144AC?OpenDocument (30.11.12).

47   Interview with Øystein Andreassen 06.08.14.

48   *The Full Picture Magazine*, January 2004: 1.

49   «Spesial Olje og Gass» article in *Teknisk Ukeblad* 17.03.13: 80.

50   «Skarv-kontroll» article in *Teknisk Ukeblad* 07.02.13: 50 and 51.

51   «Fyller opp maritime professorater» article in *Teknisk Ukeblad* 29.05.09.

52   «Jobber for å kontrollere isen» article in *Teknisk Ukeblad* 26.08.11; interview with Asgeir Sørensen 02.07.14.

53   «Remora HiLoad: En gigantisk sugekopp/a giant suction cup» article in *Teknisk Ukeblad* 17.05.12.

54   http://www.cruiseandferry.net/article/News/001184/KIMS-system-for-Royal-Caribbean (27.09.14).

55   http://www.ledelse.as/europa-m%C3%A5-p%C3%A5-skattejakt-til-havs (05.10.14).

56   http://www.ngu.no/no/Aktuelt/2012/Drofter-gruvedrift-pa-havbunnen/ (05.10.14).

57   «Tror det ligger mineraler for 1000 milliarder på havbunnen» article in *Teknisk Ukeblad* 21.05.14.

58   Kongsberg Maritime Engineering (KME) is a wholly owned subsidiary of Kongsberg Maritime.

LITERATURE

Andersen, Håkon With: «State, strategy and electronics. Research in the political economy of post World War II Norway», article in *History and Technology*, vol 11, 1994: 145–164.

Arbeidernes faglige Landsorganisasjon and Det norske Arbeiderparti: *Teknikken og framtiden.* Oslo: DNAs hustrykkeri, 1956.

Asphjell, Arne and Anne Kristine Børresen: *Institutt for teknisk kybernetikk femti år.* Trondheim: NTNU, 2004.

Balchen, Jens Glad: «Grunnprinsippene for automatiseringen», article in Arbeidernes faglige Landsorganisasjon and Det norske Arbeiderparti: *Teknikken og framtiden.* Oslo: DNAs hustrykkeri, 1956: 30–42.

Balchen, Jens Glad, Nils Albert Jenssen, Eldar Mathisen and Steinar Sælid: «A Dynamic Positioning System Based on Kalman Filtering and Optimal Control», article in *Modeling, Identification and Control* (MIC), vol 1, no. 3, 1980: 135–163.

Balchen, Jens Glad, Nils Albert Jenssen and Steinar Sælid: «Dynamic Positioning using Kalman Filtering and Optimal Control Theory», article in *IFAC/IFIP Symposium on Automation in Offshore Oil Field Operation*, North-Holland Publishing Company, 1976.

Bascom, Willard: *A Hole in the Bottom of the Sea: The Story of the Mohole Project.* New York: Doubleday & Company, 1961.

Bergbreiter, Sara: «Moving from Practice to Theory: Automatic Control after World War II», article in HIS 285S: History of Science, University of California, Berkeley, 2005.

Bjørnstad, Stein: *Shipshaped. Kongsberg industry and innovations in deepwater technology, 1975–2007.* BI, Series of Dissertations 7/2009.

Bonde, Aslak: «Våpenet som bygget allianser», in Olav Wicken (ed.) *Elektronikkentreprenørene – Studier av norsk elektronikkforskning og -industri etter 1945.* Oslo: Ad Notam Gyldendal, 1994: 47.

Brandt, Thomas and Ola Nordal: *Turbulens og tankekraft. Historien om NTNU.* Oslo: Pax Forlag, 2010.

Breivik, Morten and Gunnar Sand: «Jens Glad Balchen: A Norwegian Pioneer in Engineering Cybernetics», article in *Modeling, Identification and Control*, vol. 30, no. 3, 2009: 101–125.

Bugos, Glenn E.: *Atmosphere of Freedom: 70 years at the NASA AMES Research Center,* Washington D.C., NASA History Office, 2010.

Bush, Vannevar: *Science: The Endless Frontier: a report to the President.* Washington D.C.: National Science Foundation, 1945.

Dunham, Roger C.: *Spy Sub: Top-Secret Mission to the Bottom of the Pacific*. New York: Penguin Books, 1996.

Dybing, Bjørn (ed.): *NFA 40 år 1958–1998*. Oslo: Norsk Forening for Automatisering, 1999.

Faÿ, Hubert: *Dynamic Positioning Systems. Principles, Design and Applications*. Paris: Éditions Technip, 1990.

Furre, Berge: *Norsk Historie 1905–1990*, Oslo: Det Norske Samlaget, 1993.

Godin, Beno: «The linear Model of Innovation: The Historical Construction of an Analytical Framework», article in *Science, Technology and Human Values*, vol. 31, no. 6, 2006: 639–667.

Gotaas, Sverre: *Simulator for distribuert prosess-styringssystem*. Diploma, Department of Engineering Cybernetics, NTH, 1982.

Gulowsen, Jon: *Bro mellom vitenskap og teknologi*. Trondheim, Tapir Akademisk Forlag 2000.

Hammett, Dillard S.: «Drilling in Ultra-deep Water without Anchors or Guidelines», article in *Petroleum Engineer*, mai 1974: 60.

Hatling, Morten: *Pardans i utakt? Innovasjon mellom forskningsinstitutt og industribedrift*. STS-arbeidsnotat 7/90. Centre for Technology and Society (STS), Universitetet i Trondheim, 1990.

Ilner, Kristian: *Jacob Stolt-Nielsen. En gründer*. Bergen: Vigmostad & Bjørke, 2009.

Jenssen, Nils Albert: *Identifikasjon av dampkjelanlegg*. Diploma, Department of Engineering Cybernetics, NTH, 1974.

Jenssen, Nils Albert: *Estimation and Control in Dynamic Positioning of Vessels*. Doctoral thesis. Trondheim: NTH, 1981.

Johansen, Tor A., Thor I. Fossen and Bjørnar Vik: «Hardware-in-the-loop Testing of DP systems», Marine Technology Society's Dynamic Positioning Conference, Houston, 15.11.05.

Kalman, Rudolf E.: «A New Approach to Linear Filtering and Prediction Problems», article in the *Journal of Basic Engineering* (ASME Transactions, Part D), 1960, vol. 82: 35–45.

Kalman, Rudolf E. and Richard Snowden Bucy: «New results in linear filtering and prediction theory», article in the *Journal of Basic Engineering* (ASME Transactions, Part D), 1961, vol. 83: 95–108.

Kolltveit, Bård: *Six Decades on the Seven Seas. The Anders Wilhelmsen Group 1939–1999*. Oslo: Andresen & Butenschøn, 2000.

Kvaal, Stig: *Drømmen om det moderne Norge. Automasjon som visjon og virkelighet i etterkrigstiden*. Trondheim: Universitetet i Trondheim, 1990.

Kvaal, Stig: «Hooked on a New Technology: The Automation Pioneers in Post-War Norway», article in *Modeling, Identification and Control* (MIC), vol 30, no. 3, 2009: 87–100.

Kvaal, Stig, Torgeir Moan, Johannes Moe and Gjert Wilhelmsen (ed.): *Et hav av muligheter. Skipslinjen ved Norges tekniske høgskole og Fakultet for marin teknikk ved Norges teknisk-naturvitenskapelige universitet 1910–2001*. Trondheim: Tapir Akademisk Forlag, 2003.

Leffler, William L., Richard Pattarozzi and Gordon Sterling: *Deepwater Petroleum Explora-*

tion and Production – a Nontechnical Guide. Tulsa, Oklahoma: PennWell Corporation, 2003.

Lindøe, John Ove: *Inn fra havet. Bøyelasternes historie.* Stavanger: Wigestrand, 2009.

Løkling, Terje: *Dynamisk posisjonert modellskip.* Diploma, Department of Engineering Cybernetics. Trondheim: NTH, 1975.

McGee, Leonard A. and Stanley F. Schmidt: «Discovery of the Kalman Filter as a Practical Tool for Aerospace and Industry» NASA Technical Memorandum 86847, 1985.

McGregor, Douglas: *Mennesket og bedriften.* Oslo: Gyldendal Norsk Forlag, 1968.

Mindell, David A.: *Digital Apollo, Human and Machine in Spaceflight.* Cambridge, Massachusetts: MIT-Press, 2008.

Minorsky, Nicolas: «Directional stability of automatically steered bodies», article in the *Journal of the American Society of Naval Engineers*, vol. 34, 1922: 280–309.

Morgan, Max J.: *Dynamic Positioning of Offshore Vessels.* Tulsa: PPC Books, 1978.

Myrvang, Christine: *Troskap og flid. Kongsberg Våpenfabrikks historie 1814–1945.* Oslo: Pax Forlag, 2014.

Njølstad, Olav and Olav Wicken: *Kunnskap som våpen.* Oslo: Tano Aschehoug 1997.

Noble, David F.: *Forces of production. A Social History of Industrial Automation.* New York/Oxford: Oxford University Press, 1986.

Nordal, Ola: *Verktøy og vitenskap. Datahistorien ved NTNU.* Trondheim: Tapir Akademisk Forlag, 2010.

Overbye, Signy Ryther: *Fra forskning til industri. Utvikling av skipsautomatiseringsbedriften Norcontrol.* Oslo: Universitetet i Oslo, 1989.

Overbye, Signy Ryther: «Etablering av norsk skipsautomatiseringsindustri» in Olav Wicken (red): *Elektronikkentreprenørene – Studier av norsk elektronikk-forskning og -industri etter 1945.* Oslo: Ad Notam Gyldendal, 1994.

Poulsen, Per Thygesen: *Den samstemte bedrift. Erfaringer og prinsipper fra 18 pionerbedrifter.* Oslo: J.W. Cappelens forlag, 1987.

Priest, Tyler: *The Offshore Imperative: Shell Oil's Search for Petroleum in Postwar America.* College Station, Texas: Texas A&M University Press, 2007.

Redmond, Ken C. and Thomas M. Smith: *Project Whirlwind: The History of a Pioneer Computer.* Bedford, MA: Digital Press, 1990.

Rabben, Magne Brekke: *Langsiktig forskning og innovasjon – Tre eksempler fra NTNUs historie på hvordan langsiktig forskning har bidratt til innovasjon.* Report. Trondheim, NTNU, 2012.

Sejersted, Francis: *Teknologipolitikk.* Oslo: Universitetsforlaget, 1998.

Sejersted, Francis: *Systemtvang eller politikk.* Oslo: Universitetsforlaget, 1999.

Sejersted, Francis: *Demokratisk kapitalisme.* Oslo: Pax Forlag, 2002.

Shatto, Howard, *History of Dynamic Positioning, 2011 – The year in which Dynamic Positioning celebrated its fiftieth anniversary!* Dynamic Positioning Committee, MTS, 2011.

Skogen, Erling and Nils Holme: *Fra Forsvarets forskningsinstitutts historie*, Booklet 3, 2003.

Smogeli, Øyvind: «Experiences from five years of DP software testing», Marine Technology Society's Dynamic Positioning Conference, Houston, 13.11.05.

Sogner, Knut: »Ny teknologi i gammel næring, Staten og Simrad i samvirke 1945–1960» in Olav Wicken (ed.): *Elektronikkentreprenørene – Studier av norsk elektronikkforskning og -industri etter 1945.* Oslo: Ad Notam Gyldendal, 1994: 63–74.

Sogner, Knut: *God på bunnen. SIMRAD-virksomheten 1947–1997.* Oslo: Novus forlag, 1997.

Sælid, Steinar: *Modelling, estimation and control of a rotary cement kiln.* Doctoral thesis. Trondheim: NTH, 1976.

Sælid, Steinar: «AIM blir til» in Bjørn Dybing (ed.): *NFA 40 år 1958–1998.* Oslo: Norsk Forening for Automatisering, 1999: 88–91.

Sørheim, Hans-Roar: *Dynamic positioning in single-point mooring – a theoretical analysis of motions, and design and evaluation of an optimal control system.* Doctoral thesis. Trondheim: NTH, 1982.

Terjesen, Sven G.: «Automatiseringen i den kjemiske industri», article in Arbeidernes faglige Landsorganisasjon and Det norske Arbeiderparti: *Teknikken og framtiden.* Oslo: DNAs hustrykkeri, 1956: 43–58.

Tormodsgard, Yngvild: *Fakta 2014.* Oslo: Olje- og energidepartementet, 2014.

Verne, Jules: *L'île à hélice.* Paris: Hetzel, 1895.

Wicken, Olav: «Stille propell i storpolitisk storm: KV/Toshiba-saken og dens bakgrunn». *Forsvarsstudier* 1/1988. Oslo: Forsvarshistorisk forskningssenter, 1988.

Wicken, Olav: «Forskningsdrevet industripolitikk i Norge 1945–1970». *Fremtek-notat 21/92.* Oslo, 1992.

Wicken, Olav: «Teknologi, stat og innovasjoner. Et perspektiv på framveksten av norsk høyteknologisk industri» in Olav Wicken (ed.): *Elektronikkentreprenørene – Studier av norsk elektronikkforsking og -industri etter 1945.* Oslo: Ad Notam Gyldendal, 1994: 246–273.

Wicken, Olav (ed.): *Elektronikkentreprenørene – Studier av norsk elektronikkforsking og -industri etter 1945.* Oslo: Ad Notam Gyldendal, 1994.

Wiener, Norbert: *Cybernetics. Or Control and Communication in the Animal and the Machine.* New York: J. Wiley, 1948.

Østby, Per: *Tilfellet Comtec: Teknologispredning fra forskning til industri.* Trondheim: Universitetet i Trondheim, 1989.

Østby, Per: «En automatisk fabrikk? Bedriftsetablering i skjæringspunktet mellom vitenskap og industri» in Olav Wicken (ed.): *Elektronikkentreprenørene – Studier av norsk elektronikkforsking og -industri etter 1945.* Oslo: Ad Notam Gyldendal, 1994: 178–197.

Øyangen, Knut: *Moderniseringslokomotivet. Kongsberg Våpenfabrikks historie 1945–1947.* Oslo: Pax Forlag, 2014.

Zachary, G. Pascal: Endless Frontier: *Vannevar Bush: Engineer of the American Century.* Mass., The MIT Press, 1999.

APPENDIX

Albatross since 1975

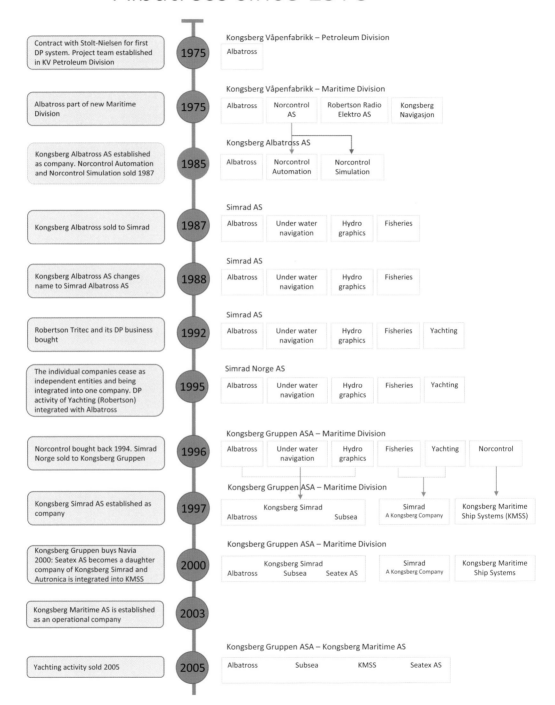

| | Contract with Stolt-Nielsen for first DP system. Project team established in KV Petroleum Division |
| **1975** | |

Kongsberg Våpenfabrikk – Petroleum Division

Albatross

| | Albatross part of new Maritime Division |
| **1975** | |

Kongsberg Våpenfabrikk – Maritime Division

Albatross	Norcontrol AS	Robertson Radio Elektro AS	Kongsberg Navigasjon

Kongsberg Albatross AS

| | Kongsberg Albatross AS established as company. Norcontrol Automation and Norcontrol Simulation sold 1987 |
| **1985** | |

Albatross	Norcontrol Automation	Norcontrol Simulation

| | Kongsberg Albatross sold to Simrad |
| **1987** | |

Simrad AS

Albatross	Under water navigation	Hydro graphics	Fisheries

| | Kongsberg Albatross AS changes name to Simrad Albatross AS |
| **1988** | |

Simrad AS

Albatross	Under water navigation	Hydro graphics	Fisheries

| | Robertson Tritec and its DP business bought |
| **1992** | |

Simrad AS

Albatross	Under water navigation	Hydro graphics	Fisheries	Yachting

| | The individual companies cease as independent entities and being integrated into one company. DP activity of Yachting (Robertson) integrated with Albatross |
| **1995** | |

Simrad Norge AS

Albatross	Under water navigation	Hydro graphics	Fisheries	Yachting

| | Norcontrol bought back 1994. Simrad Norge sold to Kongsberg Gruppen |
| **1996** | |

Kongsberg Gruppen ASA – Maritime Division

Albatross	Under water navigation	Hydro graphics	Fisheries	Yachting	Norcontrol

| | Kongsberg Simrad AS established as company |
| **1997** | |

Kongsberg Gruppen ASA – Maritime Division

Kongsberg Simrad		Simrad	Kongsberg Maritime
Albatross	Subsea	A Kongsberg Company	Ship Systems (KMSS)

| | Kongsberg Gruppen buys Navia 2000: Seatex AS becomes a daughter company of Kongsberg Simrad and Autronica is integrated into KMSS |
| **2000** | |

Kongsberg Gruppen ASA – Maritime Division

Kongsberg Simrad			Simrad	Kongsberg Maritime
Albatross	Subsea	Seatex AS	A Kongsberg Company	Ship Systems

| | Kongsberg Maritime AS is established as an operational company |
| **2003** | |

| | Yachting activity sold 2005 |
| **2005** | |

Kongsberg Gruppen ASA – Kongsberg Maritime AS

Albatross	Subsea	KMSS	Seatex AS

Facts	1975-1980	1980-1985	1985-1990	1990-1995	1995-2000	2000-2005	2005-
Accumulated number of vessels with Kongsberg DP systems	50	173	250	312	586	1169	4030
Dominant DP manufacturer	Honeywell/GEC	GEC/Kongsberg	Kongsberg	Kongsberg	Kongsberg	Kongsberg	Kongsberg
Most popular Kongsberg DP	Single ADP501/311	Double ADP503 and ADP311	ADP701 and ADP703	ADP701	SDP21	SDP21 with K-Pos DP21 taking over	K-Pos DP21
Typical station keeping accuracy	5 meters	5 meters	5 meters	3-5 meters	3 meters	3-2 meters	2 meters
Typical DP system price, including sensors and reference systems	15 mill NOK	10 mill NOK	8 mill NOK	8 mill NOK	8 mill NOK	7 mill NOK	6 mill NOK
Most common position reference systems	Tautwire, Hydroacoustics, Microwave systems	Tautwire, Hydroacoustics, Microwave systems, Radio navigation	Tautwire, Hydroacoustics, Microwave systems, Radio navigation	GPS introduced	Laser scanners introduced	GLONASS introduced	Inertial navigation sensors introduced
Applied hardware technology	ADP50x and ADP311 with KS500 mini-computer (bitslice) and random scan monochrome display	ADP503-ADP311 with KS500 and raster scan colour display. ADP 100 with SBC1000 (Intel 80186) and SBG1000 raster scan colour display	ADP503, ADP701 and ADP703 with SBC1000	ADP70X with SBC3000	SDP with SBC 400 and Windows® operating system	SDP (Green DP) with SBC500	K-Pos DP with RCU502 and RIO400
Processor memory for DP controller	128kB	192kB	512kB	8MB	16MB	32MB	64MB
Installed weight of DP system (ex HPR)	1000kg	1000kg	400kg	400kg	350kg	350kg	320kg

Through the years DP operator stations have changed significantly, and have been adopted for different types of vessels. Here we see various Kongsberg models from the early years and onwards. For instance, one notices that workstations where the operator is seated as an integral part of the station has become an alternative to the more ordinary console solutions.